Negotiated Moments

IMPROVISATION,
COMMUNITY, AND
SOCIAL PRACTICE

A SERIES EDITED BY
DANIEL FISCHLIN

Books in this new series advocate musical
improvisation as a crucial model for political,
cultural, and ethical dialogue and action—
for imagining and creating alternative ways of
knowing and being in the world. The books are
collaborations among performers, scholars,
and activists from a wide range of disciplines.
They study the creative risk-taking imbued with
the sense of movement and momentum that
makes improvisation an exciting, unpredictable,
ubiquitous, and necessary endeavor.

Negotiated Moments

IMPROVISATION,
SOUND, AND
SUBJECTIVITY

Gillian Siddall AND
Ellen Waterman, EDITORS

DUKE UNIVERSITY PRESS
DURHAM AND LONDON
2016

Printed in the United States of America on acid-free paper ∞
Interior design by Kaelin Chappell Broaddus; Cover design by Natalie F. Smith
Typeset in Garamond Premier Pro by Westchester Publishing Services

Library of Congress Cataloging-in-Publication Data
Negotiated moments : improvisation, sound, and subjectivity / Gillian Siddall
and Ellen Waterman, editors.
pages cm — (Improvisation, community, and social practice)
Includes bibliographical references and index.
ISBN 978-0-8223-6082-7 (hardcover : alk. paper)
ISBN 978-0-8223-6096-4 (pbk. : alk. paper)
ISBN 978-0-8223-7449-7 (e-book)
1. Improvisation (Music)—Social aspects. 2. Music—Physiological
aspects. 3. Sound—Physiological aspects. I. Siddall, Gillian H.
(Gillian Heather), editor. II. Waterman, Ellen, [date] editor.
III. Series: Improvisation, community, and social practice.
MT68.N33 2016
781.1—dc23   2015030877

Cover art: Film still by Carter McCall from *Big, Bent Ears*, 2015. © Rock Fish
Stew. Courtesy of Rock Fish Stew Institute of Literature and Materials.

Duke University Press gratefully acknowledges the Social Sciences and
Humanities Research Council of Canada for its support of the Improvisation,
Community, and Social Practice (ICASP) project, at the University of Guelph,
which provided funds toward the publication of this book.

To our inspiring colleagues in the
Improvisation, Gender, and the Body research group.

CONTENTS

Acknowledgments   xi

Introduction: Improvising at the Nexus of
Discursive and Material Bodies   1
Gillian Siddall and Ellen Waterman

1. Improvisation within a Scene of Constraint:
An Interview with Judith Butler   21
Tracy McMullen

PART I. LISTENING, PLACE, AND SPACE

2. "How Am I to Listen to You?":
Soundwalking, Intimacy, and Improvised Listening   37
Andra McCartney

3. Community Sound [e]Scapes: Improvising Bodies and
Site/Space/Place in New Media Audio Art   55
Rebecca Caines

PART II. TECHNOLOGY AND EMBODIMENT

4. Improvising Composition:
How to Listen in the Time Between   75
Pauline Oliveros

5. The Networked Body: Physicality, Embodiment,
and Latency in Multisite Performance   91
Jason Robinson

6. Openness from Closure: The Puzzle of Interagency
in Improvised Music and a Neocybernetic Solution   113
David Borgo

7. Mediating the Improvising Body:
Art Tatum's Postmortem Performance in a Posthuman World   131
Andrew Raffo Dewar

PART III. SENSIBILITY AND SUBJECTIVITY

  8. Banding Encounters:
     Embodied Practices in Improvisation 147
       Introduction and Conclusion by Tomie Hahn
       Essays by Louise Campbell, Lindsay Vogt, Simon Rose,
       George Blake, Catherine Lee, Sherrie Tucker,
       François Mouillot, Jovana Milović, and Pete Williams

  9. Learning to Go with the Flow: David Rokeby's
     Very Nervous System and the Improvising Body 169
       Jesse Stewart

  10. Stretched Boundaries: Improvising across Abilities 181
       Introduction and Conclusion by Sherrie Tucker
       Essays by Pauline Oliveros, Neil Rolnick, Christine Sun Kim,
       Clara Tomaz, David Whalen, Leaf Miller, and Jaclyn Heyen

PART IV. GENDER, TRAUMA, AND MEMORY

  11. The Erotics of Improvisation in
     Ann-Marie MacDonald's *Fall on Your Knees* 201
       Gillian Siddall

  12. *Corregidora*: Corporeal Archaeology,
     Embodied Memory, Improvisation 217
       Mandy-Suzanne Wong and Nina Sun Eidsheim

  13. Theorizing the Saxophonic Scream in
     Free Jazz Improvisation 233
       Zachary Wallmark

  14. Extemporaneous Genomics:
     Nicole Mitchell, Octavia Butler, and *Xenogenesis* 245
       Kevin McNeilly and Julie Dawn Smith

PART V. REPRESENTATION AND IDENTITY

  15. Faster and Louder: Heterosexist Improvisation
     in North American Taiko 265
       Deborah Wong

  16. Improvisation and the Audibility of Difference:
     Safa, Canadian Multiculturalism, and
     the Politics of Recognition 283
       Ellen Waterman

17. Performing the National Body Politic in
    Twenty-First-Century Argentina   307
        Illa Carrillo Rodríguez and Berenice Corti

    Discography   327

    References   329

    Contributors   351

    Index   355

ACKNOWLEDGMENTS

The Social Sciences and Humanities Research Council of Canada provided the funding for the Improvisation Community and Social Practice research project (ICASP) from 2007 to 2013. We deeply appreciate the material support we received from ICASP, Memorial University of Newfoundland, and Lakehead University. Special thanks are due to Rachel Shoup for her efficient formatting, to Daniel Fischlin and Ajay Heble for their comments, and to Kim Thorne for her good-humored advice. Beverley Diamond kindly lent us her cottage so that we could write the introduction. Sherrie Tucker, Julie Smith, and Deborah Wong talked over big ideas with us and made wise suggestions. Thanks to our generous contributors who demonstrated excellent improvisational skills of listening, response, and adaptation throughout the editorial process. Our families generously allowed us to "escape" for regular retreats over three long years of writing and editing. They deserve our biggest thanks.

Introduction

IMPROVISING AT THE NEXUS OF
DISCURSIVE AND MATERIAL BODIES

Gillian Siddall and Ellen Waterman

Negotiated Moments: Improvisation, Sound, and Subjectivity tests the limits of the social and political efficacy of musical improvisation by bringing it home to where it lives: in our bodies. We argue that musical improvisation is ineluctably embodied; its creative and political force is manifested through sounds and gestures that are the traces of experience at once relational and contextual. Furthermore, we contend that any argument that posits improvisation as a model for ethical human relations must take into account both theories about the social construction of bodies and theories of prereflexive experience, contradictory though they may seem. Indeed, in this book we are most interested in improvisation as a negotiation (of power, of subjectivity) at the nexus of discursive and material bodies.

The diverse contributions explore sounding bodies through creative improvisation processes ranging from free improvisation to jazz and blues, from sound art to sound walking, from political street theater to telematic concerts, and from Japanese *taiko* drumming to Iranian classical music. Our contributors analyze live musical performances and recordings, critical and creative writing, and politically engaged community projects, locating their analyses not just in artistic outcomes and social effects but also in material bodies, however mediated. This critical strategy invites us to consider representations of the body through improvisation, how bodies (gendered, sexed, raced, classed, abled/disabled) are constructed through improvisational relationships, and how mediations of the body extend its reach while seemingly causing it to "disappear." A close analysis of embodied improvisation will help us critically assess claims about improvisation's efficacy by exploring such claims as they are expressed through one of the most visceral and intimate levels of human experience: sound. Here, we explore sound's effects in terms of both signification and phenomenology.

Sound metaphors are always relational: We sound people out to get an idea of what they think or feel before we commit to a course of action; we make moral, intellectual, and emotional judgments (sounds good, sounds difficult, sounds scary); we express our anger or our strong opinions by sounding off or sounding out; we empathize with the friend who (perhaps over the phone or via the medium of text) is sounding tired or thoughtful or sad. Closely related to sound-as-metaphor is the physical act of hearing and its psychosocial complement listening: sound cannot be fully understood without considering the act of audition. "Hear me out" is a plea to be "sounded out." "Just listen to yourself" is a response to "sounding off." These common phrases demonstrate the extent to which we use sound as a signifier for our engagement with others and our world.

Sound is also a physical phenomenon: the materialities of air pressure and solid media such as strings or membranes vibrate the body through tactile impression. Sound penetrates and vibrates the body through and through. Sound is active: it travels, insinuates, reverberates, repeats, and fades away. Sound is sensual: it whispers and shouts, tickles your ear, and thumps in your chest. We embody, and are embodied through, sound. As Julie Dawn Smith writes, "Our experience of, and participation with, sound is inseparable from our experience of, and participation with, our body and the bodies of others. The resonances of sound waves register in the very fibres of each and every body in ways that confound the assumed discreteness of exterior and interior space" (2001, 32). Indeed, we agree with Smith's observation that "the invisible presence of sound" complicates representation because "it underscores the corporeal as a process of audition, (re)writing and transformation" (21). Such processes, closely tied as they are to improvisatory practices, are the subjects of this book.

In this interdisciplinary collection of essays, sounding the body is both metaphor and materiality. This book takes up the many ways that bodies can be understood as sounding, how the notion of transmitting and receiving sound occurs within bodies, between bodies, in real time, in virtual time, in memory, in history, and across space. We explore some of these themes in this introduction, which is organized in two sections. We begin by unpacking theories of improvisation and subjectivity in relation to theories of the body and embodiment to address questions of agency in improvisation. We then trace a number of crosscutting themes that organize the book and conclude with a brief meditation on the sensual nature of sounding bodies improvising.

Improvising Subjectivity

Subjectivity is a complex negotiation of lived embodied experience and social forces that work to regulate behavior and therefore shape that experience. We agree with Elizabeth Grosz that "corporeality can be seen as the material condition of subjectivity" (1995, 103); we also recognize, however, that the material body is shaped by discourse. Karen Barad's essay on posthuman performativity argues "materiality is discursive (i.e., material phenomena are inseparable from the apparatuses of bodily production . . .), just as discursive practices are always already material (i.e., they are ongoing material (re)configurations of the world)" (2006, 25). What does improvisation add to these articulations of subjectivity? Improvisation is a form of knowledge creation through expressive practice: whether we are conscious of our bodies in the moment, or transported by what psychologist Mihaly Csikszentmihalyi (1990) famously calls "flow," in improvising we experience the immediate relationships between our bodies and others. Improvisation is also a form of recollection and repetition: we call on learned repertoires of sounds and gestures and mobilize them in the moment. We cannot escape from our enculturation and our histories; indeed, improvisation is often a means of narrating the past through the filter of the present moment.

Musical improvisation makes negotiations of (material and discursive) subjectivity audible, but that is not in itself a guarantee that improvisation is transformative. Scholars of critical improvisation studies differ in the degree of social efficacy they ascribe to improvisation,[1] and we are especially concerned with avoiding reductive liberation tropes. For Daniel Fischlin, Ajay Heble, and George Lipsitz, musical improvisation enacts a politics of hope. "In its most fully realized forms, improvisation is the creation and development of new, unexpected, and productive cocreative relations among people. It teaches us to make 'a way' out of 'no way' by cultivating the capacity to discern hidden elements of possibility, hope, and promise in even the most discouraging circumstances" (Fischlin, Heble, and Lipsitz 2013, xii). For these authors, improvisation's "most fully realized forms" are often found in Afrodiasporic musics, particularly post–World War II jazz and creative improvisation broadly construed, and their politics are indexed to important struggles for human rights. But what does it mean for an improvisation to be "fully realized?" In the contributions to *Negotiated Moments* by Siddall and by Wong and Eidsheim (which we discuss in the second section of this introduction), improvisation occurs in the context of narratives that figure improvisational jazz and blues as the audible trace of trauma inflicted on female (black and same-sex) bodies. For these women, improvised music may serve as a coping mechanism, providing at least a limited space for self-expression within a repressive environment, but it is also the soundtrack for violence, for repetitive cycles of hatred passed along generations. The bruised and battered bodies of these subjects trouble liberatory claims for improvisation: although "coping" may be one step toward liberation, it may also be an expression of faint hope in the face of an impossible situation. One of the aims of this book is to examine those improvisational moments that are skewed, incomplete, or compromised to bring bodies that are often silenced into audibility. We focus less on moments of improvisational liberation and more on processes of improvisational negotiation in which agency is understood to be hard won, highly contingent, and relational.

Dance scholar Danielle Goldman (2010) describes improvisation in terms of negotiating tight places, an image that has much in common with the idea of making "a way" out of "no way." She finds political potential in improvisation as "practices of freedom" defined and even enriched by the constraints under which they operate. Goldman's thinking is deeply informed by the late work of Michel Foucault. In his "Ethics of the Concern for Self" (1984), Foucault draws a distinction between definitive moments of liberation (as an end goal) and practices of freedom (that are necessary to continue the effects of liberation) (quoted in Goldman 2010, 4). Goldman cautions, however, that "there are times when no degree of improvisational skill is sufficient to extract oneself from a situation of duress" (142) whether that situation be a nasty fall in the dance studio or a violent attack in a church. Improvisation, she contends, is "a rigorous mode of making oneself ready for a range of potential situations. It is an incessant preparation, grounded in the present while open to the next moment's possible actions and constraints" (142). From this perspective, improvisation is somewhere between assertiveness training and a survival strategy because it rests on both the acquisition of technique and a quality of constant readiness. Improvisational agency, Goldman suggests, is hard won, though it can result in "exquisite moments" that reveal "bravery, and choice, and surprise, and trust" (141).

Tracy McMullen locates agency in her term "the improvisative." Riffing on philosopher Judith Butler's influential theory of performativity, described later, McMullen's idea of the improvisative offers some hope of individual agency in the self-aware, alert subject. She maintains, "to the extent that the subject can recognize his or her own incompletion, contingency and co-arising with the other, s/he can remain open to the productive nature of discourse, allowing new meanings to emerge" (see chapter 1). In McMullen's interview with Butler in chapter 1, Butler accepts the relational aspect of the improvisative but cautions against a too volitional theory of improvisation. Describing what happens when an actor responds to a gesture in an improvisational scene, Butler insists "my agency is determined or formed in part in that exchange; it doesn't well up from within me. It's not an expression of my conscious, deliberate choice" (chapter 1). McMullen and Butler remind us that improvisational agency is both contingent and relational.

Butler has indeed had a formative influence on discursive theories of subjectivity. Her theory of performativity is especially resonant for our project because of its relationship to performance and its musical idea of repetition. Take, for example, her influential theory of gender construction in which the gendered subject is called into being by performative language; observing that the child has a vagina, the doctor cries, "it's a girl!," thus hailing that child into the social laws pertaining to the feminine gender (J. Butler 2008). Butler draws on discourse theories (especially the work of Louis Althusser, Michel Foucault, and Jacques Derrida) to demonstrate both how subjects are constructed by discourse and how they perform subjectivity within a scene of constraint. Societal notions of gender are reinforced through the subject's unconscious repetition of performative words and actions: from pronouns to clothing and makeup to compliant behaviors.

Performativity offers a limited notion of agency both when the subject transgresses expected codes (for example, cross-dressing), or by the variation— the space for newness—that is bound to creep into repetition of such codes. Butler cautions that the subject's agency is strictly limited since transgressing dominant discursive formations (for example, heterosexuality) can provoke brutal responses from the state. Performativity is useful to a theory of improvisation as social practice precisely because the citation of social codes (performative speech and actions) reveals the workings of power.

In her book *Agency and Embodiment*, Carrie Noland extends performativity to the realm of gesture, a domain that she asserts is not coterminous with language because it is embodied and kinesthetic—sensed by the body and available to the conscious mind (2009, 10). She defines embodiment as "the process whereby collective behaviors and beliefs, acquired through acculturation, are rendered individual and 'lived' at the level of the body" (9). Agency is "the power to alter those acquired behaviors and beliefs for purposes that may be reactive (resistant) or collaborative (innovative) in kind" (9). Using the analogy of throwing like a girl,[2] and describing ways this set of socially conditioned gestures can be retrained, Noland argues that—unlike biological signifiers of gender (vagina, penis)—"gestural routines are particularly vulnerable to processes of de-skilling and re-skilling; these processes undermine the culturally regulated body-discourse relation and produce intense kinesthetic and affective experiences of dissonance. . . . In short, the moving, trained, and trainable body is always a potential source of resistance to the meanings it is required to bear" (175). In our view, improvisation is the medium par excellence for the adaptable body that, however constrained, may enact potent moments of transgression and unpredictability through sonic and physical gestures that are often coterminous.

Take, for example, Clara Tomaz's articulation of learning how to speak again after mouth cancer surgery, described in chapter 10. A professional linguist, Tomaz knows numerous languages. After her surgery she underwent an intensive process of rehabilitation, learning how to speak again in English (a language secondary to her native Italian). This process involved entraining a whole new repertoire of gestures and sounds. "Having to work on each phoneme individually made me sensibly aware that language is an assemblage of sounds just as the body is an assemblage of organs" (quoted in chapter 10). Tomaz's experience of her body (taken with the adaptive experiences described by many people with disabilities) stretches our understanding of subjectivity to include not just repetition with a difference but the possibility of creating entirely new modes of speaking and acting in the world. To be sure, Tomaz is constrained by the laws of language (she wants to communicate in English), but she has also redefined what it means to speak (through new ways of forming consonants and vowels). By improvising new ways of embodying language, Tomaz refuses to be silenced and redefines fluency.

Noland's idea of gestural performativity invokes improvisational techniques of stylistic entrainment, code switching, adaptability, interoperability, close listening, and responsiveness that form the technical arsenal of any good musical improviser. Indeed, Tomaz turned to improvisation to make sense of her new adaptation. Her multimedia improvisational performance *Deviations and Straight Line* evokes her sense that "the sound I can produce as a human being is the expression of my personal consciousness. It makes all of my vibrations, emotions, perceptions and thoughts resound in the space around me" (quoted in chapter 10). Tomaz's evocative description brings us back to sound and sounding.

If, as Noland insists, embodied gesture obeys different laws than linguistic discourse does, what does the materiality of sound add to our understanding of improvisation and subjectivity? After all, in improvised musicking, sound and gesture are intimately related. In addition to the obvious gestures of breathing, blowing, fingering, and bowing, playing an instrument entails body movements that are seemingly unrelated to the production of sound (the clarinetist who employs deep knee bends at emphatic moments, for instance) and musicians in ensemble often unconsciously synchronize movements such as head bobbing or swaying in time to the music. Musical sound also participates in the discursive realm, however, since style and genre codes convey very specific gestural and affective information. Musicologists have long ago shown that by virtue of its embeddedness in culture, music *is* representational.[3] Still, sound itself is without doubt a material substance that is, paradoxically, "mysteriously immaterial" (Connor 2005, 157). Although sound vibrations are intensely physical, sounds themselves are not easily perceived as objects. We are surrounded by sound, immersed in it, vibrated by it, but we cannot easily separate sound from our experience of it. As Steven Connor explains, "how something sounds is literally contingent, depending on what touches or comes into contact with it to generate the sound. We hear, as it were, the event of the thing, not the thing itself" (157). What sound adds to the vocabularies of language and gesture is its extreme contextuality.

Ethnomusicologist Harris Berger draws on phenomenology to explain this trickster quality of sound and our ability to shift our perception of it through stance. Berger defines stance as "the affective, stylistic, or valual quality with which a person engages with an element of her experience" (2009, xiv). He follows Maurice Merleau-Ponty's influential idea that the subject is formed through acts of perception that are both partial and mobile (Berger 2009, 57). We can shift the relationship of figure and ground as we experience our body's relationship to objects and to itself (my right hand holds a cup, my left hand touches my right hand holding the cup), but we can never experience either as complete. We know the world through our body's direct and mediated experiences of the world. Furthermore, Berger explains (following Husserl's *Fifth Meditation*) that our understanding of subjectivity is relational: "I understand the type 'subject' from my direct experience of being a body in the world (of having experiences of the world, of my body's own responsiveness to my intents), and in the pre-reflexive constitution of experience, I see the body of another person as another subject" (71).

Berger theorizes that our experience of another subject (like that of our own bodies) is always partial and "constrained and enabled by the vicissitudes of communication and understanding, expression and deceit" (2009, 71). Importantly, for our theory of improvisation and sounding bodies, such stance qualities are a form of social practice, involving "those complex qualities of social relationships that are crucial to the sophisticated interpretation of expressive culture, including but in no way limited to trust and suspicion, domination and resistance, familiarity and alienation" (72).

In listening to someone play music, then, our stance affects the degree to which we perceive the other as a subject and the attitude we take toward that subject. For example, while listening to an ensemble of freely improvising musicians, your stance will be affected by your understanding and sympathy (or lack thereof) toward free-form musicking. Depending on your stance, you may experience the dense interlocking phrases, distinctive timbres of saxophone, bass, and drums, and fast tempo as liberatory or oppressive, virtuosic or chaotic. In his contribution to this book, Zachary Wallmark traces music critics' stances toward John Coltrane's saxophonic scream, which critics variously heard as hysterical noise or groundbreaking innovation. Such interpretations, he demonstrates, are not purely aesthetic but are instead imbricated with attitudes toward masculinity and race. Indeed, Berger warns, there is no guarantee that in any given situation the listener will "attend to the other as subject" (2009, 73) an idea borne out in any number of early ethnographic accounts of "exotic" music heard as "primitive" noise.[4] In this sense, Berger's phenomenology is not dissonant with discursive theories of subjectivity, for "both the significance given to stance and the interpretive processes by which the listener constitutes it in her experience are deeply informed by culture" (73). As Ellen Waterman and Deborah Wong demonstrate in their chapters, in intercultural improvisations, the stylistic and generic rules pertaining to diverse traditions deeply inform the stance of both musicians and listeners. If, as we assert, musical and sonic improvisations produce audible traces of subjectivity, these traces are seldom either direct or simple, or, for that matter, easily readable.

Of course, musical stance is further complicated by the fact that so much of our experience of music is heavily mediated. For example, musical improvisation may be recorded in concert or studio, edited in postproduction, distributed via any number of media, learned by another musician by ear, or transcribed in a score. The most spontaneous improvised solo may ultimately take on the fixed status of a composition, faithfully studied by jazz students. Improvisational performance, like all musicking, lives in the immediate experience of the listener, but the rhizophonic nature of recordings calls individual accounts of agency into question. Jason Stanyek and Benjamin Piekut define rhizophonia as "the fundamentally fragmented yet proliferative condition of sound reproduction and recording" (2010, 19), and they argue that a relational interagency is demonstrated in recordings "where sounds and bodies are constantly dislocated, relocated, and co-located in temporary aural configurations" (19).[5] Our point is that improvised music's corporeality is far from limited to nodes of performance and audition; the sonic corpus is diffused across time, space, and media. It resonates in memory and readily mutates into new contexts, new meanings. Indeed, contributions to this book by Jason Robinson and Andrew Raffo Dewar explore aspects of dis/embodiment and hyperembodiment through real-time mediations of bodies across time and space.

David Borgo, in his contribution, explores the puzzle of interagency, arguing that improvising with newer technologies can extend, but also complicate, our sense of individual authorship and control.

By gathering such disparate points of view on improvising and sounding bodies, we are deliberately refusing any singular theory about improvisational agency. Like the "exquisite moments" Goldman finds in improvisational dance, the diverse contributions to this book offer several examples of musical or sonic improvisations that change a stance, alter relationships between subjects and their social/cultural environments, and decenter power (at least in the improvisational moment). Our contributors also describe improvisational encounters in which sound overpowers and brutalizes subjects, marks the imposition of forced change, serves to consolidate hierarchies, or disperses bodies altogether. Contingent and mobile relationships in and through sounding bodies support the idea of interagency that emerges through resonance, through vibration. Throughout this collection of essays, improvisation is understood as a complex site of negotiation, and sound and music are heard as both the discursive signs and the embodied experiences of those negotiations.

Improvisation, Vibration, Resonance

Negotiated Moments is organized according to five sections: Listening, Place, and Space; Technology and Embodiment; Sensibility and Subjectivity; Gender, Trauma, and Memory; and Representation and Identity. Chapter 1, Tracy McMullen's interview with Judith Butler, precedes these five sections, standing on its own as a special challenge to think about subjectivity and agency in terms of discourse and corporeality. As already discussed, in the interview with Butler, McMullen posits her theory of the "improvisative" as a way to disrupt Butler's notion of the repetition compulsion of performativity. For McMullen, the improvisative opens up possibilities for creativity—for newness, both musically and socially. Butler, in turn, resists notions of agency, but not of possibilities for newness; for her, that newness comes accidentally and partially, when we unintentionally repeat with a difference. The tension between improvisatory agency and performative constraint identified by McMullen and Butler is a motif that appears in diverse variations throughout the five sections that make up this book. Taken as a whole, these essays remind us of what is gained when we foreground the body in critical considerations of and aesthetic responses to music and thinking about improvisation. Our ability to mobilize the political and social potential of improvisatory creative practices necessarily stems from understanding the deeply situated, relational, and embodied contexts that shape those practices. In what follows, we discuss the themes that resonate and vibrate through and across the book's sections.

Listening, Place, and Space

It is axiomatic that musical improvisation is as much a process of listening as of sounding. In the two essays discussed here, listening occurs in direct relation to embodied experiences of place and space. In her essay on sound-walking, Andra McCartney invokes Luce Irigaray's conception of love as a form of listening that embraces the unknown in the other. Irigaray conceptualizes an ethical model of intersubjectivity that denies mastery over another: "I am listening to you: I encourage something unexpected to emerge, some becoming, some growth, some new dawn, perhaps" (1996, 116–17). For McCartney, this theory of love as listening offers a new model for sound-walking, a social and aesthetic practice that involves the cultivation of a heightened awareness of sound in the environment. Her commitment to intimate listening has led McCartney to alter her career-long practice of leading people on guided soundwalks and, instead, to develop a far more improvisational form that promotes individual awareness and invites dialogue. Soundwalking is thus more than an expressive practice; it becomes a way of articulating ethical relations among subjects moving through and experiencing space.

Like McCartney, performance studies scholar and artist Rebecca Caines also wishes to employ improvisation as a methodology for making community-based sound art as a means of helping people articulate their relationships to space and place. In partnership with John Campbell, a computer programmer, Caines designed an online sound mixer that enables communities in widely dispersed locations to share sound files and create soundscape pieces as a creative response to their experiences of site/space/place. Her ethnographic collaboration with communities in Australia, Northern Ireland, and Canada involved complex negotiations of institutional bureaucracies, the vicissitudes of technology, and divisions along class, age, and cultural lines. Improvisation became not only a methodological tool for collaboration but a practice of adaptation that allowed Caines and Campbell to listen and respond to the needs and desires of the communities with which they worked. Within this improvisational practice, listening is a way to promote ethical intersubjective relations that also registers how difference and power are themselves instrumental in sounding contexts.

Technology and Embodiment

The essays in this section engage the possibilities of technological mediations of the body through improvisation from extensions of the body in time and space to the dispersal of bodies across networks and into larger social systems. They explore the persistence of embodiment as particular experience in technology (Hayles 1992).

Pauline Oliveros insists that "listening lies deep within the body and is as yet a mysterious process involving myriad time delays" (chapter 4). Her contribution to this volume traces her sixty years of improvising with audio technologies, from the variable-speed tape recorder she received as a present in the 1950s to her evolving Expanded Instrument System, which connects her performing body to digital instruments and networks. An archive of the musical examples she discusses is available online at http://www.improvcommunity.ca such that her essay encourages a full engagement of the senses, both visual and aural. Oliveros has an acute awareness of her body and of embodiment with technology. She delineates the connection she sees between the time delays that occur in the reel-to-reel tape recorders she improvised with in the 1960s (the delay between the record head and the playback head) and the embodied time delay inherent in humans producing and hearing sound. Oliveros advocates listening to the time/space between to integrate global attention with focused attention. "Balancing these two forms of attention," she declares, "is the dance of improvisation—opening to receive and focusing to a point" (chapter 4).

Jason Robinson deals with the issue of latency that occurs during telematic performances where musicians in different locations perform together in real time via sound and video sent across the Internet. The result of latency is a dislocation of sound from image that can be unsettling for players and audience. Latency is an issue that is best resolved, for some, by working toward achieving zero latency through improved technology and, for others, by adapting musical forms to compensate for sonic delays. For Robinson, latency is most productively negotiated through improvisation and expressive microtiming. His notion of the "networked body" describes the doubled experience of (dis)embodiment that marks a performance practice that, he argues, will open up a new musical paradigm and a new consciousness of embodied performance.

Andrew Raffo Dewar considers that the performing musician's body is fetishized, a concept he explores through technology developed by Zenph that extracts information from a recording in such a way that the moving keys of a Disclavier (digital piano) can replicate a piece of music exactly as originally played, in this case by jazz pianist Art Tatum. Live "reperformances" of Tatum's music have been staged with the digital piano standing in for the dead musician, and Zenph has also released new recordings that feature the digital reperformance. Dewar concludes that the primacy of the body as well-spring of creativity may well be profoundly challenged by the advent of new digital technologies that reconfigure notions of liveness and embodiment.

David Borgo goes even further in challenging conventional notions of embodied creativity by looking beyond methodological individualism. Drawing on research in social psychology, neocybernetics, and social systems theory, he argues that the human being is neither a sufficient nor a necessary entry point into understanding social and communication systems. Far from a position of hermeneutic despair, however, Borgo argues that collective improvisation affords an opportunity to celebrate the ubiquity of agency in coaction, and that looking beyond traditional understandings of communication as a form of information exchange actually moves us closer to a performative understanding of, and engagement with, the world.

Sensibility and Subjectivity

In contrast to the fragmented, distributed, and diffused bodies discussed in the previous section, several contributions to this volume focus on ways material bodies engaged in improvisatory practices can effect a reorientation of identity and community. Sherrie Tucker and Tomie Hahn invoke the dynamic idea of stretching to articulate what happens when improvising bodies engage with each other in ways that accommodate difference and expand our understanding of both sensibility and subjectivity. Their chapters share similar collaborative formats: in each case the author solicited short contributions from a number of other writers and framed those contributions with her own insights. Tucker's chapter features the voices of seven artists who work with and through physical disabilities. Hahn's chapter has nine meditations by people who participated in her workshops on improvisation and movement in the context of a summer institute on improvisation as social practice.[6] These chapters express common themes about bodily interaction and awareness.

For Hahn, improvising community is facilitated by the literal stretching of industrial rubber pallet bands. Connected by the bands at ankles and elbows, feet and torsos, necks and knees, the participants in her banding workshop improvised together, moving vertiginously through space like some many-headed alien creature with a dozen arms and legs. As the participants' journal responses attest, banding highlights—indeed, makes visible—the complex dynamics of collaborative improvisation. As one of the participants writes of the experience: "Through the push and pull practice of engagement, we found a sensibility of process" (chapter 8).

Tucker (who was one of the banding participants) extrapolates from that activity a model for improvising across abilities. Her essay reminds us that often theories of the social function and effects of improvisation ignore differently abled bodies and make an assumption about the primacy of sound based on normative notions of hearing, vocalization, and language. She asks the provocative question: "What if experimental musical communities committed to explorations of difference in realms such as harmonics, time, timbre, and form, were equally avid about the differential variable in musicians' and audience members' modes of sensory and perceptual relationships to sound waves, as well as difference in mobility, range of motion, ratios of voluntary/ involuntary mobility, multiple modes of cognitive processing and language?" (chapter 8). The artists responding to this question greatly expand our understanding of what it means to move, sound, touch, see, and be an expressive body in relation to other bodies.

One of the things that fascinates Hahn about the banding exercise is how quickly the participants achieve "flow," defined as a state of being where people are so immersed in what they are doing that they become unaware of anything else: a state of extreme attention that transcends technique (Csikszentmihalyi 1990, 4). Csikszentmihalyi studied flow in the context of elite athletes and concert musicians, but flow does not depend on any particular bodily configuration. In Tucker's chapter, David Whalen, a visual artist with paraplegia, similarly describes the conditions under which he achieves this state while digitally painting and drawing using an adaptive instrument. The state of flow implies a highly integrated mind/body connection that can facilitate a reorientation of one's sense of self in relation to others and the environment.

Jesse Stewart invokes the notion of flow in his analysis of what happens when people interact with artist David Rokeby's *Very Nervous System*. *VNS* uses motion capture technology to create an environment in which a person's movements trigger sounds in three-dimensional space, although not always in predictable ways. As with the banding exercise, participants interacting with *VNS* appear to enter into a state of flow much more quickly than would normally be the case because their bodies are put into an immediate relationship with sound, movement, and space that does not depend on specialized skills as musicians or dancers. Stewart argues that *VNS* thus democratizes musical experience, albeit within an atmosphere of surveillance: it produces its effects by literally watching (and sounding) our every move, often producing an uncanny sense that the technology reacts *before* it receives a bodily stimulus.

Gender, Trauma, and Memory

The four essays in this section bring literary analysis into contact with improvisational music by considering gendered narratives of trauma and memory. In writing about trauma and memory, Cathy Caruth identifies the paradox of the continual reexperiencing of an event that one cannot actually remember: "The final import of the psychoanalytic and historical analysis of trauma is to suggest that the inherent departure, within trauma, from the moment of its first occurrence, is also a means of passing out of the isolation imposed by the event: that the history of a trauma, in its inherent belatedness, can only take place through the listening of another" (2007, 204). For Caruth, the dialogic process of attempting to heal from trauma involves a particular kind of listening: "by carrying that impossibility of knowing out of the empirical event itself, trauma opens up and challenges us to a new kind of listening, the witnessing, precisely, *of impossibility*" (204). Her articulation of listening to what is impossible to know resonates with conceptions of improvisation that foreground listening as partial and provisional but also open to new ways of thinking. It also resonates powerfully with ways scholars like George Lewis (1996) have conceptualized African American forms of improvised music such as jazz as embodying the traumatic memory of slavery.

For a number of our contributors, improvised music becomes a means of embodying and replaying such traumatic memories. In Nina Sun Eidsheim and Mandy-Suzanne Wong's essay, Ursa Corregidora, the eponymous heroine of Gayl Jones's novel, is characterized as dealing with her ancestral history of trauma through both deliberate and unconscious acts of memorialization. Ursa responds to her personal experiences of domestic abuse and the sexual violence experienced by each generation of women in her family (dating back to her enslaved grandmother) by singing the blues, an intentional act of memorialization, and unconsciously through the timbre of her voice, unaware that to others her very voice is marked by generational traumatic memory. Wong and Eidsheim assert that "to play music, especially to improvise, is in part to bring oneself under the influence of other bodies from the past. We perform memories, our own and those of others" (chapter 12). Riffing on Foucault, they coin the phrase "corporeal archaeology," which they define as an awareness of one's own improvising body as "a living, bleeding archive of other bodies, ideologies, and values" (chapter 12).

Smith and McNeilly also explore the connections among memory, history, and improvisation in their analysis of Octavia Butler's science fiction trilogy *Xenogenesis* and jazz musician Nicole Mitchell's musical reimagining of it. They argue that "Mitchell's music materially re-members . . . the atrocities committed on black women's bodies" (chapter 14), responding to Butler's reference in *Xenogenesis* to well-known cases of black women's bodies being abused by medical science. Similarly, Gillian Siddall points to the explicit connection between trauma and improvisation in her analysis of Ann-Marie MacDonald's novel *Fall on Your Knees*. One of the most horrifying scenes in the novel is one in which a woman is severely beaten by her father in a passage that employs tropes of various musical styles to describe the brutality of the beating as well as the daughter's resistance to her father.

In these contributions, the trope of motherhood is key to the authors' conceptualizations of how memories live on in subjects across generations. As Kevin McNeilly and Julie Dawn Smith put it (invoking Julia Kristeva): "The mother subtends a concurrent existence of self and other—a paradox of 'being oneself and someone else at the same time' (Kristeva 1984, 223) and mediates mind and body" (chapter 14). Octavia Butler's narratives of interspecies survival assert motherhood as a central trope for the complexity of human identity and community and "trouble static notions of human subjectivity" (chapter 14). For Wong and Eidsheim, motherhood is the embodied trace of past trauma and resilience that lives on in the heroine's improvisational blues. In Siddall's analysis of *Fall on Your Knees*, Materia's relationship with her daughters is constrained and limited by her husband, but she and her daughter Frances in particular are connected by their improvisatory practices. Materia's improvised accompaniment to silent films allows her to define herself in the context of the call and response of community music-making—in concert with her audience. Frances employs a similarly improvisatory and ironic approach to her performances in a speakeasy, where her parodic stripteases denaturalize social categories of gender and sexuality. The figure of the mother in these chapters embodies notions central to improvisation—past and future, memory, creativity, and intersubjectivity.

As a counterpoise to these narratives of female gender and sexuality, Zachary Wallmark analyzes the critical reception to John Coltrane's saxophone playing and demonstrates how our precognitive reaction to sonic timbres can nevertheless invoke tropes of masculinity and race, as already noted. In his analysis of the saxophonic scream (an incredibly high-pitched, raw, and intense explosion of timbre first developed in the context of free jazz), Wallmark emphasizes a perceptual/cognitive approach that focuses on the degree to which the listener identifies with the sound. Citing recent research on the neurophysiology of audition, Wallmark locates a biological reason for the phenomenon of musical empathy—the perception that in listening to a sound we also participate in it. Our participation, however, is culturally conditioned. Coltrane's saxophonic scream was variously interpreted by music critics as the sound of black masculine violence and rage or as a sign of the jazz icon's spirituality, a transcendent sound. Music critics' visceral, embodied interpretations of Coltrane's saxophonic scream turned on their reactions to the birth of free jazz in the context of the U.S. civil rights movement.

Representation and Identity

The three chapters in this final section of the book situate improvisation in terms of representations of national and ethnocultural identities. Illa Carrillo Rodríguez and Berenice Corti focus on improvisational responses to the official celebrations marking the two hundredth anniversary of Argentina's first independence movement against Spanish rule that troubled (classed and raced) narratives of nationalism. Deborah Wong explores the power relations found in gender and ethnic identities in Japanese taiko drumming, and Ellen Waterman analyzes an improvisational performance by the intercultural trio Safa through the filter of Canada's official policy of multiculturalism.

Carrillo Rodríguez and Corti return us to themes of trauma and memory, this time situated in the context of historical narratives employed in the service of nation-building. They argue that the government's bicentennial celebrations served to memorialize a national history that elided the violence done to thousands of Argentine citizens during the period of state terrorism in the 1970s and early 1980s, and they argue that various improvisational artistic responses to that imposed national narrative provide a powerful counternarrative borne out of collective memory. Carrillo Rodríguez and Corti also explore "dissonant iterations of motherhood" (chapter 17) in their discussion of the Madres, mothers publicly protesting their "disappeared" children in Buenos Aires during the 1970s. The improvisational techniques of the Madres were reconstituted by the theater group Fuerzabruta in a street parade during the Argentinian bicentennial that included the responses of thousands of people who encountered this powerful commemoration with improvisations of their own, described by the authors as performances of historically charged silence.

In an essay that traces the surprising historical links between Japanese taiko drumming and American jazz, which came into contact in Japan during World War II, Wong addresses the ways in which taiko solos are both racialized and gendered. Taiko is a communal drumming practice in which players step forward to perform "improvised" solos as part of composed pieces. Depending on the confidence of the soloist, such solos may indeed be spontaneous or they may be precomposed displays of virtuosity. Wong argues that early taiko solos emulated the hard-driving beats of African American (male) jazz drum solos and have been remasculinized over time in the North American context in a complicated response to the Western feminization of Asian men. Her analysis of the gendered nature of improvised solos highlights the solo as a domain of gendered bodily anxiety.

Waterman similarly explores intercultural encounters in musical improvisation, this time through the work of Safa, an ensemble that brings Iranian classical music together with modal jazz and Latin American rhythms. Through her ethnography of a particular performance, she explores the musicians' negotiations of diverse musical styles, revealing their deep enculturation and the circulation of power involved in their elaboration. While the musicians' experience of collaboration is one of almost spiritual unity based on mutual respect and musical authenticity, members of an audience focus group interpreted the performance as a display of Canadian multicultural values that privilege the accommodation of difference within an (unacknowledged and hegemonic) norm. This dissonance invites Waterman to work out from her close reading of the performance to consider questions of selfhood and subjectivity in the context of the politically charged discourse on Canada's official policy of multiculturalism, a policy that is designed to simultaneously celebrate and contain difference.

An Erotics of Improvisation

As our summary of the contributors' diverse approaches to improvisation indicates, these essays open highly productive and crosscutting themes that reveal the intricacies of improvisational relationships through agency and interagency, body and bodies, self and selves, sounding and (other means of) sensing. One of our goals is to ensure that valences of bodies and embodiment that are not always heard in critical studies of improvisation resound in these essays: gendered and sexed bodies, differently abled bodies, and bodies that are imaginatively extended through technology.[7]

Perhaps not surprisingly in a book focused on bodies, an erotics of embodied improvisation pervades many of these essays, as they explore and assert the sensuality of musicking, of improvising bodies responding to other improvising bodies, to listeners, and to embodied histories. Sexual and/or sensual intimacy is figured in several of these essays as a profound connection that creates new, albeit partial and complex ways of being and knowing. For example, Smith and McNeilly capture this notion in their description of Nicole Mitchell's music: "Sense—as sensation and meaning—emerges in Mitchell's sound-world as a recombinant amalgam that [...] prod[s] us to question how and where our own bodies begin and end, how self and other interpenetrate, collaborate, dissolve, and (mis)comprehend, and how community can arise from cohesion and from misfires" (chapter 14). Smith and McNeilly use the word *sense* to capture the integration of sensuality—bodies—and meaning in a way that also dissolves distinctions between others and ourselves. Improvisation here is understood as a highly intimate and sensual intermingling of bodies and ideas, a process more chaotic than volitional, and the result is unpredictable but undeniably new—the very DNA of sense altered in the "recombinant amalgam" of new meaning, new identity, and new community.

In embodied improvisations, subjectivities are formed and re-formed in the profound and unpredictable dissolution and recombination of identities, whereby misfires can lead to cohesion. There is no clear sense of individual agency here; indeed, there is a sense of loss, or at least of the fluidity of identity, but also of the capacity for individuals and communities to change based on their willingness to engage with others, embrace the intimate chaos, and recognize that meaning and sensuality cannot exist separately. It is, in its own way, a hopeful means of conceptualizing improvisation, but it is founded on the necessary unpredictability of human connection. Such an erotics of improvisation, we suggest, invites us to think about the social effects of improvisation differently: they result from the complex and unpredictable interchanges between bodies and meaning, sound and subjectivity. By paying close attention to improvisation as a site of negotiation among embodied, sensing subjects, we listen for the full spectrum of ideas that sound out, from clarion calls of freedom to sounds of struggle and cries of despair.

Notes

1. This book is an extension of a growing body of literature on critical studies in improvisation. We are particularly inspired by contributions from Fischlin and Heble (2004); Fischlin, Heble, and Lipsitz (2013); Heble and Wallace (2013); Monson (1996, 2008, 2009); Rustin and Tucker (2008); Smith (2004, 2008); and D. Wong (2004). See also the early prognostications for the efficacy of improvisation as a social practice made by Attali (1985). For a good cross-section of the emerging literature see the online journal *Critical Studies in Improvisation/Etudes critiques en improvisation* at http://www.criticalimprov.com.

2. Noland is referring to the famous essay by political philosopher Iris Marion Young (1980), who analyzed the constricted physical movements of women in urban, postindustrial society in phenomenological terms.

3. McClary's landmark book *Feminine Endings: Music, Gender, and Sexuality* (2002), which stirred great controversy in academic music on its original publication in 1991, is now arguably orthodox.

4. See Bellman (1997) for a fascinating collection of essays that position "exotic" music, from the blues to Romany fiddling, as primitive and therefore a sign of Otherness to be exploited in Western art music.

5. In their article "Deadness," Stanyek and Piekut offer an intriguing analysis of duets recorded by live musicians who "collaborate" with an extant recording by a dead musician. Such recordings, they argue, trouble the ontology of deadness.

6. The Summer Institute on Critical Studies in Improvisation was organized by the research project Improvisation, Community and Social Practice (ICASP) and took place at the University of Guelph in 2011.

7. We are grateful to have been part of two large-scale multiyear grants from the Social Sciences and Humanities Research Council of Canada that enabled us to engage in sustained research on critical studies in improvisation within interdisciplinary teams and community partnerships. The International Institute for Critical Studies in Improvisation (a partnered research institute across five Canadian universities) promotes the kind of performance- and community-based research that is profiled in many of the contributions to this book (http://improvisationinstitute.ca/).

1. Improvisation within a Scene of Constraint

AN INTERVIEW WITH JUDITH BUTLER

Tracy McMullen

As a cultural theorist and a scholar in the growing field of critical improvisation studies, I am often preoccupied with the following question: "What exactly *is* improvisation?" I ask this not only in relation to musical performance but, as a student of Judith Butler and other theorists of identity, in terms of the subject and "everyday life." As George Lewis has remarked, the practice of improvisation in everyday life is ubiquitous.[1] Moment to moment we are faced with choices. Events occur and we must respond to them: from operating a vehicle, to answering a student's question, to responding to a stranger's anger erupting in our vicinity—in our moment-to-moment existence we have few formal and explicit rules to follow; rather, we acquire a "feel for the game" (Bourdieu 1993, 189). There are formal traffic laws, but no universal law on how to avoid a specific accident; we prepare for our lectures, but we must decide on the best answer to any student's question based on our perception of his or her understanding and the rest of the listening students; every day we must negotiate with other people in a variety of emotional states. In Butler's terms, this "game" we get a feel for is the "scene of constraint" (2004, 1). That is, there are certain rules about our identities. If there weren't, we would never have the feeling we were breaking them. How a black man or an Asian woman responds to anger may be informed by different "games" based on the race- and sex-based rules they have subtly intuited in culture, but as Butler argues, there *is* a modicum of freedom within our scene of constraint. Within that game, within those structures, improvisation occurs. However, it is difficult to articulate just what that improvisation is. At least in my view, to understand this space would be to unlock the secret of how the subject can undo itself and access human freedom. But this is my thinking and certainly not how Butler would put it. I wanted to better understand how this important theorist thinks about improvisation.

In her ground-breaking book *Gender Trouble* (2008), cultural theorist Judith Butler articulates how gender identity is performatively constructed. She writes, "there is no gender identity behind the expressions of gender; that identity is performatively constituted by the very 'expressions' that are said to be its results" (34). Influenced by Friedrich Nietzsche's assertion that the "doer" is a fiction that arises and coheres around the "doing," as well as Louis Althusser's explication of ideology as "hailing" the subject into being, and Austin's linguistic analysis of "performatives" (words that *accomplish* things, like the pronouncement that christens a ship), Butler argues that "the subject is retroactively, performatively 'hailed' into gender in much the same way that Austin's ship is named and Althusser's 'man on the street' assumes his subject-position in response to the policeman's call" (Salih 2004, 6–7). The subject, therefore, is brought into being in and through the other (and not just in terms of gender). The subject is produced in the doing of language, law, gender, race, culture. This is its condition of possibility. The subject may appear to be an independently operating entity, but this is only the outcome, the "subject-effect," of myriad and complex cultural operations that, in short, could be described as the "law."

Even so, all is not lost for the subject. Influenced by Jacques Derrida, Butler conceives of the operation of the law as linguistic and therefore endlessly open to citation and even misfire. Furthermore, subjects do not always answer back to their hailing in ways that perfectly repeat cultural norms. As Sarah Salih writes, Butler finds "potential for agency in the subject's response to an interpellative call that 'regularly misses its mark,' while elsewhere [she] insists that there are any number of ways in which the subject may 'turn around' in response to the call of the law" (2004, 10). Within this condition of possibility for the subject, then, there is space for productive misunderstanding, misinterpretation, misrecognition, and even conscious reinterpretation. Butler's emphasis is less on *trying* to reinterpret and more on allowing for the possibility of not knowing. To the extent that the subject can recognize his or her own incompletion, contingency, and co-arising with the other, she or he can remain open to the productive nature of discourse, allowing new meanings to continually emerge. Indeed, the solidification of rules and norms institutes the violence of identity boundaries. Butler is therefore committed to an ethics of "unknowingness" and is conscientiously nonprescriptive. She urges us "to [know] unknowingness at the core of what we know, and what we need" (2004, 39). Because decisions are made in a "lived moment" and are not the perfect enactment of rules, theoretical or otherwise, she steers away from prescribing specific steps to move toward a more livable world for all subjects.[2] This, in particular, is where her thinking dovetails with work on improvisation.

Although the term *improvisation* is not prevalent in Butler's work, her emphasis on "unknowingness," openness (incompletion), and responsiveness to the "lived moment" aligns her work with recent discussions on ethics and improvisation.[3] Furthermore, the term appears several times in *Undoing Gender* where she describes gender as an "improvisation within a scene of constraint" (2004, 1). Because Butler specifically uses the idea of improvisation here, I wanted to query her on its role in her thinking, and I begin the interview with a reference to this title. I was hoping to get answers to the following types of questions: How does improvisation accord (or not) with theories of performativity and the subject? Does the subject *do* improvisation? Or is the subject *done* by improvisation, much like it is *done* by gender? Or is it something in between? If improvisation designates a "relative domain of freedom" for the subject "in a rule-bound world," as Butler states in the interview, what is this domain? Is there a way to expand it? Where is the point where the rules end and improvisation takes over? While I think it would be a mistake to attempt to pin down what improvisation is, I do believe we need to take a closer look at how this "relative domain of freedom" is constituted.

In my efforts to query Butler on this space, she replied in ways I have heard from her before: that we cannot imagine the subject to be able to simply "step out of the rules." If the subject is constituted through the field of the Other, there is no subject who can work from outside of this system to dismantle it. There is some leeway, however, in that the law is also carried out *through* the subject. The subject embodies and repeats the law—but this repetition is not mechanical or completely predictable. The law is not perfectly repeated through the subject. In this sense, paradox is the subject's condition of possibility. The subject is constituted in and through the law, but it also *does* the law. It is being done *and* it is doing. The subject's agency, however, is too often confused with the liberal humanist individual who can pull herself up by her bootstraps and transcend every social structure as if she resides outside of it. This view does not take into account the ways the subject is disciplined for exceeding norms or the subject's own necessary perpetuation of these norms in order to be intelligible within the social field.

Nonetheless, I believe it is imperative to examine this space more closely. One way I tried to ask about this space was in relation to how "newness" enters the system—how is it, more precisely, that the law is not repeated exactly? For Butler, it is generally in the imperfect way we reproduce the law through repetition. The law is like language in that it cannot perfectly convey its message (there is always some gap between meaning and representation) and its mode of operation, reuse, opens it up to new meanings. To me, the concept of misfire in particular suggests a random error like the imperfect replication of a genetic characteristic as described by Charles Darwin. I wonder if there is something more that can be said in addition to the inadequacy of language to predictably "hit its mark." Can the subject do something to help along a result different than the repetition of the law?[4] Here Butler's and my contrasting perspectives on the predictability of the law and the repetition of discursive regimes become evident. Butler underscores the unpredictability involved in reproducing discursive regimes, whereas I envision this repetition as highly predictable. For Butler, this unpredictability is the opportunity for difference and newness to enter the system. My view is that the law can be understood as a habit that will reproduce itself quite predictably (I do not argue that it is completely predictable) because it offers a sense of security. Therefore, some effort is needed to do the unpredictable thing, an effort that is akin to some practices of improvisation. Butler and I were in agreement that improvisation can be understood as a space of "allowing," a type of openness that acknowledges an unknowingness—a refusal to cohere into a decision. I believe this space offers the moment of unpredictability within the law that constrains us. I would argue, however, that recognizing openness and unknowingness is something that needs to be practiced again and again. It involves some effort on the part of the subject, and it shifts the focus from the inability of the other (law, language) to adequately convey its message toward a focus on how the subject (self) encounters everyday experience.[5] Butler is leery of words like *effort* because she wants to avoid facile arguments about the freedom of the subject. I agree. Let us not be facile, but let us also investigate.

Judith Butler graciously accepted my invitation to do an interview and I am grateful for her time and thoughtfulness. Although we only had the opportunity for a short discussion, Butler ended it by saying, "Well, this is a beginning." I certainly hope so. As it turned out, our interview took place in the immediate wake of the killing of Osama bin Laden by U.S. Navy Seals in Abbottabad, Pakistan. As our interview came to a close, I asked her if she could comment on this event in light of our discussion.

May 2, 2011
Berkeley, California

TRACY McMULLEN: I am intrigued by a certain musicality in your book *Undoing Gender* and the way you use the term *improvisation* in relation to gender identity. For example, the book begins with a chapter entitled

"Acting in Concert," which I found to be a very musical metaphor. In that chapter you describe gender as an "improvisation within a scene of constraint," and later in the book you discuss a little boy "improvising" with putting on girls' clothes. You actually highlight and italicize improvisation as a way to understand his behavior.[6]

JUDITH BUTLER: Yes.

TM: When you speak about "improvisation within a scene of constraint" then, do you see a difference between what could be called "performance" and what could be called "improvisation"?

JB: Well, yes. Let's take performance: Performance has many different valences. We talk about people's work performance, we talk about "high-performance technology," for example, and performance studies has introduced an idea of performance that is both theatrical, in part, but also a part of everyday experience or involving modes of actions or presenting in the world that don't require a proscenium stage. If we are going to work with this latter idea of performance, then a number of questions emerge. For instance, is the human subject or the human body always performing? Is it defined by the fact that it is performing? I want to say that can't be the case if we understand performance as always active or always a question of doing something. There are domains of passivity, modes of not doing or undoing or doing nothing or being done to that clearly do not form part of a traditional idea of performance. I think that in my work I try to underscore the ways we are acted on by norms, by conventions, by prior practices, by cultural forces, that we don't choose and never chose, and that it's in relationship to being acted on in certain ways that we ourselves act. So for me the idea of performance always has to be understood in light of what acts on us. We're not just active, we're also acted on, and it's that doubleness that constitutes the scene of our acting.

Now improvisation strikes me as a very specific kind of practice because while it involves to a certain extent what it says—namely, improvisation—it also involves a certain relationship to rule-bound behavior. We wouldn't understand improvisation if there were no rules. In other words, improvisation has to either relax the rules, break the rules, operate outside the rules, bend the rules—it exists in relation to rules, even if not in a conformist or obedient relation. And this opens up the question of what leeway we have for acting in a rule-bound world. So to say, for instance, that gender rules or laws or norms precede us and act on us is not to say that we're determined in advance, that we must replicate them faithfully. And when we do replicate them, or even though we do situate ourselves in relation to those norms, rules, and practices, there is sometimes a possibility of a kind of free play—an improvisational moment. Perhaps that happens when we follow the wrong rule or we use a particular resource that's available that was not supposed to be available to us. Like the boy uses the ribbon to dance with and actually the ribbon was meant for his sister but it was still there in the room and at the moment in which he felt the need to dance he saw that ribbon or perhaps the ribbon instigated in him the desire to dance and he took it up. It's a prop that becomes a resource for a certain kind of improvisation. So for me improvisation designates a relative domain of freedom in a rule-bound world.

TM: So I often saw, and I'm wondering if you have any more to say on this, a connection—and you brought it up right now—of improvisation and play.

JB: Yes.

TM: Could you say a little more about play? You speak about the subject improvising within a scene of constraint and the subject coming into being, basically, through ideology as its condition of possibility. But there are times when you speak about the things that are in excess of subjectivity; the things that are in excess of identity. Sometimes you put it in terms of "psychic excess," sometimes you put it in terms of sexuality—spaces that are going to exceed any type of category. I'm wondering if there is a relationship there between play and the space of improvisation, that something is breaking out or not completely colonized by the realm of the Symbolic? Do you see any connection there?

JB: I guess I want to resist your question.

TM: OK, please.

JB: I say this because I feel that too often my account of gender performativity has been reduced to an idea of play that I don't really like, and that I think tends to imply that experimentation with gender norms is easier than it actually is. I mean, people who experiment or "play" in the wrong time and place can be subject to incarceration or pathologization or other forms of violence, so I don't know about play. I know that play is a very important category in the history of aesthetics. Kant makes aesthetics into a question of the play of understanding. Play is also important to [Donald] Winnicott, in his analysis of child psychology and the question of how we form attachments. Play seems crucial to that whole process. So I do not mean to demean or dismiss the concept. But I'm afraid that it takes us too quickly away from the scene of constraint, and for that reason it wouldn't be a word that I would choose.

TM: Could you say a little bit more about what you mean, then, when you talk about psychic excess or sexuality or that space that exceeds categories?

JB: Well, it's one thing to try to describe one's sexuality in terms of available categories, but then there is sometimes a bit of a joke that happens when people declare themselves to belong to one sexuality or another and then suddenly find themselves engaged in activities that don't quite comply. I don't think we can always be fully conscious and fully in control of matters like sexuality, and I'm not sure they easily conform to existing social categories. Sometimes those social categories are disrupted or abandoned or complicated in ways that make it hard to use them at all. I don't know if that's a question of play. It actually could be an experience of agony.

TM: I want to say a little bit about how I am thinking about improvisation. There is something that I refer to as the "improvisative."[7] I view the improvisative—and this is why I have been asking about this space that exceeds categories—as the opportunity to actually break the repetition compulsion of performativity. I do view performativity as a type of repetition compulsion. Performative identity can be understood as a copy of a copy with no original; and the space of agency within performativity can be found in that reduplication, that reiteration, that new copy. But for me, that theory doesn't quite get at how newness, how real creativity, how something different can enter into the picture. There are constantly things that are not colonized by language all around us and that sometimes break in. So I think of the improvisative as that space within the performative where newness can break in. I don't know if you have a thought on that at all. I understand what you are saying about play, and I do think the idea has often been too facilely employed in terms of performance.

JB: I understand. There are two points here. At least in *Gender Trouble* when I talk about a copy of a copy I think I'm dealing with the homophobic argument that gay and lesbian people replicate heterosexual structures and perform a kind of "false" or "unreal" version of heterosexuality, whereas heterosexuality is "real"—in response to this, I argue that it may be that the very genders that are formed under conditions of compulsory heterosexuality are also copies of themselves. That's different from the idea of iterability that I develop in the text, and I think repetition compulsion is part of this latter idea. It's a psychoanalytic concept that suggests that we repeat things without knowing why we do—and it could be that we repeat gender norms in general without knowing why we do. But the other thing about repetition compulsion, at least in psychoanalysis, is that the forms of repetition are never predictable; it's not mechanical, which means that things happen in the course of repetition compulsion that are unanticipated and new. So on the one hand there's no freeing ourselves of gender norms: We are going to repeat them, they work on us, they work through us, we reproduce them. But it may be that in the midst of repetition we repeat with a difference. So I want to say that there are opportunities for newness that emerge within the very practice of repetition. For me, repetition is not mechanical replication. In fact, I think that happens rarely. Your parents tell you to be this kind of girl and then you end up being a different one. You think you're obeying them, but actually you're doing something else; you thought you were doing the right thing, but it turns out you're not. Those kinds of misunderstandings are always a possibility when people take on gender norms—they think they are complying but actually they're producing a new problem.

TM: So I guess in some sense we differ there, because I do tend to see repetition compulsion for the most part as exceptionally predictable.

JB: Oh, I'm sorry.

TM: (*laughter*) No, that's great. I'm thinking of something in "Beyond the Pleasure Principle," and it is kind of an aside that Freud makes, when he discusses someone who keeps encountering the same types of difficulties in her or his life because of a quirk of personality that keeps generating the same types of scenarios and responses. A person who keeps running into that same type of alcoholic lover or whatever. He doesn't use that example, but something along those lines.[8] For me—and maybe this will connect more with some of your more recent work—this idea that the improvisative is that space, that energy, that sort of effort that it takes to *not* do the predictable thing . . .

JB: But you see, for me that makes it too volitional. That makes it really deliberate, and chosen, and enlightened and conscious. And I guess what I want to say is that a lot of us end up in non-normative or even new positions by virtue of processes and in relation to formations that we don't fully understand. We end up living out a gender norm or a bodily norm that took shape without our deciding "oh, I think I'm going to do something radically free and break the chain of repetition." We don't have that choice. It is more that we find ourselves in the world constituted in ways that don't conform or that do produce predicaments and that sometimes, yes, introduce newness into the social landscape. Then the question is, how do you navigate that? I suppose I prefer a word like *navigate*, or, how do you broker that? How do you handle being in this position that you never exactly chose but for which you are responsible, and the effects of which you have to live with? That's a different kind of agency than the one that would presume a kind of enlightened or deliberate action.

TM: When scholars discuss this idea of improvisation, however, there is often less emphasis on a typically volitional space and more on listening, on receptivity—

JB: Yes.

TM: ... on, sort of, pausing ...

JB: Yes.

TM: ... allowing for some space so that there's not just an immediate "I'm going to do this." Also, as theater, dance, and music scholars have begun to work with theories of performativity—because our work as performers is very much of an "embodied practice" ...

JB: Yes.

TM: ... many of us understand that there is a lot of knowledge that doesn't lend itself very easily to conceptual terms but that nonetheless is a type of knowing. I'm sure you have your nonconceptual knowing as well (*laughing*). So that in some sense the idea of improvisation can be almost, it is different than volitional ...

JB: I agree. The part of improvisational practice or art that I have been most drawn to is the social dimension; the fact that people very often improvise with one another ...

TM: Absolutely ...

JB: ... and that the improvisational scene, for instance, involves one person saying something and another person responding and some kind of reality being built through that listening, pausing, responding, that is a kind of "acting in concert."

TM: Absolutely.

JB: So this gives us a relational understanding of agency more than an individual, deliberate one. When I listen to another or if I'm in an improvisational scene and someone takes a move toward me or hurls an insult at me, something acts on me and I have to act in relationship to how I'm being acted on. That's part of the point I want to make—my agency is determined or formed in part in that exchange; it doesn't well up from within me. It's not an expression of my conscious, deliberate choice. It's something that happens between me and the other person. And in that sense it is something that emerges from the relationship itself.

TM: Yes. And if you can think about—because you sound to me like you are a "free collective improviser" (*laughs*)—you can imagine that when people are playing music together and they are improvising in that way and they are at a relatively skilled level of improvising, that the interesting element is to *not* do the predictable response. To do something that is going to break it open in some way. This is what improvisers would think about doing as they are practicing their art. But the way that they do that could be very surprising, even to themselves.

JB: Yes, but there are other things that happen. For instance, in jamming, in music, very often one musician has to compensate for the limitations of another—like you start jamming and you realize this person only knows how to do X (*laughs*), or that they can't really make a transition, I'm the one who has to initiate the transition. Or, say, here's a person who doesn't know how to respond to this kind of provocation but can respond to another, so you end up accommodating each other or compensating for one another and there are also questions of strength and weakness that arise; what you can be together actually has to be found out in the course of the improvisation. I don't know if that is a response to you but it just seems like—it's not always an equal or a symmetrical scene.

TM: Absolutely. For example, in *The Conquest of America* Tzvetan Todorov [1999] argues that [Hernán] Cortés was able to overtake the Aztecs and Moctezuma because the Europeans were able to improvise and the Aztecs were stuck in ritual repetition where they couldn't really go with the flow. So improvisation is not inherently some ethical phenomenon. We have to think about what we really mean with improvisation. Some people believe that improvisation means just throwing out the rulebook, a type of deregulation: a neoliberal "sure, I'm going to improvise because I know all the scripts, all the discourses, so I can just go in there and blow everybody else away."

JB: Right. I think it's tricky. We could think not only about improvisation and neoliberalism, but also about "flexibility" as a post-Fordist economic ideal. There are all these risks, I'm sure.

TM: That's why for me, I do make a distinction between this idea of improvisation and an improvisative, because "improvisation" is used in so many different ways. And if you talk about, let's say, jazz improvisation, it often is discussed in some of those terms: if you master all of these various styles and techniques then you can dominate. And that's even part of the discourse, you are a monster, a badass, you're a dominator, because you can play. But then there is another type of improvisation which, in my view, almost becomes bored with mastery.

JB: Yes.

TM: Because once you've "mastered" something then you just want to move on. You want to constantly—for me again it becomes that space of not wanting to repeat the predictable thing—you want to have that newness somehow...

JB: Yes, but wouldn't receptivity be really important...

TM: Yes, yes.

JB: . . . to the production of something new? Like letting something happen to you and being moved by something in a way that you hadn't planned? And letting something emerge as a consequence of that?

TM: Yes.

JB: It seems to me a model of agency or action that's not based on mastery.

TM: Yes! So you like this idea of receptivity, listening, awareness, allowing space?

JB: Well, I think we're acted on. We don't act without being acted on. We don't generate ourselves. We're not self-created creatures. We're always moved by something and it's only because we're moved that we act.

At this point Butler indicated that we would need to wrap up the interview. I wanted to ask her one more question in relation to an immediate turn in events: the killing of Osama bin Laden in the early morning hours of May 2 and the displays of celebration and jubilation across the United States that were currently being captured and replayed by the news media.

TM: As we wrap up, I want to take the opportunity to ask for your reaction to the very significant news that Osama bin Laden was killed last night. I've written about a kind of "martial repetition" in the United States—of perpetuating a certain type of action that then perpetuates another predictable result, instead of maybe being more receptive, more creative, more ready to do something that is not so predictable, so expected.[9] And in some sense, the killing of Osama bin Laden seems part of that same type of repetition that I discuss. I don't know if you'd have something to say about the killing in terms of anything we've been discussing on improvisation or repetition or . . .

JB: I think killing has unfortunately become a ritual form of nation-building for the United States. People cheer because he is dead and they say that justice has been done, but actually it is that revenge has been leveled. Is there a distinction between revenge and justice? I worry about how quickly we celebrate killing and how killing has become part of the way we celebrate ourselves. It's become part of our sense of the nation and it builds us as a nation every time it happens. So one can see a kind of ritual of killing that becomes crucial for U.S. nationalism.

TM: Do you see it in any way related to this idea of repetition and the idea of improvisation and doing something different or being receptive or awareness? Do you see it at all in those terms?

JB: I did think that there was something somewhat remarkable, indeed perverse, about the fact that on the one hand they kill him brutally, and then they claim that they will give him a burial that accords with Muslim law. But at the same time that they will give him a burial in accordance with Muslim law they are going, as an act of respect for the Muslim world, to drop him at sea so that no Muslim could ever visit his grave and so his grave can't become a site of mobilization or political assembly. I just think, wow, so many contradictions are manifest here. But if you want to ask what could be new? I don't know. At least [Adolf] Eichmann was brought to Jerusalem for a trial. I mean, I don't like the death penalty, although one should imagine the death penalty might be right for Eichmann, I'm not sure. But at least he was brought to Jerusalem for a trial. Here there was no code of international justice at all. This is not justice, this is nation-building, it's violence, it's revenge. And people seem to be extremely happy about it.

TM: Yes. I saw it as just a repetition of the same—both that it happened and people's reaction to it. One of the things that I have generally liked about [Barack] Obama is that, to some extent, I felt that he did step back. I felt that was very significant in opening a space for the Arab Spring, the perception that there wasn't this hovering U.S. presence like there was with the Bush administration, that there was a little bit of space, a letting go, and that allowed for a chance for democracy to bloom. That's my take on it. But then this is just more of . . .

JB: This is the Bush-Obama continuity.

TM: Yes, it is.

JB: We have a nod to multiculturalism in the midst of it, which was merely a tactical nod, so that there isn't a huge global demonstration against the United States. If there's a new twist, that's it, but it doesn't ameliorate its effect. I'm afraid I don't see anything new here at all.

Notes

1. "Improvisation is the ubiquitous practice of everyday life, a primary method of meaning exchange in any interaction" (Lewis 2008, 108). Furthermore, because improvisation is "as close to universal as contemporary critical method could responsibly entertain" it is "a crucially important site for both humanistic and scientific study" (108).

2. For Butler, "political decisions are made in [the] lived moment and they can't be predicted from the level of theory" (Butler quoted in Bell and Butler 1999, 167).

3. See for instance, Fischlin and Heble (2004) and Nicholls (2012).

4. Here I do not mean that the subject can intentionally attempt to *make* new meanings. I don't think the "subject" can. I discuss this in relation to the improvisative in McMullen (2014).

5. I describe this as a lean toward the subject rather than the object in McMullen (2014). See note 7.

6. See Butler (2004), 95–96.

7. In McMullen (2014) I argue that a focus on the notion of the performative puts an emphasis on recognition as the central modality of human life, whereas a focus on the improvisative makes generosity the pivotal modality. This is a move from the post-Hegelian construction of the subject as one that must seek, negotiate, and/or broker the recognition of an other to the idea that through giving to the other (another being or even an activity) the subject can move from a preoccupation with recognition and acknowledgment of self to a focus on the other. This focus, in fact, frees the subject from the very system of power that constructs it. As such, I argue that humans *can* function in the world without recourse to the "subject." I call this practice a lean toward the subject, however, because the focus is more on what the "self" can do (give) rather than what the "other" does (recognizes).

8. In speaking of "normal (non-neurotic) people," Freud writes in "Beyond the Pleasure Principle," "The compulsion which is here in evidence differs in no way from the compulsion to repeat which we have found in neurotics, even though the people we are now considering have never shown any signs of dealing with a neurotic conflict by producing symptoms. Thus we have come across people all of whose human relationships have the same outcome: such as the benefactor who is abandoned in anger after a time by each of his protégés, however much they may otherwise differ from one another, and who thus seems doomed to taste all the bitterness of ingratitude; or the man whose friendships all end in betrayal by his friend; or the man who time after time in the course of his life raises someone else into a position of great private or public authority and then, after a certain interval, himself upsets that authority and replaces him by a new one; or, again, the lover each of whose love affairs with a woman passes through the same phases and reaches the same conclusion" (Freud 1989, 604).

9. See McMullen (2008).

PART I

Listening, Place, and Space

2. "How Am I to Listen to You?"

SOUNDWALKING, INTIMACY, AND
IMPROVISED LISTENING

Andra McCartney

How am I to listen to you?
How am I to listen?

"How am I to listen to you?" is the question that philosopher Luce Irigaray asks at the beginning of her chapter on listening, "In Almost Absolute Silence," in the book *I Love to You* (1996).[1] Irigaray proposes that intimate listening, the special listening we might reserve for the words of a lover, ideally would be open, aware always of difference and ineffability:

> I am listening to you, as to another who transcends me, requires a transition to a new dimension. I am listening to you: I perceive what you are saying, I am attentive to it, I am attempting to understand and hear your intention. Which does not mean: I comprehend you, I know you, so I do not need to listen to you and I can even plan a future for you. No, I am listening to you as someone and something I do not know yet, on the basis of a freedom and an openness put aside for this moment. I am listening to you: I encourage something unexpected to emerge, some becoming, some growth, some new dawn, perhaps. I am listening to you prepares the way for the not-yet-coded, for silence, for a space for existence, initiative, free intentionality, and support for your becoming. (1996, 116–17)

Irigaray's conception of ethical listening resonates strongly with my own work as an artist and scholar concerned with embodied sound and listening. "How am I to listen?" is a question central to my life's work of research and creative practice in soundwalking.[2] I have a particular relationship with walking. Because of a hip disability, I did not walk until I was almost five years old, and now live with intermittent pain in one hip that sometimes makes walking difficult. I treasure the ability to move through space unaided, but never take it for granted (McCartney 2006). Perhaps because I can never take the simple act of walking for granted, I have always been acutely aware of the surrounding environment through which I move and have cultivated a practice of active listening as an integral aspect of walking.[3]

In this chapter I argue that Irigaray's conceptualization of love as involving a kind of listening that is open to what is not yet known and not yet coded provides a valuable theoretical model for approaching soundwalking. Irigaray moves active listening from a generalized environmental activity—"How am I to listen?"—toward an interpersonal ethics—"How am I to listen to you?" The approach to listening she describes has a great deal of improvisational possibility. Each subject in the exchange must remain alert and open. The future is not composed or prescribed; it must remain unsealed, as in improvisational music that is open to the possibilities of the moment. This way of listening seems ideal to me for sensitivity to the unpredictable shifts and changes of the sound environment, and it has shaped my project Soundwalking Interactions.[4]

The Soundwalking Interactions project explores the quality of creative listening interactions around soundwalk activities in different media and using varied approaches. Soundwalk recordings in the project are used to make digital videos, blog entries, and sound pieces for radio and other kinds of broadcast, and as sources for a gestural installation piece. Participants' experiences are discussed directly in conversations following each walk, and this discussion informs the sound work, video, and blog entries. A further aim of the project is to establish enduring connections with other researchers using creative approaches to walking and listening. "How am I to listen?" expresses a desire to explore a time and space through listening to the walkers, the place, the talkers, the surroundings, and the spaces between. How can we listen actively and openly, without overly didactic interventions that could limit other ways of thinking? How can this thinking about open, alert, lucid listening contribute to discourse on improvisation in listening, with a role for the participants that is creative as well as interpretive?

In what follows, I provide some background on soundwalking, after which I address the dual aspects of intimate listening and improvisational listening. I bring both of these concepts to bear on a particular soundwalk at English Bay in Vancouver, which was part of the Soundwalking Interactions project. Thinking about this soundwalk through Irigaray's approach to intimate listening allows me to reflect on the power dynamics that take place in soundwalks and the conversations that surround them, and how these dynamics shape listening practices over the long term.

Soundwalking

The term *soundwalk* emerged with various practitioners in Canada in the 1970s, and it has since become an international practice. Researchers in the World Soundscape Project, founded in the early 1970s at Simon Fraser University in Canada by composer R. Murray Schafer, engaged in listening walks, which were often undertaken for orientation purposes during initial visits to places where the group intended to document and study the soundscape. One member, Hildegard Westerkamp, created a radio program in the 1970s that took listeners on local soundwalks across the entire Vancouver listening area through broadcast mediation. Through conferences organized by the World Forum for Acoustic Ecology (which was founded in 1993 by members of the World Soundscape Project) and at many music festivals and other venues, soundwalking developed and grew. Public group soundwalks were led by acoustic ecologists to sensitize people to the sounds of the environment.

More recently, soundwalking has taken on an explicitly artistic dimension. Viv Corringham records her conversations with a person who takes her on a "special walk"; later, she retraces the walk while recording her own improvised vocal responses to it.[5] Andrea Polli traced repeated neighborhood soundwalks with GPS, the thickness of traced lines underlining her habitual walking patterns. A focus on environmental interaction in these walks is shared with other kinds of walking art, such as electrical walks (Christina Kubisch), audio walks (Janet Cardiff and George Bures Miller), micro-radio walks (Michael Waterman; Kathy Kennedy), and walking performance (Christopher Long). Participants in Kennedy's radio walks interact with the environment by singing while broadcasting to the immediate neighborhood through handheld micro-radio transmitters. In this way artists and sound-walkers become cocreators, improvising with their environments.

How Am I to Listen to You? Intimate Listening

My own approach to soundwalking is *assez particulier*, as we would say in Montréal. Particular, special, intimate perhaps. It is informed by my association with the field of acoustic ecology and several other fields of study, including feminist and critical theory. In recent years, it has also been informed by Irigaray's conception of love. For this reason, when I am introducing soundwalks,

I encourage participants to engage in intimate listening—that is, listening to the sound environment as if it were a dear friend or lover. To me, using Irigaray's theories of love as a theoretical model for soundwalking leads ideally to increased awareness and valuing of difference, a recognition that no one can be truly known or understood. Intimate listening for Irigaray is a better model than psychoanalytic or therapeutic listening, because it recognizes the potential for transference in both directions. In her exploration of an Irigarayan approach to reading art, Hilary Robinson develops the concept of the attentive audience: "the word audience has overtones of sociological surveys and of the theatrical, but does have the benefit of retaining a trace of Irigaray's interest in the practice of listening. I will call it a practice of attentiveness, as I think this suggests a combination of chosen activity, non-imposition and being-a-subject; and use the phrases 'the attentive woman' or 'the attentive audience,' on the understanding that attentiveness involves more than one sense, and presupposes a move towards intersubjectivity" (2006, 78). In this formulation, the world is not closed out or sealed away, and objectivity is possible through consideration of and respect for differences among all of us others (similar to Donna Haraway's idea of objectivity through partial connections in situated conversations, which I discuss later in this chapter). Here, I want to dig deeper into what Irigaray proposes in *I Love to You*, because of what I believe is its great potential for thinking about relationships in the intimacy of love and also in the wider world. Understanding her aim in the book as a whole is important to thinking about how this kind of listening could work. "I love to you" is an attempt to reshape the syntax of this intimate sentence that is so familiar that it can be taken for granted. I (subject) love (verb) you (object) is the traditional form that is often heard, a verbal construction in which the loved one is ineluctably an object, an other who is desired as an object, something that can be fixed in place. I love to you (*J'aime à toi*) displaces this construction, reminds the speaker that love can only be in the direction of someone else, who remains forever their own person, linked through the bridge of the *to*, the *à*, a bridge that must be maintained by both sides but, like a suspension bridge over a chasm, can only persist through growth and change if it resists being fixed too tightly.

Irigaray says in a later publication that perhaps we can approach the larger world as a different subject as well: "We have to meet the world, in particular the natural world, as other, to respect it instead of appropriating it into only one world: our world. Education ought to teach how to respect and contemplate the world, and not only how to grasp and master it, as has been too often the case in our Western culture" (2008, 234). Is it possible, however, to transpose the attitude of listening to an intimate friend that Irigaray advocates in *I Love to You*, a listening that seeks understanding without objectifying, with that kind of focus and desire for a different understanding, an understanding that makes room for difference? Is it possible to transpose and listen in this way to the world outside that intimate bond of two? Such an approach to listening would require an improviser's particular listening skills.

How Am I to Listen? Improvisational Listening

I want to listen openly, creatively, alert to the moment and to chance, improvising. I want this possibility for people participating in soundwalks that I initiate. When I am out doing individual listening and recording work for a sound project, the moments of discovery teach me the most, engage me most strongly. These moments of discovery introduce new ideas and new ways of hearing the space through listening intensively to the sound; to hear how it is being shaped by the space, weather conditions, and the sounds that are heard there at that moment; and by thinking about relationships between sonic moments. Sometimes in planned walks, that feeling of discovery is gone because the experience has become predictable, the route set. A soundwalk leader can hire musicians or other artists to perform at certain moments on the walk, creating even more of a set piece. The risk of such preplanning is that the soundwalk becomes a spectacle, the walkers more like an appreciative audience than active participants. How, then, can I maintain that level of creative listening attention that characterizes exploratory improvisational work, for myself and for those on walks with me, throughout the process of many hours of preparation and then the soundwalk itself?

For me the answer lies in thinking about listening in soundwalks as a form of creative improvising. Ellen Waterman (2008b) defines creative improvising as "an intersubjective and dialogic practice in which past histories and future aspirations are conjoined in the immediacy of musical creation." She goes on to say that "while it is almost impossible to pin down stylistically, creative improvisation by definition demands a reciprocal exchange among all participants . . . improvisation's potential to model new social relations is dependent on the degree to which it disrupts discourse while remaining fluid and unfixed" (2). I want to find a way of making soundwalks that encourage the kind of listening Waterman describes here, "intersubjective and dialogic," where the focus is less on sensitizing numbed listeners to the sound environment and more on exploring the multiple ways that people listen and how those ways of listening are conjoined, during the silence of the walk and the flow of the conversation after it, in reciprocal exchange.

All listening has the possibility of being improvisational, but as William Echard pointed out in a soundwalk discussion,[6] the potential for improvisation in listening can be dampened sooner or later by authoritative discourses that claim a correct way to listen and proper ways to focus attention. Listening is directed in different ways, through focus on certain sonic features (urban noise, silence, architectural movements of sound) or ways of listening (ecological listening, reduced listening, musical listening) and implicit or explicit discouragement of discussion in other directions; these listening methods and ideologies function as prescriptions or scores that can constrain potential for improvisation in listening. At the same time, suggestions about how to listen politically, socially, environmentally, musically, and intimately can function as supports for opening listening into new directions. What structures of listening do soundwalk participants find valuable to encourage active engagement with a sound environment and when do such supports become too constraining?

Listening is often conceived of as a receptive activity more than a creative one. In the Western hierarchical concert model, performers are up on the stage interpreting the ideas of the composer; the audience is sitting quietly in their seats, paying attention and following along, attempting to understand the musical ideas of composer and performers. Popular music can challenge this formation through greater involvement of the audience in dance and call-and-response forms. Even so, the stage, occupied only by performers, and the powerful sound system remain as structural supports for musicians to speak out to relatively quieter listening audiences, who can only match the sound en masse.

To some extent, the very idea of a soundwalk contravenes this distinction between artists and audiences. Everyone participates in the movements of a public soundwalk, and there is no clear delineation between performer and audience: it may not be immediately obvious to a passerby who exactly is the leader. Everyone listens together and performs the soundwalk together, paying attention to the sounds of the surrounding environment, sounds that are not controlled by the leader (except in particular cases where sounds are added or performers are planted in the environment).

At the same time, there is a leader, someone who plans the walk and decides on the route and approach to be used, perhaps asking the participants to be silent to facilitate unobstructed listening. Often, other participants in the walk are not aware of the route or approach until the time of the soundwalk, and so need to follow along with a preestablished program, like performers of a composition.

To animate soundwalking with an intersubjective and improvisational ethos, I have developed a three-by-three, tripartite approach to soundwalks for the Soundwalking Interactions project: overture, promenade, polyphony; soundwalk, conversation, document; listeners, makers, collaborators.

Soundwalking at English Bay

In November 2011, I led a soundwalk through English Bay in Vancouver.[7] I chose the area partly because it complicates the stereotype of sound ecology as oriented toward pristine isolated hi-fi soundscapes and as decrying urban intensities. English Bay is one of the most densely populated urban areas in Canada, a place of verticality dominated by high-rise apartment buildings, always under construction, highly trafficked. It is also what I would call an ecotonal place, drawing on ecologist James Gosz's use of the term in his article "Ecotone Hierarchies" (1993). The ecotone is a marginal zone, a transitional area where species from adjacent ecosystems interact. Some species in an ecotone are from neither ecosystem but thrive here and do not live elsewhere, because of the rich possibilities contained in such regions, which have characteristics of more than one ecosystem. English Bay is a place in which many urban ecosystems intersect and overlap: main streets, back streets, jogging paths, bicycle paths, apartment building fortresses, streets of shops, parkland, beaches and the Pacific Ocean with container ships in the distance. The ecotonality of this place, resulting from its urban complexities, makes it resistant to any extremes of sonic ideology, of representing horrible urban noise or serene wilderness quiet. With all its complexities of overlapping soundscapes, one resident told me she loved the calm of English Bay in relation to other parts of Vancouver where she had lived, and the easy access to water and parkland, its walkability and human scale, what Jane Jacobs (1961) would call urban vitality. I love to walk and listen there. Its ecotonality seems to provide a good context for engendering surprise and an improvisational approach to listening. Because of the complexity of the sound environment, it is more difficult to predict what will be heard each time a soundwalk takes place. The possibility—the likelihood—of difference keeps ears open for change.

At the beginning of this walk, I handed out a paper that introduced what we would do (excerpts from the handout are in italics). The handout provides a kind of musical structure for the walk: overture, promenade, polyphony. I wanted to mark each part of the activity as important, to bring attention to the frame of the event, and the importance of conversation before and after the walk—to remember that the walk is part of a larger conversation. The handout also included the following two quotations:

I am listening to you as someone and something I do not know yet, on the basis of a freedom and an openness put aside for this moment. I am listening to you: I encourage something unexpected to emerge, some becoming, some growth, some new dawn, perhaps. (Irigaray 1996, 116)

Encountering each other in an open field, no paths as yet defined, we follow where the sounds lead, attention given to each nuance of sound activities and interactions each moment revealing. There is no correct way to listen, except to be present, hearing. (Goldstein 1988, 11)

I encouraged participants to meditate on the meanings within and the connections between these quotations, one from a philosopher and the other from a musical improviser. I myself see interesting connections between them; both invoke openness, acceptance, and encouragement of the unexpected and surprising. Goldstein's words also invoke the spatial metaphors of open fields, undefined paths, and sounds that lead the listener to new places, all of which seem particularly appropriate to the activity of soundwalking, especially soundwalking that emphasizes listening in the moment. These quotations also imply that perhaps it is possible to hear connections between intimate listening and improvisational listening.

The following notes are also included in my handout:

Overture

con brio

Thanks for joining us on this English Bay soundwalk. I want this to be a space and time for listening. Please turn off phones and remember to hold the power of your voice in reserve for emergencies since attention to your voice will take your fellow listeners away from other listening possibilities around us. There are many ways of listening: musically (melodies, harmonies, rhythms, timbres); historically (other times you have walked here, the larger history of this place); politically (who controls the sounds and how do they shape what we hear); socially (how this soundscape reflects its urban context); evocatively (how sounds evoke other, different landscapes through features that are shared or interact); sensually (being aware of relationships among listening and other senses). Perhaps listening together and then talking afterwards about how we listened can even lead to something new, surprising and thought-provoking for each of us.

At the beginning of soundwalks, I usually suggest that people use as many of the above approaches to listening as possible. This strategy allows them to participate actively in the discussion at the end without fears concerning their expertise with fields such as music or sound ecology, allowing them to draw on historical, literary, social, political, or other competencies and knowledge as well. As Stanley Fish (1980) points out, each academic discipline or ideological grouping has established interpretive routines that are used to understand and to create works in that discipline. Suggesting a wide variety of ways of listening can bring these various ways of listening, and different interpretive routines, into productive confrontation with each other and open up improvisational conversation.

The group comprised fifteen people: some from the Vancouver soundwalk collective, several of whom were also graduate students at Simon Fraser University (SFU) in Communication Studies; some undergraduate students also from SFU; some people from elsewhere in Vancouver who had heard about the walk through Vancouver New Music advertising in newspapers; some neighborhood residents; and some scholarly visitors from out of town who had met me at SFU the day before.

The next part of the handout discussed the walk itself. I wanted to make clear to people that they could change the route by interacting with me, if they wished, or they could choose to walk alone and meet up with us at the end. Some people had arrived late and missed the spoken introduction, so the printed handout gave another method for them to learn of the planned schedule.

Promenade

andante

We will leave the Laughing Guys[8] (why are they laughing?) at 7:15 pm and start walking through the English Bay area, following our ears and exploring routes of sonic interest. I have some favourite places and sounds in this neighbourhood but am open to change, so will be listening for cues. Feel free to touch my arm and beckon if there is something you wish to draw attention to. If the group feels too large to you, feel free to break away and take your own route through the neighbourhood, focusing on listening. In any event, our route as a group will end at the Sylvia Hotel seminar room, at around 8 pm. If you have gone off on your own, please join us there to talk about your soundwalk experience.

My method in preparing soundwalks was originally as I had learned it from others, influenced in particular by the World Forum for Acoustic Ecology's approach to soundwalks. I would spend a lot of time in the selected location and would plan a specific route that showed off interesting sonic and pedestrian features of the area—architectural features of buildings that highlight sonic effects, different surfaces to walk on, ubiquitous and masked sounds. As time went on I started to think more about the pedestrian affordances of sites—how it is possible to walk in certain areas, and how some routes are barred.[9] I started to suggest different options for the soundwalk (group, individual, partial). Because most of my soundwalks are in urban areas, I also began to consider how the soundwalk can contribute to the awareness and maintenance of urban vitality.

After beginning to think more about the agency of participants in the walk, I began to experiment with ways to make the public soundwalk more improvisational, relying less on the score of a prescribed walk. To be honest, I often found it more exciting to plan the walk than to lead it, because there seemed to be more experimentation and surprise at the planning stage. Would it be more engaging for me and other listeners to leave the walk more open to the moment? How can I make sure that I am well prepared and yet still open to possibility?

At English Bay, I spent several hours on each of the previous days walking around the area and noticing sonic features. I found several sounds that I was partial to: the waves on the beach, the halyards of flags hitting the poles, a gleaner pushing a clanking cart full of bottles and cans, the electrical hum of a tram turning the corner. I also walked at night because the planned walk was scheduled to take place in the evening, and I wanted to experience the area's nocturnal soundscape. It was much quieter than I had expected, not as many people on the street. When I walked the beach that night alone, the lack of lights made me feel wary and somewhat anxious, especially when a hooded jogger passed, blocking my exit. This reminded me of earlier soundwalks at night, and how gendered experience of public spaces affects how people move through them and even whether they choose to walk in certain places (McCartney and Gabriele 2001).

Based on the knowledge I had acquired, I decided how I wanted to begin the walk but left the route open. We began by going down to the sea, stopping to listen to the lapping waves mixing with the sounds of the neighborhood. I realized that I was much more comfortable stopping there with a group of people. Walking back across the beach toward the jogging path, our footsteps were muffled by the sand, and at some points I felt the illusion of walking alone, confirming the reassuring presence of the group by turning my head. We walked up to the street, through a passageway that brought the participants into close contact with each other and with the echoes. Across the street was a small park with a bandstand that had no steps up to it, curiously. Why? We walked through wet late fall leaves back to the street.

At the corner of Denman and Beach, we entered a zone of partial listening possibility. I am thinking here of the way that Haraway speaks of the word *partial* (1988). Our partial knowledges are partial in the sense of being only part of a whole, missing certain parts, and in the sense of being focused on what we are partial to, what we like, what draws our interest. There were several sounds there that I was partial to: the flagpoles and their metal melodies, a heavy metal board covering road construction that created rhythms from the traffic, and the electrical hums of trams. Taking the group through this zone created the possibility for us to hear some or all of these sounds. How we heard them depended on the moment: if there was no wind, the flagpoles would be silent. The board had only been placed there that day and depended on traffic for its rhythms. I had not heard these particular rhythms on previous soundwalks, since the board had not been there. The trams went by on their own schedule, coloring the street differently this evening than at other times. This space sounded different now than at any other time. The pleasures of these sounds, repeated yet changed, slowed my pace in appreciation. Then I felt urged by the group to move faster, and we passed on up the street.

Walking up Denman, waiting for the lights to change, crossing with the chirping of the automated crossing sounds, we found that our route became phrased by the movement of car traffic. We walked the length of a block, no gaps between tall apartment buildings to allow a cut-through. As we turned a corner at the end of the block, there was the gleaner with his cart, at the same corner where I had seen him three hours earlier. He had tied bags of bottles and cans so that they clanked against the sides of the cart, emphasizing his slow movements through the neighborhood. This sudden and unexpected repetition of encounter felt like a cadence in my soundwalk experience. But this feeling of cadence was not shared by the other walkers, who only encountered the gleaner once and did not mention him in the discussion afterward. And while I was curious, all I really knew of him was through melodies made of glass and tin. Deeper understanding would take more time.

It was very quiet on the back streets, and one group member intermittently played the street-sign poles, making clear clanging sounds in the night around us. The sounds of a baby crying in an apartment could be heard the length of a block, and high heels outside a restaurant clipped clearly on the pavement. Noting the time, I headed back. We reached the Sylvia after about forty-five minutes.

Our route was improvised, moving through areas full of listening potential, led by the possibilities of that moment, phrased by automobile traffic patterns, architecture, weather, and the motions of the group. The group stayed more or less together, so no one left the group for a more private walk, and the overall dynamic of the group became important.

The final section of the handout reiterated the importance of the conversation at the end and promised participants the reward of sustenance if they stayed with us. In it I suggested some open questions about listening that were repeated when we arrived at the meeting room.

Dialogue (polyphony)

vivace

A seminar room has been booked at the Sylvia Hotel bar for 8 pm and snacks will be served. I am curious about your listening experience on this walk. Did you hear—feel—think anything that surprised you? How was this walk different from other walks that you have taken here or elsewhere? How did you listen?

To keep disciplinary boundaries at bay, I began the discussion with open questions like those on the handout: How is this walk different from other walks? What did you hear on this walk? Perhaps partly because we had a very comfortable space with refreshments, the discussion went on for an hour. The conversation was wide-ranging and animated. When I asked whether anyone had lived in the area for some time, two people spoke of their experience as residents. One described the urban vitality of the area, especially in the summer months, when the verticality of the apartment towers is highlighted through the sounds of activities happening on balconies at different levels. Another resident talked about the different character of winter walkers, who brave the cold and are quieter and more introspective. She focused on how friendly each encounter would be. My experience of the beach path as feeling dangerous when I was there alone was challenged by a participant who said that all of Vancouver's beaches feel safe to her at any time. However, another participant said she would not take the dark beach path at night, affirming my ideas about the gendered use of these spaces.

One listener, who had heard my talk about intimate listening the day before, wanted to address this concept directly. She said that if she thought of the sound environment heard on this walk as a lover, she would have to describe it as an uninteresting lover, with mundane sounds. I realized then that much of what interests me about the sound environment is engendered through repetition of listening, taking soundwalks over and over again in the same place. For instance, the seemingly mundane sounds of the electrical trams achieved depth for me through repeated listening. I heard how the sounds changed as the vehicles turned the corner, sped up, and slowed down, and how these electrically tethered vehicles sounded different from the diesel buses I hear in Montreal. I found pleasure in discerning these differences that only became apparent through repeated listening. The surprise repetition of the sounds of the gleaner were particularly meaningful for me because they were unexpectedly repeated in a specific location, a strange synchronicity. But repetition can also be planned as a research method, as a practice of improvisational listening in place. Repetition is an important part of intimate listening that Irigaray does not discuss in her essay: dates put aside regularly for listening to and learning about the lover, whether that is another person, a group in conversation, or the sound environment. Irigaray talks about the importance of reserving attention for listening but does not discuss the phrasing of repeated always-changing return, a theme with variations. I think the practice of listening over time, with many repetitions that pay attention to variation, is an important aspect of loving a person or place, involving deep levels of care and attention. One participant in the walk rejected the idea of practice as something imposed (like how parents insist on their child practicing an instrument when the child is unwilling). For me, however, the practice of soundwalks over and over again, with variations, in the same area is a source of pleasure and renewal, as well as a way of gradually learning more about a sound environment. This repetition—and the depth of knowledge it gives about a place—does not interfere with creative improvisation in soundwalks but enriches it. Even very mundane aspects of sound environments can thus be approached and appreciated in their daily diversity and become interesting to the lover. This richer sense of place found through repetition then informs the improvised soundwalks that take place there each time, individually or in groups.

It struck me that the group discussion format, although seeming open to all kinds of conversation, still has some limitations. Some people feel much more at ease speaking in groups than do others. One participant was clearly actively engaged in listening to the discussion, yet did not say a word until after the group split up and started to eat and engage in smaller group conversations. It turned out that she had recently moved to Vancouver and spoke English as a second language. Even though she was very good at English, she felt shy about speaking in front of this group. Once she was able to speak to me alone, she was voluble and articulate, and she has communicated with me several times through email about her intercultural artwork. This reminded me how at conferences often the most thought-provoking exchanges take place outside of sessions, in hallways and by coffee carts. It is important to provide the greatest possible variety of conversational groupings and the luxury of extended time and a relaxed setting, if the aim is intimacy and improvisation in conversation. If there had been only a short formal session, perhaps the rich exchanges with this initially shy person would not have taken place.

After the walk, in addition to blogging and other forms of documentation,[10] I engaged in an email conversation with some of the participants, focusing on issues about how to work with soundwalk material in artistic productions, as well as how this experience compared with other soundwalks that take place in Vancouver and at SFU. One listener commented that the many approaches to listening that had been introduced at the beginning of the walk helped broaden and deepen her experience. She had felt constrained on some other soundwalks because she had got the impression that she was supposed to listen in a specific way, focusing on acoustics and noise levels. The list of listening approaches that I suggested opened up possibilities of listening, thinking, and discussion for her.

This comment returned me to the question of "how am I to listen?" and how this is related to questions of participant agency. What happens when I ask people to stop talking in order to listen? To turn off digital distractions? How do the suggested listening strategies structure participant experience?

Some time ago, at a conference in Montreal, a soundwalk participant said that she thought the request for silence and establishment of a prescribed route interfered with the agency of the participants. Also, I had noticed a certain quietness and passivity on the part of soundwalk participants and wondered to what extent we were missing an opportunity for more active, engaged listening. It is sometimes as if listeners are passengers in a vehicle, paying less attention to the route and activity than if they were taking the wheel themselves. In discussions after soundwalks, there often seemed a fallback to familiar interpretive routines of sound ecology (city = bad, nature = good, etc.). It felt to me as if the leader was expected to compose the soundwalk for the participants to follow. This made me wonder about how the roles of the leader and participants could be altered and to what extent listening itself could become more active in this context, by changing soundwalk methods to focus more clearly on the listening roles of participants and facilitate a situation of openness, where improvisational listening and walking could take place.

Irigaray advocates such openness, listening as attentively as one would do to a lover: "If I am to be quiet and listen, listen to you, without presupposition, without making hidden demands—on you or myself—the world must not be sealed already, it must still be open, the future not determined by the past" (1996, 117). This articulation of intimate listening seems more open and complex than her later depiction of listening to the larger world as either focusing on respect and contemplation or on grasping and mastery: "We have to meet the world, in particular the natural world, as other, to respect it instead of appropriating it into only one world: our world. Education ought to teach how to respect and contemplate the world, and not only how to grasp and master it, as has been too often the case in our Western culture" (2008, 234).

Listening to a lover is not only about respect and contemplation, conceptualized as diametrically opposed to grasping and mastering. Think of intimate listening. Is there no touch involved, no being in touch, no grasping followed by letting go, no play with mastery, no falling onto or away from? The relations of sexual intimacy are much more complex and dangerous than pure contemplation, as others have noted. Thinking through the work of Georges Bataille and Luce Irigaray (including the same essay I discuss here), Waterman argues that, "a musical performance may encompass a number of relationships of power, discipline, and desire—some of our most potent listening pleasures (whether as players or audience members) come through the restraints imposed by those very bonds" (2008b). She adds that "creative improvisation makes high demands on the listener to 'go with' the performers, who themselves may understandably be more focused on their own interactions as musicians. . . . We need to do more work in critical studies in improvisation to account for difference in the experiences of listening subjects before we can really understand improvisation as a model for intersubjective communication" (13). Waterman notes the difficulty and importance of accounting for different listening experiences within a model of improvisation as communication. The ideal of intimate listening is both appealing and risky. Perhaps it is just not possible to take listening from one very specific context, that of concupiscence, and apply it to the whole world. Wouldn't that be exhausting, among other things? Perhaps, though, we need to take on this complexity, to listen lovingly and ecotonally, to resist simplification. Love and listening are not a simple recipe for understanding and connection, particularly if attempted in an enlarged public sphere. Sara Ahmed (2004) critiques the example of a rhetoric of love and acceptance of difference in a UK national project of multiculturalism, suggesting that in the institutional context of national multicultural policy, openness to difference is transformed into an insistence on difference as an ideology. Difference as a national policy (but in which the nation itself can only be unitary) starts to police cultural behavior (2004). This is no longer a freedom from interpretive routines, but an insistence on difference as an interpretive routine itself. Openness becomes required and therefore no longer open—a paradox of readings.

Soundwalks, however, take place on an intermediate scale, in public but repeated in always-different small groups of ten or twenty (rarely more). Perhaps in this context, intimate listening can be attempted as a goal, listening that values difference and wants connection, partial connection in the senses that Haraway means that term (partial as in a part of, not whole, and partial as in partial to, liking and desiring connection): "the knowing self is partial in all its guises, never finished, whole, simply there and original; it is always constructed and stitched together imperfectly, and therefore able to join with another, to see together without claiming to be another. Here is the promise of objectivity: a scientific knower seeks the subject position, not of identity, but of objectivity, that is, partial connection" (1988, 587). Here, Haraway is challenging the idea of partiality as prepossessed and inimical to change, far from objective and even rampantly subjective, the way it would be described in an online dictionary. Instead, she focuses on how the partial—the loved, the fragmentary, the tone within a more complex harmonic timbre—relies on connections with others for objectivity and the creation of knowledge.

This could be put another way: partiality as lack of sovereignty. Speaking of the political potential of love as a way of relating to people in the world, Lauren Berlant and Michael Hardt agree in an interview that no one can be sovereign in love (Davis and Sarlin 2011). The bridges of Irigaray, the semantic bridges of *to* or *à*, could also be considered partial connections that deny sovereignty, bridges that must be maintained by all fellow travelers for structural integrity, maintained and animated by an alert listening practice that is open to difference and change. During a soundwalk or in any kind of listening activity for which I reserve this attention, I want to keep that openness to new dawns of listening and thinking, thinking of that *to*, that *à*, as an ideal in listening that wants to keep alive and explore differences in the world and interpretation and maintain bridges to the various listeners (human or otherwise) at that time. I think part of what excites me about intimate listening is that it is neither purely about contemplation nor about mastery—it is very much an in-between place, about touching and being touched, resonating, while realizing that that moment of touching is ephemeral and partial, ungraspable in totality. The motion of love is neither the stillness of contemplation nor the strong grasp of mastery, but like walking is a combination of forward propulsive will and falling (as Laurie Anderson sings "I am walking . . . and I am falling"), repeated endlessly with shifting rhythms. In all of these senses, the omnipresence of intimate risk without security or sovereignty, the necessity for openness and flexibility in a world that is not sealed, an emphasis on listening in the moment, this seems like an ideal situation for open improvisational listening.

> So . . .
> How am I to listen to you?
> How am I to listen?
> How?

When I first read Irigaray's essay, I was excited when she said, "I am listening to you as someone and something I do not know yet, *on the basis of a freedom and an openness put aside for this moment*" (1996, 116–17, emphasis added). I misunderstood this phrase, thinking that the "for" could mean "at." I thought, yes, every time we listen attentively, we put aside openness for that moment and accept the sealed nature of the event. We accept the limitations of the listening situation: in only this place, with only these people, for only this amount of time, and with only the limited, partial knowledge I can have of these people and this place. We put aside freedom to talk while another is speaking, to do other things, to leave, to move and interpret completely openly rather than in response to the communications of other players, speakers, and walkers. In choosing to listen, we are restricting our agency to do other things. In a group soundwalk, I ask participants to facilitate the listening of the other members of the group as well as their own, balancing their own agency with that of others. Everyone makes a bargain to listen at the expense of other activities.

When I checked the French, it was clear what Irigaray meant: "a partir d'une liberté et d'une disponibilité que je reserve pour cet événement" (1992, 181). To reserve is clearly to keep something in a deep place (reservoir) to bring it into action in a special situation. It is not to give something up for that moment but to bring it into play. However, perhaps this is the surprising and productive possibility of imperfect understanding of another language, and underscores Irigaray's ideas about openness to difference. The greatest surprise for me in her essay was a moment of misunderstanding about control and desire that led to a great deal of productive thought. Hopefully soundwalks and other listening opportunities can leave space for many such moments of productive confusion and other surprises of creative listening. By thinking of the soundwalk as a tripartite activity and giving special attention to the overture and the conversation as well as the structure of the walk itself, we have been able to open up the form to think more about how to facilitate active listening, to focus on the possibilities of partial conversations. The route of the walk, the sounds of the moment, and the listening practices of particular participants all give possibilities for improvisation in listening, attention to the moment, and potential for new ways of knowledge about the places that are subjects of soundwalks.

Notes

Thanks to Kathy Kennedy, Rainer Wiens, Caitlin Loney, David Madden, Peter van Wyck, and David Paquette for discussing early drafts of the work. The editors' comments were inspiring and thought-provoking, and greatly enhanced the shape and flavor of the writing.

1. This chapter reflects at length on this part of her book as a way to think about Irigaray's approach to listening. It is not intended to be a comprehensive analysis of her

work in relation to artistic practice, which has been done elsewhere. See, for instance, H. Robinson (2006).

2. See for example, McCartney and Paquette (2012) and McCartney (2004, 2009).

3. The possibilities of conversation and the importance of active listening have deeply influenced my work for decades. Paulo Freire's (1994) approach to critical education that begins with quietly listening to people is one that resonates with hope. The contributions of feminist philosophers (Code 1991; Finn 1995; Haraway 1988) helped me think through the politics and ethics of listening, and its gendered dimensions. Ethnomusicologist Beverley Diamond's (2000) incorporation of respectful listening at every stage of ethnographic research and scholarly discourse is a profound inspiration. Pierre Schaeffer (1967, 1990) and James Tenney (1992) suggested the possibilities of listening as a basis for sonic analysis. Malcolm Goldstein (1988) and Pauline Oliveros (2005 and chapter 4) suggest tactics for improvisational listening. Agnes Varda's (2000) documentary *The Gleaners and I / Les glaneurs et la glaneuse* and its sequel are an inspiration in terms of listening to audiences and making creative conversations with them.

4. The Soundwalking Interactions project is generously supported by the Fonds Québecois de recherche sur la société et la culture.

5. Corringham discusses her soundwalking practice in an article titled "Shadowwalks: A Sound Art Project" (see Minevich and Waterman 2013).

6. The discussion took place at the Graduate Program in Music and Culture at Carleton University on November 18, 2011. See also Stanley Fish (1980).

7. The walk was programmed as part of the Soundwalking Interactions project and as part of a series of soundwalks by Vancouver New Music.

8. The sculpture *A-mazing Laughter*, by Yue Minjun, was installed in this location during the Olympics in 2010. It is colloquially known as *The Laughing Guys* since it comprises statues of fourteen-feet-tall men who are laughing.

9. The work of the CRESSON research group (Centre de recherche sur l'espace sonore et l'environnement urbain) in Grenoble, France, has been a strong influence on my approach to soundwalking, since I began working with them about ten years ago, to translate a book of theirs into English (see Augoyard and Torgue 2006).

10. After the walk, I asked Jenni Schine, a graduate student and member of the Vancouver Soundwalk Collective, to write a short blog entry about her experience, based on listening to the recordings she had made of the walk and the discussion. I gave copies of these recordings to David Madden, a PhD student at Concordia, who had not been present at the walk itself. David has taken part in many soundwalks, including leading walks for communication courses at Concordia. See Schine (2011) and Madden (2011).

3. Community Sound [e]Scapes

IMPROVISING BODIES AND SITE/SPACE/PLACE
IN NEW MEDIA AUDIO ART

Rebecca Caines

Henri Lefebvre famously contends that spatiality is made up of interconnected physical, conceptual, and lived realms that all contribute to the production of human experience. For Lefebvre, the material conditions of our spatiality (site, architecture, landscape) are accompanied by conceptual understandings of space that shape and constrain behavior (abstract space, geography, borders, place names and representations, maps, territories), and by the less measurable, embodied spatial activities of everyday citizens (lived experience, place) (1991, 38–39). All three strands are produced by society, but they also produce the very conditions on which society is based. Lefebvre believes that many people have become fundamentally alienated from taking full part in the production of space, which he sees as dominated by uneven forces of capital (48). Under his optimistic, if unfinished, conceptualization, recognizing and reuniting the perceptual, conceptual, and lived strands of spatiality could also reunite everyday citizens with the means of understanding and challenging how the spaces around them produce and control their contemporary lives (222).

One of the most fluid ways we experience spatiality is through sound. Our bodies are immersed in and penetrated by sound, and we sound out our experiences in turn. Audio artists, particularly those who record and create pieces with source material from their local environments, work across and between Lefebvre's perceptual, conceptual, and embodied realms of spatiality (site/space/place). I am interested in using audio art in community-based projects to help people critique and contribute to the production of their everyday spaces. I believe this work can help groups to achieve their own community-driven goals; to produce innovative site-specific, community-based art; and to aid in building and strengthening positive, collaborative, democratic community structures. I understand that if such an endeavor is to be successful, new methodologies must be found that can mediate the complexities of community engagement and leverage the creative potential of site-specific sound work. This chapter focuses on one project that employs improvisation as both an artistic and a social methodology.

Community Sound [e]Scapes is a new media audio art project that I designed with software developer John Campbell, working in partnership with community groups in Canada, Australia, and Northern Ireland.[1] I am a performance theorist and artist interested in the relationship between site-specific art and community building. With Community Sound [e]Scapes, I have extended my interests to include environmental sound and improvisational processes. Our initial, practice-based research question was: "Could the introduction of improvisatory methodologies into a site-specific audio art project produce new opportunities for spatial engagement in communities, and, if so, what beneficial outcomes might emerge?" We asked the participants in each location to explore how sound relates to the sites/spaces/places they live in and hope for. To help them do this, participants learned about audio art from artists and technical experts to gain experience with sound recording, editing, and mixing. Everyone was encouraged to contribute to the project website, and some participants also performed or exhibited their audio art works.

Because it emphasized participants' embodied relationships to their environments through sound, Community Sound [e]Scapes was intensely local. Each group explored site-specific (natural, urban, social, and political) environments through sound. The project also had a networked dimension, as members of each group helped create website content, discussed their projects on online forums, and posted audio and visual documentation to the project's website.[2] Campbell designed the e-Scaper to provide an online mixer through which all participants could contribute to and play with a growing archive of project recordings from all three sites. This deliberately user-friendly interface allowed users to select and mix sound samples in creative and improvisatory ways.[3]

The Community Sound [e]Scapes project began with a shared but generalized sense of improvisation, derived from the diverse creative practices of facilitators who delivered workshops and mentored participants.[4] It is fair to say that we all approached improvisation as a collaborative process of active listening, real-time decision making, risk taking, experimentation, and trust, and that we thought of "mistakes" and "failures" as potentially productive moments of re-creation and change.

Throughout the project, we used improvisation exercises in workshops on music, theater, film, and interdisciplinary arts to explore free improvisation as a means of engaging with site/space/place. By necessity, however, improvisation also became a project design methodology that created new opportunities for spatial contestation, as Campbell and I were forced to adapt to the constraints imposed by distance, technology, and culture. Participants engaged with the project in unexpected ways that exceeded our intentions and challenged our commitment to creating ethical community art. Individual and organizational "improvising bodies" interacted dynamically with both positive and troubling results. Indeed, my own improvising body is implicated in every stage of this project because I chose to work with deeply familiar sites, spaces, and places. I collaborated with my Northern Irish life partner, my Australian father, and my close friends and recent co-workers in the three countries to which I feel permanently tied by birth, blood, love, and time. However, experiences of spatial alienation, disempowerment, and dislocation also shaped the project, as I discuss later.

In what follows, I focus on three of the Community Sound [e]Scapes groups in detail: da Vinci, Ballybeen, and Woolgoolga; I then discuss the online and collaborative components that emerged across the project. Before doing so, I tease out the different disciplinary threads that informed the project. Community Sound [e]Scapes demonstrated that improvising with sound through embodied creative practices can promote different ways of contesting and engaging simultaneously with perceptual, conceptual, and embodied spatial practices. However, employing improvisation as a methodology can also have surprising, and at times problematic, impacts on community engagement.

Improvising with the Soundscape

For a number of contemporary artists, spatiality is a source of local body-based knowledge, memory, and connection and a producing, constraining political influence to be exposed and contested (Kwon 2002). I connect Lefebvre's notion of physical, conceptual, and lived spaces with concerns about physical "sites" (Kaye 2000; Read 2000), conceptual studies of "space" and spatial power (Casey 1997; Rose 1999), and phenomenological interests in embodied, emotional, and remembered "place" (Casey 1997; Lippard 1997; Nold 2009). With this project, I wanted to see how working with sound in a creative, improvisatory way might offer opportunities for participants (and for me) to engage with complex, conflicted spatial explorations and interventions. The idea of "the soundscape" provided a useful methodological framework for exploring site/space/place through sound. Canadian composer and sound researcher R. Murray Schafer first coined the term *soundscape*, an obvious aural analog to the visual metaphor of a landscape, in the mid-1960s.[5] Schafer and his team conducted empirical studies of sound in specific environments through the World Soundscape Project (WSP). Much of their work was explicitly concerned with site/space/place, from conserving heritage "sound marks" to noise pollution activism. Soundscape studies establish sound as an important marker of community, memory, and identity; such studies also investigate ways we can learn about the material conditions of a location by examining the sonic environment and emphasizing humanity's role in the construction of the soundscape (Järviluoma et al. 2009; Schafer 1977).

As conceptualized by Schafer, the soundscape is itself a "composition" that humans shape and therefore bear responsibility for protecting and preserving (1994, 205). Barry Truax (2002) notes that when recognizable environmental sounds form the basis of artistic works (known as soundscape compositions), they can link both the composer and the listener to the space where the sounds were recorded, creating new opportunities for questioning the relationship between humans and the environment. Community Sound [e]Scapes initially drew on practical exercises, techniques, and vocabularies from soundscape studies and soundscape composition, but the project did not stay focused on the methodologies envisioned by Schafer and the WSP.

Peter Cusack, a London-based sound artist, sees a number of problems with the "world as human composition" analogy common to soundscape work. He believes it places too much emphasis on preconceived ideas about what might make up a "good" composition based on "natural" sounds, distinct and in balance with one another, instead of embracing the aural complexity and creativity inherent to chaotic urban soundscapes. Cusack asks: "Should we really try to hear the acoustic environment as a musical composition when it clearly isn't?" In response, he suggests a new analogy that emphasizes process, change, and multivocality: "Free improvisation would be a more accurate musical analogy if one is needed" (2000, 8). Free improvisation is a mode of music-making in which each participant is encouraged to contribute his or her individual expressions. Musicians are not bound by genre rules, and processes of sensitive listening and responsiveness are considered central to the outcome. Free improvisation resonates strongly with the shared sense of improvisation that developed in Community Sound [e]Scapes.

Conceiving of a soundscape itself as a free improvisation with the environment is a rich recontextualization of the human–soundscape relationship that emphasizes collaboration between bodies and the environment, but it also encourages experimentation and a lack of preconceived structures or agendas for working with sound and place. It is thus a radical departure from the careful quantitative and qualitative research methods and environmental preservation aims that persevere in much contemporary soundscape work.[6] In our project, freely improvising our relationships to the soundscape encouraged us to draw on playful and transient methods and techniques for exploring sonic space. To be sure, participants engaged with their spaces partly through traditional soundscape methods, such as listening exercises and soundwalks.[7] More playful improvisations with the sound environment also occurred, however, through such diverse activities as quilt making, jamming, bicycle riding, and games.[8] Such activities emphasized the interactive, community-engaged values of Community Sound [e]Scapes.

In addition to soundscape studies, the project design for Community Sound [e]Scapes was informed by current themes, practices, and methodologies in community-based performance and theory. This impulse was drawn from my long-standing practice in community arts projects in Australia and Northern Ireland as well as my research in this area.[9] Campbell and I aimed to create work that, as Kuppers and Robertson describe it, "foregrounds concepts such as democratic ... [and] collaborative practices, everyday life, the local and the private as spaces of agency, engagement with dominant stereotypes, the merging of educative and creative aims, and the respect for multiple voices" (2007, 4). We wanted the project to be dialogical, following performance ethnographer Dwight Conquergood's use of the term (1985, 9–10). For Conquergood, ethnographers are always in a moral tension between detachment (critical and practical distance) and commitment (empathy and engagement); as such they must find ethical ways to create "dialogical performances" that "bring together different voices, world views, value systems, and beliefs so that they can have a conversation with one another ... to bring self and other together so they can question, debate, and challenge one another" (9). Conquergood sees this as a moral entailment; one must avoid plundering communities for their rich stories without providing something in return. Adopting this stance meant that we had to relinquish control of the design and the final outputs, however vulnerable that made us feel.

As facilitators following Conquergood's model, we had to keep searching with our partners for practical ways the project could be useful to each group, to clarify how we were providing a "return" for their contributions. Improvisation became a useful methodology in this process of negotiation and collaboration. The improvisatory qualities of trust, risk, active listening, collaboration, and the reconfiguring of mistakes became both methodologies and outcomes, blurring artistic and social practices. As Ajay Heble (2005) states in an essay about improvisation as a social practice, "at its best ...

improvisation can encourage us to take new risks in our relationships with others, to work together across various divides, traditions, styles, and sites . . . to foster new models of trust and social obligation, and to hear (and to see) the world anew."

In very different ways and contexts, the three community groups discussed here improvised with their sonic environments and as a result made discoveries about their relationships with site/space/place. I discuss selected moments from these richly detailed projects to highlight different strategies, challenges, and outcomes. My own improvisations with participants are threaded throughout the analysis because, for me, one of the lasting results of the Community Sound [e]Scapes project is how it transformed my understanding of community arts practice as an art form that is shaped and potentially enhanced by improvisatory approaches.

The da Vinci Project

The da Vinci Project is the brainchild of Sue Hubner and Martin Lacelle, two high school teachers in Guelph, who created an alternative curriculum based on the intersections between art and science. It provides an opportunity for a group of twenty-four adventurous grade eleven students to escape the traditional classroom for a term. Students from a range of schools and economic backgrounds spend three months at a nature center located in the University of Guelph's Arboretum, working with guest artists and scientists and taking a hands-on, interactive approach to learning.

When I met Lacelle at the campus radio station and heard about the da Vinci Project, I knew it was an ideal fit for the first Community Sound [e]Scapes project. However, with just two weeks to prepare, I was immediately catapulted into improvisational organization. I scrambled to locate ten local artists, university professors, and radio programmers who provided a series of volunteer workshops on listening, sound making and improvisation, sound art composition and graphic scores, site-specific theater, use of portable sound recorders and microphones, making sound art on specialized hardware, and editing and mixing with open-source software. In keeping with the da Vinci Project's goals, the workshops included time for unstructured exploration inside the center and out in the arboretum parkland.

There was no time to plan the workshops in detail. Implicitly, the design of the component became an improvised collective activity. The community of facilitators and participants had to listen and change, be open to new forms of experimentation, and create new opportunities from mistakes and constraints. Sometimes this fluidity produced successful, interdisciplinary results. The da Vinci sound quilt is one such success story. The quilt is constructed from twenty-four painted canvas squares, each visually representing a participant's favorite sound and place. The installation includes an electronic piano keyboard programmed with twenty-four sound samples that echo the visual images on the quilt. Since each square and each recording represents a different lived or imagined location, "playing" the sound quilt offers endless ways to combine the da Vinci spaces, foregrounding the interactive creation of site, space, and place that formed the heart of the Community Sound [e]Scapes project.

At other times, the fluid, improvisatory project design caused problems. An overemphasis on software training in workshops, for example, led to little time for teaching file formatting, archiving, and metadata. Hundreds of recordings remained untitled and unformatted, and only those students who were already the most competent and confident with technology were able to contribute their sounds to the collective sound bank for everyone to use. This omission could be seen as a failure in both ethical community-based collaboration and effective pedagogy.

Open improvisatory activity at both the organizational and individual level resulted in a variety of different explorations of site/space/place. One group of young people worked on themes of natural environments as places of peace and contemplation, in contrast to the "shallow, materialistic teenage mall culture" ("Participant Feedback 1").[10] Another group explored the fictional sound world of imaginary figures that live "beneath the toilet bowl," a conceptual space free from social expectations ("Participant Feedback 2"). Some pieces evoke spaces where ideas of city and nature overlap. Others are rhythmic. They incorporate repeated keynote sounds from the arboretum environment; at times these pieces are so processed that just the tiniest remnant of the soundscape remains discernible. Sound samples range from teacups clinking in the classroom to echoes of singing and laughing reflected from the frozen lake. Teenagers, artists, and teachers alike worked to articulate, understand, and share this precious, alternative site, conceptual space, and lived place. They thus met Lacelle and Hubner's goal to develop an effective, dialogic learning and teaching community based on "independence and creativity most of all, adaptability in dealing with challenges and new experiences" (Lacelle and Hubner n.d.).

The pastoral context of the da Vinci Project makes a sharp contrast to the Northern Ireland project in the housing estate of Ballybeen, where youth worked with very limited resources in a gritty urban location. I argue that despite their differing priorities, both groups freely improvised with contested material realities, grids of spatial power, and spatial histories.

Ballybeen

Ballybeen is a predominantly Protestant, working-class, economically deprived housing estate, the largest in Northern Ireland. The estate has been undergoing a period of significant government investment and change, which mirrors broader changes occurring across the nation since the Good Friday Peace Agreement in 1998. The estate has a history of vigilante paramilitary activity, connected to the Protestant paramilitary organization known as the Ulster Defence Association. For many of the local young people who were born after the civil conflict known as "the Troubles,"[11] the history of economic disadvantage and conflict left what they called "Ballybeen stigma"; they often spoke to me about a complex mix of pride and disgust in the history of the estate.[12] As a result of this conflicted view of the past, youth worker Robbie Rea focuses most of his award-winning projects on developing intergenerational conversation and pride in the positive aspects of Ballybeen life, as well as attempting to bridge continuing divides between the Protestant housing estate and Catholic residents in nearby areas.

I had previously worked with Rea and local professional media studio Best Cellars on a number of arts and health projects when I lived in Northern Ireland, and so I suggested that we collaborate with older teenagers in the youth programs for Community Sound [e]Scapes.[13] I was fascinated to see how these young people would engage with their unique sense of generational and geographical space in the housing estate through improvising with audio art. My own body remembered experiencing distinctive sounds echoing through the aging community hall, like the regular rhythm of footballs bouncing against the concrete outside. I smiled again at the locally specific jokes and phrases I heard so often at the local fish and chip shop, and in my mind's ear I recalled the songs and sermons that resonated in the many churches. Rea and I initially proposed that the teenagers would record sounds from around the estate, perhaps interviewing older people about the changes in the soundscape. They would then build a webpage and create an online archive of their recordings and their improvisations with the new online mixer we were building in Guelph. I sourced a small amount of local funding and scouted possible trainers, equipment, and tours of Northern Ireland sound art studios. For Ballybeen Youth Centre, the project offered new program material, access to new resources and software, and more opportunities for young people to articulate a positive sense of self and pride in place.

It is important to note that Rea deliberately recruits young people who come from a mix of religious and socioeconomic backgrounds for his projects. The participants for this project had all worked with Rea since they were children and were about to reach adulthood. These young men and women had thus been thinking in depth about what Ballybeen meant to them, and they brought a range of different experiences and hopes to the collaboration. Some had completed training and would return to become new youth workers on Ballybeen-based projects, others were looking for work, and one was planning to leave the estate and go to university. Ballybeen youth have a pervasive self-deprecating sense of humour, and I had to reach beyond this to ascertain their deepest individual motivations for choosing to be involved in Community Sound [e]Scapes. In our phone and Skype calls, they continually expressed interest in the professional audiovisual training they would receive, and all of them articulated a strong desire to be active participants in defining and representing Ballybeen, for themselves and to the outside world, in a new and positive way. In their feedback, they praised the training and citizenship elements of the project.

The design of this component developed very slowly as a result of a number of local circumstances, including complex Northern Irish paperwork and permissions and the moving of youth services from a local community center to a custom-built complex, the Brooklands Youth Centre, which opened after many delays in May 2010. During this time, Rea lost regular access to email and telephone and was forced to take on a significant extra workload setting up the new center. His participants also lost access to computers with Internet capability. Although resources were available, the project was lacking in people who were able and available to get them up and running. Consequently, Best Cellars had to take a larger role in the project. Hampered by Rea's and Best Cellars' busy schedules, and complicated by the time difference between Canada and Northern Ireland, communication among all three partners became sporadic (although rich with ideas), and everyone had to trust that progress was being made. Rea and I risked failure and possible damage to carefully constructed but fragile community relations if the project failed, but we trusted that we could keep adapting together until the structure worked. Once again, the team began to improvise at the organizational level, building relationships and ideas via indistinct phone calls and fragmentary emails, while making decisions that responded to participants' needs.

The outcomes were four soundscape compositions that challenged my preconceived notions of Ballybeen identity. As planned, the participating teens and young adults photographed their view of the estate for the website and learned to use a portable recorder, but they did not incorporate the sounds I consider distinctive to the estate. Instead, the Ballybeen soundscapes are set to a regular electronic beat track and capture the participants' interactions with the building and surrounds of their brand-new youth center.[14] After letting go of my preconceptions, I realized that the soundscapes engage directly with these young people's conceptual and lived spaces. In one piece, the rhythm evokes the flute bands that march alongside Protestant fraternal group the Orange Order every July 12 to celebrate the 1690 victory by a Protestant king, William of Orange, over a Catholic king, James II.[15] These parades and bonfires notoriously attract violence and controversy, but they are also a source of local identity and pride. All the young people had been influenced by these parades, either through their own or their parents' involvement, by participating in building the bonfire, or by being caught up in the fights and rioting that break out at this time of year in Ballybeen and neighboring estates. The bands rehearse in the spring and summer months in Protestant areas like Ballybeen and are a distinctive sound mark. Instead of the traditional flutes and Lambeg drums, however, this soundscape was made from sounds of the teenagers playing percussively on the surfaces of their new, nonsectarian youth center. They created an aural link to the Protestant history of the area, but they did it in the form of a physical interaction with a positive new space. In their words: "We wanted to include the 'drum culture' of Northern Ireland, and [we] recreated it by banging out some rhythms on a dumpster and adding some cymbal sounds from the railings around the centre. By listening carefully, you can hear the solo, flute-sound of a lone blackbird whistling for our recording session" ("Ballybeen [Northern Ireland]" 2010). This sonic work was built through improvisatory project design and made through free improvisations with the changing physical, conceptual, and lived spaces of the estate. As a result of these improvisations, a complex negotiation with past, present, and future took place, one that acknowledged and referenced violent sectarian histories but refused to be contained by them.

The project aimed to allow participants to adapt the project to their own uses to find locally appropriate ways to engage with spatiality. In Ballybeen, free improvisation with the site/space/place of the estate was mediated through complex socioeconomic factors, guided by adults who were closely involved in the teenagers' work. By contrast, the Woolgoolga project in Australia involved independent adults who already had highly developed opinions about the inequities in material, governmental, and experienced spatiality in their community.

Woolgoolga

The Woolgoolga Bike Users are a group of predominantly male, older friends who are not working because of either retirement or disability. The group's membership fluctuates depending on people's health and other family and social obligations. My father, Leigh Caines, is a prominent member, and when I go home to Australia I have coffee with the group every morning at a local café. The members come from a diverse range of cultural backgrounds and economic circumstances, but they all enjoy practical jokes and critiquing the actions of local and national government around the table. Their genuine civic commitment to Woolgoolga is expressed through volunteer activities, such as driving the bus for a local nursing home or picking litter off the beach, but bicycles are their passion. The Woolgoolga Bike Users have been building custom bicycles for over five years for and with people whose bodies and differences make using standard bicycles impossible; for example, they design specialized tandem bikes for children or teenagers who need physical therapy. The photos and videos the group contributed to the Community Sound [e]Scapes website document their ingenious work.

Campbell and I visited Woolgoolga in January 2010. We supplied audio equipment, software, and basic training, and we collected video and photographs from participants. The project seemed to suit the group's needs on a number of levels. It offered the opportunity to document their innovative work on the website, it satisfied a common interest in new self-directed projects and in new technologies, and it engaged with their concerns about contrasting current public representations of Woolgoolga. Following their usual custom, the group engaged in open discussion about the project at a local café every morning. Afterward, a few members would work actively on sound and visual documentation, followed by updates and more conversation over coffee. For some, the videos and the photographs online were the most important outcomes of the project ("Participant Feedback 4"). Despite offering helpful feedback during the development of the new online mixer, however, the group chose not to make it their main creative tool.

This fluid collaborative creative process was difficult for us to track once we were back in Canada, since the only documented evidence was each sound sample appearing in the online folder set up for this purpose. I found it difficult to inquire about progress without feeling like I was manipulating my father to support my work. I also found it very difficult to gauge other members' interest in the project because of my prior relationships with them, and I constantly worried I was forcing the group to participate because of our shared history. My hesitation to impose resulted in sporadic contact, anxiety, and alienation from the group, and after the project was over, it emerged that some members missed out on activities, particularly the chance to participate in the website launch, because of my lack of communication. In this case, my own fears and lack of trust, and the emotional strain inherent in working with close family members and friends, caused the improvisation to falter.

Like the Ballybeen youth, the Woolgoolga Bike Users improvised a much more locally appropriate design and methodology for their activities than I could have envisioned for them. On a bicycle, or in the intimate setting of the café, the most logical way for them to create soundscapes was to use the recorder as a collection and mixing device. Most of their "sounds" turned out to be short improvised collations created on the spot, using the stop and pause features on the recorder. These soundscapes tracked bicycle journeys through everyday Woolgoolga life and included conversations, native fruit bat sounds, local football, samples of favorite radio slogans, and the sounds of the bicycles on different surfaces, all combined by the recording artist in situ, an improvised interaction with embodied "place," or as Lucy Lippard describes it, "space, as seen from the inside" (1997, 8). For Lippard, the difference between "space" and "place" is the evidence of the located body and of lived, personalized, and intimate spatial practices that she collectively calls "topographical intimacy" (33). Incorporating Lefebvre's triad of lived, perceived, and conceived spaces, it is possible to read the Woolgoolga recordings of everyday activities from the seat of a custom bicycle as an attempt to reinsert lived "place" back into dialogue with what participants saw as grids of inaccessible physical and conceptual space.

In the text they submitted for the website, participants note: "The first thing people notice when they visit Woolgoolga is that absolutely everybody is friendly . . . The residents here don't want this to change and consciously work at reinforcing the feeling of community. But [it] hasn't been easy because local business people and local and state governments are pushing for much greater expansion than has already been initiated" (Caines and Campbell 2010). The activities the participants recorded included walking on the beach, riding with disabled and elderly friends, football and skateboarding contests, local Sikh markets, surprising interactions with wildlife, and café conversations among diverse groups. These activities directly contrasted with the advertising and political decision making increasingly characterizing and reshaping Woolgoolga as a site of tourism aimed at predominantly young, wealthy, able-bodied people and characterizing natural resources, religious and cultural practices, and wildlife as phenomena to be commercialized and privatized (Saddleton 2011). Of course, the Woolgoolga Bike Users' improvisations with their environment may not directly change the priorities of the local council, but the project did bring community members closer together to work on the project, celebrated their unsung achievements, documented their own audio and visual representations of Woolgoolga, and, through the online and audio work, helped sustain a strong and growing alternative site/space/place.

The Community Sound [e]Scapes project engaged communities through traditional community work, including meetings, workshops, and the facilitation of community events, but it also worked across new media formats to engage networked communities working in virtual spaces.[16] These improvisations worked inside and across community borders. New forms of sonic improvisation were created and utilized, and the various online connections enabled different types of improvisatory project design and development.

Improvising Bodies in Virtual Environments

The e-Scaper online sound art mixer was designed by Campbell as a core component of the Community Sound [e]Scapes project website. Users accessed the mixer from the project homepage. They uploaded and mixed their site-specific sounds together, drawing on an archive made up of all the project recordings. They created audio art by placing their samples (represented by colored blocks) along a timeline, layering together a mix, and then saving their experiments back to the archive. Despite such a seemingly disembodied online component, improvising bodies deeply affected how this software came into being, and the mixer became part of participants' improvised, embodied responses to site/space/place.

Members in the Canadian and Australian groups tested early versions of the mixer. As the project progressed, it became obvious that the mixer needed to be user-friendly to people with limited computer knowledge, work across different browsers and operating systems, and cater to the needs of both beginners and advanced users. The bodies of the potential users affected the design, from requiring simple adjustments of text size and color to needing mouse-over text that could be translated by audio-describing software. The ease of physically clicking and dragging was considered and adjusted. People requested different features based on their eyesight, hearing, and dexterity. Campbell responded quickly to feedback, sometimes adding requested features within hours of the request being logged on the website online forums or altering code while working directly with participants at weekly website feedback sessions at the University of Guelph. In this way, his software development was part of the collaborative improvisatory process.

The final design, with its instantaneous clear, save, loop, and reload features, encourages playfulness, speed, and the ability to build off others' sounds and mixes. Out of this responsive environment, new applications for the software soon became evident. For example, a number of participants from the Guelph and da Vinci projects began to "jam" together, and this led to public performances.[17] What was designed as a solo aid to improvisatory composition quickly became a collective performance tool. As with any musical improvisation, performers using the e-Scaper had to learn to actively listen to each other's contributions and leave room for quieter samples and soundscapes. The very different physical and conceptual spaces in the recordings sometimes clashed, overlapped, or were difficult to interpret for listeners who did not know the contexts in which they were recorded. Performers had to find live, performative ways to let each other's spaces and bodies coexist.

Conclusion: Incomplete Bodies

Community Sound [e]Scapes was publically launched on September 9, 2010, at the Macdonald Stewart Art Centre in Guelph, as part of an international colloquium on improvisation. All four community "bodies" involved in the Community Sound [e]Scapes project came together with a local audience. The final website featured pictures, texts, video, and sounds contributed by each group, as well as sections on the research components and links to the forums and mixer. The launch event took place inside an installation designed by Guelph member Nicholas Loess, made up of photomontages, video projections, and suspended headphones. Video projections displayed two live Skype sessions, controlled by Campbell, and short videos about each community. In one Skype window, six of the Ballybeen participants, accompanied by two youth workers and sound engineer Dean Llewellyn, sat in the Best Cellars media studio. They were eating pizza. In the other Skype session, Leigh Caines lay in his bed in Woolgoolga watching the sunrise. There were speeches, and each group played an example of their soundscapes, evoking, contesting, and creating their everyday spaces.

The telematic event revealed both the potential and the problems with engaging multiple improvising community bodies and spaces. This physical site, the gallery in Guelph, full of high-end equipment, emphasized the uneven distribution of resources that resulted from the fragmented, improvised project design and inherent structural inequalities. The Ballybeen youth, for example, were squeezed in front of the only computer they could access that had Internet connectivity, many of them seeing their final web page for the first time. The launch was also an unstable collection of present and absent bodies, hovering between site specificity and placelessness, between local specificity and globalized oversaturation. Bodies were everywhere, in the photographs and videos, audibly rushing against the microphones and spaces in the recordings, on the Skype sessions and in person, and yet many were missing or voiceless, lost along the way as the project shifted and turned. Some participants were unable to take time off work to continue with the project, whereas others were confused by the chaotic structures, disabled by a society that did not leave room for their differences, left behind by the complexity of the technology, or unable to find a voice in the babble of improvising sounds that emerged. As a result, dominant bodies spoke in place of those who might improvise their "community" and their sites, space, and places a little differently. As Petra Kuppers (2006) reminds us, community is "a tactical lever, utopian hope *and* oppressive regime . . . both given *and* longed for, exclusionary *and* inclusive, tradition *and* innovation, located in stories, spaces and habitus."

This project has shown me how improvisatory methodologies can productively disrupt the agendas of those seeking to dominate or control. I now believe these methodologies could also have a significant contribution to make toward disrupting power structures between academic and other communities, thus enabling collaborative, democratic research projects made with and for communities. The Community Sound [e]Scapes project entered a second phase between 2011 and 2013, working with Guelph artists and First Nations communities in northern Ontario. Throughout all our collaborations, I hope we can continue to be aware of just how fragile and uneven community spaces are. I hope that by using improvisatory methodologies, we can create more opportunities for improvisation around ownership, control, and creation of space and for engaging with community bodies in the exploration of site/space/place. Projects like Community Sound [e]Scapes, however, will always walk the risky, vulnerable, exposed line of the improvisatory—like place itself, never able to settle, always speaking *and* silencing, and always unavoidably incomplete.

Notes

1. Community Sound [e]Scapes was the focus of my postdoctoral research fellowship at the Improvisation, Community and Social Practice (ICASP) research project at the University of Guelph, Ontario, Canada. The first phase took place from August 2009 to September 2010. The project was given clearance by the University of Guelph Research Ethics Board to involve human participants in the research project (2009, 2010, and 2011). Names or surnames of participants have been withheld or changed in this chapter where necessary.

2. See http://soundescapes.improvcommunity.ca.

3. The e-Scaper is a Web 2.0 application, created with Javascript and PHP scripting languages, using a MySQL database. Users load their sound samples into the online library using the "My Sounds" upload tool on the Community Sound [e]Scapes website. Advanced users can pan between speakers, select portions of sounds, and change the time intervals. Users can also open other soundscapes saved in the library and build new soundscapes from them.

4. Project artists Rebecca Caines, Andy Houston, and Melanie Bennett cite theater artists Viola Spolin and Keith Johnstone, performance artists Richard Schechner and Tim Etchells, and relational site-specific performance artists Mike Pearson and Exeter group Wrights & Sights as dominant influences in their improvisatory performance practice (see Etchells 1999; Johnstone 1979; Hodge et al. n.d.; Pearson and Shanks 2001; Schechner 2002; Spolin 1969). Other workshop tutors and project leaders such as Michael and Ellen Waterman, Germaine Liu, and François Mouillot referenced the work of free-improvising musicians such as Fred Frith, John Stevens, Anthony Braxton, and Pauline Oliveros and improvising sound artists such as Andra McCartney in their workshops (see Lock and Braxton 1988; McCartney 2004; Oliveros 2005). Both the Australian bicycle builders and software designer Campbell refer to their work as "improvisations."

5. The World Soundscape Project was founded at Simon Fraser University in the early 1970s by Schafer and a number of colleagues, most famously Barry Truax and Hildegard Westerkamp. In 1993 the World Forum for Acoustic Ecology was founded to promote ideas about sound and the environment. Soundscape studies is thus now more commonly known as acoustic ecology. (See Schafer 1994; Truax n.d.; World Forum for Acoustic Ecology website, http://wfae.proscenia.net.)

6. For an excellent survey of contemporary acoustic ecology research, see Breitsameter and Soller-Eckert (2012).

7. See McCartney's contribution to this volume (chapter 2) for an exploration of soundwalking and improvisation.

8. I am not alone in being inspired by the relationships between improvisation and the acoustic environment; the rich intersections between improvisation and soundscape practices are the current focus of a number of scholars and artists. See Cusack (2000, 2012), McCartney (2010 and chapter 2 of this book), and Minevich and Waterman (2013).

9. See Caines (2003, 2007).

10. Exit interviews and surveys were given to participants in all three of the projects discussed here, with the names removed to preserve anonymity.

11. "The Troubles" is the name given to the civil sectarian conflict in Northern Ireland from about 1963 to 1998. During this time, Catholic Nationalist and Protestant Loyalist communities engaged in civil and paramilitary conflicts, resulting in the death of over three thousand people. Conflicts were focused on the control of the province and whether it would remain a part of the United Kingdom or return to Republic of Ireland rule. The Troubles are generally considered to have ended with the Good Friday Agreement of 1998, although isolated sectarian conflicts still break out, especially around community events like marches, parades, and bonfires.

12. See, for example, *Bap on Ballybean*.

13. Brooklands Youth Centre is the new building granted to South Eastern Education and Library Board youth workers in Ballybeen. Prior to its construction, the board delivered a range of different youth services out of rented premises inside community centers or paid part-time workers on project-based initiatives. Robert Rea has been involved in youth services in the area for over thirty years. Best Cellars was an independent music and audiovisual production company working in radio, music, youth, and community arts in Northern Ireland from 1993 to 2012. I lived in the Castlereagh area from 2006 to 2009 and worked for the local council as the community arts development officer.

14. I acknowledge the co-creation of this project by the many community participants, organizers, and tutors involved. These include staff at the South Eastern Education

and Library Board, the Sonic Arts Research Centre, and Castlereagh Arts in Northern Ireland; the leaders and supporters of the Woolgoolga Bike User's Group, including Bob McIntyre, Leigh Caines, and Rosemary Galvin; Martin Lacelle, Sue Hubner, and Violet Reid Taylor at da Vinci; CFRU.FM staff and volunteers in Guelph; and graduate students, staff, and faculty members involved in the Improvisation, Community, and Social Practice project in Guelph and Montreal. Significant contributions also came from independent artists Michael Waterman, Andy Houston, Melanie Bennett, Germaine Liu, François Mouillot, Nicholas and Rosa Loess, Mike Mucci, and Byron Murray.

15. Traditional Protestant flute bands commonly feature wooden B-flat marching band flutes and a variety of drums, including the bass drum and the larger Lambeg. They are a modern Ulster variation on drum and fife traditions; for more information see "A Brief History of the Fife and Drum" provided by prominent Northern Ireland flute makers Miller Wicks (http://millerwicksni.webs.com/historyfifedrum.htm).

16. For more details on the new media context of the project, see Badani and Caines (2009).

17. In this analysis, I have not discussed the Guelph project, which had its own moments of improvisation both hopeful and difficult. This project engaged local residents, artists, and university students, many of whom were amateur enthusiasts working with CFRU.FM, the campus community radio station.

PART II

Technology and Embodiment

4. Improvising Composition

HOW TO LISTEN IN THE TIME BETWEEN

Pauline Oliveros

Listening lies deep within the body and is as yet a mysterious process involving myriad time delays. This chapter is drawn from my experience as an improvising composer attempting to understand the process of listening that is first accessed by the nonverbal body and later understood by the verbal brain. I compare the time delay between evoked potentials and cognition identified by neurophysiologist Benjamin Libet and the time delay between the record head and playback head of analog tape recorders (and later computer-generated delays). My Expanded Instrument System (EIS), in continual development since 1967 (see Oliveros 2008), is an expression and embodiment of my interest in time delays for making music. In my long experience as an improviser, there is a gradual release of cognitive control and an increasing willingness to trust the body to respond appropriately. The cultivation of this trust is the way to greater communication between the verbal and nonverbal nature of the human being and cognitive appreciation of improvising composition.

Listening is the core process for this chapter, in both the writing and the reading. A number of examples drawn from over five decades of my music are discussed here. These examples and selected score excerpts are available at http://www.improvcommunity.ca/oliveros under Oliveros—Improvising Composition. The reader is invited to listen to these excerpts from my pieces as you read about them in this chapter. As a prelude I begin a selective retracing of my musical life with a focus on improvisation, embodiment, and technology. Following that, I discuss a particular improvisational performance with bassist Barre Phillips as a way of exploring how to listen in the time between impulse and expression. Finally, Libet's provocative work provides an entry into understanding ways that improvisation is not only cognitive but thoroughly embodied.

Prelude: A Short History of Improvising Composition

My early musical training did not include improvisation or composition. When at age sixteen I wanted to compose music, my only entry to this activity was to search on the keyboard for the sounds that I wanted to make. This approach was a kind of improvisation on the way to composition—a beginning. Gradually I learned to notate the tones I found in this way to create my first compositions in conventionally notated form for piano around 1951. These early compositions gradually included instruments other than piano and became increasingly more complicated and dissonant. I would listen inwardly and intently to perceive the timbre of the instruments I was composing for and then find the notes. When the pieces were performed I was delighted with the accuracy of the orchestration as a verification of my inner listening.[1]

In 1954, I met my composition mentor, Robert Erickson, in San Francisco. His teaching encouraged me to trust my listening rather than simply follow compositional forms. He encouraged me and my colleagues Terry Riley and Loren Rush to improvise as well as compose. In 1957, the three of us were motivated to do our first group improvisations. Terry had a commission to compose a five-minute soundtrack for *Polyester Moon*, a documentary film by sculptor Claire Falkenstein. We accommodated Terry by improvising several five-minute tracks at Radio KPFA in Berkeley, California, where Loren was working as a studio production assistant. Recording facilities were not generally available at this time, so the radio station was a great resource. Though each of us composed in differing styles, our improvisations seemed to work well together. Each of us influenced the others in a give and take of listening and playing. Terry was already an ingenious pianist, Loren was studying koto and also played percussion, and I played French horn. Terry took one of our tracks and used it for the film. (Listen to example 1: first group improvisations with Terry Riley, Loren Rush, and Pauline Oliveros at www .improvcommunity.ca/oliveros.)[2]

We decided that our experience with group free improvisation was worth repeating, and we began to meet regularly. We discovered that if we discussed what we were going to do before we played, the music usually fell flat, so we adopted the method of playing first, listening to the recording, and then discussing what had happened. This method has continued to serve me well through the years: play, record, listen, and then discuss—then play and record some more. We trusted our bodies to deliver the goods, and we considered our work to be the first group improvisations stemming from art music of the time. Indeterminancy and open form already provided for some performer choice with limited possibilities offered, but the indeterminate element was kept under careful control by composers such as John Cage, Earle Brown, Lukas Foss, and others. Improvisation was not yet a real option in this music.

To illustrate the prevailing attitude toward improvisation in new music during the 1960s, I offer the following example from John Cage. It is a well-known fact that Cage frowned on improvisation.[3] In 1964, the New York Philharmonic performed several concerts of works by experimental composers, including Cage. Perhaps because of Leonard Bernstein's perception of a certain "improvisatory" quality in the chosen works, he decided to include a separate free improvisation for orchestra. Unhappy about Bernstein's decision, Cage wrote him four months before the concert:

> Dear Lenny,
> I ask you to reconsider your plan to conduct the orchestra in an improvisation. Improvisation is not related to what the three of us are doing in our works. It gives free play to the exercise of taste and memory, and it is exactly this that we, in differing ways, are not doing in our music. Since, as far as I know, you are not dedicated in your own work to improvisation, I can only imagine that your plan is a comment on our work . . . Surely there must be some less provocative way to conclude the program, one which will leave no doubt as to your courage in giving to your audiences the music which you have chosen to present.
>
> With best wishes and friendliest greetings,
> John Cage[4]

This letter is a strong indication that, for a long time, Cage viewed his concepts of chance operations and indeterminacy as incompatible with improvisation. He also stressed that he wanted "to make improvisation a discipline" and that it would involve "doing something beyond the control of the ego" (Kauffmann and Cage 1966, 46).

The first time we encountered this limited notion of improvisation was when Lukas Foss came to town with his Improvisation Chamber Ensemble around 1958. We attended the performance in San Francisco with great excitement to hear another improvising ensemble, but we were dismayed to see music stands in front of the players. When the concert was over, we asked Foss why they used notation. He answered that without the control of guiding notes the improvisation would be "utter chaos." In my view, this dismissive attitude is reflected in the long delay in accepting improvisation as an appropriate activity or field of study in music schools.

Already present, improvisation continued to be an essential tool for my composition. *Variations for Sextet* (1960), composed for flute, clarinet, trumpet, horn, cello, and piano is an example of an early piece of mine that sounds improvised but is fully notated. There is no system involved in *Variations for Sextet* though it might sound combinatorial. I listened for what I wanted to hear next. If I got stuck, then I improvised at the piano until I got what I wanted. That is, my improvising body knew how the piece should go, whereas my cognitive side could be stuck and not know what to write next. I was often frustrated, though, because I heard in inner listening what I wanted to notate, but I had to acquire the writing skill gradually. I was not nearly fast enough to notate what I was hearing. (Listen to example 2: *Variations for Sextet* [excerpt with score] at www.improvcommunity.ca/oliveros.)

By 1953 I owned a personal reel-to-reel tape machine, then a relatively new technology. Like improvisation, it became an essential tool for composition. My first tape piece was composed in my home studio in 1960. *Time Perspectives* was originally in four channels played back on two stereo tape machines. My home studio consisted of a tape recorder, microphone, cardboard tubes, bathtub reverberation, walls as amplifiers, and found objects. *Time Perspectives* uses a variety of improvised sounds as well as improvised processing methods. Sounds include voices and whispers through different-sized cardboard tubes acting as filters, steel bowls rubbed and struck inside the bathtub for reverberation, and close microphone for very soft sounds. Long sections were improvised, then dropped or raised an octave using 3 and 3/4 IPS or 7 and 1/2 IPS reel-to-reel tape.[5] The tape could be wound by hand in record mode for variable speed effects. Improvisation proved necessary for creating the music as well as dealing with the technology of the time.[6] (Listen to example 3: *Time Perspectives* [excerpt] at www.improvcommunity.ca/oliveros.)

A big breakthrough came when I discovered how to improvise with classical electronic music studio equipment in 1965. The system I created to make electronic music consisted of tube signal generators, a patch bay, line amplifiers, and two stereo tape machines. I set signal generators above the range of hearing to generate audible difference tones from those frequencies,[7] and fed them into a tape delay system with one tape common to both tape machines. Soon, through improvisation, I was creating my first electronic music. In making my electronic instrument with the oscillators, the huge dials that had seemed so unfriendly to performance now became receivers for the musical knowledge embodied in my hands and fingers. I had created a very unstable nonlinear music-making system: difference tones from tones set above the range of hearing were manipulated by the bias frequency of the electromagnetic tape recording, and feedback from a second tape machine sounded in parallel with newly generated difference tones as I responded instantaneously with my hands on those dials to what I was hearing from the delays and as the sounds were all being recorded on magnetic tape. I had created a new musical instrument that included my own bodily input in the form of gestures mapped onto the machine for analog output to speakers. This meant that I could play my electronic music in real time without editing or overdubbing. At the San Francisco Tape Music Center I created a series of pieces titled *Mnemonics I–V* (1964–66). This series is a good example of my process at the time. (Listen to example 4: *Mnemonics III* [excerpt] at www.improvcommunity.ca/oliveros.)

During the summer of 1966 at the University of Toronto Electronic Music Studio (UTEMS), I created a large number of electronic tape pieces with an expanded version of the system that I used for *Mnemonics*. UTEMS was a more advanced studio than the San Franciso Tape Music Center. I worked with a bank of twelve oscillators, each associated with increments of a piano keyboard. I used weights to hold down keys to the oscillators that I wanted to use. Otherwise I used the same method as described for *Mnemonics* in creating this music.

I of IV (1966) was a particularly dramatic piece played completely in real time with an astonishing sound emergence—a screamer. The sound began with great intensity sweeping from very low to high in an amazing melodic arc, playing against itself canonically and eventually blending back into the sounds that had become background. It seemed like I was following as my hands reacted instantaneously in guiding the melody. I remember these moments as nonordinary—even numinous—and I was laughing in great mirth and joy as the music continued to unfold. (Listen to example 5: *I of IV* [excerpt] at www.improvcommunity.ca/oliveros.)

In 1967, I began to play my accordion with a tape delay system similar to my electronic music system. I wanted to challenge myself by dealing with more musical information simultaneously than I could play with my two hands. This was the beginning of what I call the Expanded Instrument System (EIS). I would play sounds in the present that would be returned by the tape delay in the future. I modified the delayed returns with foot pedals as I continued to play new material, knowing that the delays that return in the future would become a part of the past. With EIS I felt that I was dealing with a musical time machine. The photo in figure 4.1 shows me playing with a much later version of the EIS, which has continually evolved to adapt to new technologies over the past thirty-five years.

My notated music went through transformations that gradually led to more performer choice and improvisation and to conceptual scores meant to be orally transmitted. In the score for TRIO *for Flute, Percussion and String*

FIG 4.1: Pauline Oliveros performing "Pauline's Solo," Krannert Art Museum, University of Illinois at Urbana-Champaign, 2009. Photograph © Ione.

Bass (1963) there are composed notations, graphic indications, and space for free improvisation. You can see the score for this work online.

Sonic Meditations, composed in 1970, are instruction scores or recipes for directing attention to ways of sounding and responding. *Sonic Meditations* were also coupled with body and dream work in my research, the Meditation Project, that was carried out over four hours a day with twenty participants for nine weeks at the University of California, San Diego (UCSD), where I taught from 1967 to 1981. I learned kinetic awareness from choreographer and filmmaker Elaine Summers (originator of intermedia) and studied dream process with Ronald Nelson, a clinical psychologist at UCSD. These two practices were influential in how I began to notice bodily sensations relating to sounds I performed. I also noticed that I could change my performance by the way my body felt. I became sensitive to using just enough muscle tension, rather than too much. Kinetic and sonic awareness became intertwined for me. Noticing and recording my dreams led me to awareness of levels or atmospheres of consciousness that could also influence performance. The Meditation Project included dream awareness and kinetic awareness exercises with *Sonic Meditations.* Here is the text score for one of them, titled *Teach Yourself to Fly*.

Any number of persons sit in a circle facing the centre. Illuminate the space with dim blue light. Begin by simply observing your own breathing. Always be an observer. Gradually allow your breathing to become audible. Then gradually introduce your voice. Allow your vocal cords to vibrate in any mode which occurs naturally. Allow the intensity of the vibrations to increase very slowly. Continue as long as possible, naturally, and until all others are quiet, always observing your own breath cycle. Variation: translate voice to an instrument. (*Teach Yourself to Fly*; dedicated to Amelia Earhart)[8]

After resigning my position at UCSD in 1981, I began to improvise solo concerts with my accordion to develop my performance profession. During this period I acquired two digital delay processors and began to work more intensively on the space between sounds with EIS. As my listening deepened, I could handle more material and I wanted to add more delay processors. Because of the status of the technology of the time, additional processors required a mixing partner to configure the destinations of the different delay processors to the reverberation processors and final output to the house speakers. I developed the idea of space as a parameter of music and wanted to change the nature of reverberation much as I changed chords or timbres.

Crone Music (1989) is an example of early analog EIS. My accordion sounds were picked up by microphones, then sent to delay processors. The delayed sounds were sent back to the mixer and then to reverberators or returned to be further delayed. The configuration of delays and reverberation was varied during the performance with the collaboration of an audio engineer. The engineer was also performing by selecting sounds to be returned to me or sent on to the reverberators and out to the house system. The performing was symbiotic. (Listen to example 6: *Crone Music* [excerpt] at www.improvcommunity.ca/oliveros.)[9]

I have always been interested in the resonance of performance spaces and how the sound quality of my instrument is affected in different spaces. This interest is shared with Stuart Dempster, a longtime partner in improvisation and founding member of the Deep Listening Band. Stuart invited me to experience a very special space near Seattle, Washington. "Lear" (Deep Listening Band) is an example of a piece generated with an "acoustic time machine": The Cistern at Fort Worden, Port Townsend, in Washington. The reverberation time in the cistern is forty-five seconds. Indirect sound seems equally as intense as direct sound, so that the musicians play duets with each other and with the cistern as the sounds are continually multiplied by the acoustics. Deep Listening was born in the cistern, as was the Deep Listening Band. *Deep Listening*, the CD, was released by New Albion in 1989. "Lear" was an improvisation with the cistern, as were the other three pieces on the CD. There was no editing or over-dubbing. People often mistake the sounds as having been electronically generated. The attention already given to machine delay times in my electronic music informed the way I played in the cistern, and I understood the cistern to be an "acoustic time machine." (Listen to example 7: "Lear" [excerpt] at www.improvcommunity.ca/oliveros.)

I have continued to explore acoustic reverberation in my compositions.[10] At the invitation of Neely Bruce and Mode Records, I recorded a solo performance of "St. George and the Dragon" in the Romanesque stone Pomfret Chapel. I listened to the reflections from the walls of the chapel, locking the sound of my accordion to the sound of the chapel through the use of microphones aimed at my accordion and at the walls. The reverberation time was nothing like the cistern, and in fact was shorter than one second. However, the time difference was enough to cause interesting timbre variations depending on how I attacked, sustained, and varied the dynamics of the tones that I performed by listening to the space in between. (Listen to example 8: "St. George and the Dragon" [excerpt] at www.improvcommunity.ca/oliveros.)[11]

All of these experiences in listening to delayed sounds both acoustically and electronically inform my composition and improvisation. I have learned that the effects of different spaces are as important as instruments in making music (Oliveros 1995, 2006). Listening informs the body and the body reacts appropriately in the performance situation without cognitive recognition being necessary prior to action. Listening happens in a nonlinear way during improvisatory performances unless the improvising is highly codified such as in traditional jazz forms. Free improvisation is another matter.

Listening in the Time Between

> It is the preverbal and preliterate stage of our development
> that is dominated by musical listening.
> —Henkjan Honing, *The Illiterate Listener*

Listening inclusively to all that can be perceived in the moment (global attention) is a way to hold the space for improvisation or the readiness to create a sounding (focused attention). This listening is a process of meditation with balanced global and focal attention and becoming ready to participate with the space occupied whether as a soloist or with an ensemble. Readiness to sound or receive sound means that there is no prior commitment to any sound. One has to be open to be ready. Any prior commitment will constitute a delay in response time or spontaneity.

FIG 4.2: Barre Phillips and Pauline Oliveros performing at the Luz Jazz Festival, July 11, 2010. Photograph © Ione.

All of my solo and ensemble performances are improvised. The less I know cognitively about the music to be improvised, the better it is for me. My nonverbal body makes the music by drawing instantaneously on my wealth of experience. I trust the accuracy of my body in this enterprise. I am bypassing "thinking" my way in the improvisation. I am counting on and trusting my body to manifest the music purely and freely.

One example of such trust is my performance duo with bassist Barre Phillips at the Luz Jazz Festival on July 11, 2010, shown in figure 4.2. We had performed together only once before about ten years earlier in a quartet (The Space Between: Philip Gelb, Dana Reason, and Pauline Oliveros with Barre Phillips). Other than the sound check for the concert, we had not played together at all, nor did we need to rehearse. Our only agreement was to play shorter pieces during our hour-long set rather than one long piece. We had no other discussion about our upcoming performance.

On stage we began our nonverbal musical conversation—Barre with his wealth of experience and me with mine. Our bodies were relaxed and at home with our instruments. As the first notes sounded, I felt completely understood and well received by Barre. The sold-out audience joined us in this understanding (as evidenced by the applause and demand for encores at the conclusion of our performance). The music emerged from our nonverbal bodies since no verbal cues or notations were applied. Our musical differences were mutually absorbed and reflected back in time during the course of the pieces. There were about seven pieces within the hour, each of which had a different quality, duration, and tempo. Agreement was nonverbal and supported by deep listening. (Listen to example 9: Pauline Oliveros and Barre Phillips at the Luz Jazz Festival [excerpt] at www.improvcommunity.ca/oliveros.)

To explain why I felt such support in my improvisations with Barre, I need to provide some context about the ways I understand listening and sounding. The practice that I have called Deep Listening began with a recording experience when I placed the microphone of my new tape recorder in the window of my apartment in San Francisco in 1953. I pressed record and listened as I recorded. To my surprise when I played back the recording I heard sounds that I had missed hearing during the recording. This experience prompted me to tell myself to listen to everything all the time and remind myself when I am not listening. I have been reminding myself to listen ever since this recording experience, for the past six decades. Experiential memories persist. As I stated at the outset, the science of listening is still mysterious. Listening takes place after the ear gathers and converts sound waves to electrical energy for transmission to the audio cortex. The experience of sound waves (electrical energy) is then interpreted as attention and is directed to memory of accumulated associations (sensations, intuitions, feelings, and thoughts) and comparative similarities and differences.[12]

For me, listening and exploring new sound worlds through improvisation are inextricably intertwined as a culture of the moment. Many musicians have expanded their traditional instruments to sound in ways that are beyond the maker's intention. The use of extended techniques and ways of performing create new possibilities. Although instruments evolve over long periods of time, today's musicians may develop a new extended technique or a surprising way of playing within an improvisatory moment. These phenomena are part of the culture of free improvisation. This culture is produced by consensual understanding of common experiences even though conflict, differences, misunderstandings, negotiations, and resolutions are experienced in varying degrees on the way to consensus. In the case of our performance together, Barre and I experienced bodily the culture of the moment. Consensus arrived with our bodily interactions with our instruments. This consensus is the confluence of openness to histories, embodied musical knowledge, bodily action resulting in sound, musical give and take, and agreement to continue the flow or stop and start again.

Silence came to articulate these moments. Flow is the energy that sustains the many waves of sound that we listened to as music. The audience received this exchange, absorbed and reflected the energy back to Barre and me, the performers. We all perceived the invisible and inaudible causes and effects as well as the visible and audible ones.

How we made this music is not yet explicable.

When I established my way of working with electronic sound as described above with *Mnemonics 1–5* and *I of IV*, I was improvising with the machines. I felt a partnership that expanded my ability to make music, much as the partnership with another player does. The output of the machines seemed to be alive in relationship with a human performer. The machine energy was tempered by my human energy and vice versa. There was an experience of flow that consisted of trust (my own), simulated consensus, and the myriad tiny time delays of my human cognition in synchrony with an emergence of music.

Through my interest in the study of consciousness and attention I became acquainted with the experimental work of the scientist Benjamin Libet (1916–2007), who explored consciousness, initiation of action, and free will. Libet's experiments showed that the human brain anticipates an action to be performed that can be seen on a graphic display before the performer is aware of the action, a phenomenon known as evoked potentials. On his fascinating blog consciousentities.com, Peter Hankins explores Libet's experiments as part of a wide-ranging exploration of theories of consciousness.[13] Although an admittedly casual source, Peter's blog appeals to me because he contextualizes Libet among a wide range of thinkers in the field of consciousness. He explains Libet's findings:

> Our unconscious responses are far quicker than our conscious ones. A stimulus applied to the skin produces an "evoked potential" or EP in the brain within tens of milliseconds, and that seems to be enough for it to register unconsciously but effectively. A series of experiments have shown that we register unconsciously a whole host of things which may influence our response to events but which never cross the threshold into consciousness. Among other evidence, Libet quotes experiments which show that a conditioned response—a blink—can be created to events which the subject is never actually conscious of. The remarkable phenomenon of blindsight might perhaps be seen as a related case. (2005)

Libet's experiments showed that what was known as the readiness potential in the brain could appear as much as seven seconds before an action expressing that potential would occur as reported by the participant being measured.

Although Libet's experiments are controversial, it is interesting to note that neuroscientists have graphed evoked potentials through auditory stimuli. Kraus and Nichol measured auditory evoked potentials in their research on music and the brain:

> The firing of neurons results in small but measurable electrical potentials. The specific neural activity arising from acoustic stimulation, a pattern of voltage fluctuations lasting about one half second, is an auditory evoked potential (AEP). With enough repetitions of an acoustic stimulus, signal averaging permits AEPs to emerge from the background spontaneous neural firing (and other non-neural interferences such as muscle activity and external electromagnetic generators), and they may be visualized in a time-voltage waveform. Depending upon the type and placement of the recording electrodes, the amount of amplification, the selected filters, and the post-stimulus timeframe, it is possible to detect neural activity arising from structures spanning the auditory nerve to the cortex. (2005, 214)

Sharma et al. have shown that "passively elicited" AEPs provide a "reliable objective measure of cortical auditory function" (1997, 541).

The time delay of one-third to one-half second between evoked potentials in the brain and cognition discovered by Libet is fascinating with respect to my trust of bodily response before cognitive recognition during improvisational performances. Discovering the similar time delay between the record head and playback head on tape recorders in the early 1960s presented a wonderful creative resource that I have used and elaborated on for nearly half a century (Oliveros 1984).

Both external delay times of machines and the delay times of perception are resources and causes for improvisation. The time delay between the record head and playback head of an analog tape machine focused my attention on the possibilities of layering, phasing, and spatializing sound. The time between the initial sound monitored at the record head and the delayed sound monitored at the playback head was crucial in terms of the next initialization of sound at the record head. Myriad inaudible decisions were made and integrated in the space between the record head and the playback head and stored as possible bodily reactions. Just as many possible outputs would come from the machines. As the improvising composer of many pieces of electronic music, I was most comfortable listening to the output of my tape delay system without knowing what would emerge so that I could react spontaneously with my hands and fingers.

I have progressed through many changes in music technology from the end of the 1950s to the present. Along the way I developed a bodily relation to machines for making music. It has always been necessary for me to have a bodily performing relationship with sound. I now understand this to be so because of the essential knowledge of the body that is preconscious and nonverbal.

Although I have constructed many compositions systematically and conceptually, I believe that my true knowledge of music is bodily in equal measure or more than my intellectual knowledge. Both are necessary. However, intellectual knowledge without bodily knowledge remains rather dry. This does not mean that there is no intellectual excitement. There is! Something such as a eureka-type moment when a problem is solved brings a bodily rush of such excitement. In such moments I experience integration and bodily/intellectual attentional fusion.

Attention is often highly focused for language, manifested as written and spoken words, mathematics, notated music, and programming. This kind of focused attention can split itself off from open or global attention. Global attention may perceive all sensations in all directions, both inner and outer. Integration comes when there is a fusion of both kinds of attention. Balancing these two forms of attention is the dance of improvisation—opening to receive and focusing to a point. Focused attention must go point to point to maintain continuity, but global attention is always expanding and receiving, although blurry on detail.

The nature and number of decisions made by a performer during the course of an improvisation is, so far, immeasurable. A sounding happens. The sound continues or is followed or joined by another sound. The trajectory of soundings gradually constitutes a long line of soundings that is perceived as a shape or form that is music. Within that trajectory are myriad decisions that are intuited and join to refer back to the initial sounding and forward to the ending sound. Each sounding has its own shape, which we might describe as attack, sustain, decay, release or as articulation, dynamic, energy, rhythm, timbre, and frequencies or pitch. All these components integrate to form a sounding, yet there are time delays within the smallest components of a sounding and our own delay in awareness of the sounding. All this happens, to evoke Libet again, from the readiness potential in our own brains to the action that causes the sounding to the awareness that the sounding has happened. The awareness of being aware, and of the musical implications past and future, is part of this space between.

There are many studies on hearing. The functional operations of hearing and the mechanism of the ear are measurable. What is not measurable in physical terms is the experience of listening. Listening remains mysterious unless experience is described and understood in consensus. Consensus listening took place in the examples of the first group improvisations that we performed in 1957. There was consensus after the action of making the music together. What remains mysterious is how the myriad decisions and actions that make the music happen during the space between the readiness potential and the performing are coordinated so spontaneously.

As I discovered and worked with time delays, I came to regard my EIS as a very crude model of how the brain works. Sound is initiated in what we consider to be the present moment. That sound comes back in the future; when it comes back, it is part of the past. Thus I am improvising in the past, present, and future simultaneously. We are made of time delays from nano- or pico-seconds to years for the whole of our lives. Coordination of trillions of time delays makes up improvisation and makes it possible to improvise composition or compose improvisation. Thus the nonverbal body informs the verbal mind and vice versa, eliminating the so-called mind–body split.

In the 1960s, when using tape machines for delay processing, the problem of interface was paramount. The electronic music studio was an improvised collection of machines adopted and adapted from post–World War II surplus test equipment and telephone exchanges that were not intended for music making and especially not for performing. Machine operator interfaces are often very limited. Threading a tape for use on a reel-to-reel tape machine took time. The speed and the length of the tape limited performance time. Thus my tape pieces were often no longer than thirty minutes (7 IPS). All of my electronic music was performed live in real time in the studio, including the examples discussed in this chapter. Because I was listening to and between delayed sounds, I began to have aural experiences resembling after images. I remember taking a break from a live session, walking outside, and hearing the delay repetition patterns sounding in the environment.

I began to perform with a tape delay system on stage with my accordion in 1967. Lugging two heavy tape machines around for my performances was difficult but necessary. There was no other way to accomplish the way I wanted to make my music. In 1983 I replaced tape delay with digital delay processors and began to talk about the EIS, although I consider the system to have been initiated in 1967. The delay processors gave me more performance controls than did the tape machines. By the 1990s computers began to be an option that gave me even more control possibilities. Currently the EIS is programmed to run on my laptop and allows for me to have up to twenty delays per hand. These delays are modified by foot pedal and by algorithms allowing me to deal with many more voices than would be possible without the technology. My sounds also may be spatialized so that sound in space and space itself are parameters of music and of my performances. The development and performance with EIS over forty years has given my body plenty to absorb and "think" about at the nonverbal level as well as the conscious verbal level. I could not deal with the complexities of the performance system without trusting my body to react appropriately and drive the improvisation of composition or the composition of improvisation.

It is undeniable that my improvisations are informed by a lifetime reservoir of experience informed by Deep Listening. What this means to me is releasing conscious control to my nonverbal body so that my music can be present in the performance gestures I make. These gestures are shaped by my inner experience interacting with the present feelings arising from the situation of inflow from the environment, other musicians, and audience members. I attend to all of this as a listener. The body, so far inexplicably, knows how to compose and improvise and releases this information through words and physical gestures if one is open to receive the constant vigilance and output of neuronal activity that is not consciously willed. Paradoxically, it takes will to be open and trust the body to deliver and integrate that which is needed in the moment of performance and yet unknown to the verbal mind.

Perhaps there will be a new understanding of how the body knows so much more than is possible to bring to conscious awareness as new evidence accumulates in cognitive and neurosciences. For now, I consider my task to be to increase my conscious awareness as much as possible each day of my life and respect what the body signals to me through sensations and feelings just as much as what my verbal mind tells me through thoughts and intuitions. Synthesis and integration of all of these modes of perception and knowing empowers my musical being in the world.

Notes

1. Some of Oliveros's early scores are available at the Geisel Library, University of California, San Diego.

2. All listening and score examples are copyright Pauline Oliveros unless otherwise noted.

3. See Feisst (2009) for an extended discussion of Cage's ambivalence toward improvisation.

4. John Cage to Leonard Bernstein, October 17, 1963, Bernstein Collection, Library of Congress, Washington, DC.

5. Tape drive speed is measured in IPS or inches per second.

6. See my article "Tripping on Wires" (Oliveros 2004b) for a more extended discussion of *Time Perspectives*.

7. The Simon Fraser University *Handbook for Acoustic Ecology* offers a good definition of difference tones: "When two tones are sounded simultaneously, other tones can sometimes be heard, the frequency of one of which is the difference between the frequencies

of the two tones being sounded. For example, if the two tones are 1500 Hz and 2000 Hz, the difference tone will be 500 Hz, if the two original tones have sufficient intensity—over about 50 dB. A police whistle, for instance, blown loudly enough will produce a difference tone which is heard as a low buzzing sound" (Truax 1978). This is why I could produce an audible difference tone by having two tones set at a higher frequency than the human ear can hear.

8. From *Sonic Meditations I–XXV*, copyright Smith Publications, 54 Lent Road, Sharon VT 05065. Used by permission.

9. The sound excerpt from *Crone Music* is used by permission of Lovely Music.

10. "Lear" was originally published by New Albion Records which, sadly, went defunct in 2012.

11. The sound excerpt from "St. George and the Dragon" is used by permission of Mode Records, copyright 1994.

12. This complex process is described by Stephen Handel (2006) in his book *Perceptual Coherence* and more recently in *Musical Cognition: A Science of Listening* by Henkjan Honing (2011b).

13. In "Libet's Short Delay," Hankins carefully points out that in the past few years, Libet's ideas have been variously challenged *and* supported by scientists who created new versions of his experiments using functional magnetic resonance imaging technology. See, for example, Soon et al. (2008), who determined that the body responded fully ten seconds before the mind, and Trevena and Miller (2010), who determined that there was no demonstrable connection between evoked potentials and decision making. Libet's theory resonates with my own lived experience as an improviser.

5. The Networked Body

PHYSICALITY, EMBODIMENT, AND
LATENCY IN MULTISITE PERFORMANCE

Jason Robinson

In recent years, an increasing number of concerts have occurred that involve performers at multiple locations linked in real time through emergent Internet-based networking technologies. Commonly called "telematics,"[1] these events reflect a broad range of conceptual, compositional, and performative approaches, and many feature audiences at distributed performance locations. One such concert, titled "Inspiraling: Telematic Jazz Explorations,"[2] took place on June 13, 2010, and featured performers at New York University and the University of California, San Diego.[3] The event was organized by conductor and composer Sarah Weaver and bassist and composer Mark Dresser, both important advocates for networked music in the United States. As an audience member at the San Diego location, and as a frequent performer and composer of networked music, I was struck by how the event captured the complex yet subtle ways that networked music challenges certain ideas about synchronicity, improvisation, and the body, while also reflecting deeply held values about the nature of musical performance.

I am interested in the ways our bodily understandings inform cognitive processes during networked performances. Indeed, the relationship between the physical world and "virtual worlds" offered by emergent telecommunications and Internet-based technologies foregrounds questions about human embodiment.[4] In this chapter, I argue that an important dialectic tension exists in telematic music performance, a doubleness of dis/embodiment, produced in large part through generative fissures of latency, the body, and improvisation. Despite its technological innovations, telematic performance remains deeply connected to a persistent desire to reinscribe telematics in the cognitive modes of traditional, in-the-same-room performance.

Networked music offers tremendous new opportunities for collaboration from afar, yet these opportunities are often mediated by prevailing historical understandings of embodied musical performance and the necessary immediacy of visual and auditory interaction. Latency, or time delays resulting from the transmission of data, is a constant feature of networked music. Cognitive dissonances produced by latency emanate from the relationship of distant bodies in networked performance, as well as common futurist (and perhaps utopian) visions of a time when zero latency (or absolute synchronicity) will become a reality. From this cognitive dissonance emerges the question of embodiment, or perhaps more accurately, disembodiment: What is the nature of this peculiar telematic dis/embodiment? How might networked improvisation act as a kind of theorizing of embodiment? Finally, how might traditional notions of in-person, face-to-face, corporeal performance limit the ways we imagine the boundaries of networked music?

I explore these questions by analyzing two works from "Inspiraling: Telematic Jazz Explorations," but first it is important to make a clear distinction between the experimental musical aesthetics of indeterminacy and improvisation. Broadly stated, *indeterminacy* refers to a compositional strategy whereby chance elements, beyond the control of the musicians, are allowed to affect the musical outcome. Improvisation likewise courts the unexpected, but it does so via the intentional choices of musicians. Latency adds a certain degree of indeterminacy to networked performance, and many composers have factored this into their pieces as part of their aesthetic. I nevertheless find that the agency and intense interactivity characterized by George E. Lewis's notion of "Afrological" improvisation are especially pertinent to networked performance.

Lewis coined the terms *Afrological* and *Eurological* to serve as heuristic frameworks for parsing the varied ways that improvisation has been described in scholarly writing about experimental music. In his influential essay "Improvised Music after 1950," Lewis (1996) argues that the indeterminacy that featured strongly in experimental music by John Cage and his followers was applauded for its bold innovation but that the improvisational explorations of groundbreaking jazz musicians such as Charlie Parker were either ignored or discredited in academic circles as repetitious and therefore unoriginal. Lewis posits that indeterminacy was acceptable because it fit the cult of originality that marks the European tradition of composition. He therefore terms it a Eurological compositional technique. In contrast, jazz improvisation, with its indexing of riffs and styles, draws on personal and collective histories that are brought to bear on the immediacy of musical interaction, oral histories that resonate with the music's African American roots. Because of its dialogical essence, Lewis refers to improvisation as Afrological and, in my view, "Inspiraling: Telematic Jazz Explorations" stems from this tradition. Emphasizing the Afrological in telematics helps position new forms of technology-enabled performance within larger historical and cultural networks of meaning.

That improvisation weaves prominently in networked music should come as no surprise. Indeed, as I argue, networked performance privileges various improvisational strategies, including "free" or "open" improvisation as well as improvisation situated within groove-based rhythmic structures and predetermined harmonic forms. Improvisation often occurs within compositional frameworks, complicating any binary opposition between improvisation and composition. The two pieces I analyze here are best considered as compositions for improvisers. In the context of networked performance, Sara Weaver's *Telein* and Gerry Hemingway's *OilEye* display features of indeterminacy, but the musicians' successful negotiation of these works owes more to techniques of Afrological improvisation.

Improvisation in networked performance reveals "expressive microtiming," Vijay Iyer's term for "extremely deft manipulation of fine-scale rhythmic material" (2002, 411). Iyer is primarily concerned with groove-based music that features "a steady, virtually isochronous pulse that is established collectively by an interlocking composite of rhythmic entities" (397). The ability to "groove together," while also negotiating the latency inherent to networked performance, structures how some musicians conceptualize the aesthetic potential of telematic music. My analysis of the groove-oriented sections of Hemingway's *OilEye* suggests that musicians distributed across a latent network execute expressive microtiming to great effect. Furthermore, I argue that we can expand Iyer's notion of expressive microtiming to include improvisational choices made during more open contexts for improvisation, such as those contained in Weaver's *Telein*, where rhythmic placement still matters even in the absence of an isochronous pulse. In both works, improvising musicians must exercise agency in dialogical interactions.

Aiming to Groove: Latencies, Cognitive Dissonances, and Telematic Improvisation

> The paradigms of existence on the Net
> make the lines of musical experience more visible.
> —Dante Tanzi (2001, 435)

In most cases, though not all, telematic concerts feature academically affiliated performers and composers utilizing institutionally mediated access to

Internet2,[5] specialized performance venues outfitted for technology-laden events; a vast array of audio, video, and computer equipment; and free or open-source audio and video networking software. A major trope within telematics celebrates the gradual elimination of latency and, as a result, new possibilities for collaboration with others at great physical distances. The new potentials afforded by the telematic medium are articulated in a number of forms: a way to avoid increasing costs of musician travel,[6] a format for continuing immersive collaborations from afar, a rehearsal tool, a way to circumvent physical disabilities or conditions that might prevent travel, and, in a broader sense, a way to build and maintain community.

One of the prevailing software platforms used to provide robust, uncompressed, full-quality audio networking traces back to 2000, when Chris Chafe and a small team of researchers at Stanford University were awarded a National Science Foundation grant to help develop new audio technologies for application on the Internet.[7] The project ultimately led to the creation of SoundWIRE (Sound Waves on the Internet from Real-time Echoes[8]), a research group at Stanford's Center for Computer Research in Music and Acoustics, one of the leading academic research institutes for music technology in the United States. An early part of the project consisted of developing software to send uncompressed, high-quality audio through a two-way (full-duplex) networked connection across the Internet. In 2004, this software was named JackTrip, a contraction of *Jack*, the audio software connection toolkit, and *triple*, a reference to the synchronous three-location concert for which Chafe developed the final version of the software. Since then, JackTrip has become the software of choice for a growing community of improvisers and composers exploring networked performance.[9]

Despite the new opportunities afforded by JackTrip, telematic music is accompanied by aesthetic and technical issues that make it inherently different from traditional performance. These issues are generated in large part by the unavoidable presence of latency in available networking platforms. Latency—the time it takes for sounds (or video, or any other data) to traverse the Internet from one location to another—is determined by a complex combination of transmission and signal-processing delays (Oliveros et al. 2009). Transmission delays result from the distance that data must move across fiber optic networks and the various switches, other hardware, and "traffic" that compose and affect the network signal path. Processing delays, on the other hand, occur when sound and video are transformed from their performed, audible modalities at each network node into their traveling form (data on the network) and back again at each remote location (what is often described as analog-to-digital and digital-to-analog conversions). Although latency can be minimal in connections between close network nodes, it is more often a significant factor. Inevitably, these delays affect the nature of music itself, especially in contexts that privilege a high degree of interactivity, real-time decision making, and finely nuanced senses of synchronicity (rhythmic, melodic, harmonic).

Jonas Braasch suggests that "performers tend to agree that the threshold above which it is difficult to play in sync between two remotely located sites is about 25 milliseconds" (2009, 423). When performers are distributed between two or more networked locations, our understanding of this threshold becomes more complicated. For example, a performer responds to an incoming musical gesture only after it has already become latent; as a result, their response is then doubly latent by the time it reaches the location of the performer who created the original gesture. At the same time, however, studies indicate that very low latencies in networked performance often create tempo accelerations in music with a steady beat.[10] Such findings reiterate the fact that latency is already present in all in-person performance contexts.[11] As the improviser and composer Pauline Oliveros, an important proponent of telematic music declares, "we're dealing with latency all the time . . . it doesn't seem like such a foreign thing" (personal interview with Jason Robinson, Skype, May 17, 2011).

Although latency may be ubiquitous in musical performance, the goal of zero latency (to be achieved through future technological improvements) is nevertheless fetishized in telematic music. The trope of absolute synchronicity may be found in most descriptions of networked performances, especially when they are considered "successful." This focus on absolute synchronicity likely emanates from the central role of interactivity in improvisation and groove-based music. English percussionist Eddie Prévost, for example, describes improvisation as the "inter-active dialogical relationship between performers," something that seemingly privileges zero latency cognitive immediacy (quoted in Mills 2010, 188). At the same time, Oliveros suggests that absolute synchronicity in networked performance is "born out of people who are thinking about keeping a beat" (interview). To be sure, for Oliveros, whose networked music is often based on drones and expansive notions of listening and time, the relationship between latency and expressive microtiming is broad. As I illustrate in my analysis of Hemingway's piece *OilEye*, however, rhythmic synchronicity and isochronous pulse ("keeping a beat") can be particularly complex processes, especially in African American–derived rhythmic traditions—"cyclical rhythms and polyrhythmic [music]" that Michael Dessen calls "rhythmic counterpoint" (personal interview with Jason Robinson, Skype, June 1, 2011).

Issues of synchronicity were central to "Inspiraling: Telematic Jazz Explorations." Separated by more than three thousand miles of fiber optic cable, the concert included networked audio using JackTrip over Internet2 and high-definition video via the LifeSize videoconferencing platform. Each location featured a small group of performers; trumpeter Amir ElSaffar, alto saxophonist Oliver Lake, pipa player Min Xiao-Fen, percussionist Gerry Hemingway, and conductor and event coordinator Sarah Weaver were in New York, while tenor saxophonist Hafez Modirzadeh, trombonist Michael Dessen, bassist and co-coordinator Mark Dresser, and percussionist Alex Cline were in San Diego. Large projection screens placed behind the ensembles at each location presented composite images of the performers at the remote venue for viewing by the audiences (figure 5.1). In New York, additional side-stage video projection screens allowed the performers to see their remote counterparts in comfortable sight lines (figure 5.2). Similarly, in San Diego video monitors were placed strategically on stage, allowing local performers easy viewing of their New York counterparts, including Weaver's conducting (figure 5.1).

Video networking provided crucial theoretical dimensions to the performance. Weaver conducted throughout the concert, and while she was physically present at the New York location, her image was the central component in the video feed sent to San Diego. In New York she faced coterminous performers, arms often stretched above her shoulders, while she used various hand gestures to signal musical phrases. The video feed sent to San Diego was filmed from the perspective of the audience in New York; the San Diego audience and performers viewed Weaver's conducting gestures from behind her body. As a result, the conducting gestures could be used as visual cues for both ensembles. Much like the "telematic space" engendered through the audio networking of the concert, the visual representation of her conducting—her arms, hands, and bodily movements—contributed to a networked, nodal, or virtual space. She conducted an ensemble that existed *in*, yet *beyond*, each physical location.

From the perspective of the audience, however, minor latency differentials became apparent through subtle divergences in the arrival of sonic and visual information. For example, in her piece *Telein*, Weaver used several physical gestures (reminiscent of conduction or soundpainting[12]) to signal performers at both network nodes (Weaver, personal interview with Jason Robinson, Skype, May 10, 2011). At the San Diego location, the audible musical figures often seemed as if they arrived before the completion of her bodily gestures visible on the projection screens and video monitors. Such latency differentials between audio and video are common in almost all telematic music concerts that use different networking systems for audio and video.

FIG 5.1: View from the audience at the San Diego location of "Inspiraling: Telematic Jazz Explorations," showing the remote performers and conductor Sarah Weaver on the large screen placed at the back of the stage. Courtesy of Mark Dresser and Sarah Weaver.

FIG 5.2: Side view of the New York location of "Inspiraling: Telematic Jazz Explorations," showing a side-stage screen and video monitor providing easy sight lines for the musicians. Courtesy of Mark Dresser and Sarah Weaver.

Common systems that integrate audio and video such as iChat and Skype are considered unreliable for high-end telematic performance because of their compressed audio and video signals. Using independent systems enables higher quality audio (JackTrip) and video (via proprietary video systems such as LifeSize, used in the concert discussed here).

However, latency differentials in parallel audio and video networking systems often affect audience perceptions. For example, in an earlier collaborative project by Michael Dessen and Mark Dresser, audience members at one of the performance locations experienced a one- or two-second delay between the arrival of audio and video.[13] The physical gestures of percussionist Billy Mintz arrived *after* the sounds that were produced by those gestures.[14] According to Dessen, "when audience members see that, it sort of reveals the illusion in too stark a way for them, all of the sudden, this illusion of the technology . . . And then it just distracts them from the flow of events, so they're not able to concentrate on what you're actually doing because they're seeing the mechanics of it too much . . . I think to minimize that is really important" (interview). In this example, expectations of absolute synchronicity guided the audience's aesthetic experience, in turn shaping what was believable.

Stemming from perceptions of togetherness in traditional in-person performance, absolute synchronicity becomes the defining criterion for believability in networked performance. Such expectations catalyze a kind of hyper-embodiment in telematics; for many listeners and musicians, networked performance must capture and extend the timing and interactivity of a "hyper-real"[15] potential, even if the performers are aware of or are playing on differences between networked and traditional performance.

"Inspiraling: Telematic Jazz Explorations" illustrates various compositional and performative approaches that mask audio and video latencies. The compositional strategies employed by Weaver in *Telein*—strategies largely based on visual cues and flexible, rhythmic structures played rubato by the performers—obfuscate such latency differentials by prioritizing loose rhythmic relationships. For much of the piece, the two drum set players, one at each location, improvise sustained cymbal gestures while other performers enter and exit using flexible, pre-determined melodic and rhythmic figures. After several minutes, bassist Mark Dresser begins to improvise freely, using the continuing ensemble accompaniment as a melodic, harmonic, and textural reference. Dresser's improvisation contains many aesthetic qualities for which he is well known, including double amplification of each bass string (creating a peculiar overtone-like timbral effect). Rather than using a predetermined harmonic or rhythmic form for the basis of his improvisation, Dresser instead responds to the evolving, modular, networked ensemble accompaniment using his distinctive vocabulary. His personal and dialogical relationship to the ensemble codes this improvisation as Afrological.

Even though *Telein* contains certain predetermined musical structures— it is most definitely a composition—it is nevertheless deeply informed by Dresser's free improvising. Alain Renaud (2010) notes that "free improvisation has been a practice often employed in NMP [networked music performance] due to its emphasis on musician-to-musician interaction and flexibility of materials; thus providing a good basis for developing musical strategies for interacting over a network regardless of its latency."[16] Indeed, Weaver's *Telein* is successful largely because of its sophisticated combination of rhythmic rubato, modular ensemble accompaniment, and free improvisation. Such a combination mitigates the perceptible impact of latency within the performance of the piece. Instead, it makes the piece "about" something other than rhythmic synchrony.

Gerry Hemingway's composition *OilEye* offers a different, decidedly groove-based strategy for negotiating latency, with striking effect. *OilEye* was inspired by the catastrophic April 2010 BP oil spill in the Gulf of Mexico. On a rather veiled conceptual level, the piece plays with the juxtaposition of oil and water (Hemingway, personal interview with Jason Robinson, June 24, 2011). This analogy emerges in the first moments of the performance, in which Hemingway, who mainly plays percussion throughout the piece, triggers various electronically enhanced samples of bird and water sounds. This surreal soundscape is gradually coupled with bowed cymbals, pipa (Chinese lute), and vocal improvisations, and other musical material, much of which is cued by Weaver, who conducts the piece. The piece is structured around three distinct notated sections, which punctuate various duo improvisations and other more openly improvised passages.

Much of the piece seems aimed at negotiating the latencies of audio networking. Based on conversations with the event coordinators, Hemingway expected a twenty-five-millisecond delay in the audio and a fifty-millisecond delay in the video between San Diego and New York (Hemingway, email correspondence with Jason Robinson, June 21, 2011).[17] Based on this information, Hemingway developed several notated sections to be performed with a steady pulse shared across the distributed performance sites. The first notated section (which begins at approximately 4:14 in the online documentation video of the project) begins with Weaver conducting a recurring beat (quarter note at seventy-two beats per minute) visible at both locations. Hemingway divides the networked ensemble into two units. The horns and bass at the San Diego location play a synced figure in contrapuntal rhythmic synchrony with a figure played by the horns and pipa at the New York location. At the same time, the two percussionists, one at each site, improvise together (see example 5.1).

Distributed across the two performance sites, this first notated section groups musicians by location, requiring each to play in rhythmic synchrony with the other. To audiences at both locations, the combined effect produced

a distinct feeling that both ensembles were playing completely in time, with no perceivable audio latency between the two locations. Dresser credits this effect to a "hocketing" approach that was achieved by having a regular rhythmic pulse visibly conducted by Weaver and maintained independently at each location (Dresser, personal interview with Jason Robinson, Skype, June 1, 2011). Indeed, close analysis of the score and recording reveals that the two locations are playing at the same tempo, but they are rhythmically displaced by a consistent (latent) interval with a strategic mathematical and metric relationship— the two ensembles are displaced in a dialogic way. Although happy with the outcome, Hemingway was nevertheless surprised that his compositional planning produced the desired rhythmic synchronicity. Somehow the inherent and unpredictable latency present in the networked connection functioned smoothly with the rhythmic pulse of the piece (Hemingway interview).

Yet despite such compositional planning, I contend that the musicians' ability to "groove together" in the performance of *OilEye*—to play in rhythmic synchrony without simply duplicating each other's rhythms—owes more to improvisational and expressive traditions associated with African American music than perhaps to any compositional imperative. The indeterminate latencies inherent in the performance of *OilEye* required remote performers to adjust to "temporal granularity" (Schroeder and Rebelo 2009, 139) through close listening and expressive microtiming. Returning to Iyer's insightful analysis of microtiming, we find that "individual musicians can improvise at this microrhythmic level to create an attentional give-and-take [what may be called 'streaming']" (2002, 402). For Iyer, this is a skill and aesthetic quality generated from the relationship between groove-based African American music and dance, a culturally and historically emergent bodily orientation toward rhythm in music. I contend that the performance of *OilEye* articulates this deeper history of bodily oriented groove through the agency of the improvisers, through their ability to negotiate latency by using microrhythmic placement of individual sounds across the network.

My argument rests on two assumptions. The first concerns the nature of the heuristic framework of the Afrological. The majority of the performers featured on "Inspiraling: Telematic Jazz Explorations" are deeply invested in jazz and other musical forms closely related to the development of African American music, even if their work resists simplistic categorizations. As such, the pieces performed at the event illustrate qualities associated with Afrological musicking: an expression of agency, the activation of personal and collective histories, and a focus on intense interactivity. This is not to say that all or even most of the performers are African American. It is crucial to note that for Lewis, Afrological and Eurological are "historically emergent rather than ethnically essential" frameworks that, among other things, help us understand "the reality of transcultural and transracial communication among improvisers" (Lewis 1996, 93).

The second is that I have deliberately resisted drawing a genre boundary between free or open improvisation and more groove-based improvisation because I think that such a distinction would be facile and problematic. It would betray the breadth and depth of African American expressive traditions while potentially relegating open forms of improvisation to a state without history or culture. Although I have employed a series of binaries to deepen my analysis—Afrological/Eurological, composed/improvised, free improvisation/groove-based improvisation—it is, nevertheless, important to view these formations as continuums, as overlapping, non–mutually exclusive positions designed to illuminate aspects of musical practice rather than to provide decisive mappings.

In the broadest sense, I feel that both free improvisation and groove-based improvisation are particularly compelling musical approaches in the telematic medium. These highly interactive modes of musicking that require real-time personal decision making both highlight and conceal the reality of latency in networked performance. At the same time, this focus on negotiating latency illuminates fundamental aspects of music whether performed telematically or in the traditional, corporeal manner. Thus, as Dante Tanzi suggests in the epigraph, networked music provides key insights for all music making.

Disembodiment or Hyper-embodiment?
The Body in Multisite Networked Improvisation

> To be a body is to have a space where the materiality of this body
> can be endowed and where its existential potentiality of movements
> and hence actions can be exercised.
> —Btihaj Ajana (2005)

The nature of "space" is especially slippery in networked audio and video. Performers in the telematic medium describe this virtually manifested environment using a variety of terms, including "telematic space" and even "real space."[18] All of these names are aimed at understanding the differences and similarities between the physical spaces of traditional performance and the new modalities—a new "materiality," to borrow from Ajana—manifested in networked performance.

For some, "presence" is fundamental to the distinctions between these different spaces. Pedro Rebelo, for example, writes that "notions of presence and environment become central to performance that is characteristically multi-nodal. . . . Presence, in this context, relates to how remote participation is rendered in multi sites/nodes" (2009, 389). Similarly, Oliveros prefers the term *telepresence* to capture the peculiar "materiality" of the body in networked performance: "I really prefer telepresence because we're making our presence manifest over distance. And telematic is another way of talking about it but I don't think I prefer that, even though I use it. I prefer telepresence because I teach, for example, using Skype, and that means I'm present in the distant classroom and the classroom is present to me. So that makes sense to me. . . . [And] we all use the telephone. So 'tele' is in our genes these days" (interview). Oliveros's focus on "presence" intimates a long view of the development of networking technologies, including the telephone and the Internet. She downplays the newness of Internet networking platforms; for her, telepresence occurs in many different forms, only one of which is specific to the Internet.

Oliveros also suggests that different spaces exist for the expression of presence. These include dream space, meditation space, and groove space; as

Oliveros argues, "there are all kinds of spaces that you can be inhabiting" (interview). In networked music, a fundamental dichotomy emerges between telematic space and real space. In-person, embodied music-making takes place in real space, where musicians perform in close physical proximity. For Oliveros, telematic space identifies both the platform and the various aesthetic qualities of interaction, presence, and musicality engendered in networked music.

Interestingly, Oliveros's real space sharply contrasts the use of the same term by Weaver and Dresser. Weaver and Dresser measure real space by the degree to which networked performance feels believable. As networked performance begins to exhibit its inherent latencies and trans-spatial qualities, it becomes less believable to audiences conditioned to the normalcies of in-person performance.[19] As such, telematic performance becomes indexed to "liveness," and audiences are encouraged to reflect on the ways that such performances are mediated through networking technologies.[20]

This tension between real and telematic senses of space foregrounds issues of embodiment. As music technologist Miller Puckette maintains, "when not approached carefully, distributed performance . . . is aesthetically dangerous ground. If you see someone on a screen, does that mean the person is really thousands of miles away, or just in a nearby closet?" (2009, 411).[21] Indeed, seeing and hearing operate as two crucial markers of embodiment in networked music performance. They serve as the primary modes through which Dresser and Weaver's notion of believability take place as well as the fundamental contours of Oliveros's telematic space. Moreover, that which is believable is directly related to our prior experiences listening to and performing music in the same room, an experience that we understand as authentic. The knowledge and understanding of networked bodies is extended through the prism of co-located bodies.

For this reason, networked music necessarily involves embodiment, or what I call "the networked body." I contend that all networked performances carry certain theoretical expectations for both performers and audiences. These expectations may be divided into two rough, overlapping hermeneutic formulations: networked audio-embodiment and networked video-embodiment. In both of these modalities, in-person (or embodied) performance acts as a standard against which the intrinsic technical qualities of networked performance are measured.[22] As latency and audio/video quality attenuate, a sense of disembodiment becomes apparent for performers and audiences. Consequently, embodiment and disembodiment function as interdependent potentialities. For some, embodiment acts as the consequential quality of believability; for others, dis/embodiment shades networked music performance with special aesthetic and artistic possibilities that, in the words of Oliveros, "need to be developed and experimented with" (interview), even if such new creative possibilities have yet to be more fully realized.

The possibility of audio- and video-embodiment is closely connected to constantly evolving networking technologies. Today, most networked performances use special software and hardware that make high-fidelity audio and video network connections possible between remotely located performance sites. Although JackTrip is available free of charge, its functionality is largely dependent on Internet2 access and, usually, a large collection of digital and analog sound equipment. First made functional in 1999, Internet2 was created to serve the needs of institutional (governmental and educational) partners and requires membership to the official Internet2 consortium for access.[23] The reduced traffic and considerable bandwidth provided by Internet2 make it ideally suited for certain intensive applications, such as audio and video networking.

In many respects, the high quality, low latency, and easily manageable audio networking enabled by JackTrip has yet to be matched by readily available video networking platforms. Some projects use platforms such as iChat, Skype, or other consumer-level software that provides relatively easy video networking, but with much higher latencies (and lower resolutions) than the audio networking offered by JackTrip. Other projects invest considerable time and resources in using proprietary video networking platforms, such as Access Grid, UltraGrid, and Ultra-Videoconferencing, most of which offer high-definition resolution.[24] In some cases, these professional-level video networking platforms offer distance-to-latency ratios that match those of JackTrip.[25] Yet these systems also usually require a significantly higher level of production support. Indeed, although decreased travel cost is sometimes cited as a reason for developing these new performance platforms (Dresser interview), the amount of support necessary to successfully present a networked concert may far overshadow the real costs of traveling to distant concert venues (Puckette 2009, 409). This may be why others have turned to low-technology versions of networked performance that use iChat, Skype, and combinations of primarily consumer-level audio and video software.[26]

For example, a low-tech approach may be found in Oliveros's "Deep Listening Convergence," a three-day concert in 2007 that brought together forty-five musicians from three countries for in-person performances that had been developed and rehearsed using Skype (Dalton 2007; Oliveros interview). Centered on Oliveros's Deep Listening practice and improvisation, the participants used Skype audio and video networking to develop pieces in a networked context that were then performed in person.[27] For Oliveros, such "low-tech" approaches to networked music represent a "participatory technology": "For the low-tech connection, at least everybody that has a good laptop and camera and an Internet connection can participate. So it's a participatory technology. Whereas the Internet2 is more specialized and reserved for, say, university situations, situations that can afford to have it. And it's not public. So, I prefer to work with both. Developing both of them as best I can" (interview).

If low-tech options for audio and video networking represent a "participatory technology," such opportunities might be considered as what David Kim-Boyle calls a "democratization of performance." In his essay "Network Musics: Play, Engagement and the Democratization of Performance," Kim-Boyle writes, "Just as much of the work of this earlier generation was motivated by social and political ideals, composers of network-based music often share a common interest in democratizing performance through establishing musical environments that are expressed through playful exploration and interaction among participants" (2009, 364). Kim-Boyle analyzes projects developed by composer Atau Tanaka and the group Metraform, but his findings also apply to more improvisation-oriented contexts. The notion of democratizing musical participation has at least two disparate historical threads. One emphasizes the relationship between agency and improvisation, especially that found in African American improvisatory forms of the 1960s (Attali 1985, 138–40). Another thread, albeit of a different nature, relates to the potential of new digital music recording and production capabilities of the 1990s, which were often accompanied by promises to "democratize" recording through the advent of the "home studio" (Homer 2009, 89).

In a certain sense, then, the idea that telematics might have a democratizing effect on music-making could relate to both the improvisatory nature of much music that is performed during networked concerts as well as the very technology that makes such performances possible. Both eJamming (an online database model introduced in 2008 by Alan Gluckman, Bill Redman, and Gail Cantor) and NINJAM (a client server model introduced in 2004 by Brennan Underwood and Cockos International) might lend credence to the notion that networked improvisation democratizes collaboration (Mills 2010, 188–89) because they lower or eliminate technical barriers to participation and reduce hardware and software costs. Despite such remarkable new modes of music making, the necessary connection between participatory technology and democratic engagement remains to be fully articulated. Participation may not equal democracy.

Indeed, an interesting tension coalesces around participation, notions of professionalism, and differences in working methods in various interdisciplinary, networked collaborations. Dresser, for example, articulates his preference for high-tech, low-latency networking with a playful phrase: "for me, it's . . . a pro shop or no shop" (interview).[28] For Dresser, the audio quality and latency benefits of using JackTrip and professional-level audio equipment are essential to his telematic work.[29] Alternative methods of networking using low-tech solutions fail to provide such benefits and Dresser has access to the necessary institutional support.

These new contexts also introduce a variety of interdisciplinary concerns that significantly change the performative experiences of musicians accustomed to in-person music-making. It is common for networked musical performances to take on more theatrical dimensions in their production, such as staging, lighting, blocking, and scenery. In a recent project, the tension between different disciplinary performance aesthetics posed special challenges for Dessen, which seemed at odds with his more immediate expectations as an improviser:

> The challenge for me is that this puts the music that we're doing into a whole different environment. Because you're dealing with people who are coming from a more theater or dance type background, where they have a certain set of expectations about the polished visual nature of what's happening. How we look is important. Where exactly you stand on stage. You've got to stand on your position. I can't tell you how many times during the sound checks and all the tech rehearsals they were telling me "get back on your" . . . You know, they had to spike where I was standing because I kept moving around. My mic has to be right here . . . That's very difficult for me . . . I don't mind staying more or less in the same place, but the idea of really thinking, as I'm performing, [about] conforming to a certain set of visual expectations and almost theatrical kind of expectations about how to use my body . . . it became an interesting constraint to work within that I was not accustomed to, and that I really had to get used to because I felt like it worked a little bit against the kind of improvisational nature of the music we do. (interview)

For Dessen, the relationship of the body to performing and improvising is centrally important. As expectations about the networked body diverge from his experiences in other improvisatory contexts, the very nature of performance itself shifts. Although deeply interested in the new practical and aesthetic performance options offered by telematics, Dessen confesses that he is nevertheless "mostly a concert musician" (interview).

While Dessen's analysis might apply to any theatrical context, his comments here are nevertheless directed at the process of capturing and distributing the video image of the bodies of remote performers in telematics. His perspective emphasizes the relationship between the body, improvisation, and networked performance and illustrates the complex interdependence of audio-embodiment and video-embodiment (as well as the disruptions caused by disembodiment). This may be a necessary component of networked performance. I agree with Simone Osthoff, who suggests that distributed musical performance is "part of contemporary art's natural development towards immateriality" (1997, 279). Similarly, Giuseppe Longo argues that "the effects produced on the body by information technology are particularly interesting. *Telematics* and *virtual reality* produce a communicative, perceptive, and functional diffusion of the body" (2003, 26). Audio-embodiment and video-embodiment in networked music rearticulates the body as a location for meaning that is referential, necessary, and contingent.

Such a perspective is not new. The relationship between the body and new technologies was a central question during the heyday of discussions about the possibility of virtual reality and the nature of cyberculture, discussions now largely associated with the 1990s. The body also factors prominently into the cyberpunk genre of science fiction popularized in the late 1980s and 1990s, in which characters move easily between real, in-person identities and imaginative, online identities replete with cyber-enhanced capabilities that blur the boundaries between real and artificial. In a similar manner, Donna Haraway's commonly cited "cyborg" provides a feminist challenge to traditional assumptions about the naturalized body; in short, Haraway argues that "we are [all] cyborgs" (1994, 150); we are all socially constructed bodies in dialogue with technology.[30]

Since the virtual reality debates of the 1990s, technology has certainly continued to provide new models of bodily engagement with the world. For some, this has led to the notion of the posthuman. In his essay "Technologies of Post-Human Development and the Potential for Global Citizenship," Mike Featherstone draws connections between new telecommunications technologies and bodily potentials: "If technology is increasingly embedded in our everyday activities, from means of physical communication involving movement, to mediated forms of communication at a distance (telephone or Internet), then technology is part of the material structure of everyday life in the sense that it provides a familiar range of objects with which we associate and that our bodies have become accustomed to feeling at home with" (2003, 228). This increasingly intimate relationship with technology has produced compelling new ideas about both technology and the body. For Don Ihde, this is summarized in his concept of the "technological body," or "embodied experiences in and with technology" (quoted in Yurtsever and Tasa 2009, 2).

In the context of telematic music performance, such a technological body involves performing across vast geographical distances by relying on audio and video networking technologies—a kind of extension of the body through telematic prosthesis.[31] As Braasch suggests, this might be viewed as "a new type of musical instrument or instrument extension" (Oliveros et al. 2009). I maintain that cognitive assumptions about networked audio- and video-embodiment in telematic performance derive in large part from the bodies of performers and audiences, bodies that occupy specific spatial coordinates, even while participating in or witnessing spatially distributed performance. Thus embodiment and disembodiment in telematic music are largely derivative of traditional understandings of in-person music-making. In this way, dis/embodiment in networked performance is best viewed as a form of hyper-embodiment; the assumptions and expectations of in-person, in-the-same-room performance become the necessary conditions of believability for the networked body. Such a reliance on traditional embodiment creates a technological conundrum: "the ultimate goal of virtual embodiment is to become the perfect simulacrum of full, multisensory [*sic*] bodily action" (Ihde 2002, 7).

Telematic Music for the Improviser-Composer

The ramifications of this conundrum are rather startling. Is telematic performance aimed at replicating "full, multisensory bodily action?" In other words, are telematic performances shaped by an implicit goal of replicating in-person performance? We may indeed conclude that some telematic performances strive to make their very networked nature invisible and inaudible. As future technologies continue to decrease latency, this goal will become more attainable. Real (embodied) and virtual (disembodied) bodies may become so closely connected that, as I suggest here, a new hyper-embodiment becomes the measure on which networked performance is constructed and judged.

For "Inspiraling: Telematic Jazz Explorations" and many other telematic concerts, a more subtle reflection on the nature of latency and performance is taking place. Musicians are asked to play in time, but to do so requires that they draw from their extensive experience as improvisers. Grooving together in Hemingway's *OilEye* challenges musicians to engage one another interactively across a latent network: to play in time in this way is to improvise toward a negotiated, dialogic rhythmic relationship through expressive microrhythms. Performers feel their way toward compelling rhythmic relationships—toward a groove—with their networked collaborators. At the same time, Weaver's *Telein* combines modular compositional techniques with free improvisation, effectively obfuscating the presence of disruptive time lags between networked sites. In both cases—free and groove-oriented improvisation—latency and improvisation make for strange yet inherently related bedfellows. Perhaps it is this way in both networked performance and traditional in-the-same-room performance.

From this perspective, the believable is always relative and reflects deeply held beliefs about the nature of musical performance. Indeed, the believable itself may be used as a robust compositional and improvisational tool in telematic music. Illusions of rhythmic synchrony shift as performers and audiences are distributed across multiple network nodes. Each node, each perspective on the aggregated performance, presents a special opportunity to construct and deconstruct synchrony, to embody distant performers, to create "real space," and to articulate conceptual nuances of embodiment and disembodiment. Rather than simply striving to re-create the real, I hope that telematics opens new creative strategies aimed at understanding time, the body, and dialogism. Whether through free improvisation, expressive microtiming in groove-oriented improvisation, or other improvisatory practices, I believe that improvisers are uniquely positioned to help catalyze these new potentials.

Notes

I am grateful for the insightful comments from the reviewers of this volume and to many friends and colleagues for important feedback that has helped shape this essay, including Ellen Waterman, Joseph Moore, Eric Lewis, and the participants at "(Re)Thinking Improvisation," an interdisciplinary conference that took place in November and December 2011 at the Inter Arts Center, Malmö Academy of Music, University of Lund, Malmö, Sweden. A special word of thanks to Michael Dessen, a longtime musical collaborator whose ideas about telematics have surely influenced mine.

    1. The history of the word *telematics* traces in part to Simon Nora's and Alain Minc's 1978 report to former French president Valéry Giscard d'Estaing, published in 1980 as *The Computerization of Society*. Their sprawling account of the impact of new technologies on life and politics introduces the term *telematics* (*télématique*), which refers to the "conjunction of computers and telecommunications" (Shanken 2000, 65).

    2. "Inspiraling—Telematic Jazz Explorations," networked performance, Vimeo video, June 13, 2010, http://vimeo.com/15069197.

    3. Partners in the "Inspiraling: Telematic Jazz Explorations" concert included the Steinhardt School of Culture, Education, and Human Development at New York University and the Conrad Prebys Music Center at the University of California, San Diego. The event was sponsored by the Music Technology Program at New York University, CalIT2 and the Center for Research and Computing in the Arts at the University of California at San Diego, and Roulette Intermedia.

    4. "Embodied cognition" has received considerable attention from analytic philosophers and cognitive scientists, among others. I use the terms *embodied* and *embodiment*

in ways that reference this discourse, yet also more loosely relate to what is recently called "kinesthetics." For a more recent discussion and challenge to psychological studies of embodied cognition, see Adams (2010). For an application of kinesthetics in the context of theater, see McConachie (1993).

5. The technology of Internet2 goes by different names in different countries and regions: Internet2 (United States), Canarie (Canada), GEANT2 (Western Europe), and CERNET2 (China), for example.

6. Bassist Mark Dresser notes the "pragmatic need to find an alternative way to perform, due to the worsening restrictions in travel with a double bass since 9/11" (Oliveros et al. 2009).

7. The project aimed to "create a sonification tool for fine-grain flows on the Internet" (Chris Chafe, personal interview with Jason Robinson, Skype, June 8, 2011).

8. In a personal interview, Chafe gives a slightly different articulation of the research group's acronym: Sound Waves on the Internet for Recirculating Echos.

9. This essay primarily focuses on the telematic projects of Michael Dessen, Mark Dresser, Chris Chafe, Pauline Oliveros, and Sarah Weaver, all of whom were interviewed by the author. Oliveros is also deeply interested in low-tech networking options, such as Skype and iChat, as I discuss later.

10. See Chafe and Gurevich (2004); Chafe, Cáceres, and Gurevich (2010); and Mills (2010, 187).

11. See Bartlette et al. (2006). As Braasch maintains, "we tend to forget that every performance involving more than one musician is a distributed performance. . . . The acoustic information needs time to propagate from the musical instrument to the ears of the participating musician(s)" (2009, 423).

12. Soundpainting and conduction refer to conducting languages developed for improvising ensembles by Walter Thompson and Butch Morris, respectively.

13. "Multiplicities: An Inter-arts Telematic Performance," October 25, 2008, Visual Arts Black Box at the University of California, San Diego, and CalIT2 Auditorium at the University of California, Irvine (video excerpt available at http://vimeo.com/8589093). Dessen, Dresser, and Joachim Gossman codirected the event.

14. Audience perceptions were corroborated by casual comments and, more formally, by polling them after the event. The relatively latent Quicktime Broadcaster was used for video networking and AULab was used for audio networking (Michael Dessen, email correspondence with Jason Robinson, December 21, 2011; Mark Dresser, email correspondence with Jason Robinson, December 21, 2011).

15. For a more extended discussion of hyper-realism, see Baudrillard (1988).

16. My use of the term *free improvisation* here is meant to refer to its open, nonpulsed quality as compared to groove-based music, rather than to any historical style. For this reason, I use both "free" and "open" interchangeably. It must be noted, however, that these terms have varied histories. See Derek Bailey (1993) for a more detailed discussion of free improvisation as a practice that emerged in Britain in the 1960s in which he distinguishes between idiomatic and nonidiomatic styles.

17. These estimated delays are seemingly based on distance only; processing delays would surely increase the actual latencies.

18. "Telematic space" is offered by Pauline Oliveros (interview); "real space" is a term used by composer and conductor Sarah Weaver (interview) in her collaborations with Dresser to refer to "the perception that you're in the same room, but not in each other's room."

19. Dresser calls this the "believability factor" (interview).

20. For "liveness," see Auslander (2008), Blau (2011, 246–63), and Crisell (2012). For insightful analyses of the relationship between "liveness" and "deadness," see Novak (2013, 28–63) and Stanyek and Piekut (2010).

21. Puckette illustrates this by offering an anecdote from the 1997 meeting of the International Computer Music Conference, where a group called the Convolution Brothers revealed a supposed "remote" performer from behind a curtain in the same the room (2009, 411). Puckette now performs with the Convolution Brothers (Puckette "Biographical Note," http://crca.ucsd.edu/~msp/bio.htm [accessed May 30, 2011]).

22. In his influential book *The Audible Past: Cultural Origins of Sound Reproduction*, Jonathan Sterne emphasizes the complex interplay between sound and vision through his critique of what he calls the "audiovisual litany," which "idealizes hearing (and, by extension, speech) as manifesting a kind of pure interiority" (2003, 15). Sterne's project aims to center the importance of sound in human experience. I contend, however, that for many audiences the visual takes priority over the sonic in telematic performance, especially when slippages occur because of latency differences in the video and audio networking.

23. See "Internet2: The First 10 Years," Internet2, http://www.internet2.edu/about /timeline (accessed May 29, 2011).

24. Access Grid is "an ensemble of resources including multimedia large-format displays, presentation and interactive environments, and interfaces to Grid middleware and to visualization environments" developed first at the Argonne National Laboratory in Chicago (AccessGrid.org). UltraGrid is a subset of the Dynamic Resource Allocation via GMPLS Optical Networks project, a National Science Foundation–supported research consortium that includes members at Massachusetts Institute of Technology, NASA Goddard Space Flight Center, and elsewhere, and which interfaces with AccessGrid technology ("HD-CVAN < DRAGON < TWiki," *Dragon—Dynamic Resource Allocation via GMPLS Optical Networks*, http://dragon.maxgigapop.net/twiki/bin/view/DRAGON/HD-CVAN [accessed June 1, 2011]). Ultra-videoconferencing is currently in development at McGill University in Montreal by a research group drawn from the Centre for Interdisciplinary Research in Music Media and Technology of the Faculty of Music ("McGill Ultra-Videoconferencing Research Group, see http://ultravideo.mcgill.edu [accessed June 1, 2011).

25. This was the case with the April 16, 2011, performance of the project titled "Tele-Motions: A Networked Intermedia Concert," which featured pianist Myra Melford and bassist Mark Dresser at the University of California, San Diego, and trombonist Michael Dessen at the University of California, Irvine (Dessen interview; Dresser interview; "Tele-Motions: A Networked Intermedia Concert," networked performance, YouTube video, April 16–17, 2011, http://www.youtube.com/watch?v=qVVW9301huA).

26. In this context, "high" and "low" might have several connotations. Although they position certain technologies in relationship to recent innovative developments ("high-tech" versus "low-tech"), it is hard to deny the class implications also intimated by these qualifiers. For example, the significant institutional resources usually required to use "high" technology might correlate to "highbrow" and "lowbrow" distinctions that emerged in American culture in the nineteenth century (see Levine 1990).

27. Deep Listening is both a musical system and a philosophy that is premised on the idea of listening actively to everything all the time. See www.deeplistening.org.

28. The "professional" also has a second nuance for Dresser. He views telematics as an opportunity to create new working contexts for professional musicians: "I'm really seeking

pro-level stuff. For really pragmatic reasons. I want musicians to be able to work. I see less opportunities for our profession and I think this can be an exciting artistic potential" (Dresser interview).

29. He maintains that "without it, it's not good enough" (Dresser, personal interview).

30. See David Borgo's contribution to this volume (chapter 6) for a related discussion of improvisation and neocybernetics.

31. For other forms of technological prosthesis in musical performance, see Rebelo and van Walstijn (2004) and Schroeder (2006), the latter an editorial essay of a double issue of *Contemporary Music Review* dedicated to the issue of the "technologically informed body."

6. Openness from Closure

THE PUZZLE OF INTERAGENCY IN IMPROVISED
MUSIC AND A NEOCYBERNETIC SOLUTION

David Borgo

A particular joy of making improvised music is not knowing precisely the relationship between one's thoughts and one's actions (one has to surprise oneself, after all) and between one's actions and the actions of other improvisers (did you do that because I did that, or did I do that because you did that?). Improvising in electro-acoustic situations can heighten the joy (by extending one's musical resources and horizons) and the complexity (by introducing additional technological actors and agency) of an already puzzling situation. Kent De Spain describes the complex agency involved in improvised performance rather succinctly: "There are things that we *do,* things that are *happening* that we feel we are a part of, and things that feel like they happen *to* us" (2012, 29).

Writing on improvisation tends to engage these issues either by exploring the interrelationship between mind and body or by theorizing the interpersonal and intersubjective dynamics of performance. However, after one comes to the realization that the mind is in the body and the body is in the mind (or, more precisely, that our conceptual, sensory, and motor capacities are intertwined and have coevolved), and that the mind extends beyond skin and skull into the social, cultural, physical, and technological environments that influence human experience, it can be unclear where to go next.

One route has been to theorize an emancipatory quality to improvisation, to view it as a liberating force in people's lives.[1] I will not be following this particular route, although I do not deny improvisation's uplifting potential. Another route has been to theorize an anticipatory quality to improvisation, to posit improvisation as a form of social practice and project this onto political problems yet to be solved.[2] Again, this will not be my chosen trajectory here, although learning about the trials and tribulations encountered by improvising musicians and about their personal ideas and ideologies can certainly rub off on devoted listeners, just as creating new venues for and attitudes about the practice can have an effect on community dynamics and desires.

Instead, I start from a point of questioning what and how exactly improvisation communicates, and, by connection, who or what exactly is doing the communicating. I begin by exploring the puzzle of interagency alluded to at the outset. Along the way I share my experience working in the realm of electro-acoustic improvised music with trumpeter and computer musician Jeff Kaiser in a duo called KaiBorg. This work, as much as my theoretical reading, has influenced my belief that we must shift from viewing tools as extensions of the human to a condition where nonhuman networks of tool-systems instrumentalize the human. Donna Haraway's (1994) well-known theorization of the cybernetic organism, or cyborg, along with Andy Clark's (1997, 2003) equally influential work on distributed cognition, are both reminders that to be human is already to be extended and posthuman.

If we are not careful, however, this approach tends to spread the notion of agency rather wide and thin, and it runs the risk of privileging information over substance, pattern over matter (as Katherine Hayles, among others, has often pointed out).[3] As a way forward, I turn to neocybernetics, which offers a somewhat counterintuitive but I believe ultimately compelling alternative.

Cybernetics is an umbrella term coined by Norbert Weiner (1948) in the 1940s to describe the study of regulatory systems and feedback mechanisms. It brought together an unruly subset of approaches and fields, including, in its first stage, mathematics, engineering, robotics, and information theory, and later psychology, brain science, the arts, education, management studies, and spirituality, among other things. At its best, however, cybernetics established a pioneering transdisciplinary approach. According to Andrew Pickering (2010), cybernetics studies systems that learn to adapt to a world that can always surprise them.[4] From the field's inception this meant a special focus on the adaptive brain, but subsequent extensions of cybernetics looked beyond the biological brain into the realm of the self and social relations.

In the current moment, cybernetics can appear simultaneously nonmodern and postmodern, in part because it is *nondualist* and *nonrepresentational*. It rejects the modernist dualism of things and people, which is now institutionalized as the natural and social sciences. It argues that science, like the arts, is a performative engagement with the world. It abandons simplistic understandings of cause and effect—that something already identifiably present causes things to happen this way or that—and champions a world in which reality is always "in the making." Its ontology is performative and its epistemology is radically constructivist. Cybernetics, much like improvisation studies, insists that "we" are plunged in medias res into a lively world that we cannot control.

Cybernetic research began during and after World War II, and the field's early proponents have sometimes been criticized for the military, industrial, and managerial applications that emerged in its wake.[5] In the decades that followed, however, a second-order cybernetics proposed a self-reflexive turn away from the tendency toward instrumentality and control that arguably did dominate early research. It symbolized a new level of attention being paid to the environments and embodiments of systems, to their media and not only their forms. I have chosen to use the term *neocybernetics*, recently championed by Bruce Clarke and Mark B. N. Hansen (2009), among others, in part because I believe a critique of both first- and second-order cybernetics is still in order. Also, given the conceptual baggage that tends to accompany the term *cybernetics*, and the fact that it never found a comfortable home in the academy (for reasons that we should probably celebrate rather than condemn), adding a "neo-" prefix seems like a good idea.

A basic tenet of neocybernetics is that a system is open to its environment in proportion to the complexity of its closure. "Environmental entanglement," write Clarke and Hansen, "correlates with organismic (or systemic) self-regulation" (2009, 7). In place of a humanist conception of autonomy that insists on a subject in which perception and communication are unified, neocybernetics approaches the "human" as a self-referential system that involves an amalgamation of multiple observing systems. It extends the biological insight that living systems are open to energetic exchange but "operationally closed" (i.e., they are self-producing and self-maintaining systems) into the cognitive and social realms.

In this chapter I use the notion of "openness from closure" to interrogate how systems of improvisation, both human and nonhuman, natural and social, are established, engaged, and maintained. Although I believe that this insight applies broadly to the question of improvisation in the arts and in human experience, due to the nature of my own background as an improvising musician working with open forms (what is sometimes called "free improvisation") and now often in electro-acoustic situations, this chapter will most directly engage with and be inflected by these practices. Briefly, I argue that it is only through the interrelated operational closures of individual musicians' bodies and psyches, the "staging" of the performance event, and the self-organization of the artwork itself that improvisation is able to open itself up to and productively engage with the hypercomplexity of the world.

Jazz and improvised music are frequently heralded for their high degree of interactivity. Musicians listen, relate, and respond to one another while performing together. Audiences, too, can influence the musical proceedings through explicit vocal interjections or by more subtle means. Terms such as *flow*, *groove*, or *vibe* circulate among practitioners and scholars to get at the complex connections and emotions generated in improvised performance.

This focus on interaction tends to assume a unified and fully autonomous human subject as its common denominator. Psychologists focus on how an individual extracts and represents information from the sonic environment and in turn responds to or acts on these representations.[6] Ethnomusicologists tend to adopt this general orientation while focusing on how these abilities are shaped by cultural conventions, usually conceived of as a model or referent stored in long-term memory.[7] Some researchers shift the focus from the performer to the listener, noting that music perception is partially volitional: we can selectively choose what we wish to focus our attention on.[8] Still others with interests in phenomenology or cognitive science focus on the instrument itself as a kind of structured environment for the human actor to explore.[9] There is much to be gleaned from these approaches, but taken together they highlight the influence that methodological individualism has had on the field of improvisation studies (and the study of creativity writ large), as well as the tenacity of the representationalist cognitive paradigm.

What if our sense of agency or personal authorship is not so easily or fully explained by a representationalist paradigm? According to a recent neuroscience study, musical improvisation dramatically reduces inhibitions and conscious awareness (seen as a decrease in activity in the dorsolateral prefrontal cortex), while ramping up regions of the brain (the medial prefrontal cortex) associated with storytelling, dreaming, and other expressions of personality (Limb and Braun 2008). Recent experimental evidence also demonstrates that one's actions are often initiated from below the level of conscious awareness. For instance, a baseball player deciding to tip his bat up or down as the ball crosses the plate is acting faster than conscious thought allows (D. Ross 2007, 4). In a gun-slinging duel, the one who responds to seeing the other person draw first actually pulls his weapon about 10 percent faster, a phenomenon known as the "reactive advantage" (Welchman et al. 2010). It makes sense as a survival strategy that our bodies can initiate quick actions in response to the environment before our conscious mind has had time to weigh all the alternatives. David Rokeby (1998), writing about his experience performing with his installation work *Very Nervous System*, found that the system (which involved video tracking his movements, linked to computer-generated audio) often responded *before* he had realized he had started moving.[10] Much of what we do and why we do it seems to elude our conscious awareness.

In an article titled "The Puzzle of Coaction," social psychologists Daniel M. Wegner and Betsy Sparrow (2007) use some deceptively simple alphabet pointing experiments (involving paired participants working simultaneously as well as in leading and following arrangements) to explore how fine differences in the timing of action and gaze can radically alter perceptions of "authorship" or the feeling of who is in charge. It turns out that one's experience of authorship can be enhanced or undermined relatively easily by externally directed attention or by manipulation of environmental and social conditions.

Wegner and Sparrow argue that people come to understand their actions as their own by: (1) using proprioception or introception (i.e., learning from the body and visceral sensations); (2) establishing how the mind may have contributed to action (via intention, planning, or premeditation); and (3) incorporating external information about the social circumstance of the action (i.e., the presence and potential contributions of other agents). For them, these three indicators of authorship may add to or subtract from each other such that the experience of conscious will is the final common pathway that produces the sense of "I did it," "I didn't do it," or any gradation in between.

In this light, recall briefly De Spain's description of agency in improvisation: "There are things that we *do*, things that are *happening* that we feel we are a part of, and things that feel like they happen *to* us" (2012, 29). Improvisers also combine informational pathways from proprioception (including one's visceral connection to an instrument and the surrounding soundscape), intention/planning/premeditation, and the social circumstance of the action (which would include both human and nonhuman agents participating in the performance). For De Spain, "the trick to staying in the intimacy of the moment is not to care where we are on that spectrum, but rather to value each place for what it offers us as creators and performers" (2012, 29).

In place of a "ghost in the machine"—a mind that is "self-luminous," knowing all that it does, including its causation of action—Wegner and Sparrow envision a conscious will that emerges from the mind's efforts to understand its own authorship. Seeking to extend and contextualize their experimental findings, Wegner and Sparrow argue that authorship judgments have evolved to account for agency in a social world where agency in coaction—or what I am calling *interagency*—is the measure of all things. It may be that improvised music offers an experience by which we can, at certain times, and perhaps only fleetingly at best, lessen our grip on social accounting and celebrate rather than merely puzzle over interagency and coaction.

In my work with Jeff Kaiser as the duo KaiBorg, our reigning aesthetic has been to devise hybrid instruments that both extend and complicate our sense of personal agency and control. While the name of our duo is on the one hand a simple contraction of our last names, it is of course meant to evoke the well-known (and well-trodden) image of a hybrid biomachine, a cyborg. Images of cyborgs are frequently intended to incite fear by combining flesh with metal or implanting brains with electronics. We subscribe to Clark's (2003) notion that we are all "natural-born cyborgs." Our remarkably plastic brains have co-evolved in tandem with a shaping environment to prime us to seek out and incorporate nonbiological resources and the cultural practices that surround them into our very existence. The transition from notepad to notebook computer, Clark argues, is one of degree, not kind.

In KaiBorg we extend our acoustic instrumental resources with digital sound processing techniques controlled by various video tracking methods and hardware controllers (primarily foot pedals and pressure-sensitive pads). As improvisers, we desire an action/response time that is comparable to that of purely acoustic performance. We also insist that all aspects of sound production and electronic processing happen in the moment of performance (i.e., we do not use any prerecorded samples or precomposed musical materials). But we seek, to paraphrase Haraway's discourse on the cyborg in her book *Simians, Cyborgs and Women* (1991), the pleasure in the confusion of boundaries, even as we accept the responsibility for their construction. Ultimately, we are after a relationship by which the organism becomes one part of elaborate feedback mechanisms and the cybernetic, in turn, incorporates the sophistication of the organic into its systems.

On a technical level we use a variety of timbral, temporal, and pitch manipulations (using MaxMSP) in tandem with multichannel spatialization effects (using Ambisonics). Our particular aesthetic is to have the acoustic and electronic components of our hybrid sounds exist on an equal footing and surround ourselves and the audience with complex, often rapidly moving and highly fractured sounds. As a result, there are times when it is unclear to us as performers, and undoubtedly to listeners in the audience, from which musician or from whose "system" sounds are emanating. A saxophonist who enjoys extreme dynamic and register shifts and a variety of overtone, articulation, and fingering devices, playing with a trumpet player who explores a similarly wide range of extended techniques, along with complex layerings of material recorded and looped live in performance, produces a combined soundscape that can get rather dense. Ultimately, however, it is the combination and creative blurring of intentions and boundaries within a shared and interactive soundscape that defines our duo performances above and beyond the specific type or density of sonic materials used.

The notion of interaction implies that the actions of two or more individuals are observed to be mutually interdependent. The related term *interactivity* is frequently used to describe the measure of a medium's potential ability to let the user exert an influence on the content or form of the mediated communication in real time. Interactivity, however, often gets treated as a quality that is designed into technical systems a priori (as is the case in most video games, for example).

For Werner Rammert (2008), *interagency* refers to situations that involve humans with technical systems capable of actively searching for new information, either to select behavior or to change a pregiven frame of action. Portable digital devices that alert users to predicaments or possibilities based on geolocation and various information culled from sensors, the Internet, and an individual's past use or stated preferences would already seem to be engaged in a relationship of interagency with their human "operators." With regard to music performance, Joel Chadabe writes of "shared symbiotic control" when discussing the relationship between "interactive composing instruments" and their performing partners (1996, 201).

I am less interested, however, in the specific technical configuration of any particular system and more interested in the ways users, technologies, and environments *configure* one another (Borgo and Kaiser 2010). In an article exploring "system-environment hybrids," Hansen poses a pressing question to contemporary cultural theorists that frames the remainder of my discussion: "How can one recognize the certain consistency, perhaps even the autonomy, of the human mindbody and at the same time account for the certain non-autonomy that accrues from its unavoidable reliance on the agency of informationally complex environments to achieve its cognitive tasks?" (2009, 117).

Somewhat paradoxically, the way forward may be to insist on the operational closure of the individual's consciousness and on the self-organizing dimensions of the artwork itself, even as these emerge out of and are structurally coupled to environments compounded by social and technological systems. In the next section I suggest neocybernetics as a possible solution to the puzzle of interagency.

Openness from Closure

Cybernetics comes from a Greek word meaning "the art of steering," as in a boat. The relationship between feedback and control (that one intimately feels when piloting a boat) became something of a unifying thread that ran through cybernetic theory at this time. On the whole, the field aimed to shift the focus from the building blocks of phenomena to the form of behaviors: from what things are made of to what things do and how they are observed. Unlike conventional engineers, who design systems able to withstand environmental fluctuations (i.e., to be indifferent to their environment), cyberneticians were interested in modeling and building systems that could adapt to their environment by being sensitive and responsive to changes in the world around them. The adaptive brain was viewed as a cybernetic system par excellence, and research in the field was some of the earliest to demonstrate the constructedness of our thoughts and observations: that there can never be a one-to-one correlation between perception and world.

Grey Walter's mechanical "tortoises" were the product of one of the more memorable cybernetic projects from this early period. They were designed so that their behavior, when set down in the world, was based entirely on whatever the tortoise found in its environment. In addition to highlighting the field's emphasis on feedback and adaptation, the tortoises also exemplified its concern with viewing performance as *performance*, not as a pale shadow of representation. "The tortoises engaged directly, performatively and nonrepresentationally, with the environments in which they found themselves," writes Pickering (2010, 21).

The related notion of a black box with input and output but unknowable internal workings emerged as another key concept in the field, especially in the work of William Ross Ashby (1956). The idea of a black box may suggest for some a deficient understanding lacking in important details. Modern science tends to operate this way, with a determination to strip away the casings of black boxes to understand their inner workings. It assumes that eventually all black boxes can be opened and assimilated to its representational schema. But a black box requires a fundamentally performative engagement: it is something that does something, that one does something to, and that does something back.

Ashby insisted that black boxes are ubiquitous in our daily lives. He was a psychiatrist by training, engaged on a daily basis with the inherent unknowability of psychological states. This likely influenced his views, but in his book *An Introduction to Cybernetics* he deliberately gives a mundane example of a black box to highlight its ubiquity: "the child who tries to open a door has to manipulate the handle (the input) so as to produce the desired movement at the latch (the output); and he has to learn how to control the one by the other without being able to see the internal mechanism that links them. In our daily lives we are confronted at every turn with systems whose internal mechanisms are not fully open to inspection, and which must be treated by the methods appropriate to the Black Box" (1956, 86).

We gain knowledge (or not) of the workings of a black box through a performative engagement; knowledge of its inner workings is not intrinsic to its conception. Much of the time we establish a satisfactory performative relation with black boxes such as doorknobs—or musical instruments for that matter—long before we have a need or a desire to figure out the specific mechanisms involved. After decades of playing the saxophone, I am still unable to decipher how all of its key mechanisms work or understand all aspects of its physical design. Pickering usefully describes black boxes as partners in a dance of agency, stating that "we are indeed enveloped by lively systems that act and react to our doings, ranging from our fellow humans through plants and animals to machines and inanimate matter, and one can readily reverse the order of the list and say that inanimate matter is itself also enveloped by lively systems, some human but most nonhuman. The world just is that way" (2010, 20).

Cybernetics refuses the detour through knowledge conceived of as representational on which nearly all modern science relies. It argues that much of our being does not have a representational aspect. To put this somewhat differently—and in a way that avoids a "deficient" reading of cybernetics— Pickering argues that modern science entails "a detour away from performance and through the space of representation, which has the effect of veiling the world of performance from us" (2010, 20). For Pickering, modern science stages a modern ontology that veils the performative aspects of our being, since it is precisely these performative aspects that are unrepresentable in the idiom of the modern sciences: "Theoretical physics tells us about the unvarying properties of hidden entities like quarks or strings and is silent about the performances of scientists, instruments, and nature from which such representations emerge" (21).

Cybernetics upholds a vision of the world as a place of continuing interlinked performances. In my reading, it is compatible with an ecological approach to the perception of musical meaning that insists we resonate with environmental information and do not simply decode, represent, and compute.[11] Although the theoretical aspects of cybernetics may receive the most attention, its performative ontology can be best appreciated through its experimental leanings. Gordon Pask, to offer only one example, designed and created an impressive array of cybernetic machines involved in education, architecture, and interactive arts, among other things. His Musicolour Machine, for instance, turned a musical performance into an electrical signal that modulated a show of light and motion. The relationship between the sounds and the visuals, however, was nonlinear. In other words, the various visual effects responded based on the previous history of a particular performance. The machine would eventually get bored, as Pask was fond of putting it, and stop responding to specific stimuli until the performer came up with something new to wake it up and get it performing again in a lively manner. In essence, the performer trained the machine and the machine trained the performer. Any given performance was a joint production involving a reciprocal adaptation of the human and the machine.

Pickering argues that the actual construction and implementation of cybernetic projects helped bring the field's ontological claims down to Earth; they simultaneously offered "aids to our ontological imagination" and provided "instances of the sort of endeavors that might go on with a nonmodern imagining of the world" (2010, 22). I like to think that free improvisation offers its own "ontological theater" in precisely these ways. It is a music of imaginative possibilities that is also wrapped in the rather matter-of-fact reality that it relies on and stages ongoing interlinked performances between various black boxes, both human and nonhuman.

Let's unpack this notion of black boxes in improvised music a bit more. Before doing so I introduce one more wrinkle in our cybernetic story. A second wave of cybernetic thought emerged in the period from the 1950s through the 1970s and is associated most often with the work of physicist and philosopher Heinz von Foerster, biologists and neuroscientists Humberto Maturana and Francisco Varela, social scientists Gregory Bateson and Margaret Mead, philosopher and management specialist Stafford Beer, and sociologist Niklas Luhmann, among others. Second-order cybernetics is often described as a shift from a cybernetics of *observed* systems to a cybernetics of *observing* systems. It maintained the performative ontology and the cognition-centered focus of first-order cybernetics. "All doing is knowing, and all knowing is doing" (Maturana and Varela 1998, 27) became a credo for Maturana and Varela, but it also involved an increased awareness of the role of the observer. "Everything said is said by someone" was another of their guiding maxims (27).

Consider that as we go about our lives we encounter a nearly infinite reservoir of possible experiences, each one different from the next. Our sensorimotor interface is extraordinarily complex and massively parallel, but by necessity our conscious mind must filter these perceptions. One strategy our psychic system uses is "filling in the blanks" through prediction and expectation. Another strategy is to integrate information into a more unified experience. For instance, we cannot easily separate the sound of a word from its meaning or separate the color of an object from the object itself, nor can we easily separate out the various components of a musical tone (although musicians train for many years to be able to counter some aspects of our ecological hearing). To be conscious is to bring to every situation a preexisting orientation. Yet this preexisting orientation allows us to become so entangled in our various communicative environments: openness from closure.

With second-order cybernetics, researchers abandoned the subject/object distinction that was still implicit in a first-order cybernetics of observed systems in favor of the system/environment distinction. Because of grammatical conventions we tend to think of systems "within" or "surrounded by" environments, but in second-order cybernetics to say that a system is "within" an environment is only to say that it functions while other systems function simultaneously. For example, a body can be viewed as comprising organs and the various connections between them—a whole made up of parts. But a body viewed as a living organism is a series of nested systems functioning simultaneously, including circulatory, digestive, immune, reproductive, and respiratory systems, among others—a whole made up of other wholes. The immune system, for instance, cannot be precisely located *in* the body, nor is it transplantable or able to be amputated, yet it only works in the complex environment *of* the body, simultaneously with the other systems just mentioned.

The "interior" of a system in second-order cybernetics is not defined by a structural boundary, but by a zone of reduced complexity. In other words, communication within a system operates through a particular medium and by selecting only a limited amount of all available information. Systems are able to increase their internal complexity only by recognizing external irritations; in other words, they construct their interactions with their environment as information. Communication is both subjectless and actionless: it is *coordinated selectivity*. Meaning does not emerge, for instance, as an individual creates or receives information; rather, it involves the linkage of a given message to subsequent communications.

The prolific, dense, and still rather controversial writings of German sociologist Niklas Luhmann in social systems theory offer perhaps the most detailed examination of these ideas. Briefly, Luhmann is critical of the "transmission" metaphor for communication: "The entire metaphor of possessing, having, giving, and receiving" is unsuitable, he writes (1995, 139). He conceives of communication not as an action performed by an actor; rather, it is a selection performed by a system.

For Luhmann, only communication communicates. I will try to explain this rather counterintuitive notion. Biological systems operate through life processes, such as blood circulation, nervous activity, digestion, reproduction, and the division of cells. Mental systems operate through mental operations, including thoughts, feelings, and emotions. Since at least the time of Descartes, Western thought has struggled with how to reconcile this dualism. Instead of challenging the mind-body split—and risking the ever-present danger of simply flipping the conventional valuation of these terms by celebrating notions of embodiment—Luhmann asks us to embrace a mind-body-communication plurality. Society neither digests nor thinks; social systems communicate.

It is here that neocybernetics—and from here on I use my preferred term—engages with posthumanism, although from an empirical rather than a rhetorical stance. According to Luhmann, neither body nor mind nor society are the definite "home" of the human being, and therefore the "human being" is neither a sufficient nor necessary entry point into understanding social and communicative dynamics. Rather than describe society on the basis of its members, Luhmann attempts to describe society on the basis of its events: to look empirically at what actually happens.

Just as systems biologists would describe the functioning of the various subsystems within a body and their mutual dependence and feedback, or an ecologist might investigate various niches and the environmental resources that both differentiate and support them, Luhmann seeks to describe the functions of the various communication systems in society. In the economic system, for instance, money and financial values circulate. In the political system, power is generated and perpetuated. The legal system operates by establishing and enforcing a legal code. The art system operates around judgments of beauty. Each of these communication systems, and many others, have reached a level of complexity in the past few centuries, according to Luhmann, such that they are best understood as operationally distinct even as they function simultaneously and in constant mutual influence. To use the language of neocybernetics, they are structurally coupled but operationally closed.

To say that systems are structurally coupled but operationally closed implies that they need one another in their environment to exist and persist, but there is no explicit causality between them. Without thinking about it, we tend to look for causal links. Either social change provokes musical change, or musical change provokes social change. Either the mind tells the body what to do, or the body leads the mind. But thinking about blood circulation, for instance, does not produce nor halt the circulation of blood. The various systems of life, consciousness, and communication use and rely on resources from their environment, but those resources do not become part of the systems' operation. A passage from Hans Georg Moeller's useful *Luhmann Explained* may help to ground these ideas:

Is it really more convincing to describe what happens when one buys a chocolate bar at a store or stock on the Internet as instances of "human interaction" than to describe them as events in the function system of the economy? On what factual grounds can one hold that zapping to a TV channel or acting in a soap opera is a way of taking part in the life of a community rather than taking part in the system of mass media? And to what extent is the mechanical counting of a vote in an election more an act of recognizing the individual intentions of a citizen than an element of a social procedure to distribute power? If one opts for the second description in each case, one steps towards social systems theory and one of its most basic assumptions: *human beings do not and cannot communicate—only communication can.* (2012, 6)

Human beings and their thoughts are necessary for communication to take place, but they are inaccessible within communication. We can, in communication, only connect to the communication of others, never directly to their minds or brains, much less to the "human being" as such. Luhmann avoids speaking of communication in terms of "expression," "exchange," or even "agency." In their place he borrows terminology from Maturana and Varela's theory of autopoiesis and insists on perturbation/compensation. In common parlance, to be perturbed is to be unsettled or anxious. Someone or something has provoked a heightened response, but the mechanism of the influence and its repercussions are not entirely clear. Perturbation contains the root word *turbid*, meaning opaque.

This essay, for instance, is a communicative product that does not express all of the mental activities (not to mention the bodily processes) that were going on as I wrote it. My thoughts may perturb the communicative system through the medium of language, and, in turn, these words may perturb some thoughts in you, but they will not be the same thoughts. Only communication communicates. Similarly, a music performance can perturb the biological and psychic systems of those within earshot, but the responses will not be the same, nor are they predictable in their entirety. Edgar Landgraf writes, "All of us who have fallen asleep at the opera, were bored in a museum, distracted during a concert, or simply annoyed by a particular performance will know, no work of art and no performance can determine if and how it will be perceived by the psychic system it finds in its environment" (2009, 195).

To define communication in terms of thoughts and ideas is as misleading as defining mental processes in terms of brain physiology. There may be correlations between the two, but correlation does not imply causation. Within the traditional semantics of communication, this operational closure might be viewed as a form of hermeneutic despair. Even the most intimate lovers, for example, cannot literally exchange their ideas or feelings. It is important to note, however, that the performative ontology of neocybernetics is in no way synonymous with the "linguistic turn" in the humanities and social sciences (associated with poststructuralism, among other things). The linguistic turn maintains (and in many ways strengthens) a fundamental dualism since it insists that while we have access to our own words, language, and representations, we have no access to things in themselves. It is an epistemological argument that essentially forbids discussions of ontology. Second-order cybernetics also "talked itself into a corner" in Pickering's view by intensifying its emphasis on epistemology (2010, 26).

Neocybernetics insists that only through operational closure are systems able to increase their own internal complexity, but operational closure is not seen as an endpoint; rather, it is the precondition for openness, which is to say for any cognitive capacity whatsoever. The neocybernetic emphasis on perturbation/compensation underpins its performative ontology, an ontology that resists the detour of knowledge through representation. For this reason, Landgraf finds Luhmann's social systems theory especially useful to understanding art in general and musical communication in particular. "The neocybernetic discourse," he writes, "allows us to understand the 'experience' created by a person's cognitive engagement with art without having to assume a representational or an interpretive stance toward the work of art or performance" (2011, 150).

We can think of an interpretive stance on improvisation as a "first-person" perspective and a representational stance as a "third-person" perspective. First-person accounts include reflections by improvisers on their practice or thoughts from listeners about a given performance. Third-person accounts involve descriptions of repeatable measurements of phenomena, such as a technical analysis of a recording, a transcription, or a musical score. Both the first- and third-person accounts, however, follow a detour through either verbal description or symbolic representation.[12]

A neocybernetic orientation does not need to supplant modern science, verbal description, or symbolic analysis. It is clear that first- and third-person accounts of music are useful and will continue to proliferate. It can, however, draw back the "veil" that, according to Pickering, the modern sciences have cast over the performative aspects of the world, including our own being (2010, 21). Insisting on the operational closure of cognizing systems as they reduce the chaotically complex to the manageably complex also somewhat paradoxically prevents agency from being "overrun," following Clarke and

Hansen, "by the technoscientific processes that are everywhere transforming the material world in which we live" (2009, 2). For me, the provisional closure of improvised music performance—it begins, it ends, it starts anew—can celebrate our fundamental and shared humanity even as it tracks the alterations imposed on it by our ever-accelerating environmental complexity.

Final Thoughts

It has become increasingly difficult to maintain the conventional binary between humans and their technological environment: between what we make and who we (think we) are. Working as KaiBorg, I find that the process involves strange loops in which envisioning, designing, testing, discussing, refining, exploiting, and at times abandoning approaches, and playing in/with spaces and with/for other people, is inextricably linked to (albeit not in linear or predictable ways) the types of sounds, behaviors, interactions, expectations, insights, and sometimes disappointments that I experience as an improvising musician. As I continue to refine an "interface" with the digital world and the electronic soundscape—through, I might add, constant collaboration with other flesh-and-blood humans—my view of myself has become less unitary, more protean. I find myself straddling the presumed divide between human intention and the material and systemic forms of agency that perturb my psyche and body and percolate through the music. Perhaps it is possible, as both Landgraf and De Spain allude, to experience agency as both the source of improvisation and its effect.

To be clear, I am not interested in arguing for a facile posthumanism that reproduces and vilifies a unified human subject as its other. It is still material brains, material bodies, and the complex cultural and technological environments whose looping interactions generate human thought and reason that matter. By describing society on the basis of its events rather than its members, however, we can circumvent the vexing question of where exactly resides "the human": in its biological, psychic, or social identity?

In what is perhaps his most radical move, Luhmann insists that we must "de-anthropologize" the description of society. He calls this the fourth insult to human vanity. The first insult, the cosmological insult, came from Copernicus, who argued that the Earth is not the center of the universe. The second biological insult, associated with Darwinian evolution, demoted humans from the crown of creation. Freud's psychological insult was to our human ego, highlighting how it is often trumped by unconscious drives and forces. Last, Luhmann's sociological insult argues that human society cannot steer itself. "Just as we cannot control the universe, our bodies, or our minds," writes Hans-Georg

Moeller in *The Radical Luhmann*, "we are also unable to shape the social world we inhabit according to our ideals, wishes, or intentions" (2012, 28).

Overcoming the anthropocentric tradition of European and North American social philosophy is no small order, of course. As long as we maintain an anthropocentric view, we are doomed to vacillate between the poles of humanist pessimism, the machine as dehumanizing, and humanist optimism, the machine as expanding what it means to be human, extending our biological, intellectual, and communicative capacities. In both cases, putting the ill-defined notion of "the human" center stage prohibits more nuanced theorizing about systems of communication and ultimately keeps us mired in a dialectics of matter and form, substance and pattern, in which the immaterial wrests agency away from the embodied (Clarke and Hansen 2009).

Improvisers are interested in placing themselves in situations and among fellows and objects that can always surprise them. Even as they gain experiences and forge relationships with their human and nonhuman coparticipants, any given performance remains a dance of interagency about which not all can be known or anticipated. We are effectively black boxes engaged with black boxes in an exceedingly complex dynamic of perturbation/compensation.[13] By substituting the neocybernetic notion of perturbation/compensation for communicative exchange, "we can comprehend the psychic and the nervous system as observing and relating to their environment," Landgraf writes, "long before comprehension mediated through language and abstraction is initiated and yet, without having to ignore the laws of iterability or the idea that 'experience' is necessary for the appreciation of art" (2011, 150).

The act of improvising together produces a temporal and sensual immediacy, allowing complexity to emerge from a simple and contingent beginning. Improvisations create a movement whose direction we want to see continued, but critically this movement occurs through the increased narrowing of possible choices. One's playing draws a distinction that is condensed, confirmed, canceled, or compensated by subsequent distinctions (made by either oneself or others). These sounds and situations also perturb the psyches of listeners (those in the audience and those performing) into compensating and (potentially) reorganizing the orientation they brought to the performance. In this sense, the music and the performance itself stages particular constraints that encourage the emergence of something new or inventive.

At its core, neocybernetics asks us to rethink our fundamental theories of knowledge. Knowledge is not passively received but actively built up so that "we" can adapt *with* the experiential world. Social systems theory also insists that to understand how society functions and operates we cannot reduce it to the broad and ill-defined notion of the human being. Doing so may offer a way to understand how complex social systems, including music and art, can function without a legitimating consensus of citizens, without the idea of a common morality or a shared democratic ethos.

Where does this leave us with regard to traditional humanist ideas about morals and ethics? For an ethics of improvisation compatible with neocybernetics, we might be well served by the writings of Emmanuel Levinas.[14] According to Levinas (1969), we do not choose to be responsible. Responsibility arises as if elicited, before we begin to think about it, by the approach of the other. Language and communication are not the site in which existence arises, nor do they begin by reaching out to the other: rather, they begin in a responding-to-the-other. Levinas was interested in intersubjectivity as lived immediacy, as a precognitive sensibility, a responsibility in responsiveness. The very meaning of being a social subject is to be for-the-other. For Levinas there is no authentic sociality apart from ethics, and there is no ethics apart from sociality. His writings often stepped out of philosophical reasoning into a more performative register.

As an improviser, a performative ontology or an ontology of unknowability clearly appeals to me. I am also fond of arguments that resist modernist views that value representation, musical or otherwise, above and beyond the performative. Cybernetics is not much discussed these days, and the temptation is to assume that it died of some fatal flaw, but it is in fact alive and well, living under a lot of other names. Revitalizing its lineage may provide models for future practice, as Pickering suggests. Even if we are unable to shape the social world we inhabit according to humanist ideals, as Luhmann insists, how we act in the world and how we imagine it inform one another.

Notes

1. See, for example, Nachmanovitch (1990).

2. See, for example, Heble (2000).

3. "Pa-ttern" (masculine) over "ma-tter" (feminine) may even reinforce a conventional gendered dualism.

4. One of the more fascinating aspects of Pickering's account is the relationships he uncovers between books by cyberneticians and the writings and activities of Aldous Huxley, Timothy Leary, William S. Burroughs, the Beats, and others from the psychedelic 1960s, as well as links to Eastern philosophy. To a certain extent the antidisciplinary orientation of cybernetics—running roughshod as it did over traditional academic departments and divisions—explains its continuing marginalization in established institutions. Pickering calls cybernetics a "nomad science" in the Deleuzian sense of the phrase that would contrast it with "royal science," which functions to maintain a stable social and political order.

5. Pickering (2010) unpacks several lines of critique of cybernetics—that its approach to modeling cognition demeans key aspects of our humanity; that it intensified control of

workers by management; that it is primarily a science in bed with the military; or more generally that it involves a political valence of control—but he insists that the military and industrial applications do not come close to exhausting the range of cybernetics, nor should a "guilt by association" critique lead us to condemn cybernetics out of hand.

6. See, for example, Pressing (1988).

7. See, for example, Nettl (1974).

8. See, for example, Monson (2009).

9. See, for example, Sudnow (1978) and Iyer (2002).

10. See Stewart (chapter 9) for a detailed account of *Very Nervous System*.

11. See, for example, Eric Clarke (2005). Cybernetics is arguably more "ecological" than work in the field that maintains distinctions between natural, human, and social systems.

12. Music notation is literally a symbolic notation, but recording also involves a transduction of acoustic signals into electrical signals, and now often a conversion of these into a digital code.

13. My current electro-acoustic set-up, for instance, involves a foot controller with ten pads that each send controller data based on foot pressure and position to a different signal processing subroutine or "patch." I have a certain amount of practiced control with each pad individually, but in performance I can also choose to cover three or four different pads with each foot and "roll" them in various directions with varying amounts of pressure, producing rather complex and inherently unpredictable results, all of which perturbs my simultaneous saxophone playing.

14. Heinz von Foerster's (1984) often-quoted ethical imperative for cybernetics is to "act always so as to increase the number of choices."

7. Mediating the Improvising Body

ART TATUM'S POSTMORTEM PERFORMANCE
IN A POSTHUMAN WORLD

Andrew Raffo Dewar

A piano sits on an otherwise empty stage, lit dramatically from above, as the audience waits in quiet anticipation. The setting is Los Angeles's historic Shrine Auditorium on September 23, 2007. The occasion is a performance by virtuosic jazz piano legend Art Tatum. The conundrum, of course, is that Tatum died of kidney failure in 1956. The piano, a Yamaha Disklavier Pro, begins to play "Tatum Pole Boogie," and the spectral sounds of Tatum's improvisations resound in the Shrine, fifty-eight years after their original performance on April 2, 1949. Zenph Sound Innovations, a technology start-up based in Durham, North Carolina, produced this phantasmic 2007 event using its groundbreaking and controversial "re-performance" technology actively developed between 2005 and 2012.[1] Zenph extracts and separates the performance from the recording medium to reanimate it, using a robotic piano—the Disklavier Pro—so a listener hears the actual source of the sound (in this case a piano, but other instruments were in development), and not a reproduction of the source, as in a traditional recording.[2] As Zenph's promotional materials state, this technology generates a "live realization of the original interpretation."[3] The performance information extracted by Zenph's proprietary hardware and software is exponentially more complex than the standard MIDI (Musical Instrument Digital Interface) information commonly used in the music industry. Zenph uses a high-resolution MIDI format that captures a wider range of dynamics, attacks, releases, and pedal information to "re-perform," according to Zenph founder John Q. Walker, "exactly" what Tatum played.[4] Zenph has not only produced concerts such as the one described here, but has also released recordings of their re-performances of previously recorded music. As the company described on its website, "Our process frees artists from 'frozen audio recordings,' precisely replicating what they originally recorded and turning the audio back into a live performance."[5] This technology, then, complicates and arguably elides traditional distinctions between an original performance and its copy, challenging conventional notions of performance and embodiment, since the re-performance features a piano with expressively moving keys and pedals that produce a physically generated sound without the corporeal presence of a musician.

In this chapter I argue that Zenph's technologies allow us to reconsider the notion of loss implied by the reproduction of a live performance, and to conceptualize the ways many performances are in a sense re-performances, whether performed by their creator for the first time, improvised or notated, recorded, or reproduced through data analysis with the technology Zenph and others employ. I suggest that contemporary listeners' comfort with the disembodied sounds of twenty-first-century music listening practices render the conventionally understood binary of "original" and "copy"—with the fetishized performing body given primacy—as an outmoded approach to the ontology of human creativity. I contrast Zenph's spectral re-performance of Tatum with classically trained pianist Steven Mayer's embodied re-performances of Tatum to examine the complex roles of corporeality in performance. As outlined here, even so-called original performances by artists such as Art Tatum are still complex composites of a multitude of borrowings and self-consciously stylized reproductions of the self. In place of the "original" and "copy," I instead propose the idea of a "spectrum" of ontology that allows for a diverse range of representations of a given flesh-and-blood artist's creative "essence," some of which may be embodied, others virtual or facsimiles, but all of which are more than simply "copies" of an unadulterated "original." The ontological issues I engage with confound dismissal of a "copy" based simply on the presence or absence of Tatum's body. I suggest that there is an ontological spectrum to consider, with layers and degrees of Tatum's presence in Mayer's and Zenph's approaches to his music, and, moreover, that Tatum's presence and performance of himself was complex, even when he was in bodily attendance of his music-making.

Original and Copy

The attempt to capture the "original" has a long history in audio recording. A number of scholars have written at length about the history of the listening public's acceptance of audio recordings as plausible surrogates of a live musical performance.[6] Emily Thompson's work on the Edison "tone tests"— performances during which a live singer was juxtaposed with an Edison gramophone "performing" the same work—"to convince the audience that it was actually impossible to distinguish the singer's living voice from its re-creation in the instrument" is one illustrative moment in this history that, as she writes, "helped to transform musical culture in America" (1995, 132).

While trying to minimize the difference between an original performance and the recorded copy to market its product, the music industry's marketing nonetheless relies on the assumption that there *is* an original to be copied, but that the copy is so good one cannot tell the difference. This strategy is epitomized in a 1913 Victor Records advertisement for their Enrico Caruso catalog. In the ad, Victor announces that both the opera singer's recording and Caruso himself *are* Caruso, and that you "hear him just as truly as if you were listening to him in the Metropolitan Opera House."

In addition to the early Caruso print advertisements, there are several contemporary examples of our cultural preoccupation with the original as referent and its often enmeshed relationship with emerging technologies and capitalist interests. One example from the mid-1970s features legendary jazz singer Ella Fitzgerald in a Memorex advertisement for a new cassette tape formulation that, according to the commercial, allows a listener to ask "now more than ever . . . is it live, or is it Memorex?" Fitzgerald appears with trumpeter Chuck Mangione in a second Memorex commercial from the same period in which she is asked to listen for the difference between a live and recorded performance of Mangione and band, to which she responds, "beats me!" Two television advertisements from 2010 featured contemporary analogues of Fitzgerald, pop singers Beyoncé Knowles and Ciara Harris. In both cases the artists are used as control references to illustrate the vibrancy of audiovisual reproduction with new technologies—a Vizio television in the case of Knowles, and an LG mobile phone in the case of Harris. These examples emphasize the depth at which this trope of the original and the copy is ingrained in our cultural consciousness.

Zenph's technology takes the fetishization of the original to a new level. The technology creates the illusion that the original artist is performing the original piece by manifesting a physical surrogate. Is it, then, performance or re-performance? When presented with the uncanny sound and ghostly keyboard mechanics of Tatum, coupled with the conspicuous absence of his physical being, what are we, as listeners, experiencing? While exciting for some, the idea of experiencing a re-performance of a dead musician's work—such that the illusion is created that the musician is alive and in the room even though he or she cannot be seen—may be repellent, a position encapsulated in one prominent jazz scholar's off-the-record dismissal of re-performance as "making dead people do what you want." Indeed, it is interesting to consider why some listeners who have embraced audio recordings, the most commonly encountered re-performance, as acceptable proxies for an original performance, have not (yet) accepted this emerging form of performance as credible. Reviews in the popular press of Zenph's Art Tatum CD have been overwhelmingly (and in a number of cases ardently) positive, with *Stereophile* reviewer John Swenson (2008, 9) remarking, "this is a crucially important release in music history." The discrepancy, then, between the way some audiences might reject the Zenph-produced on-stage re-performances as ghoulish, and yet embrace audio recordings produced with the same technology suggests that it is the disembodied public performance that is at issue. The moving keys and pedals, which I witnessed at Zenph's headquarters, give a fascinating and unnerving illusion of musical corporeality. Mark Katz has identified the "invisibility" of the performing body and source of musical sounds as one of the hallmarks of recording technology, which was "once a source of great anxiety" (2004, 19). In fact, Katz reports, an English music critic in 1923 explained that some listeners could not "bear to hear a remarkably life-like human voice issuing from a box. They desire the physical presence" (2004, 19). Although many listeners have now grown comfortable with the disembodiment of recorded audio, the same kinds of anxieties Katz identifies as being prevalent in the early days of recorded music come to the fore again with Zenph's staged re-performances of artists like Tatum and Gershwin. With Zenph's technology, we have the enigma of a disembodied reproduction of a piece that sounds as though Tatum himself were playing it, and one even has the remarkable sense of his ghostly presence through the nuanced movements of the piano's keys. The question raised here is whether there are degrees of separation between originals and copies. Does having the keys of a grand piano moving precisely the way they would have if Tatum himself were playing them produce a copy that is closer to the original than an audio recording would be? How important is the presence of the musician's body to our assessment of the veracity of a performance?

Steven Mayer's Re-performance of Tatum

In answering that question, it is useful to compare the Zenph re-performance of Tatum's work to the work of Steven Mayer, a classically trained concert pianist who has been performing Tatum's music for more than two decades. Working primarily from detailed transcriptions of Tatum's improvisations made by Felicity Howlett, J. Lawrence Cook, and Jed Distler, Mayer memorized them for performance. His virtuosity is evident, and his dedication to performing Tatum's work is without question. What is interesting, however, is a comparison of his performances with Zenph's. Mayer plays memorized versions of Tatum's recordings, producing an excellent facsimile. Furthermore, at his concerts there is a living, breathing musician actually playing the piano. Presumably, audiences at his concerts would not feel the ghostly presence of Tatum in the same way as they would in the Zenph performances, as they are well conditioned to hearing living musicians play the work of those now gone. On the other hand, audiences are not hearing Tatum's work as it was actually played by Tatum, whereas with the Zenph re-performance they experience something quantitatively much closer to Tatum's original performance mechanics, with a precise replication of details from Tatum's originally recorded performance, such as the attack of each key and the choreography of his piano pedaling. Which performance, then, is closer to the original?

Some critics argue that the need for audiences and musicians to be physically present at the same time is paramount. Richard Leppert, in *The Sight of Sound*, has written that "precisely because musical sound is abstract, intangible, and ethereal—lost as soon as it is gained—the visual experience of its production is crucial . . . for locating and communicating the place of music and musical sound within society and culture" (1993, xx–xxi). Composer Igor Stravinsky has also weighed in on the importance of the performing body to musical meaning, stating, "the sight of the gestures and movements of the various parts of the body producing the music is fundamentally necessary if it is to be grasped in all its fullness" (1936, 122). Neither Leppert's nor Stravinsky's remarks, however, take into account the discarnate sounds of the twenty-first century, where the majority of the Western world's musical performances now emanate from headphones embedded in the private concert halls of listeners' ear canals. Certainly embodied performance can still be of great importance, conveying more information and providing a broader context than a recording, but a convincing case can be made that music technologies and evolving listening practices have rendered the modern music listener, in practice, all but ambivalent to the reality of disembodiment in contemporary musicking—at least in theory.[7] That said, a contemporary listener's comfort level with recorded music does not necessarily translate into an audience at ease with the singularly complex entanglements of a staged Zenph re-performance, as my own difficulty with quantifying a response to witnessing one attests. Perhaps it is a deeply rooted socialized expectation that a live performance will include a performing human—a variation on the unease of the "uncanny valley" that roboticists strive to overcome when developing technologies that mimic the human form.[8] It is therefore still fruitful to examine Mayer's performances in light of arguments by Leppert and Stravinsky.

If, for example, we consider Leppert's assertion that audiences need to see the musicians performing to assist them "in locating and communicating the place of music and musical sound within society and culture," what does that suggest about Mayer's performances of Tatum? Thinking of Mayer as a surrogate for Tatum foregrounds the complexities of the politics of identity in public re-performances and profoundly delimits the performing body in sociocultural and historical contexts. For example, while Mayer's performances have been widely well received, some critics have taken issue with the notion of a Euro-American classical pianist playing memorized improvisations of an African American musician. Reviewing a 1990 performance by Mayer of Tatum's work at Alice Tully Hall in New York City, John Rockwell (1990) wrote: "The prospect of a white classical pianist mimicking the improvisations of a black jazz icon, however well-meaning his intentions, fills some jazz aficionados with dread and disdain." Rockwell's comments point to additional complexities in theorizing the notion of the original. When the body of a Western-trained white musician playing to primarily white audiences performs work originally produced by an African American musician in very different venues, suddenly the notion of the body becomes central to the dialogue, and the music, however much it may sound like the original, cannot easily be divorced from the contemporary social/historical context in which it is being performed.[9] Mayer himself speaks openly of the racial complexities of the "specter of a white pianist playing Tatum" (Steven Mayer, telephone interview with Andrew Raffo Dewar, March 2, 2011), but the specter is even more multifarious than Mayer intends, as Tatum actually "had aspirations to perform on the traditional classical music circuit, though he probably would have been denied access to it, as were so many early black musicians" (Watrous 1990). Ghoulish and politically complex as it may be, Tatum finally tours as a classical concert pianist, entangled in Mayer's corporeal performance of his work—a complex and problematic case of coming full circle, and a resolution more bitter than sweet.

In a phone interview with Mayer, he admitted that re-performing Tatum has been good for his career, and he does not feel the recordings of these performances really needed to be produced, since we have the original recordings by Tatum himself, but he acknowledges that there were career considerations to be made. This situation is, of course, precarious, given the context and history, both perceived and real, of musical appropriation between various ethnic groups in the United States. In Mayer's case, he is very forthright about these complexities, stating that the "two recordings that I made [of Tatum's work] was because they were so helpful to my own career . . . and in a way I can say that's a sin against Art Tatum." Humbled by the limitations of his re-performances, he hopes his love for and hard work re-creating Tatum's solos outweigh negative perceptions, because, he says, "I think I do enough that it has some validity" (Mayer).

Based on some of the critical response to Mayer's performances of Tatum, in particular Rockwell's review, it would seem that the presence of a musician's body playing Tatum's music does not produce an experience that is perceived as any closer to the original. Indeed, race and class differences between the original performer and the re-performer highlight the extent to which all performance is partisan, and thoroughly grounded in a network of physical, social, historical, and political contexts. Arguably, then, however well intentioned, a white classically trained musician playing memorized performances of an African American musician, in very different venues and to disparate audiences, is far removed from the original performance and would suggest that we cannot divorce the music from the originary context in which it was played. Would Rockwell have raised the same issues if Mayer was African American and the concert had taken place at the Apollo Theater and not at Lincoln Center?[10]

Mayer makes an interesting observation that highlights yet another question about the relationship between original and copy. In reproducing Tatum's work, Mayer says "it's not physically possible . . . to do it exactly right," also asserting that "there's a lot in Tatum where he doesn't do it 100 percent either." When asked to expand upon the idea of Tatum himself "not doing 100 percent" of Tatum, Mayer explained that "there are little imperfections in things he's doing . . . things which can be construed as wrong notes, and 'getting out of wrong notes'—meaning [Tatum would] do something he wasn't exactly sure was what he wanted, and then will change a little bit to get out of it and get back into where he was."

Although one might consider Mayer's statement emblematic of a fundamental misunderstanding by a classically trained pianist approaching the work of a jazz artist like Tatum, where perceived imperfections and wrong notes are part and parcel of the performance process, Mayer in fact comes very close to describing what ethnomusicologist Paul Berliner has called the "musical save" in jazz performance, or musical solutions to "spontaneous compositional problems" (1994, 210). In conversation with Berliner on this issue, trumpeter Tommy Turrentine noted that sometimes he will "go for one note and hit another . . . and say to myself . . . how am I going to get out of this one?" (211). This fascinating issue of wrong notes in relation to the concern of preservation of an original performance also reared its head during Zenph's work on Glenn Gould's iconic 1955 recording of Bach's *Goldberg Variations*. It was made clear at one point in Zenph's coding process that Gould's finger had come down slightly askew to punctuate an articulation, hitting two keys instead of one, creating a dyad not present in Bach's score. Zenph, in its attempt to be true to the original, decided to leave the extra note in the performance. Of course the primary difference between Gould's mistake and Tatum's is that in the former we have Bach's score as referent, whereas with Tatum we have only a listener's perception of what he might have intended in a particular improvisation. In both cases, however, the performative body intrudes on an "ideal" performance—a quintessential goal of repetition-obsessed recording culture.

Despite Mayer's function as a corporeal embodiment of Tatum's music, there is still an obvious ontological issue here, in that Tatum's work incorporated improvisation, with most performances never having been conceived as fixed entities, as they are currently performed by Mayer and Zenph. So in asking the question "Where is the body?" in these re-performances there is a dual issue, both corporeal and aesthetic. Where do we as listeners locate what we might think of as Tatum's ontological essence? Is it in the recorded, static performances he left us, or was it really only accessible through listening to his virtuosic praxis as a living improviser, responding to musical (and extramusical) stimuli at the moment of creation?

Tatum Re-performs Tatum?

The above question is complicated by the fact that we know Tatum himself re-performed others' improvisations. Felicity Howlett (1983), who has transcribed and analyzed hundreds of Tatum improvisations, describes how Tatum was known to memorize and perform piano rolls by Fats Waller and James P. Johnson, a practice in a number of fascinating ways similar to Mayer's re-performance of Tatum. Tatum's mastery of re-performing piano rolls was such that his childhood friend Francis Williams reported "he simply could not tell, from the next room, whether it was Art or a piano roll he was listening to" (quoted in Lester 1994, 44).

Howlett also asserts that in some of his interpretations Tatum's improvisations became quite fixed, including his performances of "Tiger Rag,"[11] an iconic piece in Tatum's oeuvre. Howlett states that "the difference between the 1933 recording and later recordings are those of velocity and virtuosity, rather than any significant changes in material or texture," and that "by 1933, Tatum's structural arrangement of materials [in 'Tiger Rag'] was as set as if he had been performing a written composition" (1983, 90).[12]

These historical pieces of information add a new layer of complexity to this consideration of original and copy and of the artist's role in their production. If, as suggested, the essence of the artist is present only in a real-time improvised live performance, then where is Tatum's essence in his recordings, his own re-performances/fixing of previously improvised music, and his re-performance of music learned from piano rolls?

The issues raised by these questions set into relief the possibility that the conception of original and copy, conventionally understood as a binary relationship, is perhaps more akin to a spectrum of ontological multiplicity that human creativity can fluidly inhabit, occasionally at more than one point simultaneously. This concept of a spectrum of ontology is relevant to my argument because through Tatum's re-performance of Tatum we can see that even his original performances lie somewhere on this spectrum between the original and the copy. They are a composite of, among many other things (including his peerless invention), the memorization and re-performance of piano rolls by Waller and Johnson and the fixing of his own originally improvised interpretations of tunes. As we examine Tatum re-performing Tatum (and Waller, and Johnson), we learn that his creative essence is more complex than a facile application of the term *original* would suggest.

Humanness in Creativity

If one concludes that musical essence is present only in the live real-time performance of music, then one must deduce that Zenph's technology eradicates the essence of the musician, and simply provides an impressive but ultimately nonhuman or robotic copy of the sound produced at the time of the original performance, and not the synergistic theurgy that can only happen as the music is being created in real time in front of a live audience. One would further have to conclude that this creative essence is absent from even Tatum's own recordings. However, if we accept the idea of a spectrum of ontology or essence, we can refigure the notion of a clear distinction between human creativity and technologically produced musical performances in a way that also dismisses the argument that re-performed music, whether by a human being or facilitated through technology, is somehow deficient compared to an originating performance. Instead, both forms of performing Tatum are simply cohabiting at different points on a spectrum that encompasses the totality of what we might call Tatum's ontological essence as an improvising musician, with one end of this spectrum being a flesh-and-blood Tatum performing live for an audience and the other being the quantifiable sonic aspects of a Tatum performance perfectly replicated by a Zenph-powered Disklavier Pro, and Mayer's embodied re-performance located somewhere in between.[13] All these performances of Art Tatum's music are indisputably representations of Tatum's musicality, and they are also indivisibly dependent on one another for their existence, in a discomforting dance of ontological symbiosis. This is a situation that Jonathan Sterne has succinctly described: "without the technology of reproduction copies do not exist, but then, neither would the originals" (2003, 219).[14]

David Cope, a composer and prolific creator of artificial musical intelligences, complicates the notion that there is something unique about human creativity and originality, rooting the activity in positivist biomechanical activities. For the past several decades, Cope has been building artificial intelligence engines with the capability to model musical creativity.[15] Though Cope and Zenph approach the computer modeling of musical creativity in differing ways, they both, broadly speaking, share as a conceptual departure point the idea that human creativity can ultimately be reduced to a complex quantitative interaction of biology, physical mechanics, and neural networks, rather than intangibles such as spirituality, inspiration, intuition, or even Walter Benjamin's beloved aura.[16] That said, Zenph's John Q. Walker acknowledges that these biological systems exist not in a binary world of ones and zeros or absolutes but "in the varied tonalities of greyscale" (Walker, telephone interview with Andrew Raffo Dewar, August 25, 2010). Both Cope and Zenph use the artificial intelligence community's concept of the uncanny valley and the Turing Test (the point at which indistinguishable humanness is achieved) to support their view of creativity. Cope, for example, "wonders if . . . those who agree with [romanticized definitions of creativity] could recognize these ingredients . . . in a test of human versus computer output?" (2005, 8).

Composer, musician, and scholar George Lewis has also written extensively about the computer modeling of musical creativity, chiefly drawing on his decades-long work with *Voyager*, a custom software program he designed that functions as an improvising partner to his own trombone, in what he characterizes as a "nonhierarchical . . . subject-subject model of discourse" (2000, 34). In this nonhierarchical mode, Lewis has attempted to provide *Voyager* with its "own sound . . . in tandem with a kind of technology-mediated animism" (37). According to Lewis, "*Voyager* is not asking whether machines exhibit personality or identity, but how personalities and identities become articulated through sonic behavior. . . . Rather than asking if computers can be creative and intelligent . . . *Voyager* asks us where our own creativity and intelligence might lie" (38).

In outlining aspects of the relevant discourse on what constitutes an original performance, I have invoked Cope's and Lewis's challenging viewpoints to illustrate the complexity of valorizing original performance and bodily authenticity and to refocus the discussion on issues of "where our own creativity and intelligence might lie" instead of on "whether machines exhibit personality or identity" (Lewis 2000, 38). For example, we might argue that the neurological impulses that form before the triggered gestures that cause sounds are the ultimate original performance. From this perspective we could argue that musical performances are already translated and mediated. Furthermore, whatever we might decide on as the original performance—be it brain activity, the body, the sounds captured by microphones or on paper—the sounding result is ultimately an infinite number of performances filtered through each listener's mind to give it meaning, with each interpretation as unique and valid as the next, transforming the sounded original into its own mediated reproduction via interpretation.

Futurities

Zenph planned a future that would continue to vex traditional notions of creativity in relation to originals and copies. They even imagined creating the technology to re-perform orchestras of instruments.[17] Their plans were curtailed, but in 2015 Zenph's technology was incorporated into Steinway and Sons' Spirio player piano system. Zenph also planned to make performance data available, in addition to recordings, that could be manipulated by the end user to generate real-time improvising performances of their own design, constructed from self-emergent artificial intelligence—evolving cellular automata modeled on the data extracted from iconic performers, with hopes to take into account transformations in various periods of an artist's work. In August 2011, Zenph released their first attempt at this new software platform, dubbed RePerform, which allows end users to manipulate performance data, whether generated by Zenph or by the users themselves. One interesting implication with RePerform is that it displaces (or even transmigrates) the creative body from one physical home to another, much in the same way DJs and producers shape, re-perform, and recompose samples using existing media, making new work entangled with both their own bodies and the bodies of others, in a manifestation of what Stanyek and Piekut in their discussion of "deadness" have designated a "co-laboring" of "distributed personhood" (2010, 14).

In addition, Zenph began to work with video material, synchronizing re-performances of pianist Oscar Peterson with film footage to create an audiovisual re-performance. With advances in holographic video technology and computer-generated video manipulation, it is not difficult to project where this technology is headed—one day, you may walk into a club to hear an artificial intelligence–powered, three-dimensional hologram of John Coltrane performing "Giant Steps" with a live band accompanying him, the now quasi-corporeal "Trane" generating endless new variations on the piece.[18] This kind of development, of course, would take things in a direction decidedly similar to Cope's work, applying generative tools to model compositional style and creative problem solving, but for real-time improvisatory interactions. In this only slightly hyperbolic example, most of the elements of an embodied performance exist—a human form that gestures and mimics the physicality of instrumental performance and real-time decision making. What will audiences make of this surrogate? One need only watch the screaming crowds in video footage from deceased rapper Tupac Shakur's triumphant comeback at the April 2012 Coachella festival, which featured a new performance by a holographic Shakur, who died in 1996.[19]

In fact, even before Shakur's somatic return, there was already a working prototype of this kind of real-time generative virtual performance in Japan's virtual pop star Hatsune Miku (literally translated as "first sound of the future"), who has played sold-out concert tours in Japan. In addition to Miku being projected onto the stage as an eight-foot-tall three-dimensional hologram, her voice is entirely synthesized in real time, not built from samples of a human voice. As a result, in a concert performance, for example, if the band (made up of humans) changes tempo, Miku will compensate to keep the song's structure together. In addition, because Miku's voice is not sampled, but completely synthesized, and her body is entirely digitally generated, the original voice and body is Miku herself, sui generis. All of these emerging technologies likely lead us as a society toward not only redefining what constitutes humanness in musical creativity but also questioning whether that concept is even relevant any more, as long as audiences are satisfied with their listening experience.

In her interrogation of the "posthuman" condition, Katherine Hayles incorporates Baudrillard's concept of "hyperreality." Hayles describes this process of social implosion "as a collapse of the distance between signifier and signified, or between the 'original' object and its simulacra," contending that "the terminus for this train of thought is a simulation that does not merely compete with, but actually displaces the original" (1999, 250). With the manifestation of Hatsune Miku on the world's stages, we have a simulation for which there is no original. Of course, in the case of Tatum all we have are varying degrees of simulation that exist in relation to the original. Returning to the question of the uncanny valley, the sheer amount of disembodied musicking in contemporary life, and in light of Zenph's speculative future in artificial improvising musical intelligences, how many listeners would hear the difference if placed, blindfolded, in a room with Tatum himself?

As twenty-first-century listeners increasingly accept the uncanny valley of acceptable musical humanness through the digital creation, distribution, and performance of reanimated and newly invented artificially intelligent music-makers in human form, we also cross the horizon of plausibility in critically discussing outmoded binary ideas of the original and copy as conceptualized by Benjamin and others in the twentieth century, and should instead consider the possibility of the ontological corpus of human creativity as a variegated spectrum that encompasses multiple cohabiting ontologies. The days by which the assumption of the primacy of the human body as indispensable origin and wellspring of musical creativity may very well be numbered—in the binary code of zeros and ones.

Notes

1. Zenph Sound Innovations ceased development on most of these technologies when the company declared bankruptcy in the summer of 2012. The company's intellectual property was purchased by a relaunched Zenph that is leveraging "the extensive intellectual property, including patents, music learning software and digital signal processing algorithms, acquired from Zenph Sound Innovations, Inc." to launch ZOEN (Zenph Online Education Network), an interactive, online music education tool. "Zenph Does Retake, Launches ZOEN," Reuters.com, http://www.reuters.com/article/2012/08/15/idUS126819 +15-Aug-2012+BW20120815 (accessed October 7, 2014).

2. Of course every piano is different, so despite Zenph's attempt to reproduce the source in their re-performances, they cannot reproduce the actual source instrument. However, because they successfully commissioned the invention of technology for converting any grand piano into a Disklavier, if they have access to the original instrument it could be used for a re-performance.

3. This tagline is attributed to Canadian music writer Kevin Bazzana and is used in Zenph's promotional materials. "Zenph Technology," http://www.zenph.com/company /technology (accessed November 4, 2012).

4. For example, where typical MIDI has 128 degrees of "NoteOn" and "NoteOff" information, the high-resolution format Zenph employs has 1,024 degrees.

5. "Zenph: The Music," Zenph.com, http://www.zenph.com/the-music (accessed May 26, 2013).

6. For more on this see Sterne (2003) and M. Katz (2004).

7. Of course, the ubiquitous consumption of disembodied recorded music does not erase the multiple significations of any recorded sound, which can trigger for an imaginative listener any number of identity markers, such as the race or socioeconomic background of a performer.

8. The "uncanny valley" concept references Jentsch (1906) and Freud's (1925) essays about "the uncanny," but the term was coined by roboticist Masahiro Mori in "Bukimi no Tani Genshō" (1970; see Mori 2012) to describe the "sense of eeriness . . . that protects [humans] from proximal sources of danger," such as "corpses and members of different species." According to Mori, crossing the uncanny valley in robotics design is the point at which an artificial life form can "pass" as human in a society.

9. Rockwell's final statement alludes to one way Tatum had already been "semi-legitimized" through apocryphal anecdotes of classical pianists hearing Tatum's virtuosity and being deeply moved. Most famous among those is Vladimir Horowitz, who was known to

have "entertained friends with an arrangement of 'Tea for Two' employing showy double thirds," which may be evidence of Tatum's inspiration to the pianist (Giddins 1998, 440).

10. Interestingly, Zenph engaged with some of these issues by staging a live theatrical production of their re-performance of Tatum's *Piano Starts Here* album at the Apollo Theater in Harlem on July 2, 2009. In Zenph's show, African American actor Trevor Johnson performed as fictional jazz club owner Doc Henley, who reminisces about Tatum in between Zenph re-performances of Tatum.

11. The study and performance of solo transcriptions, from recordings or otherwise, has been a fundamental practice for musicians studying jazz for decades, which actually highlights the importance of wrestling with this issue.

12. This seems to be a fairly common issue among improvising musicians, especially those who have become known for signature gestures, techniques, and so on. On one hand, there is the obvious fact that praxis reinforces an individual's prevailing musical characteristics and responses, but there is also the audience factor—giving assembled listeners the sounds they expect to hear.

13. Jonathan Sterne argues that the kind of fidelity Zenph pursues in their re-performances "is much more about faith in the social function and organization of machines than it is about the relation of a sound to its 'source'" (2003, 219). Nicholas Seaver expands on this idea, suggesting that "the faithfulness that 'fidelity' indexes is not between sources and copies but rather between us and our copying machines" (2011, 56).

14. Sterne reexamines Walter Benjamin's (1969) seminal essay on mechanical reproduction, illustrating that rather than simply disparaging reproductive technologies, a common reading of that piece, Benjamin also notes that in fact it was reproduction technologies themselves that introduced us to that distinct "aura" of the "original"—a situation we might summarize in the vernacular as "you don't know what you've got till it's gone."

15. One of Cope's earlier projects, for example, had computers composing new works in the style of old masters like Bach and Mozart by analyzing their compositional language and algorithmically generating new pieces based on each composer's aesthetic.

16. Benjamin describes his concept of the "aura" as "that which withers in the age of mechanical reproduction" (1969, 221). The "aura" includes a work's "authenticity" or "essence," which Benjamin characterizes as "all that is transmissible from its beginning, ranging from its substantive duration to its testimony to the history which it has experienced" (1969, 221).

17. As of 2011, Zenph was in the process of developing a virtual string bass by reverse-engineering the physical and gestural mechanics of jazz bassist Ray Brown's playing.

18. They have also partnered with Japanese pop star Seiko Matsuda, filming a music video that incorporates Matsuda's voice with a piano re-performance of Duke Ellington and Quincy Jones playing a bartender in the video's storyline.

19. The surprise appearance by Shakur, who performed a song with the living rapper Snoop Dogg, was orchestrated by hip-hop producer Dr. Dre and the San Diego company AV Concepts. AV Concepts are currently developing a holographic Elvis Presley they hope to tour in the near future.

PART III

Sensibility and Subjectivity

8. Banding Encounters

EMBODIED PRACTICES IN IMPROVISATION

Introduction and Conclusion by Tomie Hahn

Essays by Louise Campbell, Lindsay Vogt, Simon Rose,
George Blake, Catherine Lee, Sherrie Tucker,
François Mouillot, Jovana Milović, and Pete Williams

> I felt stable and secure just a moment ago, both feet firmly planted on the ground.
> Then something pulled my left elbow back and upwards, causing my torso
> to torque enough that both feet uprooted. Equilibrium shift. An out-of-control
> sensation quaked my settled state. A low voice growled so close to my ear I felt
> the warmth of breath, while from below someone whistled sweetly through their
> teeth. How quickly disorientation ensued—and my small world, altered.
> —Hahn, field notes, 2010

In this chapter, nine improvisers reflect on their encounters with one another while literally connected by large rubber pallet bands. "Banding" is an experimental exercise in movement and sound improvisation I developed since 2008. During the 2010 Improvisation, Community and Social Practice Summer Institute for Critical Studies in Improvisation in Guelph, Canada, more than a dozen improvisers explored new ways of connecting, communicating, improvising, discussing, and writing about their banding improvisations. To reflect the diversity of experiences and perspectives during banding, multiple voices needed to come together. Encouraged to give voice to oddly playful yet profound moments, participants stepped forward to contribute their words and visual responses. We offer banding as a case study in our collaborative essay, hoping readers will explore similar visceral, experimental improvisations of their own creation—involving play, intuition, physicality, and music-making—and then step back and contemplate the deeper issues that arise during improvisation.

The form of this chapter mirrors the collective that arose in late summer in Guelph—the writings appear in a variety of styles, lengths, and points of view, yet all stem from shared experience. I marvel at the diversity. The texts impart theoretical considerations, contemplative introspection, passionate reflection, colorful whimsy, social issues, and personal insights. Nearly everyone struggled with the challenge of putting words to the experience, yet I believe that through the effort a host of new creative outpourings emerged. Although the words/visuals in this chapter hardly reproduce the actual experience, we strove to emulate the essence of banding so that readers would be inspired to experiment in similar ways.

Through our banding explorations, we quickly learned how our bodies became sensorially heightened; our physical awareness of movement, touch, sound, spatial sense, as well as an awareness of our inner emotional states, had shifted. Banding requires more than one body. Communities and relationships flourish. In a slippage of words, banding transforms to bonding. The bands visually display the bodily connections to others in space, and the physical dependency on others becomes starkly clear. Adding vocal improvisations to the movement experience overlaid another quality to our already fully engaged movement improvisation so that tactile, kinesthetic, and visual experiences left aural traces we could hear intertwined in the space. A community emerged, now voicing identity.

Through working with this group I found myself asking: what theories arise from embodied practices? Problematizing the relationship between embodied practices and theory appears to be a current theoretical challenge—from research on consciousness and embodiment to phenomenological approaches. The body, so unstable, fickle, and malleable, simultaneously stands as an individual with agency and as a member of multiple communities, located in diverse contexts, and intricate relationships. The personal, social, and cultural complexities of the situated body make embodied practices even more difficult to comprehend. I see banding as an embodied improvisatory practice, a mini-laboratory for gaining insights into the dynamic complexities of improvisation.

Banding makes visible the "social potential of improvisation" (as this volume's editors, Waterman and Siddall, put it) for both outside observers and improvisers.[1] For those engaged in banding, the connections between performers provide direct tactile, sonic, kinesthetic feedback to orient themselves to one another. Physical orientation in space and time, with people and things, can be realized through disorienting experiences—what I have referred to as "orientation through disorientation" (Hahn 2006, 2007). On a physical level, the bands create a new experience that is curious, yet disarming. Precisely because the encounter with the bands in improvisation is foreign, a period of uncertainty ensues. The disorientation provides an opportunity for each person to observe exactly what the nature of his or her disorientation might be. Observing and identifying what is foreign about the experience orients the body. A contrasting example may help. Imagine I offer you a bowl of something that you have not tasted before—perhaps *kanten* (a seaweed gelatin, also known as agar). The flavoring is green tea. You try it. Although it reminds you of the Jell-O you had as a kid, something's different and you are taken aback. A subtle disorientation. "Gee, it looks like Jell-O," you think, "the texture is similar . . . hmm, but green tea?" and so on. After eating several bites to observe and identify the differences, you ask me what it is and I tell you. At this point you have compared the texture, taste, look, behavior, and other characteristics of this green jelly-like food and learned the word *kanten*. Clearly, we use our past experiences as a baseline to compare new encounters. After observing the nuances of a new sensation, we incorporate it into our expanding experiential vocabulary, and voilà—mystery solved—orientation!

In *Sensational Knowledge* I explored notions of orientation through disorientation for body-mind practices, "Orientation through disorientation occurs as a disruption of normalcy, followed by a clarity that signals a re-orientation and comprehension of one's sense of place, literal or otherwise" (2007, 154). Although I was writing about Japanese traditional dance, a style that is not improvised, I propose that orientation through disorientation provides a meaningful perspective of the social, embodied, emotional, and mindful process experienced during improvisation. I believe for all the banding improvisers, finding orientation through disorientation meant simultaneously a physical orientation in space and time and an orientation of subjectivities within the larger community. Consequently, the social potential in improvisation during banding is observable to onlookers and improvisers—as if what normally is hidden in the experiences, inside bodies, reveals itself. In other words, the variety of unseen (or unnoticed?) social connections during improvisation suddenly becomes exposed and obvious. Transparent. The bands demarcate and potentially blur boundaries as well. "Support" is visually displayed. Active and passive qualities of the physical and psychological kind surface.

Improvisers are already familiar with being sensitive to others during their (nonbanding) improvisations. With banding, performers find multiple sensory modes available to communicate/receive their creative connections with others. In a way, the experience of such elastic relationships offers a sensory enhancement for expressivity and communication. I found this particular group fascinating because of the disciplinary mix—some participants are dancers/movers and others musicians. Literally rubber banded together, everyone experienced a *dis*orientation at first because no one expected the dynamic, sensory enhancement or the clearly visible connections of their improvisations. Through the multisensory banding experience a new kind of expressivity emerged via orientation with others. Musicians found themselves experiencing the physical bonding that dancers commonly experience, while dancers found themselves exploring a sonic agency or "sonic mask" (Hahn and Bahn 2002) bonding with others. We stood back. Was this "performance"? Was it an improvisatory exploration without concerns about reception? In the end, we did not care. After presenting the nine short essays by the participants, I suggest ways banding illuminates theory as embodied practice. First, allow me to introduce the simple recipe for banding, followed by the essays. I return at the close with theoretical considerations.

BANDING RECIPE
Ingredients

- 10 or more large rubber pallet bands
- 10 or more improvisers
- An open space

The Mix

Place large pallet bands in the middle of the floor.

Round 1: "the sensitizing level." Working in pairs, place a band around an arm, elbow, or wrist and attach it to your partner's arm, elbow, wrist. Start by turning away from each other and exploring various levels of pull via the band. Start very slowly. Can you sense your partner's subtle movements? What are the qualities of movement that you can sense? Changes in body positions, such as an angling upward or to one side? Speed of movement? Can you also sense other qualities, such as fatigue, reluctance, enthusiasm? Does closing your eyes change the experience? Explore the slow dynamic of improvisation as you gain trust and awareness.

After a period of improvisation (ten to twenty minutes, depending on the group), sit and quietly write. If possible, everyone transitions from banding to writing without conversation. Freewrite about anything that comes to mind. Include drawings or other forms of creative expression reflections in your notebook.

Round 2: "safe play, eyes open!" Working in groups of three to five people, attach bands to any appendage: legs, arms, neck. Now facing in any direction,

FIG 8.1: Photo taken during a banding exercise at the Summer Institute for Critical Studies in Improvisation, 2010. Photo by Tomie Hahn.

eyes open, explore the dynamics of a group in flow—with no limitations of speed, direction, or where the bands are attached. What are the mechanics of pull when there are several people in a group connected by bands? What is the difference between round 1 and 2?

Round 3: "sound banding." Continuing Round 2, or beginning a new round, everyone now adds sound to their movement. Does the addition of sound change the experience? Does the movement improvisation change with sound? Free write/draw.

Louise Campbell

Rubber band Dance—moving and being moved. Literally. Tangible feeling of connection, being in group. Self feeling strong in group. Pulled into the middle of it, into the thick of things and luxuriating in movement. Rubber bands dictate a certain fluidity, suppleness, connectivity in movement. An instant object to

play with. Fun and funny—we all play with these as kids! Unexpected . . . Quick
abandon into spontaneity and fun.
—Field notes written immediately after the first banding experience.

My memories of the banding reveal a sensual experience—the feel of the tough, practical fabric of the band, the sound of my own breath and that of the three other people in my group, glimpses of the shifting shapes of the others, and time slowing down as this four-headed, amoeba-like life-form half-oozes, half-flies through space.

The bands are striking as objects. Strong, tough, flexible, and heavily textured, the bands support a great amount of weight and invite exploration through touch. I find them unusual since they are not at all like little rubber bands that hold together a stack of cards or like ropes used to close a cardboard box or create a handle. I explore and discover these curious things through playing with them with the other members of my group. The bands become a powerful metaphor for community, as the banding experience makes the connections between self and the group unmistakably visible and tangible.

As a musician, I continually seek out the experience Tomie Hahn calls "orientation through disorientation" (2007, 154). I crave experiences that put me out of my comfort zone and enjoy the pleasure of exploring creativity outside my "trained" discipline of music. I relish discovering new ways and means of creating through feeling disoriented, to the extent that I now consider myself an experienced mover and interdisciplinary artist. I also recognize that for some musicians the feeling of disorientation is highly unpleasant, and the resistance to working outside of one's comfort zone is very strong.

The bands almost instantly created a sense of play and safety. As a group of musicians, we interact with objects all the time in the form of musical instruments to create music. The bands tapped into this shared experience directly, as objects with which we could play, explore, and interact with each other. For me, this sense of play and safety facilitated a strong sense of self within the group. This is major for me, since much of my work as a musician revolves around facilitating others' music making, such as teaching adult amateur musicians or leading workshops in improvisation. I am comfortable as a facilitator, and it is far less obvious for me how to *not* take on this role and fully participate in a group without silencing or curtailing my own voice. The bands put me at ease instantly as I explored the constantly changing resistance and tension in the bands, trusting that I could enjoy and take care of myself, and that the others in the group were doing the same. The metaphor for community is clear—regardless of the type of community in which we find ourselves, musical and otherwise, the vitality of a community is reflected by the vitality of its members, a dynamic that is in constant flux.

Lindsay Vogt

The band is a technology that permits so many things—

It is a technology of letting. Of letting muscles become, somehow, unbounded by bodies. And fastened to the tendons that usually stay inside of other bodies. By the band, which is itself another tendon.

They say the small intestine is about ten times the length of the human body. DNA, if unraveled and assembled into one tiny string, would reach the moon—and this is from any body. How long, then, is my supraspinatus after it is hooked up to the muscle machine that belongs to you? To twelve of us put together?

The band itself is the first part of the letting. Industrial strength, this thing has been made to hold the stuff of freight and machine—the weight of a human becomes but a matter of play.

The question: Me? You? Us? becomes at once appropriate but totally unanswerable. As I cannot feel any differentiation—I *am* me. You. Us. I *feel* it. Your pulse rocks the band that nudges my ankle that glides across the floor that takes your belly with it. And down to the ground you go. And then I. And you. And I. And you. Us. I. Continually.

It is at the point where: We have become the same project.

This is a tiny, localized preview of what it's like to be a fish. To *feel* like a fish—

Except it would be that sensation more subtly (but you would be attuned to those subtle variations) and all along your body. And it wouldn't be drawing you into connection with just the ground and the bodies that are touching it, but *all displacement* and movement going on around you.

I can't help but think there is something absolutely aqueous about this whole thing. A particle system turns to a wave.

We are so mixed up in each other that you, I, *we*, incur the complicated consequences of any action. Made unto, made within, this collective system.

Did you know that every time you take a step, you fall?

I need things to be big and deep, sometimes fast, to feel them.

The strange angle of the femur to the hip + the knee + the foot catch it every time.

. . . talking about having so much energy, about having hard and fast and big energy and how sometimes that's hard on other people—he feels overridden by it, pressured to elevate and escalate to that level . . .

Play with that the next time you go for a walk.

For all Thoreau got right, he certainly didn't seem to deal with movement carefully enough. He says, "but superficial, it was!—only another kind of politics or dancing. Men were making speeches to him all over the country, but each expressed only the thought, or the want of thought, of the multitude . . . No man stood on truth. They were merely banded together, as usual one leaning on another, and all together on nothing" (Thoreau 1906, 470–71).

No, *superficial* is not the word.

Simon Rose

FIG 8.2: Saxophone: *Solo for a band*. Courtesy of Simon Rose.

Transferring embodied experience/understanding to understanding in words is not a straightforward translation. In trying to accurately explain the experience of banding, how close do you ever get? The inadequacy of words emphasizes the body expressing. Perhaps this is why I have become drawn to making music with an instrument that has such an uncompromised relationship with the body—the sound only exists in relation to the body's essential process of breathing and the contours of the sound directly reflect the internal contours of the body. The graphic image of the sound shares the same origin as the experience of the movement. As the sound is created by breath and saxophone, the image is a direct representation created from inside the body involved in improvised sound making, by means of the saxophone expressing the embodied, in the embodied.

George Blake

When you are making friends with a classroom of academics and musicians, pallet bands don't usually enter the picture. Creating a band of humans with huge rubber bands was new and unexpected. It involved reading others in different terms and on a different register. Through the push and pull practice of engagement, we found a sensibility of process.

In "the sensitizing level," my taken-for-granted self felt discommoded. My common sense was ruffled and a hilarious feeling took over. I sensed a different way of knowing. I could feel myself quaver and was closely attuned to slight shifts in direction from my partner. Of course, my mind did wander. I was not always exactly where I was. I would catch myself ignoring all the nuance I had just begun to sense. I would check the time or think about lunch. Then I would return to how much I knew and didn't know from what I was sensing. I was refreshed and frightened.

With "safe play, eyes open!" I lost familiarity with my body, regulated only by self-restriction. Instead, I was a cocreator of a web of sensibility. What others did became a constitutive part of my own experience. However, banding was a process of considering possibilities that involved testing boundaries. We had to create a solid base of rapport from which exploration and difference could exist. It was a performance inextricably linked to others. I couldn't formulate my next move without taking into account if and how new energy would impact the group.

I found it hard to legitimate extremes. No movement would have been tedious, while too much movement would have been aggressive. At moments, banding was like sailing with gusts of wind coming from all sides. We were a heterogeneous group and we had to feel through possibilities. While the power relationships in the group were complex in the merry band without a center, it did become apparent through the tension of the bands that awareness of others was central. These links and energetic intermingling were both a process of learning through sensitivity and invention. We became an animated constellation, mobile yet structured by the constraints we found together. This was not simply individual expression or group expression, but somewhere in between. Although I had space for myself, group expression also expressed me.

I was bewildered in important ways by this particular presentation of self in academic life. Banding did not require a formal mask, nor was it surreptitiously an evaluation process. Instead, it provided a glimpse of what an open learning community might look like. Everyone was involved and the group experimentation at play was as sensitive as it was exciting. After the banding encounter had ended, I was alert and sensitized in new ways, but I found that I could not immediately apply my new sensibility. In fact, it was hard to enjoy anything else for the next few hours.

On a basic level, banding was about learning delight. It was an open-ended process of formulating questions through the collective handling of whirling pools of energy. It was disorderly and was about making time for disorder. By moving out of the regularity of our lives, we could improvise new routes, create new ways of interacting, and find new sensibilities of imagination.

Catherine Lee

Journal writing after banding:

It was amazing how it developed. I ended up with my eyes closed the whole time, and it really felt as if I was inside the movement. Similar to how I feel when I am playing my instrument and am inside the sound or tone. I could not tell if I was moving or being moved. Such an incredible feeling of trust and beauty: the four of us moving together.

The introduction of improvisation with an object was novel to me. The elastic allowed me to have much more freedom and to really play. It was much easier for me to get past inhibitions of being wrong or what people would think of me as we were all playing together. It has made me realize that when working with something that we have preconceived ideas about, such as an instrument, it can be difficult to enter into play; using an object that is new allows a freedom that in turn opens new ways of experiencing relationships and situations.

During the explorations with movement and sound, the two felt inexplicably linked. The sensation was similar to how I had felt earlier during the banding when I was not sure if I was moving or being moved. It felt like a manifestation of the same thing, though rather than linking me with others this experience joined two systems that coexist within me. I was not sure if my movement was informing the sound or the sound the movement. They were one and the same, inseparable yet at the same time each with their own agency creating a dance of sorts.

I.
Four bodies moving as one,
a loop of industrial elastic,
creating intimate connections between acquaintances.

Eyes closed, senses heightened,
a gentle soundscape accompanies our movements.
Our breath,
rustling of clothes,
soundings of the walls and carpet.
The space is alive,
a primordial creature emerges.

II.
Being inside the movement,
the most amazing thing.

Am I moving,
or am I being moved?

III.
We sit side by side in a circle,
tears prickle my eyes,
no idea why.
The beauty of the experience astounds me,
intimacy and play.
The urge to reach for my instrument,
overpowering.
I am sure my voice will be clear,
inhibitions left behind.
I have found a part of myself I did not know was there,
precious, strong.

IV.
Months later,
walking down the street,
I revisit the sensations.
Hurried steps are transformed,
becoming fluid,
connected,
with beauty.

V.
Pencil gliding on my notebook,
fingers tapping a keyboard.
Thoughts in my head,
become tangible, expressed,
as I reveal parts of myself to you.

Your words resonate,
I felt that too,
You felt like a fish,
I, an inexplicable floating entity,
cradled by gentle resistance.
I had no idea.
I am surprised by the connections,
as our private thoughts are transformed,
into a written elastic.

Sherrie Tucker

Banding notes:

At first I experienced choices.

The choice to yield, to pull, the moments when I felt others yield or pull—then, we all became a body/organism and I stopped thinking in terms of what my own impulses were, which had been quite conscious—give, pull back, step over this one, lie down and roll with it—and tuned in to what the organism was doing. Then I noticed when subtle changes took place in patterns. I still anticipated snaps, the sonic-tactile ramifications of playing with rubber bands, and prepared to yield in these moments—but sensitivity to patterns felt different than choices, as listening is to sounding. It wasn't a passive experience to fold into the organism, but a different way of being. Senses attuned to bubbling and flowing, not to mention the smell of rubber, the unexpected pleasure of not consciously thinking through my steps and rolls in strands of rubber.

Later, I thought this experience of letting go of conscious choice is probably illusion—do I, perhaps, attain this *release* in remembering it this way? If I can remember the shift from conscious choice-making to balance within the organism—and I do—then it wasn't a loss of consciousness, or awareness of the bodies, my own and those of others, the room, the furniture, gravity, safety. But there was a shift in consciousness. Maybe it was a reorientation from self-consciousness to group-consciousness? Whatever it was, it happened in the bands and was extremely pleasurable, even restorative. I couldn't wait to do it again.

François Mouillot

As a twenty-nine-year-old suffering from cerebral palsy, my relationship to my own body had always been at the same time complex and very simple. On the one hand, my physical day-to-day activities have always consisted of dealing with obstacles in a never-ending search for balance (in a constant process of improvisation); on the other hand, I never believed or really felt that my body was itself an obstacle to leading an active life. In short, I never dreamed of having a different body.

Given the particular limitations and possibilities offered by my body, I tend to have a fairly fixed idea as to what it can or cannot do. Control over my own physical balance is always a fleeting goal and a temporary state of being.

By contrast, the banding experiment struck me as an exercise in "letting go," and perhaps in a novel way for me, "letting go" of the urge (that I am so typically used to) to control my body. Through the gentle pushes and pulls inflicted on the rubber band, banding became an experience of listening. First, listening to my partners' suggestions as to what my body could do and where it could go, but also listening in the most straightforward sense: eyes closed through most of the session, I felt very much aware of and guided by the sounds of our breathing, and of my body "cracking" and stretching. Quickly enough, however, (as a telling sign of my own physical comfort zone) I took the banding exercise closer to the ground, where maintaining a stand-up balance was less of a problem. For me, banding then also became a process of "grounding," on a literal level (using the ground to compensate for my own lack of balance standing up) as well as on a more abstract level, forcing me to ground my experience of the world in my body again (as part of dealing with my own physical situation has involved engaging much of my time in more intellectual pursuits, and in a way "bypassing" my body).

The particulars of my relationships with my banding partners added more depth to the session: with me in this trio were a longtime mentor (Ellen) and a good friend (Rebecca). Their presence added a dose of comfort and upped the personal stakes in the exercise. From my perspective, through banding, an unexpected form of intimacy with Ellen and Rebecca emerged, one that was not necessarily comfortable from the get-go (self-conscious thoughts racing through my head: "What will my body allow me to do? Will I even be able to walk within this band? How limiting will I be to Ellen and Rebecca? What will our interactions be like after we are done?") but which turned into a profound exercise of bodily communication through the gradual erasing of my initial anxiety. As my mind and body wandered about in our collective movement, banding first was about guessing, feeling how Rebecca and Ellen would react to my inflexions on the band, and how I could let my body become as reactive as it could to their movements. Then, a gradual sense of ease and familiarity (perhaps even an intuition?) with my own, as well as with Rebecca's and Ellen's movements began to take over the mental process. I cannot say it ever felt quite like a "collective consciousness," but it certainly started to feel like I was thinking through my body. Inside the band, I interacted with Rebecca and Ellen on a much different level that I am used to, entering into a form of dialogue mediated through the body, breaking down some of the hierarchical and emotional boundaries that may be present in other forms of communication with them. I first had to allow myself, and allow them, to interact with my body. In a sense, I felt like the bands themselves materialized the extension, tensions, and releases of the preexisting bonds I had with my banding partners.

Jovana Milović

For me, the experience of the banding exercise made explicit the connections between people and our responsiveness to one another. The elasticity of the band allowed for improvised movement of all the interconnected participants, while the resistance of the band enforced cooperation. As the connections became more intricately intertwined, the undulating collective began to move as a wave—with each member of the group moving of her own volition, and with each movement sending reverberations to the others and back again. My idiosyncratic movement was concomitantly a part of and informed by the movement of the collective. I was free within the restraints and bounds of the group, while the group itself was responsible for my freedom.

The bands were thus both the precondition and the limitation of freedom and movement. Within the parameters of their elasticity and resistance, we tested the power and influence of the other bodies around us and became utterly and unmistakably *receptive*. This receptivity to the other—physical, literal, embodied—resonated through the remainder of our days together. We could not untwist from the bands that strung our thoughts into a dense constellation bright with creativity.

Months later, I am on a subway car as it lurches forward, moving all the occupants in sync. Muscles strain to keep the bodies upright, still, appropriately dispersed. The corners of mouths curl upward uncomfortably as, here and there, people wince. I'm sorry. I touched you. Curt nods forgive the transgression. The activation of the receptive realm is truncated by this place, as it is by so many of the places we inhabit.

Watching people move in public places, I am fascinated by how effortlessly receptivity is foreclosed. After disturbances strangers silently renegotiate their space and retreat to their private sphere. Now, even shoulder to shoulder, we are disparate—each in a different sensory environment. But there was an instant when we were together and we knew it. When I was right here—and you, you were right here with me.

Pete Williams

As a scholar interested in the bodily experience of improvisation, I welcomed the opportunity to experience banding. I entered the activity with this sense of excitement, but I also had some trepidation or anxiety about my own bodily experience. As someone who is not all that athletic or limber, I worried about how I might look, how my weight might possibly endanger the group if I fell or moved too quickly, whether I was wearing clothes that would allow me to move freely, and so on. Was it possible to get hurt working with the bands? I didn't know.

Despite these worries, I managed to join a group that was playful and eager to experiment with movement. We put bands around our own and each others' arms, shoulders, wrists, knees, and ankles. Someone tied the end of one band to my ankle and the other to someone else—I lost track of who was attached to whom.

At first, I tried to keep track of my and others' movements by sight, noting when someone's arm moved in response to my pulling. But I soon realized that the influence I had on their movements was more subtle and less like a puppeteer's control over his puppet. I might pull against someone's arm, but the bands were loose enough that my pulling may have little visible effect on that person's arm. So I just gave up watching and tried to feel how my body was moved and how I moved it. I felt connected, manipulated, too, but subtly, and not by any single individual. I could also subtly or more overtly move my body or resist the manipulation, and that movement wouldn't upset the integrity or balance of the group drastically. I soon discovered that I had freedom of movement within some constraints. At times, I experienced those constraints as a source of collective strength, when my prior trepidations about my body faded away and I could rely on this strength to keep me and the group safe.

As we began to move, I noticed that my sense of balance was somewhat altered. I struggled to stay on two feet sometimes, when I felt the band around my left ankle pull that ankle off the floor. At first, I was determined to remain fairly stationary and grounded to the floor. But as soon as I lifted up a foot (that was attached to someone else somewhere else), I noticed that my balance shifted but did not totally destabilize as it might when I was moving by myself. This gave me a sense of safety and comfort, and so I began to experiment a bit with my balance, leaning into bands that were near my body but not attached to me, lifting a hand or foot and letting the band pull that body part wherever it went. I noticed that the network of bands supported me no matter how much I leaned, pulled, or loosened my own grip; what constrained me could also support me.

Parting Thoughts

What theories arise from embodied practices? I realize that this question assumes a separation of theory and practice—a culturally constructed, historically reinforced, bifurcation that magnifies the separation of mind and body. I suggest that although in some situations theory arises from practice (and vice versa), theory and practice are often inseparable. Similarly, if thought resides within our entire body, then theory shares that living space along with practice.[2] Have you ever felt at a loss for words to describe an experience, however meaningful and profound the encounter? Not having words for an experience does not devalue or negate the lived moment. An orange bird flies to a nearby branch and seems to stare through me, then chirps and twitches wildly—the extraordinary experience does not cease to exist just because it left me speechless, or because I don't know the Latin name of the bird. Words can even seem to shortchange the moment until I push to find a creative way of translating one set of sensory modes to another. I am not slamming the theory-practice dichotomy. I am musing the existence of a liminal, blue-gray zone, where theory and practice dwell within the body. Perhaps the very struggle of comprehending experience allows us to grow and creatively convey what we know in an embodied sense. If discourse consists of meanings related by text or spoken word, then the awareness and processing of sensory experience is vital.[3]

While collaborating with artist Melanie Klein for a sculptural performance rig one summer,[4] we experimented with pallet bands. Once I extended the use of the bands to other improvisers, I immediately realized the potential for multisensory improvisation. The common yet surprisingly oversized and whimsical nature of pallet bands attracts people to the activity. Even the few timid onlookers who choose to sit out often eagerly jump in after the first session. Donning a rubber band *with* other people—attaching to them, supporting them, letting go—swiftly becomes a palpable coordination challenge. In the Guelph workshop, some banders, even the seasoned improvisers, left the space astonished by the depth of insights gained. How funny that I needed to remind them that *they* discovered these insights together, and the bands only enabled the awareness. The individual contributions in this chapter offer a variety of such insights: realizations concerning social interactions, awareness of a collective, heightening of embodied sensibilities, energy, balance and groundedness, and issues of control, to list only a few.

Banding appears to usher the body back into the discourse on improvisation. Frankly, it was always there. As Siddall and Waterman put it, "the improvising body sometimes seems to disappear . . . in discourses that disassociate sound from source, ideal from real."[5] Banding draws attention to the notion of body-as-instrument as well as the social, interactive nature of bodies during improvisation. Bodies and our experiences create and inhabit discourse. I propose that improvisers embody and enact discourse in ways that spoken word and text cannot. As Wittgenstein acknowledges in *Philosophical Remarks* no. 54, "What belongs to the essence of the world cannot be expressed by language. For this reason, it cannot *say* that all is in flux. Language can only say those things we can also imagine otherwise" (quoted in Stern 1995, 161). If we consider that language cannot represent *all* that is experienced, I propose we recognize the "articulate sensate body" as a vehicle for discourse. This means that gesture, gaze, sound, touch, taste, and movement convey "something" that contributes to, or *exists as*, discourse. After all, prior to language, communication most likely existed as an embodied code. Currently, with the variety of ways of transmitting information and communicating ideas, we continue to rely heavily on the literal nature of discourse, leaving many sensory modes of experience unwritten. If we cannot find words to adequately describe our experiential encounters, especially those that fall below the threshold of what is considered "discourse," how might these experiences emerge in/as discourse? What of orange birds twittering on branches? I posit that bodies carry discourse codes; finding ways to tap into embodied dialogues is the challenge at hand. I ask, are we able to draw on embodied sensibilities—embodied metacognitive sensibilities—to note and "read" them, to fully enrich our (theoretical) discourses?

As vehicles for discourse, bodies carry stories. The banding experiences that participants struggle to find words for reveal the difficulties in "translating" sensation, yet, as I intimated earlier, the activity of attempting to articulate the experiences reveals fascinating results. What might experimental practices in improvisation contribute to the discourse, the stories, on the sounding body and embodiment? In sharing stories one moves from a profound solipsistic sensibility to acknowledge that others meet with similar experiences.

Upon hearing a high-pitched squeal from three banders, what sound might I add, or do I decide to stay silent? The stream is time-based. Jump in—or observe? Shall I lower my torso downward in reaction to a tug, or allow the pull to sweep me up in a more passive way? A keen awareness of the moment-to-moment (ex)changes of movement and sound helps one make creative choices about how to contribute. Improvisational contributions can seem rapid in the progression of time. Is the improvisatory action conscious in a "thought out" way or intuitive? Because improvisers contribute to the stream of sound/movement in real time, their improvisations can appear ad libbed, or without any preparation. This is far from the truth in most cases! Their contributions emerge extemporaneously, meaning their skills have been honed through extended embodied experience and practice so that their improvisations appear spontaneous, without preparation. I propose that the embodied knowledge that improvisers accumulate through experience and practice allows them to improvise fluidly in the moment. Such improvisatory outpouring dramatically exemplifies Mihaly Csikszentmihalyi's concept of "flow"—or "optimal experience"—in the sense that an improviser, fully immersed, achieves a state of flow during their practice (Csikszentmihalyi and Csikszentmihalyi 1988; Csikszentmihalyi 1990). Csikszentmihalyi argues that when a person is completely absorbed in an activity or idea with single-minded, focused attention, a sense of "flow" exists. He finds that this state of complete concentration is the result of a delicate balance between the difficulty of the task and the individual's skill level. People experiencing flow can often work intuitively, because of their skills, depth of experience, and awareness, combined with the new challenges they are presented with.

Stepping back, the number of potential choices one is faced with during improvisation is mind (-body) boggling. Infinite even. The options are compounded by the more subtle qualities of *how* one improvises at any given moment and the ever-changing degree to which other banders also feed into the decision process. One decision alters the entire banding improvisation. Because of the complexity of the body-mind decision-making task, "flow" is vital. Let me explain. For multifaceted operations, a carefully thought out, logical decision-making process is basically impossible. Instead, I offer that a reliance on the flow of embodied knowledge needs to kick in. There is, simply, no time to consider the infinite! Complex activities demand and rely on embodied knowledge—those abilities that an individual has learned and embodied and can perform "without thought." Performing multiple activities, multitasking intricacies, requires considerable processing. Embodied knowledge, such as the multiple embodied skills used to ride a bicycle, must engage. If I considered every action needed to ride a bicycle, I would not get far. Too many cognitive and psychological processes are necessary. However, through gradual learning and practice the body-mind acquires knowledge, enabling embodiment of skills or abilities. The embodiment of skills while banding with others is often just the challenge needed to supply that extra effort and heightened awareness, to create a flow experience. The process of gaining orientation through disorientation contributes to a flow experience, as it provides the challenge needed for the experience. For example, while working in pairs in round 1, banders orient themselves with only one individual. At this sensitizing stage, I have observed there is a more cautious quality of movement—a subtle disorientation perhaps—as banders are tuning into the process as well as their partner. But very quickly this mini-disorientation dissipates and a greater challenge is needed. The leader needs to be aware of when the banding encounter ceases to be a challenge. At this point I usually combine pairs of banders and suggest increased movement in the group. Disorientation returns through increased complexity, but soon this skill will become incorporated. Challenges such as disorientation, technique, or awareness keep moving the level of facility forward—and through that challenge an experience of flow may arise.

During focused awareness, ideally an improviser's body-mind complex has flow and the body-mind improvises as one. A different viewpoint: hesitation, or "thinking" through a decision, often blocks flow. How interesting that themes of water, fluidity, and flow recur as common metaphors throughout the banders' reflections. Csikszentmihalyi notes that during flow states, individuals find the experience enriching, gratifying, and pleasurable. I hope readers picked up the pleasurable, even ecstatic atmosphere of banding through the contributors to this chapter. I wonder if flow experiences are transmitted between people—fluidly running through the bands as extensions of sensory, embodied knowledge?

Allow me to add another facet to the considerations on embodied knowledge and improvisation practices. Consider the many objects that you physically encounter in any given day. Some you manipulate, others support you, and others aid your communication, health, food intake, and so on. For performers and artists, many objects in the real world serve as expressive tools—musical instruments, paint brushes, fans, or costumes, for example. In my experience most artists/performers form unique relationships with the objects they use. I want to highlight the particular body-mind-object relationship that develops between artist and instrument. The relationship often deepens over time, beginning as a physical, pragmatic, task-related connection, but often leads to a bonding where the specific qualities of the object become a necessity for expressing oneself. How does this happen? I find the initial stages of interacting with a new instrument quite clumsy, physically. My dexterity—the body-mind-tool connection—lacks facility, and my orientation to the object feels awkward and pedestrian. However, as my abilities grow with experience, I notice an alignment with the object as well as the activity. At this time my predilection for particular tools that feel right, that flow with *ki*, begins to cultivate body-object relationships. Bonding. Motivated by my desire to express something in the real world, I seek the specific objects to suit the nuances of my expressivity. The affinity links me to the object.

The physical connection to an object and how energy flows from body to object is culturally constructed and even transmitted via the learning stages. For example, in *Sensational Knowledge* I wrote about the Japanese concept of *ki* and how dancers learn to direct the flow of this vital energy from the body's core *into* dance props, such as a fan (Hahn 2007, 8–9, 65). I call objects employed for creative expression "sensible objects," noting that as the body extends itself through objects, it also learns new sensibilities from interactions with "things" (Hahn 2011). The physically expanding body often transforms, revealing knowledge gained through experiential encounters with objects in performance and everyday life. Sensible objects enable an expanded sensory presence—objects that extend the senses, expand expressivity and the expressive self through these objects. Imbued with energy, sensible objects become animate or are considered already animate. They engage and inform aural/oral and enactive knowledge (knowledge learned through movement). These *things* teach us about matters of the outside world, of the self, and the relationships between them. Sensibly.

What does this have to do with banding?

To be honest, banding took me by surprise several years ago. The improvisers included in this chapter revealed the potentials, as well as new practices, for this quirky exploratory improvisation. These banders quickly pointed out the unique qualities of the bands themselves, and how they encourage community building. I learned how the bands embody liveness. These bands, as sensible objects, convey energy from person to person.

Although different from the objects created specifically for art practices (such as a banjo, pen, or knitting needle), the bands seem to invite participants into the activity precisely because of their seemingly commonplace yet oversized and outlandish quality. After enclosing participants in their elastic grasp, bands telegraph and display energy. I noticed that a curious pattern typically repeats during workshops. The gradual acquisition of fluency with an instrument or prop I discuss here normally takes years. Surprisingly, the developments in banding follow the same order as other practices—stages of disorientation to orientation and fluency to creative skillfulness—but often occur within a two-hour session. During workshops I draw attention to the process because the quickly formed body-mind-object relationship and skills might be overlooked in the wild fun-loving context. However, exploratory improvisations with others can potentially mirror a wide variety of insights. For me, the heightening of awareness, observing relationships, broadening expressivity, creativity, and embodied knowledge lie at the core, and I have been fascinated by how simple rubber bands enable insights on many levels.

New experiences provide opportunities for growth—however disruptive or disorienting—jolting us from our comfort zone, away from our expressive habits. Banding serves as a lens to look deeper into our improvisations as social interactions, particularly magnifying our habits, what seems comfortable, and within our set vocabularies of expressivity. The banding authors so clearly convey the diversity of perspectives using this lens. Themes highlighting the social potential of improvisation emerged through such words as *negotiation, trust, resistance, allowing, relaxing, intimacy,* and *balance*—not a surprise, considering that the texts were written by individuals connected by rubber bands. I primarily took the role of facilitator, creating a physically and socially safe space for banding to take place. During the improvisations, I observed the participants bonding with a mindfulness of others in a multisensory mode. Banding, as a truly disorienting experience at first, heightened awareness to sound, touch, movement, gaze, balance, and even smell. The sheer quantity of multisensory information had the potential to be overwhelming, but I/we noticed a period of settling into the improvisation arising over time. Perhaps disorientation was transforming to orientation? I am not sure.

> Rolling on the floor, I saw you all from a new point of view. A banded trio lumbers along the carpet as if an amoeba, amorphous and fluid. Humming and buzzing. Now a high-pitched long tone rides above! Was that an orange bird fluttering by? Oddly, the amoeba sprouts an appendage extending a length of band around my torso and I am incorporated. Str-e-tch. Corporeal attachments. (Hahn, field notes)

Notes

1. Gillian Siddall and Ellen Waterman, Call for Papers, "Sounding the Body: Improvisation, Representation, and Subjectivity," 2010.

2. For examples of theories concerning embodied cognition see: Briñol and DeMarree (2012), Clark (1997), Damasio (1999), and Gallagher (2005).

3. Banding has a family relationship to other embodied improvisational practices that focus on building a heightened sensory awareness such as Deep Listening and contact improvisation. See Oliveros (2005) on Deep Listening, and Pallant (2006) and Novack (1990) on contact improvisation.

4. Tomie Hahn and Melanie Klein, "taut," performed and filmed at the Feminist Theory and Music Conference, Greensboro, NC, May 29, 2009; video at http://www.arts.rpi.edu/tomie/interactive.html.

5. Siddall and Waterman, Call for Papers.

9. Learning to Go with the Flow

DAVID ROKEBY'S *VERY NERVOUS SYSTEM*
AND THE IMPROVISING BODY

Jesse Stewart

Visitors to an art gallery enter what appears to be an empty room. A spotlight illuminates an ellipse on the floor. Perplexed, the visitors move further into the space. The sudden sound of a streetcar halts them in their tracks. The sound stops too, as abruptly as it began. After pausing for a moment, they begin to move again, only to hear the sound of crinkling cellophane mixed with the sound of splashing water. Before long, they realize that their own movements are triggering the sounds they are hearing, and they begin to respond accordingly, improvising with their bodies to sculpt the sound.

I have witnessed this scenario many times in different exhibitions of David Rokeby's *Very Nervous System* (*VNS*). First developed in the mid-1980s, when interactive art, computer-based art, and sound art were emergent fields, *VNS* uses video surveillance technology, synthesizers, a sound system, computers, and image-processing software designed by Rokeby to translate movement into music and sound. The movements of gallery patrons are monitored by an inconspicuously placed wall- or ceiling-mounted video camera. The video signal is routed to a hidden computer where the image-processing software divides each frame into an 8 × 10 grid. A different audio file is linked to each of the grid's eighty cells. The software compares each video frame to the previous one. When it detects even a slight difference between two adjacent frames, it triggers the playback of the sound(s) associated with the part(s) of the grid in which change has occurred. The sound is spatialized such that movements taking place on the extreme right of the space trigger sounds that are played back on a speaker positioned on the right side of the gallery and left-sided gestures are played back on the left. Due to the relative compactness of the video grid, even small gestures can trigger multiple contiguous sounds.

Remarkably, the sounds are played back into the space through the sound system in roughly one-twentieth of a second, creating an almost instantaneous biofeedback loop between the technology and the improvising body.

Very Nervous System opens a critical space for those who interact with the work to reflect on the inherent tensions and contradictions between the logic of the computer binary code that underpins the piece and the intuitive, embodied improvisatory gestures that activate it. The piece inverts the traditional relationship between movement/dance and sound/music: instead of the body responding to music, the movements of the improvising body cause the sounds, in effect orchestrating the music one hears. The work thus functions as what Rokeby has called a "transforming mirror." "The medium not only reflects back," he writes, "but also refracts what it is given; what is returned is ourselves, transformed and processed. . . . To the degree that the technology transforms our image in the act of reflection, it provides us with a sense of the relation between this self and the experienced world" (1995, 133). By reflecting and refracting our actions in space and time, and by encouraging an intuitive process of bodily improvisation, *Very Nervous System* provides unique opportunities to become fully immersed—in both mind and body— in the moment, entering into what psychologist Mihaly Csikszentmihalyi has called a state of *flow*, "the state in which people are so involved in an activity that nothing else seems to matter" (1990, 4). Through an analysis of several incarnations of *VNS*, the present essay examines some of the ways the work alters our awareness of our bodies and encourages a state of flow through embodied forms of improvisation.

The very title of the piece alludes to the human body, to the nervous system that transmits signals between different parts of the body, coordinating our actions. Marshall McLuhan famously suggested that all technologies are extensions of the human body: the shovel extends our hands and arms; the microscope, telescope, camera, and television extend our eyes; the microphone, radio, amplifier, and speaker extend our ears. The computer, according to McLuhan, is the extension of our central nervous system. "The important thing to realize," he explains, "is that electric information systems are live environments in the full organic sense. They alter our feelings and sensibilities" (McLuhan and Fiore 1968, 35–36). In both name and structure, *VNS* realizes McLuhan's dictum in a provocative way.

The experience of improvising with *VNS* is more complex than one might think. The relationship between bodily gesture and auditory response does not feel like a unidirectional form of mimesis in which gesture x causes sound y. Having spent extended periods of time interacting with different versions of the work, I have noticed that *VNS* heightens not only my awareness of the sonic environment, but also my perception of the relationships between my body and the sonic environment. This heightened perception often continues for some time after I leave the gallery—walking to my car or down the street, I remain keenly aware of the sounds around me, sometimes continuing to perceive them as being connected to my own movements. Of course, they are connected, though not in a causal way as they are inside the gallery. They are connected in the sense that our bodies constantly act as transducers of the sounds around us as sound waves come into contact with different parts of our body, including our eardrums. *VNS* draws our attention to this fact, focusing our aural senses in a particularly embodied way.

When interacting with *VNS*, I sometimes get the feeling that the system actually anticipates my bodily movements. It becomes difficult to discern who is leading, human or machine. Rokeby has commented on this phenomenon as well, describing his early attempts to "out draw" the system in his studio. Of course, the system cannot really anticipate our gestures, but the speed with which it responds seems to be faster than our ability to process what is taking place in an analytical, left-brained manner. This phenomenon enables the improvising mind/body to become fully immersed in the moment, to "let go" and enter the flow state.

Csikszentmihalyi identifies eight components that are often associated with a sense of enjoyment and flow:

> First, the experience usually occurs when we confront tasks we have a chance of completing. Second, we must be able to concentrate on what we are doing. Third and fourth, the concentration is usually possible because the task undertaken has clear goals and provides immediate feedback. Fifth, one acts with a deep but effortless involvement that removes from awareness the worries and frustrations of everyday life. Sixth, enjoyable experiences allow people to exercise a sense of control over their actions. Seventh, concern for the self disappears, yet paradoxically the sense of self emerges stronger after the flow experience is over. Finally, the sense of the duration of time is altered; hours pass by in minutes, and minutes can stretch out to seem like hours. (1990, 49)

Very Nervous System provides opportunities to experience virtually all of these flow factors. However, unlike many other improvisatory modes of music-making that require years of training and the internalization of a myriad of genre-specific rules, *VNS* allows us to enter into a flow state very quickly.[1] In *VNS*, there is only one rule: move your body to hear sound. All of the other constraints governing the interaction are beyond our control, having been established in advance through lines of computer code. Under these circumstances, our embodied gestural vocabulary—which is shaped by our physiology, our cultural environment, and the totality of our past physical movements—becomes the "knowledge base" that allows for improvisational interaction with *VNS*. No one can really be "better" than anyone else at improvising with *VNS*, at least not musically. However, repeated and/or sustained interactions with the work do allow performers the opportunity to develop and refine the nature of their movements in dialogue with *VNS* so that the visual/kinesthetic dimensions of their interactions can become more nuanced. This has been my experience, having had multiple opportunities to interact with different incarnations of the work over the past fifteen years. Moreover, sustained interaction with *VNS* allows us to deepen our experience of the flow state, which might be thought of as part of the process of becoming a more adept improviser. One of the unique things about *VNS* is that it provides opportunities for musicians and nonmusicians alike to develop an embodied improvisatory practice through movement and sound, thereby democratizing musical experience.

Virtually anyone—even individuals with limited motor control, cognitive ability, and/or sensory integration—can enter into embodied improvisatory dialogue with *VNS*. This feature of *VNS* has profound implications for differently abled persons and their bodies. In *Disability Aesthetics*, Tobin Siebers "conceives of the disabled body and mind as playing significant roles in the evolution of modern aesthetics, theorizing disability as a unique resource discovered by modern art and then embraced by it as one of its defining concepts" (2010, 2–3). He continues: "Disability aesthetics refuses to recognize the representation of the healthy body—and its definition of harmony, integrity, and beauty—as the sole determination of the aesthetic" (2–3). *VNS* similarly refuses to valorize the "healthy" body. By creating a space (literally and metaphorically) for bodies and minds of all types to engage with the software, Rokeby's work further inscribes bodies of difference into the contemporary art world—not as things to be represented but as active and constitutive agents in the aesthetic experience.

Disabilities studies scholar Alex Lubet has argued that music and dance are essential human rights and the "denial of such rights is nothing less than an atrocity, inexcusable when visited upon even one person" (2009, 128). *VNS* is not merely inclusive, it is empowering. Indeed, the *VNS* technology has had numerous practical applications outside of art gallery contexts. For example, *VNS* has been used extensively in rehabilitation centers to allow people with physical and/or mental disabilities, including those with extremely limited motor control, to create music and sound using their bodies as musical instruments (Leech 2002). In 1989, *VNS* enabled members of a Vancouver-based group called Supercussion, which consisted of four quadriplegic musicians, to perform with celebrated Canadian jazz fusion group UZEB. In the late 1980s, Rokeby modified *VNS* to help a paralyzed woman, whose only form of motor control was the movement of her eyelids, to communicate. By calculating the changing distance from her eyelash to her eyebrow, the *VNS* software enabled her to communicate in binary code. Raising her eyelids for long or short periods would enter single bits of information: zero or one. Because spelling out words in binary would be extraordinarily time consuming, Rokeby worked with a company specializing in assistive computer technologies to increase her speed based on the probabilities associated with the next letter in a given letter combination and on her word usage history as gleaned from letters and essays she had written prior to her injury. As in *VNS* itself, all of the feedback was in sound; this was necessary because her eyes roved in an involuntary manner, making it impossible for her to concentrate on a screen. A MIDI synthesizer indicated successful communication of long and short eyelid raises, along with some other basic sonic indicators and word suggestions. This system provided a much faster input process than a straight binary or Morse code system, allowing her to communicate up to fifteen words per minute.

In addition to adapting the *VNS* technology for use by people with disabilities, Rokeby has continued to develop the technology for use within his own creative practice. Advances in video technology and image processing capabilities over the work's twenty-plus-year history have made *VNS* much more sensitive. Where earlier versions of the work responded best to large, dramatic gestures, the current version rewards minute movements, creating a heightened sense of intimacy between the participant and the work. Now the installation actually gets quieter if it detects an overabundance of movement in the space. In a sense, the system has become somewhat less nervous over time. The sonic dimension of the piece has changed, too. In its early incarnations, the sound was more traditionally musical in nature, using different synthesizer patches to allude to a variety of musical traditions. In recent years, Rokeby has replaced these explicitly musical sounds with more intimate sounds that do not signify particular musical or cultural traditions to the same extent—the sound of paper crinkling or a roll of duct tape being unrolled, for example. Many of these sounds have an almost tactile dimension, further complicating the interplay of gestural discourses involved in the work and heightening the intimacy of the experience. Because of the increased emphasis on the tactility of sound, it is almost as if Rokeby is compensating for the work's lack of a physical presence, highlighting instead the improvisatory movements of the bodies that engage with the work and activate the empty space in which it is shown.

The immateriality of *Very Nervous System* deserves further comment. Invisibility has a surprisingly rich and varied history within contemporary art,[2] beginning perhaps with French artist Yves Klein's 1958 exhibition titled *La spécialisation de la sensibilité à l'état matière première en sensibilité picturale stabilisée, Le Vide* (*The Specialization of Sensibility in the Raw Material State into Stabilized Pictorial Sensibility, The Void*), an empty white-walled room that featured what Klein described as "immaterial pictorial sensibility." Tom Friedman's 1992 work *Untitled (A Curse)* features an area of empty space that has been cursed by a witch hired by the artist. In exhibitions of the work, the zone of cursed space sits atop an empty sculpture plinth (or so we are told). Jeppe Hein's *Invisible Labyrinth* (2005) features an invisible maze that visitors must learn to navigate by wearing helmets that trigger a small electrical pulse whenever they bump into an invisible wall. Rooted firmly in the conceptual art tradition, such works privilege the idea behind the art and the experience of the visitor over aesthetics. They also draw our attention to the limits of visual perception and to the myriad unseen factors that shape our encounters not only with art but also with various aspects of our daily lives. *VNS* has a similar effect that is achieved by creating a space in which the performing body is mediated and transformed by video surveillance technology. Participants quickly become acutely aware of the fact that their movements are being monitored in some way, even if they don't know by what mechanism. Just as the work heightens our perception of the relationships between our bodies and the sounds around us, it also draws attention to the various forms of invisible surveillance (including video and computer monitoring) that now permeate our lives. This subtext of surveillance complicates the more playful aspects of the work, affecting the ways in which some people interact with the work—even to the point of choosing not to. In a way, *VNS* necessitates that we tacitly accept the fact that our movements are being covertly observed, especially if we hope to enter a flow state while interacting with the work.

The dual themes of interactivity and surveillance are integral to many of Rokeby's subsequent works as well, most of which incorporate and build on the *VNS* technology. For example, *Watch* (1995) features a live surveillance camera feed that is processed in such a way that two representations of the same scene are projected into the gallery space: in one version, all of the objects that are moving disappear; in the other, all of the objects that are static disappear. The degree to which our bodies (or portions thereof) are represented in the video images depends on the nature of our movements while we are within the video camera's field of vision. More recently, *Dark Matter* (2010) uses infrared video cameras to survey movements within a darkened gallery from four angles. These cameras divide the space into thousands of three-dimensional zones, some of which trigger the playback of particular sounds when activated by movement in those areas. Visitors to the space feel their way around the space in darkness, discovering the form of Rokeby's invisible interactive sculpture by encountering pockets of sound. Unlike the delicate sounds of the current version of *Very Nervous System*, *Dark Matter* uses very physical, often startling sounds, such as falling rocks or flame bursts, endowing our actions and interactions with an elemental, almost mythic quality. At the same time, the piece reminds us that surveillance technology has advanced to the point that even in total darkness our actions can be monitored and observed. In *Discipline and Punish*, Michel Foucault persuasively demonstrates that surveillance and punishment have been fundamentally linked historically, as embodied in the concept of the Panopticon, a prison designed to enable one watchman to observe all the inmates, who each become "the object of information, never a subject in communication" (1995, 200). Participants surveilled by *VNS* software invert Foucault's theory because they are simultaneously active subjects of a technologically mediated form of instant communication. Their movements are observed and rewarded with an aesthetic response.

In a sense, the *VNS* software (now known as softVNS) has become something of a transforming mirror within Rokeby's own creative practice, and it has transformed, and continues to transform, the field of interactive media art and sound art more generally. A growing community of creative practitioners is using softVNS, which now operates as an external object within the graphical programming language known as MaxMSP, to create interactive systems of their own. For example, Toronto artist Nina Levitt's 2004 installation *Little Breeze* includes an audio transmission of Morse code. When a viewer enters the room, a webcam connected to a computer running the *VNS* software triggers Maurice Chevalier's 1929 recording of "Louise," which emerges from the sound of the Morse code, only to disappear when the viewer stops moving. In her 2004 piece *Direct Cut*, Belgium-based artist Alexandra Dementieva used softVNS to create a form of interactive cinema. The installation includes two video projections, each featuring a character involved in a complex and at times antagonistic relationship with another. Through softVNS, the movements of spectators' bodies in the space, as well as the proximity of the spectators to the projected characters, trigger different video clips, affecting the behavior of the characters and influencing the story line that unfolds. In these contexts, the *VNS* software engages participants' bodies in a less explicitly dialogical manner than in Rokeby's work. Instead of emphasizing the improvising body and creating opportunities for participants to experience a flow state, these works tend to situate the body in particular ways in relation to their visual and narrative elements, which remain the primary focus. The *VNS* software functions less as a transforming mirror than it does as a door that opens onto new narrative threads within the works.

Clearly, the *VNS* software is versatile enough to facilitate a wide range of artistic practices and intents. My own experiences with *VNS* have made it clear that the work can accommodate a wide range of musical sensibilities as well. In the winter of 2011, I was invited to guest-curate an exhibition of *Very Nervous System* at the Carleton University Art Gallery in Ottawa, Canada. In addition to curating the work, I organized a series of performances to take place in conjunction with it: a performance by alto saxophonist, composer, dancer, and intermedia artist John Oswald; a performance by baritone saxophonist, composer, and martial arts expert David Mott; and a solo percussion performance by me. Oswald began his performance by standing motionless in the center of the space. Before long, a small, possibly involuntary gesture triggered a response from the system. Oswald quickly turned his head to look at the speaker that produced the sound, eliciting a further series of sounds in the process. Jerking his head to the other side resulted in another burst of sound. Alternating from left to right, his axial head movements gradually developed into an improvised dance that involved his whole body, delineating and activating the area under surveillance by the *VNS* camera. Sometimes his movements elicited a cacophony of rapidly changing sounds; at other times, he seemed to react to particular sound configurations, repeating certain physical gestures and their concomitant sounds. The performance culminated in an improvised solo on alto saxophone, the movements of Oswald's fingers on the instrument's keys continuing to elicit percussive responses from *VNS*. In much the same way that his improvised dance movements created a figure/ground relationship between his body and the white walls of the gallery space, the improvised squeals, pops, tones, and groans of his saxophone became a shifting set of aural figures set against the ground of sounds emanating from *VNS*.

Mott brought a different aesthetic sensibility to *VNS* and a different approach to the physicality of embodied improvisatory performance. In addition to his background as a composer and virtuoso improviser on the baritone saxophone, Mott is an eighth dan black belt in Uechi-ryu karate and a highly accomplished practitioner of qigong, the Chinese practice of merging movement, breath, and awareness. Having performed with Mott in multiple improvisatory contexts for over a decade, I have witnessed firsthand some of the ways his background in martial arts informs his improvisatory musical practice: in his posture, in his awareness of and attention to breath, and in the physicality of his embodied performative gestures when improvising.

However, to my knowledge, he had never combined his dual background in the martial and sonic arts in performance in an explicit manner, so I invited him to do so in conjunction with *VNS*. He began by performing several acoustic solo baritone pieces out of the range of the system, using circular breathing and multiphonic techniques to create a rich, polyphonic texture. Putting down his horn, he ventured into the video camera's field of view and performed a series of qigong-inspired movements, the fluidity of his improvised motions generating a fluidity of sound from the installation that created a sense of phrasing both visually and sonically. Picking up his horn once more, he concluded by combining the sound of his baritone saxophone with that of *VNS*, merging movement with both acoustic and mediated sound.

It is difficult to judge the degree to which another performer has attained flow in performance, given that it is a highly subjective interior mental state. Based on my own experiences as an improvising musician and on discussions with many other improvisers and audience members over the years, there does seem to be a correlation between a performer's (or group's) experience of flow in performance and an audience's perception of the quality of that performance. Performances in which there is a clear sense that musicians "are so involved in an activity that nothing else seems to matter" tend to reach further into the consciousness of listeners, sometimes even inducing something akin to a flow state at the site of reception. From my perspective as an audience member for both Oswald's and Mott's *VNS* performances, it seemed as though the two performers entered a flow state very quickly. I suspect that multiple interrelated factors contribute to the speed with which a performer is able to achieve flow in performance, including years of performing experience, confidence level, technical proficiency, knowledge of repertoire, audience attentiveness, and so on. Physiological factors may play a role as well. For example, Mott's extensive use of circular breathing (and his awareness of breath in general) likely contributes to his ability to achieve and maintain flow.

Reflecting on his *VNS* performance and on his experiences as an improvising musician and martial artist more generally, Mott's perceptions of his own state of consciousness during performance seem to resonate with Csikszentmihaly's concept of flow, with one notable exception. "I don't agree at all with Csikszentmihalyi," Mott explains in email correspondence (December 17, 2012), "where he states that after emerging from Flow one feels a greater sense of self. For me the loss of self-identification while in Flow requires that I actually reinstall a sense of self. I can go on and on afterwards without the impinging sense of self." This suggests that some performers can attain a sufficiently strong sense of flow while improvising that it can extend well beyond the duration of a performance, influencing their consciousness more generally. This is not unlike the residual heightened perception of sound and movement that I have felt after interacting with *VNS* for extended periods of time.

My own experience of flow was complicated by the *VNS* technology—or, more correctly, by my attempts to control the technology—during my performance. For my solo performance, I set up a single snare drum at the back of the gallery space, just beyond the camera's field of view. This allowed me to play acoustically on the drum, using an array of extended techniques to create different sonorities and rhythms, such as playing the drum with my fingers, hands, chopsticks, and other unconventional striking agents; using the resonance of the drum to amplify and modify the sound of a variety of small percussive objects placed atop the drumhead; and scraping, rubbing, and plucking the metal wires of the snare on the underside of the drum. Part of my intention in using a minimal set-up was to emphasize the visual and kinesthetic aspects of the performance, allowing my performative gestures to be read more clearly by the audience without the added visual distraction of superfluous percussion equipment. From my liminal position, I was also able to trigger *VNS* by moving a drumstick or my hands in the space just beyond the drum, which corresponded to the rear edge of the video camera's field of view. In this way, I was able to juxtapose acoustic and mediated sounds, blurring the boundaries between the two. Several people commented after the performance that they were unsure at times whether the sounds they were hearing were being generated by me or by *VNS*. As the performance developed, I gradually extended the scope of my movements further into the camera's field of view. At first, I did so by sending various objects, including drumsticks rolled across the floor and wind-up toy marching drummers, into the center of the space, their movements triggering additional percussive sounds. Eventually, I left my seat behind the snare drum and ventured into the illuminated performance area, continuing to blur the boundaries between acoustic and mediated sounds. Dragging a rubber superball mallet across the wooden planks of the floor, for example, elicited moans from the floorboards that were answered by a variety of moan-like sounds from the speakers.

My performance ended with a duet between waterphone and *VNS*. Invented in the 1960s by Richard Waters, the waterphone is an experimental percussion instrument that consists of a stainless steel vessel with bronze rods welded around its perimeter. The steel vessel amplifies the sound of the bronze rods when they are struck or bowed. A small amount of water inside the instrument creates an eerie glissando effect when the instrument is tilted while sounding. I had poured water into the instrument prior to the concert. However, I used *VNS*'s recorded sound of trickling water to add a theatrical element to the performance: I determined in advance the precise location that I needed to move my hands to elicit the water sound from the installation, marking the position of the shadow that my hands cast on the gallery floor in chalk. This would enable me to find the water sound during performance without having to search for it, or so I thought. One reviewer summarized the results as follows:

> At one point in the performance, Stewart was playing the waterphone . . . and was trying to coax a specific reaction out of *VNS*, namely, the sound of water trickling. The first two attempts were successful, Stewart mimicked filling his cupped palms with water and *VNS* reacted to these movements with soft swishing sounds. On the third attempt, he cupped his palm and recreated his movements in the exact same space as he had just moments ago, but silence followed. Again he tried—silence. He paused, tried once more, and an unruly growl emerged from the speakers. Stewart looked quizzically at the audience for a quick instant, which provoked a burst of laughter, and then the performance continued. Such are the difficulties of manipulating an "instrument" which is both invisible and intangible, and exists in a space of unclear boundaries. (Webb 2011)

Like a human improvising partner, *VNS* does not always respond the way we want, but the indeterminate aspects of the encounter create additional opportunities for improvisatory dialogue between body and machine. However, unlike generative computer programs such as George Lewis's *Voyager*, which improvises in the sense of not only responding to musical inputs from human performers but also generating new musical ideas, the indeterminate aspects of *VNS* do not generally stem from the system itself but from the considerable difficulty of a performer consistently locating an unmarked place in an empty three-dimensional space. By marking my shadow on the floor to help locate the zone of interaction associated with the water sound, I essentially collapsed a three-dimensional space into two dimensions. However, moving my hand even an inch or two toward or away from the camera lens resulted in a similarly positioned shadow on the gallery floor, but a different hand position in three-dimensional space and within the zones that are delineated by the video camera and image-processing software.

When I described my experience to Rokeby, he commented that throughout the history of *VNS*, most attempts to control the system in such a manner have often resulted in frustration on the part of the person(s) trying to do the controlling. This frustration likely stems from the fact that when we attempt to achieve a particular sonic result from *VNS*, we tend to be less receptive to the system's sonic responses; we are not as fully "in the moment." Certainly in my performance, the fact that the system did not respond as I expected it to pulled me temporarily out of the immersive flow state I had been experiencing. I have experienced something similar on numerous occasions when improvising in other contexts as well: during the course of a performance, the moments in which I try to insert a musical idea worked out in advance of the performance into the flow of musical events tend to be precisely the moments when the music—or at least my role therein—starts to unravel. The reason for this, I think, is that such thoughts often have the effect of pulling one's mind (and body) out of the improvising moment and out of the state of flow. I suspect this is why so many musicians caution younger improvisers to "not think" too much about playing in the moment of performance, but just play. Learning to let go, to give up the quest for control and just move our bodies, listen, and react is part of learning to flow. *Very Nervous System* provides opportunities for musicians and nonmusicians alike to develop this skill by sounding the body through a process of improvisatory play, deepening our awareness of our body's relationship to sound and technology in the process.

Notes

1. In this way, *VNS* behaves like a high-tech version of the simple elastic pallet bands that Hahn suggests help movers to achieve flow in chapter 8 of this book.

2. At the time of this writing, the Hayward Gallery in London is presenting a retrospective of invisible art titled *Invisible: Art about the Unseen 1957–2012*.

10. Stretched Boundaries

IMPROVISING ACROSS ABILITIES

Introduction and Conclusion by Sherrie Tucker

Essays by Pauline Oliveros, Neil Rolnick, Christine Sun Kim,
Clara Tomaz, David Whalen, Leaf Miller, and Jaclyn Heyen

Opening Parameters

Stretching exercise. What are the parameters of a community, a space, a performance opportunity? What happens if everyone touched (caressed, blocked, recognized, or ignored) by those parameters—the insides and outsides, soft centers and sharp edges—accessed ways to touch back and change its shape? And what if those lines yielded, responding not by shoring themselves up but by stretching to all of our different needs, desires, modes of contact? With no imperative to deny, elide, or escape our different orientations, we stretch the boundaries as we encounter them, all at once, receiving, at the same time, the tugs and twists from fellow stretchers from different directions. It's like Tomie Hahn's "Banding Encounters," discussed elsewhere in this volume (see chapter 8), only with everyday social, cultural, political, geographic, architectural, and institutional parameters (such as concert production!) to stretch, rather than giant rubber pallet bands. Across difference, we apprehend the boundaries as we perceive them, and s-t-r-e-t-c-h. What changes in this multidirectional and multisensory stretching encounter with boundaries—the "borders, frontiers, and diasporas" that David Borgo has described as "semipermeable musicking membranes" (2010, 131)?[1] Who are "we" who gather in this proposed dance of parameter-pulling and how do "we" connect? What does our stretching do to the sonic boundaries among differently sounding and perceiving bodies? As we stretch, what happens to the multiple perceived boundaries among us and between us, the slash between the "us"/"them," not to mention the unevenly palpable boundaries of the utopian "we" with room for all (except for the unnoticed others who didn't get in)? Let's stretch again. Observe. Repeat. What happens to communities, social relations, performance spaces, and opportunities if improvising across abilities is taken as an important precondition for stretching the boundaries? (What doesn't happen if it isn't?)

This chapter pulls at themes of "stretching boundaries" and "improvising across abilities," beginning with a specific set of parameters: eight people reflect on their participation in one or both in a series of two concerts, featuring artists of all abilities, called *Stretched Boundaries*, curated by Pauline Oliveros in March and June 2011. Coauthors were invited to contribute artist statements and/or essays that were related to the boundary-stretching performances of the concerts. Ostensibly, any event programmed by Oliveros— even a Skype meeting or conference panel—could go by that title; she is, after all, someone who has been stretching boundaries in performance, classes, workshops and intensives, research, and invention for over sixty years. Although the two concerts that provide the jumping-off point for this chapter certainly continued the "stretching" she is known for—expanding the horizons of what is listening, what is sounding, what composition can be, what technology can do—these particular concerts also stretched perceptual, social, and conceptual boundaries of ability/disability on an improvisatory sonic landscape. Building on insights from the social model of disability developed primarily in the field of disability studies and the disability rights movement, *Stretched Boundaries* takes "disability" as "a largely oppressive practice that cultures visit upon persons with, or regarded as having, functional impairments," to quote a leading scholar in disability studies of music (Lubet 2004, 133).[2] What if that culturally drawn oppressive line between "ability" and "disability" becomes the thing to sound by improvisers across abilities (not in one "voice," but in critical dissonance from many modes of sending and receiving, sounding and perceiving)? What new consciousness may emerge from sounding these borderlands?[3]

Again, this stretch is an extension rather than a break from Oliveros's ongoing exploration of the depths of listening and consciousness: "All cells of the earth and body vibrate," she reminds us. "Humans sense the sonosphere" in complex and multiple ways, according to the bandwidth and resonant frequencies and mechanics of the ear, skin, bones, meridians, fluids, and other organs and tissues of the body as coupled to the earth and its layers from the core to the magnetic fields as transmitted and perceived by the audio cortex and nervous system (Oliveros 2011, 162) (all of this with great variation, of course). What if the boundaries, not only of the most rigid social constructs but also of the most intentionally inclusive of our experimental, improvisatory communities, were conceived as cultures and practices in need of stretching?

What if improvising across abilities—or across differential modes of transmitting and perceiving in the sonosphere—was conceived as a precondition for critical dissonance? What if experimental musical communities committed to explorations of difference in realms such as harmonics, time, timbre, and form, were equally avid about the differential variables in musicians' and audience members' modes of sensory and perceptual relationships to sound waves, as well as differences in mobility, range of motion, ratios of voluntary/involuntary mobility, multiple modes of cognitive processing and language? What if this stretching, as with artistic exploration, was conceived as never finished; the embodied knowledge pooled in communities never wholly inclusive? Even my stretch to multiply *language* in the previous sentence privileges the linguistic. Stretch that to what Harter, Scott, Novak, Leeman, and Morris call "embodied rhetoricity"—a framework that does not presume every kind of knowledge stems from the verbal world, thus blocking the knowledge of nonverbal people and the collaborative potential of improvising across multiple modes of "sense-making" (Harter et al. 2006, 5).

The boundaries observed, reset, and stretched in the *Stretched Boundaries* concerts include bodily parameters; social, cultural, and medical definitions of abled/disabled bodies; improvisatory communities; and concert protocols and spaces. Whose improvising bodies come into contact with one another and whose don't, and how might these be stretched in intermedia performances? The concerts featured sound artists with disabilities as well as sound artists who are not considered as such by the normative standards of the society in which they operate (in disability studies, "able-bodied" is often replaced by "temporarily abled" to get at the social construction of this divide). *Stretched Boundaries* provided occasions for stretching the consciousness of concert goers, artists, technologists, and scholars, who shared prepared pieces, improvised across abilities, and reflected on the concerts' abilities to stretch our thinking about sound, bodies, and difference.

Not all of the people who performed in the concerts or spoke on the post-concert panels are included in this chapter—an effect of the boundaries of publication space. Those who appear together in this gathering-on-the-page comprise a diverse combination of sound artists, composers, scholars, and technologists, most with multiple orientations, for instance, a lawyer/inventor and an occupational therapist/drummer. Pauline Oliveros begins as she did in concert, by introducing the artists. Then four of the performers—Neil Rolnick, Christine Sun Kim, Clara Tomaz, and David Whalen—stretch out on the themes, identifying some shared and some different boundaries toward which they direct their sonic practices as artists. I return briefly *soto voce* to provide brief concert notes for the final act, in which two performers, Leaf

Miller and Jaclyn Heyen, share their off- and on-stage memories of what it meant to stretch concert boundaries in collaboration with young musicians from Abilities First, a school for children with disabilities in Poughkeepsie, New York. I return at the end to reprise my role as one of several after-concert panelists, pulling at themes from my place in the web as a scholar whose interest in improvising across abilities is connected to questions about communities of difference.

Pauline Oliveros: Curating *Stretched Boundaries*, the Concerts

The first *Stretched Boundaries* concert occurred on March 31, 2011, at Rensselaer Polytechnic Institute. The concert featured Tintinnabulate, an improvising ensemble of students and faculty that I direct at Rensselaer, along with guest artists with disabilities.

This concert of mixed abilities provided a public forum for artists with disabilities and artists without disabilities to share an evening of music-making together with their compositions and improvisations.

The inaugural *Stretched Boundaries* concert included MONO *Prelude* (solo for laptop and voice) composed and performed by Neil Rolnick, who suffered sudden hearing loss in his left ear one morning in his studio between 9:30 and 11 AM. It also included *Binary Reality with a Delay* (solo for transducers and delay pedals) composed and performed by Christine Sun Kim. Deaf since birth, Kim gave the audience a visual experience of the space they are in through surface noise that can be heard through her speaker-functioning head in *Binary Reality with a Delay*. Transducers, delay pedals, and microphones are among the instruments Kim used to explore media's practice of delaying live material, known as a broadcast delay. The standard delay time is seven seconds; she tripled this time to twenty-one seconds, indicating a reflection of her everyday communication. The concert also included *Configured Nights* (for Tintinnabulate with video), composed by Jonas Braasch; *Tai / Pi* (solo for analog electronics), composed and performed by Matthew Azevedo; and *Prometheus I* (for Tintinnabulate and digital painting), composed by Deborah Egloff with digital painting improvised by David Whalen. Whalen, injured in a ski accident at age nineteen, presents with quadriplegia. He is a musician, artist, and inventor. He improvises using his JamBoxx interface to play music and do digital painting. Shaped like a harmonica on a neck brace, the JamBoxx has a fully rotating mouthpiece that glides easily along a track. Breath and head movement provide an alternative for the pen and the hand.[4] Last, the concert featured *Collaborative Beats from Inside and Outside* (for dancers and Tintinnabulate) composed by Christine Sun Kim, who also danced, joined by Deborah Egloff, as well as *Deviations and Straight Line*, composed by Clara Tomaz, which is an experimental video piece that was adapted and performed with the live voice of the speech-impaired artist and improvised music by Tintinnabulate. Tomaz is an Italian new media artist producing videos and installations on themes of perception and point of view. She poses anthropological inquiries into areas of handicap, disability, life-threatening diseases, and corporeality in general.

The second *Stretched Boundaries* concert was included in Electroacoustic Music Studies 11, an international conference, at the Cell Theater in New York City on June 15, 2011. The concert included Neil Rolnick's *MONO Prelude*, Deborah Egloff's *Prometheus* with David Whalen, Clara Tomaz's *Deviations and Straight Line*, and also included the Play the Drum Band, comprising three children with disabilities from Abilities First School in Poughkeepsie, New York. The students performed with drums and AUMI (Adaptive Use Musical Instrument).[5] AUMI is a software interface developed by the Deep Listening Institute that affords access to musical sound-making for those with extremely limited movement. In addition to the students, the Play the Drum Band included Leaf Miller, occupational therapist and drummer/musician, and Rona Mannain, a teacher, both from Abilities First School, and Jaclyn Heyen, composer/singer and music technologist on staff at Deep Listening Institute.

The objective of the *Stretched Boundaries* concerts is to include artists with disabilities in more mixed-abilities public concerts and presentations to bring this population forward and also to bring artists without disabilities into contact with artists they might otherwise miss in an ableist culture. The boundaries that are stretched are multidirectional. To include the children from Abilities First also stretched boundaries of concert programming that typically separates artists from amateurs, masters from students, and adults from children. The musicians in the Play the Drum Band played like professionals and received an ovation from the audience of sophisticated electroacoustic artists, technologists, and listeners. They were a hit. They had never had an experience like this. Their performance in the second *Stretched Boundaries* concert succeeded in showing them, their fellow performers, and the audience that they are musicians.

Neil Rolnick: Composition in Perceptual Motion:
MONO Prelude (2009)

If we listen to the same piece of music, do you hear what I hear? When we look at a red stop sign, do we actually see the same thing? If we each take a bite of the same apple, do we experience the same taste sensation? Even if we agree we're both hearing a Bach fugue, looking at a red stop sign, and tasting a sweet apple, how do we compare our actual perceptions? As far as I know, we have no way to know someone else's actual sensation of sound or sight or taste.

On March 31, 2008, between 9:30 and 11:00 AM, I lost all hearing in my left ear. The loss is permanent and is accompanied by a loud white noise tinnitus where the left ear should be. With only one ear, I now hear the world monophonically. There is no stereo or surround sound in my world. Much of what I do hear I identify as distorted and unclear compared to my memory of what I heard before.

This experience heightened my awareness that our perceptions are indeed different, because my perception of sound now is quite different from what it was. I wanted to see if this was unique, so I started asking around—first to friends, then to a wide range of contacts on the Internet—to see if other people experienced similar changes to their perceptions of the world through their five senses. What I found was a flood of people who identify one of their five senses as impaired. They are aware that they see, or hear, or smell, or taste, or feel the world differently than others. When you listen to this piece, there's no way to know if you hear what I hear. Probably not. And if we're not hearing the same sounds, how can we agree on the music? Yet for the most part, we do. We may not like the same things, but we agree enough on what we hear to be able to discuss it, comment on it, and refer to it. The more I think about this, with the huge number of people in the world who identify their senses as being impaired in some way, the more amazed I am.

Several years later, I've collected and compiled some of these stories into an evening of music and media performance called MONO.

MONO is a series of musical meditations on the fragility of perception: its appreciation, its loss, and our capacity to adjust to changes in our perceptual abilities. MONO is a consideration of how our perceptions shape us. It is a series of twelve pieces that explore the loss of perceptual ability and the subsequent changes in how we relate to the world in response to that loss.

The MONO Prelude is a little foretaste of the larger work. It describes my experience of the initial few days and weeks of discovering and adjusting to the change in my hearing. Unlike in the larger piece, which involves instruments, singers, and various media, I perform Prelude alone, talking to the audience, controlling the laptop computer that modulates my voice.

Rather than trying to re-create exactly what I hear with my damaged ear, I take my listeners on a tour of my changing sonic and psychic perspectives as I discover the loss and come to the realization that it may not get better. I could have just given everyone an earplug with an embedded white noise generator, told them to stick it in their left ear, and been done with it. But it seems more meaningful to use the interplay of melodic material derived from the rhythms of my speaking voice, and real-time looping and processing of my voice, to try to capture the conflict between the unrelentingly negative developments of my condition, and my resolve to keep focused on what I can do to find a positive outcome for the experience.

Christine Sun Kim: Sound under New Ownership

I use the medium of sound as my voice because it gives me the most direct connection to society at large.[6] Sound carries a lot of status. Because I was born deaf, my learning process is shaped by American Sign Language (ASL) interpreters, subtitles on television, written conversations on paper, emails, and text messages. These communication modes have often conveyed filtered and limited information, which naturally leads to a loss of content and a delay in communication. Hence, my art practice mainly deals with socially informed ideas surrounding sound, and that entails processes of what I have called "unlearning sound etiquette" and challenging "vocal authorities."

My trajectory as an artist began with a simple question of sound ownership, since society places so much value on sound and vocal languages, leaving little room for visual languages. By contrast, within the culturally Deaf community, there is a sense of resentment toward sound as we are protective of our nonvocal language—there is a great need to insist on its social legitimacy. To use our voices is not a priority. I perceive this stance as an important attempt to secure a clear place for visual languages in society. My exploration of sound ownership has put me in a rather complex relationship with Deaf culture. It is my intention to approach sound by constantly pushing it to a different level of physicality and attempting to conceptually and physically translate my evolving relationship of sound into performances (and drawings), while unlearning society's views and etiquettes around it. Using my conceptual judgment and compromised understanding, I challenge and question the visual absence of sound and language, which I call two things: ghost and currency. Fortunately, with today's advanced technology, I claim alternative access to sound—not to a mere substitute sound.

One of my earliest performances (an untitled experiment that predated my later *Binary Reality with a Delay* by about two years) consisted of a recurring theme of embodiment and everyday communication; I used and amplified my own voice box through a transducer that was placed on my throat and used a delay pedal as a means of translation that resulted in my vocalization with a ten-second delay. This awakening experience allowed me to recognize the limitations within languages and the need to put my cultural identity aside to study my own vocalization, as I sometimes forget what originates internally. The idea of "a voice box" can be politically charged to both signers and nonsigners. I would like to resituate the box, take it away from politics, and bring it into the realm of a personal and intimate understanding. The transducer method offered a tool to signify my presence from within and my whole being and presented delayed sound as a memory. This formed an internal and closed feedback system with my own body, widening the distance between the audience and myself.

I did a choir project called *Face Opera* where I had my deaf friends "say" rhythmic concepts with their faces only and their hands tucked in their jacket pockets. It was a commentary on ASL as a nonlinear and spatial language. There are multiple layers happening simultaneously, and it is highly inflected compared to linear English. Grammatical aspects of ASL could be likened to keys on a piano. Imagine that each aspect correlates to a key: one key is placement, another key is space, another is facial expression, hand shape, repetition, and so forth. When played together, each of these aspects simultaneously combines with others to form a word or concept. In this project, we took turns in conducting and shared conducting four separate scores that I had composed, which were displayed on an iPad. The scores were developed from the different parameters of ASL (placement, space, etc.). My intention was to tune out of linguistic machinery through the removal of grammar to maximize the sonic materiality of the experience. Roughly 30–40 percent of ASL is the manual production of the language, while the rest is expressed on the face and through body movement. This performance indicates the multiple layers that are lost when societies privilege spoken languages at the expense of visual and spatial languages.

I also produced a series of study drawings by appropriating notational elements from three different systems and one language—graphic notation, musical notation, ASL, and ASL "glossing" (a somewhat written system with English words, but not translation)—to reinvent a new syntax and structure for my compositions. Like sound, ASL cannot be captured on paper; thus, I combined these various systems in an attempt to open up a new space of authority/ownership and rearrange hierarchies of information.

Someone once asked me, "How do you capture your position in this world through your work?" That very question sums up both my constant dialogue with society and my practice as an artist.

Clara Tomaz: *Deviations and Straight Line*

My personal interest in language as a sonic resource was generated by a speech impairment I developed in 2007. The rehabilitation process I went through after a major mouth surgery made me consider the real nature of language and transfer those considerations into my art practice. With the help of several speech pathologists, my voice and speech rehabilitation required me to train my vocal cords to be able to produce some basic sound and modulation of pitches; find alternative solutions with lips, palate, and throat for the pronunciation of phonemes that could not count on a functioning tongue anymore; practice with the coordination of phonemes for the formation of words, and with words for the formation of sentences. In this personal experience, my perception of language and sound changed dramatically; having to work on each phoneme individually made me sensibly aware that language is an assemblage of sounds just as the body is an assemblage of organs.

The idea of language as an assemblage of sounds is creatively expressed in my work *The IPA Keyboard* (2009–10),[7] a MIDI keyboard that plays the forty-four phonemes of the American language and can be used at three different levels. In the first two levels the musician's objective is using phonemes for the obvious formulation of recognizable words and a nursery rhyme, whereas at the last level the musician uses the phonemes as pure sounds and musical notes, with the result of a very unusual interpretation of Schumann's scores for *Dichterliebe*, Opus 48.

Later I decided to work directly with my own voice and sound articulation. The sound I can produce as a human being is the expression of my personal consciousness. It makes all of my vibrations, emotions, perceptions, and thoughts resound in the space around me. And if my body (speech-impaired or not) is the instrument that allows me to play the sound, then the sound I produce becomes a vehicle for the expression of my consciousness.

My video with performance, *Deviations and Straight Line* (2010–11), explores language as a major sonic resource and expression of consciousness. The Tintinnabulate ensemble improvises music through traditional instruments and electronic devices while the speech-impaired vocalist performs preverbal sounds, phonemes, isolated words, sentences, and finally a whole narration. The vocalist uses language in all its aspects, from pure sound (preverbal modulations), to fundamentals of language (phonemes), association of meaning (words and sentences), and organized speech (narration). The choice of guided improvisation for the ensemble, in place of traditional composition, contributes to the definition of language and sound as vehicles for the expansion of consciousness in the external space. The Tintinnabulate musicians accompany the vocalist by interpreting their own individual consciousnesses in the moment. Consciousness is in constant becoming because it reacts to the external world that it perceives through the body, and the sound that interprets such reaction (and is performed by the body as a musical instrument) ends up being connoted by different qualities of rhythm, pitch, and color, depending on the moment it is performed. The narration performed by the vocalist, and reiterated by animated writing on the video visuals, is about acceptance of others' disability and societal assumptions connected to diversity and disability: whether following a *Straight Line* obsessively in life or accepting diverse *Deviations* is a personal choice that should come from our consciousness as human beings.

David Whalen: Digital Art and Music for People with High Levels of Disability

There's a quiet moment at the start of a new digital painting or musical performance when you get to enjoy concentrating on the countless options that digital technologies allow—not at your fingertips but in your consciousness. When you paint digitally with a computer, you may question if you are *actually* painting. Yet—pulsing with satisfaction and submerged in fun—I feel that I am. The same is true when I trigger my virtual electric guitar synthesizer. What I hear is what any electric guitarist would hear. We're both thinking about the next note—but I use a controller that is activated by head and breath.

As a quadriplegic for over thirty years, and as someone who aspires to art and music, I have experienced obstacles as well as pathways opened at a breathtaking pace by technology. I write this essay with voice recognition software, an extraordinary change from the past, but now just another tool that is widely available, even on my cell phone. Alternate controllers reduce exclusionary requirements of fine dexterity in art and music; software allows people to trigger notes, phrases, and loops with a single switch. There is a tremendous sense of empowerment when you have the right controller. For me, the use of breath and head movement provides an alternative for the pen and the hand.

Scanning techniques allow people with low dexterity to expand and shrink areas of the work as needed. Software such as Artrage (a commercial product with a free version) increases participation by people with limited mobility through features that allow for changing scale, rotating, shading, layering, and independent set-up. Digital art allows for reiterations in the development of a project. Because you can go at your own pace, fatigue can be reduced. There is no cost for canvas, no cost for ink, no cost for recording tape; in fact there is an infinite number of canvases and unfathomable recording space with which to be creative. You can collaborate with people all over the world by transferring files and working on projects simultaneously.

FIG 10.1: *Wings & Digital Things*: Adaptive art using digital medium and breath-controlled joystick. Photo by David Whalen.

Persons with locked-in syndrome or high levels of quadriplegia may capture musical expressions through preplanning and recording. A complex musical score could be performed using one switch to trigger parts that were weeks in the planning. I may not be able to shoot my fingers across a piano keyboard; nevertheless, I want to play complex melodies and change scales, so the use of presets is very important. I'm also not averse to triggering samples and preprogrammed phrases, but it lengthens set-up time and also triggers questions about notions of performance versus recording. I feel that it depends on people's abilities and the types of music they wish to perform and explore. Single-switch inputs can be encouraged and viewed as part of the performance as a whole.

It energizes you to share your work with other people. In the first *Stretched Boundaries* concert at Rensselaer, I painted live on stage in multimedia improvisation with Tintinnabulate.[8] The bowed and wind instruments, grand piano, and experimental electronics in *Prometheus I* brought deep levels of emotion and feeling, sped up the sense of time, and heightened the senses. The sound worked to push away other concerns, and I could focus more deeply on painting. I also performed at the Cell Theater via Skype. Skype is very useful, but the interaction can be isolating. It is different from the immersive and intense experience of performing onstage with the musicians.

The Rensselaer concert was also special in that it was the first time we used a large screen, away from the solemn usual activities generated at the computer. You try to share an emotional state at some level in the process. Usually my painting involves many iterations; I return to the medium again and again in quiet. Only after I have the satisfaction of completeness would I dare share my work. There is a feeling of risk in painting live in a matter of minutes in front of many individuals you may not know. The reward is simply to enjoy the process and find a shared emotion with others present.

Leaf Miller: "Goin' to New York City, Play the Drum"

For the second Stretched Boundaries *concert, the* Play the Drum Band *made its performance debut, using drums, percussion, and the* AUMI, *an excellent example of the stretching of home computing to musical instrument developed by the Deep Listening Institute. (The* AUMI *is a free-download software interface that turns any computer with a plug-in or built-in camera into an extremely flexible musical instrument that adapts to users by tracking even the slightest movement). The* Play the Drum Band *consists of students from Abilities First School in Poughkeepsie, New York, and is led by led by musician and occupational therapist Leaf Miller and assisted by Jaclyn Heyen. The* Play the Drum Band *was created for people of all abilities to come together in a welcoming and inclusive musical community. Miller shares what it was like for her to prepare the Abilities First community for this unprecedented trip for three of the students to play in the New York City concert and what happened.*

Preconcert Stretching

It was really important to me for the students to take ownership of the whole experience and the process. This was the first time they were performing as members of a band, going out into the community and actually putting themselves out as musicians. It was also the debut public performance of the AUMI.

Musically, I demanded a high level. I wanted the audience to have a great musical experience and not just say, "That's good for a bunch of kids with disabilities." I didn't want our musical performance to be in a different category from other performances on the program. The band included three students, D and R on drums and percussion, and A on percussion and the AUMI, and three adults: myself on drum, Jaclyn Heyen from the Deep Listening Institute on the AUMI, and Rona Mannain, a teacher from Abilities First, playing percussion. So we are an intergenerational all-abilities band.

The logistics were challenging. They involved the kids, the parents, teachers, social worker, nurse, getting funding for the trip, making arrangements, every detail down to "Where are we getting the lunches?" We have one student who uses a wheelchair and has intense medical needs. She was in on the early development of the AUMI, and we wanted her to be part of this concert. She rehearsed with us, but she could not make that trip physically. Another parent was not willing to let her daughter go with us to New York City. When you are a parent of a child with a disability, you are just that much more protective. Then I come along saying, "Oh, come on, let her go, this is a great opportunity." It took me a while to really comprehend where that parent was coming from, and that child did not end up going.

Stretching the Audience

At the Cell Theater, the Play the Drum Band members were all doing very different things, and they were able to express themselves individually, while working collectively in the group. Unfortunately, many people tend to put all these kids with special needs in a box because it's what we do as a society with people who are "different." This time the audience had to see them as *musicians* and as *unique individuals*, and that is definitely a way to stretch people. In the beginning we all played drums and percussion. Then A moved to the AUMI. Her playing was projected on a huge screen for the audience. At that point, the audience joined in, clapping and being part of the rhythm, and the line between audience and performer disappeared.

Stretching Ourselves

I am so proud of the students and what they were able to accomplish. We have come a long way. This public concert was an amazing acknowledgment of years of hard work for all of us. The *Stretched Boundaries* concert was not just about pushing the audience to new and unexpected places. I know all of us in the band and connected to the band got really stretched. Maybe that was what Pauline Oliveros had in mind all the time, because while it seems like it's about stretching other people's boundaries and blowing other peoples' minds, it actually totally blew our minds.

The next step is to try to open future opportunities for these young musicians. The big question is: What place do these exceptional kids have in our world when they get out of school and become young adults? Are they included in our thoughts, in our hearts, in our lives, in our communities?

Jaclyn Heyen: Wanted, Room to Stretch

Jaclyn Heyen also participated in the Stretched Boundaries *concert. The music technologist shares her perspectives on the challenges of seeking a venue that can accommodate musicians of all abilities.*

Accessibility is a more complex issue than many people realize. It was a challenge to find an appropriate venue for the *Stretched Boundaries* concert, but it was also an opportunity to broaden the understanding of venue owners and managers. Even after we selected a space and discussed set-up for the artists, when we arrived, there were no spaces in the audience for wheelchairs. When I said there needed to be at least one, the person in charge of setting up the space asked if I was expecting anyone in a wheelchair. I said, "I didn't know people in wheelchairs needed to make reservations!" Space was cleared, but only after I spoke up. In staging a concert that would work for as broad a range of bodies of musicians and potential audience members as possible, we were also creating awareness about abilities.

Preparation at every level was needed to create as inclusive a concert environment as possible. This meant not only inquiring about accessibility but asking for exact measurements of doorways and aisles and bathrooms. Not all wheelchairs are the same size. People aren't the same size, so chairs aren't the same size. Even if the space had an accessible bathroom, some of the students would also need a changing table. Some students would need to be taken out of their chairs every few hours to lie down and be fed via feeding tubes. And each chair works differently. Some have a really good turning radius, some do not. M was one of the three students who helped develop the software and had the most experience, and it was her senior year. We really wanted her to come, but her chair could not be accommodated along with other needs, so it wasn't possible.

At Abilities First, we prepared the students (who were able to make the trip) to do something they had never done before. We prepared ourselves for what it meant to bring students to New York City and how to keep everyone happy and safe. We also had to prepare the other performers. The Abilities First students needed to travel a long distance. It made sense for them to have the last sound check. Because sound checks never stay on time, and the students had never performed in public, it was important for everyone else to try especially hard to stay on time. I had to make sure there were no wires on the floor, because somebody could trip.

I wanted the students to be treated like professionals. When they arrived, I first welcomed them into the space, and then I made sure to introduce them to all of the other performers (all of whom were adults) as fellow artists. They had a lot of questions and they wanted to see what was going on. But the space was not conducive to their experiencing part of the concert from the house. Audience conventions in electronic music are somewhat more relaxed than in classical music. Even so, there is an expectation that people will sit still and listen. If the students joined the audience, they would not have been able to ask questions, access the bathrooms, or leave if they didn't like it (some of them had sensory issues). Instead, they listened from backstage.

Their part of the performance was truly amazing. I played AUMI along with one of the students. A is an amazing performer, and she connected with the audience as soon as she started playing the AUMI. Her performance skills made me come out of my shell of hiding behind a computer. Her range of mobility is narrower than my own, yet I had to stretch my own boundaries to dance and play right along with her. We couldn't have asked for a better response. It was such a great experience that I will remember for a lifetime.

Conclusion: Pulling at Themes

In this chapter—as in our bodies, communities, and sound practices as artists, inventors, therapists, teachers, technologists, and audience members—we begin and end in different places and contingent places. An appropriate conclusion would not try to crunch these together. But leaving us all to dangle in our separate stretching exercises does not seem right either.

Let me stretch my notion of "conclusion" to a situated response about how I am pulled by the pieces and where I am moved to pull.

It seems as though what we share is a process-approach to continually stretching boundaries in improvised sounding from multiple orientations to sonic vibration. Conceptually, a stretched boundary is not the same as a crossed boundary (someone from one side crosses over to improvise within the parameters of the other side), or a violently erected/resisted/endured/ unnoticed ever-shifting boundary, or even a brand-new boundary. It isn't like lines redrawn on the map to codify the seizing, withholding, and otherwise redistricting of power, wealth, and rights, or in the sand that we know will wash away at the end of the afternoon, or a new set of labels on the record bin separators. What calls to me, as I ponder our many perspectives side by side, is the sense that we share differently situated commitments to "improvising across abilities" as a rich site for boundary stretching that pulls at paradoxes of identity, community, and difference.

Each author identifies and seizes a boundary and stretches it, both in sound practice, and in these pieces of writing. Neil Rolnick stretches composition to account for difference and changes in sound perception, in his own experience of hearing loss, and in the inability to really know whether how we perceive sound is the same as anyone else's perception (the auditory portion of what neuroscientists and philosophers refer to as the "qualia problem").[9] In other words, his piece is specific to changes in his own relationship to hearing, and how that affects him as a composer, but it is also about the myth of sameness in hearing that is seldom addressed by composers, musicians, and audiences who are not people with disabilities.[10] Christine Sun Kim stretches the boundaries of "sound ownership" in ways that confront both the dominant cultural primacy of sound while also pulling at the limits of Deaf culture's rejection of sound, motivated by the struggle for recognition of visual language. At issue is not the fact that she is deaf, but the solipsism of the "hearing world" that privileges one kind of sound processing, and the oppositional stance in sound politics in Deaf culture, both of which render the Deaf sound artist a controversial figure. Clara Tomaz turns our attention to the phenomenology of contingent, shifting boundaries, staging encounters between two kinds of simultaneously operating orientations—straight line and deviation—as modes of navigating space, language, and consciousness. David Whalen shares strategies for breaking boundaries of access to digital music and painting for people with high levels of disability made possible by new technologies that stretch the boundaries of affordable home computing. Leaf Miller and Jaclyn Heyen reflect on the multidirectional stretching demanded by, generated in, and extending outward from the process of creating a public piece for the second *Stretched Boundaries* concert with the students from Abilities First School.

It doesn't worry me that the boundaries in this chapter are not always the same. Taken together, these pieces suggest that embodied knowledge of boundaries is neither singular nor plural but multiple and differential—and that improvisation across abilities is a way to mutually benefit from and share in doing something together that we couldn't do alone. And, if we do it well, we make a new "we" to stretch next time around. Improvisation across abilities gets at the necessary differential multiplicity of critical stretching—a practice for working out the tautness that sets in around difference in cultures plagued by habits of (illusory) sameness and other violent policing borders dividing bodies into norm and Other. The boundaries are never quite right— but the goal of getting them so beckons. Improvising across abilities seems a promising method for developing stretchable, adaptable boundaries that are up to the task of constant recalibration for differential usability and consciousness. Improvisation across abilities is a methodology for identifying and adapting boundaries, tight or slack, noticed and unnoticed, carefully, so as not to break their potential for connectivity.

Boundaries are deceptively active, even when they pass invisibly under our feet. Boundaries organize ways of knowing—writing can be stretching. I just used the phrase "under our feet," unconsciously shaped by an ordering system that presumes a particular kind of body and mode of mobility. I started to edit that sentence to "feet or wheels" and immediately deleted it, wishing not to elide the difference it makes in navigation and analysis of boundaries to be a wheelchair user. Stretching is not just obeying rules of "political correctness," or wanting not to "offend." Tomaz and Kim, in different ways, help me to understand that language always needs more curb cuts—and these are not achieved through rule-making alone but through improvisatory exploration, performance, practice, perceiving, and stretching into/against/and out from many cultural, social, political systems through which people encounter and try to order the sonosphere. When the earth moves, those closest to the fault lines are more likely to detect shifts in plate tectonics that displace some, while passing undetected to others. Societies are variable, but tend to be erected on many fault lines, many orientations to noticeably shaky or seemingly stable ground. We need each other, and we need to send and receive each other's stretch.

Whether encountered as built or natural, enabling or disabling, boundaries often masquerade as solid, still, intractable objects. But check back later—or listen deeply, as Oliveros might say—and *whoosh*, they are someplace else, grumbling or silent, depending on where you are situated in the wake. Sometimes boundaries shift without much fuss or notice, sometimes with tumult, disorientation, and displacement. Sometimes a change in boundaries opens pathways, reconfigures social relations, and even transforms social consciousness. New placements may constrict or expand—but always, they reconfigure. We will not perceive the full range of effects of any given shift from the surface, and we will not perceive them in the same ways. Zoom earthward to the lines on a map—and attend to the breath that emanates from those shape-shifting lines: how do boundaries differently interact with those who encounter them? What difference does it make to be this body, at this border, with this trajectory, this ability, at this historical moment?

Consider the space in which you read this book, or in which you improvise with others—what boundaries have already shifted in the history of this environment? What social justice movements, technological innovations, creative thinking/tinkering, passage of bills and laws and policy papers, and other embodied improvisatory activities have resulted in stretching the boundaries so you and I and the people with whom we collaborate may gather in this space? What would it take to stretch these boundaries to accommodate a (wider) wheelchair, an increased or decreased range of mobility, all degrees of voluntary and involuntary movement, an endless variety of ways to perceive and produce sound vibrations, an overall multiplication of sensory difference and modes of cognitive processing? What would it take to question and stretch the boundaries of our most precious, experimental, adventurous containers, make them even better? If the room we love most already seems inclusive, it takes courage to ask who isn't here who could bring another stretch to this space, extend the improvising community even further. Who would the "we" be then, and what could "we" do together that we don't do now?

To stretch a boundary is to extend or twist its implications to make something new. Improvisers are, among other things, stretchers of boundaries.

To improvise across abilities is to stretch sound, communities, and consciousness.

Notes

1. For an excellent introduction to the varieties of boundaries engaged by "musickers," see David Borgo's (2010) introduction to a special issue of the *Journal of Popular Music Studies* (which he guest-edited with Kenneth S. Habib), based on papers from the IASPM-US, 2009 conference, " 'Don't Fence Me In': Borders, Frontiers and Diasporas."

2. For more scholarship in disability studies and music, see Lubet (2010) as well as his coedited "To Dance beneath the Diamond Sky with One Hand . . ." (Lubet and Sheffi 2008), a two-part special issue of the *Review of Disability Studies: An International Journal*. See also Davidson (2008), Lerner and Straus (2006), and Straus (2011).

3. I do not take this reference to Gloria Anzaldúa's (1987) new mestiza consciousness lightly—through writing specifically about queer Chicana subjectivity, her theoretical analysis of critical transformations of consciousness that may emerge from subjects who live not on one side or the other of a boundary but operate in liminal spaces yields important insights for scholars in disability studies. See, for example, Ramlow (2006).

4. See http://www.jamboxx.com for more information.

5. See http://www.deeplistening.org/adaptiveuse for more information, a tutorial, and free download. For more on how it is being used and studied, see Oliveros et al. (2011).

6. For more information on this artist, please visit http://www.christinesunkim.com.

7. Documentation of *The IPA Keyboard* and other original work mentioned in this article can be found at http://www.claratomaz.com.

8. See a video of the performance by Clara Tomaz on Vimeo, "David Whalen in Stretched Boundaries 2011," http://vimeo.com/29467494.

9. See, for example, Nagel (1974). For recent work on improvisation, music, and qualia, see Borgo (2005). Musical perception is not only different across different perceivers, but on different listenings by the same perceiver. See Monson (2008).

10. For an excellent discussion of varieties of hearing and other registers of sound perception, see Glennie (1993).

PART IV

Gender, Trauma, and Memory

11. The Erotics of Improvisation in Ann-Marie MacDonald's *Fall on Your Knees*

Gillian Siddall

Ann-Marie MacDonald's novel *Fall on Your Knees* underscores a nexus of improvisation and bodies in ways that posit human engagement as always provisional, sometimes joyous, and often violent.[1] Noisy bodies sound and re-sound in improvisational relationships shot through with desire but forcibly constrained by race, gender, sex, and class. The novel juxtaposes the kind of improvised music that Materia and her daughter Frances perform with the classical, notated music that James insists their daughter Kathleen pursue in her professional career, although Kathleen later embraces jazz and blues.[2] Both Materia's and Frances's performances are characterized as experimental—interpolating fragments of popular and classical music in ways that not only subvert classical musical forms but also subvert, or at least disrupt, prevailing power relations that privilege white, male heterosexual identity. The political work that Materia's performances do is very much a product of co-creation with her audiences, in that she eschews the formal separation of performer and audience and instead engages the audience in the production of her music, very much in the style of burlesque performers of that time. Frances's performances as a striptease artist engage differently with her audiences, as she subverts their expectations by parodying conventional representations of sexualized female bodies under the male gaze. Both Materia's and Frances's performances destabilize notions of meaning and identity as coherent and unitary, and they thereby open up the possibility of what Judith Butler calls "political resignification"—the potential for new meanings, new forms of signification (1993, 191). Their performances also assert a profound and complex connection between bodies and signification, sensuality and meaning, what Ellen Waterman and I have referred to in the introduction to this collection as an erotics of improvisation. This notion is explored even more fully in the complex relationship that unfolds between Frances and Teresa Taylor, the latter a black West Indian woman, who, in a magic realist moment, impregnates Frances with a bullet, an action that surprisingly leads to an affirmation of the Piper family that has suffered so much violence.

While musical improvisation, especially free improvisation, is sometimes seen both as an example of and a model for articulating social and political resistance to oppression (Fischlin, Heble, and Lipsitz 2013), improvisation is not, as these authors acknowledge, impervious to oppressive discursive forms. Improvised music does, indeed, have a significant historical connection to African American resistance to oppression. George Lewis and others have done important work on this history and the ways it continues to resonate for contemporary musicians. Scholars such as Lisa Barg, Sherrie Tucker, and Julie Dawn Smith also remind us that female musicians have been marginalized within jazz culture, and consequently not given full access to the resistant potential of jazz and improvised music, and that marginalization persists today. Clearly, and not surprisingly, any kind of political work that can be done by improvised music is always fraught, caught up as it must be in the complexity of discursive formations in which it is created. *Fall on Your Knees* situates the liberatory potential of improvised performance very clearly in the context of the violent oppression that often mutes it.

To situate the analysis that follows, I provide some context for the trauma that unleashes the cycle of violence that James perpetrates on his wife and daughters. *Fall on Your Knees* is an epic story of the life of James and Materia Piper and their daughters in New Waterford, Cape Breton, at the turn of the nineteenth century. Primarily a mining town at that time, New Waterford is characterized in the novel as a fairly diverse community comprising immigrants from Scotland, Lebanon, and the Caribbean. This diversity serves as an important component of the novel, as it foregrounds issues of race and ethnicity and of the ongoing negotiation of power in the context of identity politics. James's overriding concern throughout the novel is to elide ethnic difference within his own family—to underplay his wife's Lebanese heritage, not only in terms of her own markers of identity but, even more urgently for him, in terms of his four daughters' identity, especially his eldest daughter, Kathleen.

James's relationship with his wife and daughters is often mediated through music. Indeed, in the opening paragraph of Book 1, the narrator tells us that James's mother taught him to "read the classics, play piano and to expect something finer in spite of everything. And that was what James wanted for his own children" (MacDonald 1997, 7). For James, then, the significance of music and the literary classics is that they are forms of social currency, and for this reason he wants his children to have access to them. Interestingly, however, as a young man, James has a glimpse of music as a politicized entity, when his abusive father leaves him and his mother, but not before dismantling the piano—a move that profoundly and literally silences the house and foreshadows the kind of silencing James himself later attempts to impose on his own family. At this point in his life, however, he resists this form of oppression and spends six months reassembling the piano: "All he wanted at fifteen and a half was to hear his mother play the piano once more, but she was dead of a dead baby before he finished the job" (8). The narrator's bald statement makes a clear link between the father's destruction of the piano and the toxic environment he created in the home that culminates in the death of James's mother in childbirth. James's response to his mother's death is characterized in relation to the piano. Before he leaves the family home, he takes a moment to play the piano, but in a way that suggests a highly emotional response to it: "He came back in, sat down at the piano and plunged into 'Moonlight Sonata'. Stopped after four bars, got up, adjusted C sharp, sat down and swayed to the opening of 'The Venetian Boat Song.' Satisfied, he stopped after five bars, took the bottle of spirits from his mother's sewing basket, doused the piano and set it alight" (8). His abbreviated versions of Beethoven's and Mendelssohn's pieces are suggestive of his foreshortened emotional well-being and social responsibility. His need to burn the piano is a violent response to the loss of his mother, and an annihilation of the recuperative possibilities offered by music. Although he continues for a while to work as a piano tuner, his own relationship with music remains dysfunctional.

After James and Materia are married, he takes on an authoritarian role in the house, pushing Materia to read the classics and insisting they stay at home rather than going out to dance and socialize. Soon she is pregnant and crying all the time, her only two activities walking on the shore and playing the piano. James is busy taking night classes at Saint Francis Xavier University, with a view to becoming a lawyer and a respectable, "cultivated man. A gentleman" (MacDonald 1997, 21). For him, reading the classics is a key way to do that; as he puts it, "Books were not an expense; they were an investment" (21). For him canonical literature is a signifier of class; he is not looking for an intellectual or emotional experience, but wants to acquire the demeanor of the learned and thereby improve his socioeconomic status.

Materia's response to James's drive for respectability is to shift from playing classical music to experimenting with improvisation: "lately she'd begun playing whatever came into her head whether it made sense or not—mixing up fragments of different pieces in bizarre ways, playing a hymn at top speed, making a B-minor dirge out of 'Pop Goes the Weasel', and all with the heavy hand of a barrelhouse hack" (MacDonald 1997, 24). When James hears her playing, he describes it in a way that dismisses it as simply noise: "Pound, pound, pound on the piano keys in the middle of the night. No wit any more, however juvenile, no naughty ditties, just discords. Tantrums. Fine, let her exhaust herself. *Plank, splank, splunk* into the wee hours" (24). To him, the sounds Materia makes are a discordant manifestation of childish anger. For Materia, however, this playing marks the beginning of her move to a very different ethos of meaning-making from James's, one that eschews linear, notated music and instead explores a highly physical relationship with the piano—she is pounding on it—a fragmentary and dissonant approach that juxtaposes fragments of preexisting musical forms in an experimental manner.[3]

Although the novel does not explicitly historicize Materia's musical style, it is reminiscent of emerging experimental music of the time. Consider, for example, composer Charles Ives, whose turn-of-the-century pieces are filled with juxtaposed fragments of hymns and brass bands, church bells and Beethoven sonatas (Burkholder 1996). Viewed in this light, Materia's improvising may be seen as part of a significant shift in European and American music occurring at the beginning of the twentieth century, a shift that proved challenging to many listeners. In this context, James's characterization of her music as "noise" calls to mind Jacques Attali's argument that historically music that was initially regarded as noise has been a harbinger and even an agent of social change. As Attali provocatively states, noise can destroy "orders to structure a new order" (1985, 20). Indeed, he sees music as a significant indicator and purveyor of changing power relations:

> Music is prophecy. Its styles and economic organization are ahead of the rest of society because it explores, much faster than material reality can, the entire range of possibilities in a given code. It makes audible the new world that will gradually become visible, that will impose itself and regulate the order of things; it is not only the image of things, but the transcending of the everyday, the herald of the future. For this reason musicians, even when officially recognized, are dangerous, disturbing, and subversive; for this reason it is impossible to separate their history from that of repression and surveillance. (11)

Whether one agrees with these provocative assertions, they provide a useful critical framework for the novel's representations of the potentially subversive effects of music. James's violent reaction to Materia's music mirrors the larger social and historical power struggles around music identified by Attali. James finds Materia's music "disturbing," so much so that he eventually locks up the piano so she can no longer play it. When he does finally allow her to play again, it is only to accompany their daughter Kathleen, a promising classical singer, and she is to play "exactly what was put in front of her" (MacDonald 1997, 36).

James's move to repress her musical sensibility is thwarted when Materia begins, without telling him, to work at the local movie theater, accompanying silent films on the piano and playing for vaudeville troupes. Although the novel does not give the precise date for these activities, it is clear that she takes on this work sometime between 1907 and 1909. Rick Altman, in his history of sound and silent film, identifies this period as a transitional one from the prominence of vaudeville and burlesque theaters, which first introduced silent films, to the establishment of small nickelodeons and then more formal movie theatres (2004). The style of music initially used to accompany silent films was drawn from burlesque. The role of music in burlesque theater, Altman argues, "strongly contradict[ed] today's assumptions regarding narrative causality, textual coherence, and musical integration. Driven by financial considerations and interpersonal machinations, the late-nineteenth-century theater not only allowed but virtually required the regular use of interpolated songs and dances throughout theatrical performances of the most varied nature" (33–34). Altman calls this an "aesthetic of discontinuity" (51), whereby "theaters systematically supported interpolated performances of songs, dances, or variety acts entirely unrelated to the plot of the play" (52). Tim Anderson argues that this kind of accompaniment also predominated in presentations of silent film, and he emphasizes the importance of the collaborative role the musician and audience developed in producing meaning: "The noisy conduct of these urban audiences and their effect on the nature of musical performances within these spaces reveal quite a bit about the potential power of the audience in early cinema. Not only could these audiences influence what selections the musician made, but they could alter the meanings found in the dominant narrative of the film. It is no secret that skillful improvisation can be a powerful and humorous form of critical commentary that assists in discovering unmined possibilities of signification" (1997, 15).

Materia's style of playing, whereby she juxtaposed fragments of diverse musical pieces and styles, positions her as being historically consistent with burlesque and silent film accompaniment at the turn of the century, and the novel characterizes her as having the kind of cocreative relationship with her audience described by Anderson. What James regarded as noise in her playing becomes an important part of a process of signification in concert with the audience members. Consider, for example, the following passage, which describes Materia's accompaniment of film and live acts in a vaudeville theater. She begins to interpolate fragments of diverse musical forms and genres in a way that has no obvious link with the visual narrative. Indeed, her playing provides an ironic commentary on the predictable plots and characters: "Now and then a locomotive sped towards the audience through 'I Love You Truly,' and ran over them to 'Moonlight Sonata.' Villains struggled with virgins to 'The Wedding March' and tenors saved the day to 'Turkey in the Straw'. Performers complained, but the audience ate it up when rabbits emerged from the top hats to discordant splats and women were sawn in half to 'Nearer My God to Thee'" (MacDonald 1997, 53).

Materia is engaged in a lively and profound process of cocreation with her audiences, as they challenge traditional narratives and the ideology contained within them. Instead of the expected loud, fast music to accompany the hurtling train, she plays a lilting "I Love You Truly." Perhaps the most telling decision she makes in this particular accompaniment is to play "The Wedding March" while "villains struggle with virgins," suggesting, perhaps, her own disenchantment with her marriage; certainly it is an indictment of the power imbalance between men and women and a critique of conventional ideas of romance. The hero rescues his damsel in distress to the tune of "Turkey in the Straw," a nineteenth-century folk song, whose nonsensical lyrics are spoken by a hapless rural dweller. The villain, the music would suggest, rather than the hero, gets to marry the girl. The woman about to be sawn in half, presumably by a magician, is accompanied by "Nearer My God to Thee," a dour prediction of the outcome. Through the repetition of narrative conventions, complicated by the improvised interlacing of musical and visual systems of signification, Materia and her audiences are able to disrupt dominant social codes in noisy and unpredictable ways.

Materia's improvised accompaniment serves to point out the ambiguity of music as a representational system: "The audience leans slowly back as the locomotive appears on the horizon, tinkling towards them at first, birds singing— just another day in the country—then the first hint of doom as the train looms larger; a switch from major to minor, chugga chugga, here it comes rattling and rolling whistle screeching, punctuated by the warning *woo-woo*, escalating through the landscape in a melody of mad elation, hurtling over the keys till all erupts in chaos, notes and birds fly asunder and the speeding iron horse thunders right over our heads and past us" (MacDonald 1997, 46). On one hand, this description of Materia's playing suggests the ability of the music to mimic the action on the screen: the classic move from major to minor to connote an emotional change from normalcy to terror, the "melody of mad elation" capturing the runaway train, which is described as "hurtling over the keys." Indeed, one could argue that the conflation in that final image of her playing and the film's narrative, where the train, rather than Materia's hands, is described as moving the piano keys, signifies that the two artistic forms, music and film, are so stable as signifying systems of meaning that they can merge as one. On the other hand, the use of tropes in this passage simultaneously asserts and troubles the notion of film and music as stable reflections of reality. For example, the description of the train hurtling over the keys can be read in at least two ways. One way is to see it as indicative of the intimate connection between the music and action, which is further signaled by the continued merging of the two toward the end of that passage, when not only birds, but also "notes" "fly asunder" (46). Another way is to argue that as the two artistic forms merge, they actually highlight the instability of both forms; that is, they draw attention to each other as culturally contextual, and thereby unstable, systems of meaning.

Indeed, as the passage continues, the conflation of the film's narrative and Materia's accompaniment is represented in a way that draws attention to the constructedness of both:

> The next scene is more terrifying. A man in evening clothes has cornered a young woman in a slinky nightgown halfway up a clock tower. No narrative preamble is required, *all ist klar*, the shadows lurk, the tower lists, the music creeps the winding stair, the villain spies a grace-note of silken hem and he's on the chase in six-eight time up to where our heroine clings to a snatch of girlish melody, teetering on the precipice of high E, overlooking the street eight octaves below. Villain struggles with virgin in a macabre waltz, Strauss turned Faust, until, just when it seems she'll plummet, dash her brains on the bass clef and die entangled in the web of the lower stave, a vision in tenor crescendos on to save the day in resolving chords. (MacDonald 1997, 46–47)

The notion of musical notation as space disrupts the filmic illusion of reality. The recognizable conventions of classic melodrama—the villain, the damsel in distress, the clock tower, the rescue at the last possible minute—are exposed as conventions by the interpolation of musical metaphors into the narrative. Materia's approach to accompanying film disrupts not only the narrative but also the very notion of stability of meaning that underwrites the films she is accompanying. In the theater, at the piano, she is able to exercise the kind of discursive agency that is forbidden, indeed punished, in her marriage.

In addition to accompanying films, Materia performs with vaudeville troupes, initially all-white troupes coming to Nova Scotia, but all-black troupes start to arrive as well: "Materia couldn't figure out why they too performed under cork with giant painted-on mouths, but she did know she preferred them. She acquired a big collection of ragtime, two-step, cakewalk, processionals, sorrow songs, plantation lullabies and gospel" (MacDonald 1997, 52). Materia's confusion about the black performers' decision to perform in blackface gestures to a highly complex history of minstrelsy, a ubiquitous component of vaudeville shows. The novel is relatively silent on the politics of this history, but the emphasis on the use of cork and the painted-on mouth— that is, on black performers using the white markers of blackness to signify racial identity—foregrounds the deeply troubling representations of race perpetrated by the white performers in blackface as well as the instability of race as a category of identity.

Materia's preference for performing with the black minstrel performers suggests that although she may not consciously recognize the complex politics of their reproducing, and thereby potentially disrupting, the racialized representations of minstrel shows, she does feel an affinity with the black performers that she does not feel with the white performers with whom she works, who are irritated by her style of playing and interactions with the audience. As she performs with the Blackeville Society Tap Twizzlers, a trio of African American vaudeville performers, she "just watched their feet and let her hands go, chunks of *Rigoletto* colliding with 'Coal Black Rose,' 'Una Voce Poco Fa' on a see-saw with 'Jimmy Crack Corn,' all slapped up against her own spontaneous compositions—just as for the moving pictures, only with the dancers there was a two-way feed. They hounded, flattered, talked back and twisted—ebony, ivory, and nickel clickers grappling till there wasn't even any melody, just rhythm and attitude" (MacDonald 1997, 52). The codes of white dominance built into minstrelsy shows are here disrupted by the collaborative performance by a Lebanese woman pianist, three African American performers, and an audience that was likely predominantly working class and ethnically and racially diverse.

Altman notes that film producers began to take steps to make the accompaniment more predictable, based on notated music and much less on improvised music. He argues that the gradual shift away from musical accompaniment as participatory critical commentary constituted a loss of agency for the audience. He quotes a piece written by early film producer Clyde Martin in 1911 in which Martin bemoans what he saw as the disruptive effect of such undisciplined accompaniment:

> In several picture theatres I found that the piano player had a tendency to try and make the comedy pictures funnier than the authors intended, by adding music in contrast with what the scene portrayed. . . . This is not

all; in some places I found that the piano players were taking advantage of some dramatic scenes and getting a laugh up by springing comedy music or effects during a dramatic production. Such practice is a great detriment to any house, and the sooner the manager dispenses with the services of such persons the better it will be for the business in general. (quoted in Altman 2004, 280)

Altman's narrative of the history of sound in silent film suggests that Materia's approach to accompanying film, based on the traditions of vaudeville, would eventually have been suppressed by the tide of change in Hollywood, but it also serves to highlight the extent to which she participated in a tradition of vaudeville musical accompaniment that celebrated the audience's participation in the production of meaning, and that she employed the same approach to her accompaniment for film. James's eventual refusal to allow Materia to work as an accompanist anticipates the coming changes imposed by the film industry that asserted the primacy of the film's narrative as the source of meaning, and thus fundamentally changed the experience of attending films as a collaborative process of meaning-making that, in its noisiness and unexpected interpolations, produced productive disruptions to dominant social discourses.

Materia still finds access, however, to another mode of improvised music, this time in the context of her relationship with her daughters and very much in the context of the connections between bodies and intersubjectivity. Although we learn very little of the musical training Materia received as a child, at one point in the novel it becomes clear that the Western European tradition of music is not her only influence. While James is overseas during World War I, Materia, the narrator tells us, "comes to life" (MacDonald 1997, 86) and starts to teach her daughters about Lebanon, her birthplace. She begins to teach them Arabic and tells them stories about the "Old Country." Perhaps most significant, though, is the Arabic record that Materia's sister Camille sneaks to her one day, its cover bearing "a water-colour of Beirut by night" (89). Materia plays the record at least once a week, and she and her daughters dance the traditional Lebanese *dabke*:

At least once a week, Materia takes the record from the hope chest, carries Kathleen's gramophone down to the kitchen and winds it up. She aims the brass bloom and places the needle on the spinning wax:

First the antechamber of snowy static, airlock to another world, then . . . open sesame: The *deerbeki* beats rhythm, ankle bells and finger cymbals prance in, and the *oud* alights and tiptoes, a woodwind uncoils, legless ancestor of the Highland bagpipe, rising reedy to undulate over thick strings thrumming now in unison. It all weaves and pulses into a spongy mesh for the female voice to penetrate—no words yet, a moan between joy and lament; the orchestra suspends itself below, trembling up at the voice, licorice, liquid, luring, "dance with me before I make love to you later, later, soon." (89)

The sense of solidarity among Materia and her daughters is here achieved not only by celebrating and sharing music and dance from Materia's own ethnic roots but in the very nature of the music. Its sensual, erotic description emphasizes rhythm and emotion and highlights the extent to which improvised vocals are an important component. It also imbues the female vocalist with sexual energy and offers a figurative queering of conventional Western music, as the female voice "penetrate[s]" the "spongy mesh" of the music. Music here is embodied and figured as an erotic encounter between female voice and eroticized female music, and accompanied here by women, Materia and her daughters, dancing together.

In the end, however, Materia succumbs to the violent and oppressive domestic environment in which she lives with James. After the brutal scene in which she chooses to save Kathleen's unborn children (one of whom is breech), thereby sacrificing Kathleen's life, because she believes that is what her daughter, who has been raped by her father, wants, Materia takes her own life at the age of thirty-three. Frances is just a child at this time, but as a teenager, she embarks on a musical path reminiscent of her mother's foreshortened career in vaudeville and film.[4] Frances gets a job stripping at a speakeasy, but develops an ironic improvisatory approach that leaves no doubt she is well aware of the social power dynamic in which she is performing, one that constructs the performing woman as sexual object, subject to the male gaze. Her performances draw on the vaudeville tradition in terms of the music she plays on the piano—she plays her mother's old vaudeville music—and in terms of the juxtaposition of diverse musical traditions: "Frances is a bizarre delta diva one night, warbling in her thin soprano 'Moonshine Blues' and 'Shave 'em Dry.' Declaring, an octave above the norm, 'I can strut my pudding, spread my grease with ease, 'cause I know my onions, that's why I always please.' The following Saturday will see her stripped from the waist up, wearing James's old horsehair war sporran as a wig, singing, 'I'm Just Wild about Harry' in pidgin Arabic" (MacDonald 1997, 292). Frances's strategic performances echo her mother's improvisatory performance style. Frances and Materia resist established codes of music and performance that often interpellate both performers and audience as autonomous individuals rather than as performers of socially scripted roles in an unequal power dynamic.

Frances begins stripping not long after she receives a severe beating from her father for something she has not done but for which she takes the blame to protect her sister Mercedes. The description of the beating takes up very powerfully the trope of improvisation, making it starkly clear that if improvised music can potentially be a harbinger for liberation, this function is not inherent:

> On Water Street, the outside walls of the shed thump now and then like a bass drum with a foot-pedal at work inside it keeping the beat. In the shed the performance has begun. The upbeat grabs her neck till she's on point, the downbeat thrusts her back against the wall, two eighth-notes of head on wood, knuckles clatter incidentally. In the half-note rest he lights up her pale face with the blue wicks of his eyes, and the lyrics kick in *con spirito*, "what right have you, you have no right, no right to even speak her name, who's the slut, tell me who's the slut!" The next two bars are like the first, then we're into the second movement, swing your partner from the wall into the workbench, which catches her in the small of the back, grace-note into stumble because she bounces, being young. *Staccato* across the face, then she expands her percussive range and becomes a silent tambourine.... "I don't want to hear you speak her name," accidental note to the nose resolves into big major chord, "Do—You—Understand—Me?" We've gone all stately; it's whole notes from here on in. She flies against another wall and he follows her trajectory, taking his time now because we're working up to the finale. One more clash of timbers and tissues and it's finally opera, "I'll cut the tongue right out of your head." She sticks her tongue out at him and tastes blood. Cue finale to the gut. Frances folds over till she's on the floor. Modern dancer. (MacDonald 1997, 262–63)

This passage is reminiscent of one I discussed earlier, which describes Materia's piano accompaniment to a film scene about a man terrorizing a young woman in a conventional melodrama narrative, featuring a villain, a helpless virgin, and her last-minute rescue. Both passages describe a woman being brutally assaulted, and both conflate musical notation and performance with narrative action. In my analysis of the earlier passage, I argued that the conflation of signifying forms served to highlight the instability of both modes of signification: music and visual narrative. Materia's piano playing foregrounds systems of meaning as culturally contingent and constructed, allowing her to challenge or disrupt the dominant notions of gender embedded in them. In this description of James beating Frances, however, the effect of the stylistic approach is much more unsettling, since the action being conflated with improvised music is an actual domestic assault. Unlike the woman in the film, who is in danger of "dashing her brains on the bass clef" (46–47) but is rescued in the end, Frances has no escape from her father here.

The cavalier description, however, interestingly echoes Frances's improvisatory strategies as a burlesque performer. Horrific as this description is, she is not wholly passive, as is made very clear by her sticking her tongue out at James. Her discursive resistance is also evident in the descriptions of her that suggest that she is actually, in a way, participating in this improvised performance and thereby troubling the power dynamic. For example, she is described as expanding "her percussive range" to become a "silent tambourine," and even the phrase "she flies against another wall" uses the active rather than the passive voice and makes her the subject engaged in action, rather than the object on whom her father's violent actions are imposed. Indeed, the use of language throughout the passage—the rhythms, the images, the swift movement from image to image, and the juxtaposition of disparate and fragmented musical styles—is much more aligned with Frances (and Materia) than with James, and suggests a counterintuitive notion of agency whereby Frances cannot escape the violence enacted on her, but can disrupt it in this complex musical and discursive performance. This passage reminds us that power is always at play in any negotiation of meaning and relationships, and that aesthetic tactics of engagement, such as improvisation, figured here as an act of violence, will not reliably lead to change based on principles of social justice.

The violence inflicted on Frances by Teresa, which occurs a couple of years after Frances starts stripping, resonates altogether differently. There is no musical connection between these two women, but the erotics of improvisation are manifested in a fraught but deeply embodied connection between them. The scene in which Teresa shoots Frances in retaliation for her seduction of Teresa's brother Leo initiates a profound shift in Frances's life that ripples out to the remaining members of the family. From a very early age, Frances has been mesmerized by Teresa: "What she wants is everything about this fabulous woman" (MacDonald 1997, 121). Just before Teresa shoots, Frances sees her from a distance and is enraptured: "Frances looks up and experiences an arrow through her heart at the crucivision. The arrow is love, its pain spreads outward and the pain is faith, the source that launched the arrow was sorrow. 'Teresa,' thinks Frances, and her lips move around the name as she stretches her arms up and holds them out to the woman standing far above" (399). This moment halts Frances, shifting her out of her fast-paced sardonic self-positioning and enabling an alternative discursive mode focused on ecstatic love and desire, sanctified by the religious resonance of the "crucivision." Seen within the context of embodied improvisation, this scene asserts a highly sensuous and intimate communication between Frances and Teresa, poignantly illustrated by the description of her lips moving around Teresa's name.

The relationship between Frances and Teresa is a complex one that highlights one of the primary claims of the novel—bodies are performative and engaged in ongoing improvisatory relationships with other bodies and discursive systems. Teresa's act of shooting Frances, undoubtedly violent, surprisingly initiates a disruption of the discourse of hate that permeates the novel. Teresa is furious with Frances for tricking her brother into impregnating her, but the novel suggests that when Teresa shoots Frances, the bullet penetrating Frances's body, while violent, is also loving if not erotic. Indeed, in Frances's mind, it contributes to her successful impregnation; when Mercedes asserts that Frances could not possibly be pregnant after having been shot, Frances replies that she has become pregnant "Especially after what happened" (MacDonald 1997, 416). The relationship between Frances and Teresa confounds James's violent opposition to miscegenation; as I discuss later, Frances's son becomes a key component of affirming a family tree that, with its inclusion of lesbian mixed-race relationships, would have horrified James had he lived to see it.

For Frances, Teresa evokes a conflation of erotic and maternal desire. Frances has a strong memory of Teresa giving her a candy when she was a child, which we know to be true, but also of Teresa singing her a lullaby, which according to Teresa is untrue (it was Materia). When Teresa comes to see Frances in the hospital after having shot her, she ends up softly singing a West Indian lullaby to her, replaying, in a sense, Frances's memory but also standing in here for Materia, allowing Frances to have the lost memory of her mother. This scene highlights the sensual intimacy of these two women.

We also learn that nine and a half months after the shooting incident, Teresa herself is pregnant, finding the desire, finally, to have sex with her husband, long disabled both physically and cognitively after a work injury. Teresa's pregnancy is clearly aligned with Frances; it is after Frances tells the police that she shot herself, even though Teresa has just confessed, and the narrator tells us that "That's how Frances took Teresa's hate away" (MacDonald 1997, 411), that we learn of Teresa's pregnancy. The full complexity of Teresa's hatred is not articulated here, but the point is that Teresa and Frances find a way to engage in a reciprocal relationship of maternity and spirituality.

Also significantly, Frances, while pregnant, develops a different awareness of and relationship with her body than she has had before. Whereas prior to this incident she had ironically positioned herself as a juvenile, literally sporting a girl guide outfit and making this persona part of her act at the speakeasy, now she is described as sexually mature. The description of her pregnant body, which occurs in the section titled "The Bullet," is sensuous and erotic, and she is described as being "in love. With her body, and what it is bringing forth" (MacDonald 1997, 416): "[Mercedes] has been washing, stroking, feeding, drying a woman who is blooming like a hothouse rose. The nipples look ready to burst and scatter seed, the russet pubic hair hangs proud like a bunch of grapes. A fig leaf would not do in this case—ripe and uncooked, pink and grainy as that fruit, clitoris in the prow, is in constant rockabye motion in response to the new deeper tides of her body. She is almost always somewhat aroused, can feel her soft-sided barque opening, closing taking on water from within. Her body is making love to itself. Until now, Frances had no idea what all the fuss was about" (416). This image provides one of the most sensuous descriptions of a body in the novel. The description evokes Hélène Cixous's notion of "writing the body," and, indeed, the entire exchange between Frances and Teresa initiated by the shooting evokes Cixous's theory of *l'écriture feminin*, with its emphasis on women writing about other women in a non-linear discursive form that disrupts the dominant mode of discourse in which women are figured as Other. Teresa and Frances inscribe each other's bodies in a way that frees them to refigure themselves and to disrupt the culturally coded identities against which they have been struggling. In their relationship, then, the novel posits a nexus among the body, erotics, and improvisatory modes of communication that enables new or alternative ways of conceptualizing identity.

After much loss and suffering, the novel concludes with the intersection of family, love, survival, and, significantly, music. The child to whom Frances gives birth is taken from her; Anthony grows up in an orphanage not knowing his lineage or his mother. The trope of child loss occurs throughout the novel. As I have discussed elsewhere, Frances's sister Kathleen also gives birth out of violence: her father rapes her when he discovers that she is in love with the black jazz pianist Rose (Siddall 2005). Although she carries twins, Lily is the only one who survives. Now that he is an adult (it is now the 1950s), Mercedes gives Anthony a family tree to take to Lily, who now lives with Rose, Kathleen's former lover. The novel ends, then, with Anthony's discovery of who his parents are: he is the son of Frances and Leo Taylor (Teresa's brother), but also, as I have argued above, of Teresa. In the end, James's desire for racial "purity" is overridden; the family is now interracial, intercultural, and the notion of family is queered not only by the notion that Anthony is the son of Frances, Leo, and Teresa but also by the presence of Rose, who now identifies as Doc Rose, a "jazzman." Rose is explicitly linked with Kathleen in the family tree, archival evidence of the complexity of this family and its history. In a sense, Anthony's arrival, with family tree in hand, asserts and celebrates diverse forms of identity and love, although very clearly contextualized by struggle and trauma.

Although the novel remains circumspect, then, about the capacity for improvised music to make social change, its ending gestures to the fact that change does happen—albeit often in the face of much violence—and the connections among music and social resistance and change are made right up to the end. Significantly, Anthony is also a musician, and he teaches ethnomusicology (MacDonald 1997, 564). One of the final lines of the novel has Rose ask, " 'What the hell is ethnomusicology?' " as she wanders off to play the piano. Rose's question may be dismissive, but the question, coming right at the end of the novel, foregrounds an important development in intellectual thought. Ethnomusicology pays careful attention and respect to the diverse origins of music; Anthony emerges at the end of the novel, then, as a signpost for the kind of scholarly work that will be done in the decades to follow, work that will interrogate notions of race, gender, class, and ethnicity in the context of music. At its conclusion, then, the novel affirms the possibility for improvised musical performance to be potentially socially disruptive in productive, always embodied ways, but the family tree reminds us of the violent deaths of Materia and Kathleen, for whom improvised music was not ultimately a means to personal freedom.

Notes

1. Ann-Marie MacDonald is an award-winning Canadian author and playwright. Her publications include the play *Goodnight Desdemona (Good Morning Juliet)* (1988) and the novels *Fall on Your Knees* (1996), *The Way the Crow Flies* (2003), and *Adult Onset* (2014). She has also been the host of *Life and Times* and *Doc Zone* for the Canadian Broadcasting Corporation.

2. I have dealt with the relationship between Kathleen and Rose elsewhere. See Siddall (2005). This paper includes an analysis of the American cultural context in which women's blues challenged dominant notions of race, gender, and sexuality.

3. See Kristen Poluyko's (2001) analysis of Materia's playing as noise, as well as of the significance of the dance scene with Materia and her daughters, in the theoretical context of the work of Jacques Lacan and Hélène Cixous.

4. Materia's suicide is the almost inevitable result of the long, complicated chain of tragic events that mark her brutal marriage and mar her relationship with her daughters.

12. *Corregidora*

Mandy-Suzanne Wong and Nina Sun Eidsheim

To play music, especially to improvise, is in part to bring oneself under the influence of other bodies from the past. We perform memories, our own and those of others. My body and my bodily practices are partly molded by memories personal and cultural—which means that my body, my practices, are not wholly mine. To improvise, then, is to call on the resources of our bodies and catapult ourselves beyond the confines and capacities of our singular bodies.

In the words of Michel Foucault, the modern body is "manipulated, shaped, trained" by social institutions, and is thus an "object and target of power" (1995, 136). Our bodies are living evidence of social geographies and ideological regimes, harboring, in addition, "counter-memories," personal experiences of which official archives are unable or unwilling to offer account (Foucault 1977). An individual *embodies*—gives a living body to—the personal and cultural memories that "shape and train" her living body. Thus, she interacts continually with memories that are themselves breathing, pulsating, affective bodies, and, as they interact, they impact and move her *bodily*. Hence, from Foucauldian "archaeology," a method that attempts to elucidate the historical and cultural forces determining the concepts available to individuals, we derive "corporeal archaeology." Corporeal archaeology attempts to understand how sociohistorical concepts and events, retained and transmitted through shared, cultural memory, influence the way an individual understands her bodily capabilities, how she and her society value her body, and therefore how she uses her body—particularly, in this chapter, when she improvises music.

In what follows, because we understand the improvisational aspects of performance to be deeply personal, we consider their role in the transmission of cultural memories through music. If we listen closely, improvisation may even be found in the most rigorously predetermined performance of a notated composition. Improvisation may indeed occur at the level of form and style, as in jazz performance, but the more subtle aspects of any musical performance may also be improvised and thus, we argue, molded according to personal and cultural memories. Examples include the grain of the voice, emotional inflections, and temporal impulses, all micromusical details that are dependent on and respond to the immediate performative context. Corporeal archaeology therefore provides a lens through which any improvised performance may be analyzed. It may yield insights distinct from, and possibly unavailable to, analyses based in sonic or cultural-historical generalizations. If we "listen back" toward sounds' origins in musicking human bodies, we may sense living memories that can be traced to other bodies and even beyond them to entire peoples. In other words, the repository of experience harbored in each musicking body is revealed in the sonic results of improvisatory music-making practices.

The first part of this chapter draws on what Jann Pasler calls "writing through music" (2007, 4). Pasler's primary argument is that "writing through music" is a kind of writing that forms unique perspectives on nonmusical aspects of the world *by considering music*. Music thus functions as a "critical tool, activating and developing multiple layers of awareness" (4). Gayl Jones "writes through" the blues in her novel *Corregidora* (1975), articulating a corporeal archaeology that enacts the performance of personal and cultural trauma through song. *Corregidora* testifies to the existence of bodily memory and its transmission through music. In the novel, bodily memory crosses generations and geography, tracing an Afrodiasporic route from Brazil to the U.S. South.

The second part of our chapter shifts from literary analysis to ethnographic analysis. We consider the extent to which such transmissions are intrinsic to real musicians' bodies and to what extent they are made by choice. To do this we consider the testimony of African Brazilian musicians, as interviewed by ethnographer John Burdick. Burdick's informants recount their experiences of racial and cultural memory in gospel and gospel rap, two African American musical genres that have found voice in African Brazilian musical culture. Whether the music in question is experienced in live performance, via recordings, or as part of a narrated account, fictional or otherwise, we believe that music can open up perspectives wherein it may be possible to discern the nuances and subtleties of extramusical phenomena like embodied memories—phenomena that might otherwise remain in shadow. In that regard, corporeal archaeology is an instance of successful thinking and writing "through" music.

Bearing Witness through Music in *Corregidora*

Corregidora is the first novel by the Kentucky-born, African American author Gayl Jones, and it was controversial when it was published in 1975. Its exhaustive descriptions of sex and violence shocked readers and reviewers (Clabough 2006, 649). Jones claimed, however, and reviewers agreed, that in part *because Corregidora* is about "love and trouble," memory and trauma, it is also a novel of the blues, a performance of an improvised musical form that was itself born of the violence of slavery (Jones and Harper 1977, 700). Reviewers call her a "blues woman," and Jones herself calls *Corregidora* a "blues novel" (700). It is by singing the blues that Jones's protagonist, Ursa Corregidora, tries to learn to live with memories of recent trauma and the "cultural violence of the past" (Clabough 2006, 653). These memories of rape penetrate and scar Ursa's body, so that every aspect of her singing—from her original lyrics to the timbre of her voice—is audibly influenced by these memories. In other words, her blues singing manifests her embodied memories.

Corregidora chronicles Ursa's attempts to recover from an abusive relationship with her first husband, Mutt. Resentful of the fact that she holds a nightly singing job, a drunken Mutt throws her down a flight of stairs. As a result, her womb is irrevocably damaged: she can never have children. Despite cautions from her doctor and her new husband, Tadpole, Ursa goes back to work soon after her release from the hospital. Having lost the ability to have children (which was for her the most important, creative function of her body), all she can do to "give back," to "leave evidence," is sing, to create using her voice (Jones 1975, 14). "It was as if I wanted them [the audience] to see what he'd done, hear it. All those blues feelings" (50). This statement implies Ursa's conscious use of performance as an audible, visible conveyance of her memories to listener-viewers.

That aspect of her performances may be the reason Mutt disapproves of her singing. This compulsive, almost physical need of hers to reveal her "blues feelings," feelings about "love and trouble," to strangers in public—in performance—must have been mortifying to him. "He didn't like for me to sing after we were married because he said that's why he married me so he could support me," Ursa recalls (Jones 1975, 3). "I said I didn't just sing to be supported. I said I sang because it was *something I had to do*, but he never would understand that" (3, emphasis added). Mutt also fails to understand when Ursa tries to communicate her feelings to him alone, when she "asked him to try to understand [her] feeling ways" (50). From Mutt's point of view, then, Ursa's desire to sing her memories and feelings *to other people* both excludes him from her confidence and puts him on display as the root of her "love and trouble."

It becomes clear, however, that Ursa also musically embodies trauma in her performances in ways that are unconscious. After Mutt attacks her, her voice, like her womb, is no longer the same, but it is far from barren; it is full to overflowing with new timbres. Audiences hear these new sounds as direct consequences of Ursa's recent trauma. One such listener remarks on the change, in conversation with Ursa:

> "Your voice sounds a little strained, that's all. But if I hadn't heard you before, I wouldn't notice anything. I'd still be moved. Maybe even moved more, because it sounds like you been through something. Before it was beautiful too, but you sound like you been through more now. You know what I mean?"
>
> "I know what you mean, but it's still changed" [Ursa replies].
>
> "Not for the worse. Like Ma [Rainey], for instance, after all the alcohol and men, the strain made it better, because you could tell what she'd been through." (Jones 1975, 44)

Ursa is apprehensive here because her voice seems to have changed of its own accord. Despite her efforts to sing as she normally would, "it's still changed," she says. Because of its inadvertent quality, the change can be likened to a scar, as something left unwanted in and on her body, like the physical consequences of violent rape. Try as she might to move beyond the trauma by going back to work, Ursa's body retains and betrays, in her singing, working voice, the memories of the trauma. She worries about how audiences will receive her, but to listeners her voice actually sounds "better" *because* it has been inadvertently traumatized, *because* memories of pain have imposed themselves on it and melded with it. Other listeners also report being more affected or "moved" by her scarred timbres, drawn in by them, perhaps drawing some empathetic relationship between their own pain and her vocalized agony. "You got a hard kind of voice," someone says. "You know, like callused hands . . . The kind of voice that can hurt you. I can't explain it. Hurt you and make you still want to listen" (96). As memories infuse, penetrate, and wound Ursa's performing body, physically scarring it and timbrally altering her voice, those memories become crucial to her performance.

It is not only her own personal trauma that is embodied in Ursa's singing. She is constantly haunted by the traumatic memories of her female ancestors, all of whom, for three generations, were horribly sexually abused. Her enslaved great-grandmother, Dorita, was repeatedly raped and prostituted by her master, "Old Man" Corregidora, a Brazilian plantation owner (Jones 1975, 8). Then Ursa's grandmother, Dorita's daughter by Corregidora, was raped by the same man, producing Ursa's mother, Irene. Indoctrinated by her mother's and grandmother's dogmatic retellings of their horrifying stories, Irene is unable to maintain healthy sexual relationships and contrives to have Ursa because her ancestors have branded her with the idea that she must produce a daughter to whom she, too, can transmit their memories. As Ursa describes it, "my great-grandmama told my grandmama the part she lived through that my grandmama didn't live through and my grandmama told my mama what they both lived through and my mama told me what they all lived through and we were suppose to pass it down like that from generation to generation so we'd never forget. Even though they'd burned everything to play like it didn't never happen" (9). The novel suggests that the continual retelling of generational trauma inflicts its own kind of trauma on Ursa; as she herself says, it is "the kind of [telling] that can hurt you" (96). So we use the word *branded* deliberately: Irene's mother and grandmother repeat their traumatic stories so often, and in such harsh detail, that they leave impressions on Irene's *body*, to the point that when she recounts her ancestors' stories for her daughter, it is as if her ancestors' voices elide her own (124), and even before having Ursa, she continually suffers from a physical compulsion to make a girl-child who would bear witness as she did to her ancestors' suffering (114). "It was like my whole body wanted you, and knew it would have you, and knew you'd be a girl," she tells Ursa (114).

There's a specific reason for this: a specific obligation is the price of existence for every generation of Corregidora women. Because there are no *official* histories of their suffering—all written accounts of Corregidora's slave-prostitution operation have been burned—with Ursa's ancestors' *orally* transmitted legacy comes a duty "to pass it down like that from generation to generation so we'd never forget" (Jones 1975, 9). "And I'm leaving evidence," says Dorita, violence pouring out of her mouth as she cradles a tiny Ursa in her lap, "I'm leaving evidence. And you got to leave evidence too. And your children got to leave evidence. And when it come time to hold up the evidence, we got to have evidence to hold up. That's why they burned all the papers, so there wouldn't be no evidence to hold up against them. . . . The important thing is making generations. They can burn the papers but they can't burn conscious, Ursa. And that what makes the evidence. And that's what makes the verdict" (14, 22). The duty to "make generations," a filial duty that has nothing to do with love, is branded into Irene to such an extent that she's unable to love any man, yet her body feels compelled to make a daughter (114). The imperative to pass on Great Gram's memory becomes the desire and movement of each descendant's body.

Because Ursa is unable to fulfill this physical imperative once Mutt destroys her womb, she becomes the first to transmit the Corregidora women's memories beyond the family by performing them publicly through music. Consider this pair of blues verses from Ursa's own composition that she sings to herself while daydreaming:

[1] While mama be sleeping, the ole man he crawl into bed
While mama be sleeping, the old man he crawl into bed
When mama have wake up, he shaking his nasty ole head
[2] Don't come here to my house, don't come here to my house I said
Don't come here to my house, don't come here to my house I said
Fore you get any this booty, you gon have to lay down dead . . .
(Jones 1975, 67)

The "old man" referred to here is probably "Old Man" Corregidora. "Mama" may refer to any one of Ursa's female ancestors. Notably, although Ursa herself tries to hold off Corregidora ("don't come here to my house"), he sneaks into her anyway, slithers into her body through her indoctrinated memories. "Fore you get any this booty, you gon have to lay down dead"—and dead he is, though he makes his mark on her nonetheless. She dreams of him even in the daytime, as she leisurely undresses, peeling off her "wedding suit" right after her marriage to Tadpole (67). Why should she think of Corregidora then? To the revulsion of both her husbands, Corregidora is always in her thoughts, and to be intimate with Ursa (in bed or in her music) is to rub up against the old man with and through all her female ancestors. She is physically compelled to sing their memories in the same way as Irene was bodily compelled to make a daughter-as-archival-transmitter. Ursa's improvised blues lyrics, based on her ancestors' tales of rape and fear, demonstrate the extent to which their memories have become her own: *they* are what she sings.

She sings them in her genre of choice: the blues, which, although it is the musical vernacular of her Kentucky audiences, takes after the call-and-response structure typical of slave songs. As a relatively open form, the blues leaves room for the improvising musician to perform what she, personally, has lived: there is plenty of space between the preestablished chord changes for the Corregidoras' memories to ring out. The repetitiveness inherent to the form also aligns it with memory and mourning and calls to mind the repetition of Ursa's ancestors' stories, which each generation is born to hear and transmit. That said, she gives voice to her memories, not only through selecting certain words, pitches, and forms, but also and primarily through the sensual aspects of her performance: the timbre of her voice and the appearance of her body. "They squeezed Corregidora into me, and I sung back in return . . . I mean in the tune, in the whole way I drew out a song. In the way my breath moved, in my whole voice" (Jones 1974, 103). In *the way* she sings, as in *what* she sings, Ursa embodies and lives out a response to her inherited memories.

Indeed, the improvised aspects of Ursa's music include her decisions about pitches, timing, ornamentation, and in some cases lyrics. Additionally, her bluesy improvisations comprise personal and interpersonal histories, counterhistories, and abstractions. We have seen how her recent personal traumas determine the timbre of her voice, and how the interpersonal past, which her ancestors brand on her body, gives her lyrics, dreams, and compulsions. We know from African American history that in the blues, Ursa draws on a musical form developed during and in response to slavery. The blues, then, invoke the collective, cultural memory of slavery with which many African Americans live. We have also seen that the history of Corregidora women is not an official, recorded history. Instead, Ursa sings "counter-memories": experiences remembered by individual bodies that contradict recorded history and are irreducible to linguistic generalizations. Such histories, although deeply personal, collectively define the concepts known as "African American history" and "African American culture," which are themselves inseparable from the violence of slavery in all its forms. Several scholars, such as Clabough (2006), Griffiths (2009), and M-S. Wong (2012), hear in Ursa's singing the intersubjective, general, and abstract (that is, terminological and at times obscure) phenomenon called "black culture."

Ursa therefore turns "writing through music" into "bearing witness through music," a kind of corporeal archaeology that is not only discursive but also performative, embodied, and sonorous. Pasler takes music as a lens through which unique perspectives on other, nonmusical experiences may form. Likewise, in the formal, sonic, and visible aspects of her performance, as in her performing body itself, Ursa musically testifies to what befalls Corregidora women *besides* music. She sings, she enacts, she *is* these memories: as her musical performances bring her audiences to a sensory awareness of her embodied memories, her body itself, her activities and capabilities, form a living record—which, thanks to Gayl Jones, is also and at last a written one.

If we think *through* Ursa, which is also to think beyond her, we might find that her musical experiences, though they are certainly extreme, constitute part of every musical, improvisational experience. To be sure, many of her embodied memories are horrifying, but we would like to suggest that as a concept, embodied memory may also apply to nontraumatic relationships with history and help us describe how the past and present bodies of *other* people, themselves laden with memories, may affect one's own physical practices. Listening through Jones's novel, we may also find that just as music may point the way beyond itself toward other inquiries, bearing witness through music—or, retrospectively, an archaeology of the memories that form and stimulate musical performance—may give analytical discourse a "way into" those aspects of music that are too personal to be notated or generalized (a musician's personal "sound," for example). To acknowledge the musicking body's formation by the past is also to admit that music may perform familial, cultural, ideological, even religious work—albeit not without ambivalence.

Musicking as "Discourse-Practice"

Because each of us performs with and through a body formed by a process of the technology of social life (to adapt Marcel Mauss's [1979] terminology), and because it is that body we call on in musicking, we ask whether every musicking body is *bound* to bear witness to its direct and indirect experiences through musical expression. Do our personal and collective experiences encompass not only the musical horizon but also its end and purpose?

Daphne Brooks calls the musicking body a "sonic archive": a body marked by its past, that thus keeps track of its own history. Just as a pair of scholars may derive two different arguments from the same archival evidence, two performing bodies, although they might share certain significant experiences, may not assimilate or communicate them in the same way. In this analogy, a performer is a historian who selects aspects of her history to communicate to audiences through music. Accordingly, sounds emitted from her body are evidence of past events.[1] The selection may be deliberate but—here the analogy falls apart—as Ursa's "changed" voice evidences, certain parts of a performer's history are liable to slip into the open whether she wants them to or not. In that sense, what she communicates through music is and is not her own choice.

The notion of discourse-practice, from Foucault's *History of Sexuality* (1990), may be useful here. Discourse-practice signifies communication that isn't simply about other kinds of activity but is itself a bodily, interactive practice. Musical performance and the musicking body qualify as discourse-practices: communications of (inter)personal histories and other information, that are also creative, bodily endeavors. Because they reflect and internalize shared histories and cultural conditions, the terms of the discourse, and the practice by which every discourse-practice is conveyed, are and are not matters of choice.

To an extent, an improvising performer may decide her attitude toward her past, and thence theoretically musically bring out or repress what she has gained from her forebears. However, Ursa's negative feelings toward Old Man

Corregidora do not prevent her from embodying his history. Inadvertently, and thus with an air of inevitability, she reproduces his story, singing it forth. Her body is the living evidence that nurses her ancestors' tale. Though her injury prevents her from having a baby girl, she nonetheless makes generations, every night and with each sound of her voice. She alone plays every role in the reproductive drama. The Corregidora story is the embryo nourished by her dreams and lyrics; it impregnates her voice with a spectrum of sonic color, and with that sound she penetrates her audience.

While she sings of Corregidora in her own compositions, Ursa *chooses* other songs for the café, songs like "Open the Door, Richard," "Broken Soul Blues," and certain songs by Ella Fitzgerald (Jones 1975, 152–60).[2] She *chooses* when to sing about Corregidora: when she's alone—though the songs sometimes creep into her nightmares. The implication is that singing memories is not always inevitable, although it may be.

Charlie Parker said, "Music is your own experience, your thoughts, your wisdom. If you don't live it, it won't come out of your horn" (quoted in Lewis 1996, 119). What you live, and what others live, sounds in your music. The story need not be expressed as a time-based narrative; rather, it could simply be present in the sound born of the air expelled from the body. Take, for example, the short note values, quick tempos, and complex rhythms that generate the percussive timbres of bebop. In this music, the performed/performing body is a beaten body. According to Frank Kofsky, bebop's origins lie in "the police beating Negroes' heads . . . that old club says, 'BOP! BOP! . . . BE-BOP!' . . . That's where Be-Bop came from, beaten right out of some Negro's head into them horns" (1970, 270–71). *That* beaten Negro's body continues to blow that horn, through today's bebop musicians.

George Lewis believes that it would be irresponsible for an African American improviser not to express her African American history as part of her identity, as though living the past and performing histories are obligations (1996, 109). Indeed, Kofsky and others comment on the strong presence of history and memory in jazz improvisation, manifested in the musician's choice of sonic material, social position, and corporeal relationships with her instrument and other players, but the obligatory element is absent from these thinkers' analyses. Lewis himself goes on to suggest that *denial* of history's present relevance is in fact valid response to past events (109).

So far, the question of embodied memories' ineluctability in musical improvisation remains unanswered either by Ursa Corregidora or by the "real-life" musicians and scholars discussed here. To visit examples of performers who explicitly position themselves and their voices in relation to Afrodiasporic history, we return to Brazil, Corregidora's homeland. In contemporary Brazil, we find African American musical forms that have traversed the Corregidora women's route in reverse. Rap and gospel made their way to Brazil from the United States. These musical forms allow plenty of room for improvisation, despite their strict parameters. In what follows, we read John Burdick's ethnography of Afro-Brazilian gospel and rap discourse-practices in terms of corporeal archaeology, in hope of discerning the choices and inevitabilities at work in improvisation and the music-making body.[3]

In Burdick's interviews with "real" musicians, we read exemplars of the ideas that Jones articulates in her novel. The authors' aims are of course distinct—Jones aims to enact shared embodied memories of enslavement and violence through a fictional blues singer, Burdick to analyze the relationships that real improvising musicians have with their bodies and cultural memories—but they both infer the legitimacy of what we're calling corporeal archeology: an awareness of a musicking body as a living archive of other bodies and experiences, which are audible in the musician's improvisations. Although we could have chosen any number of sites to which to apply corporeal archeology, we found Burdick's work particularly engaging because of a certain experiential similarity between blues and gospel (as they are described in Jones's novel and by Burdick's informants): both genres offer fairly strict musical forms that nonetheless leave room for improvisation. In other words, both are heavily steeped in tradition but equally reliant on individual expression, which we believe includes the performance of personal and collective memories via improvised elements (ornaments and cadenzas in gospel, phrases and rhymes in rap). Rap and blues also share an emphasis on narrative and reflective lyrics, which makes them amenable to comparison with literature.

Burdick examines how Afro-Brazilian gospel and rap vocalists understand their own vocalities. His first case study is a close reading of a gospel performance, informed by interviews with gospel singers, both men and women. The vocalist follows a common gospel pattern wherein the performed song consciously attempts both to transform (to comfort and soothe the doubts of the audience) and narrate a journey from hell to heaven. For gospel singers and church parishioners, this narrative also embodies the Afrodiasporic community's journey from slavery to freedom, and the voice with the capacity to engender transformation by summoning the Holy Spirit is heard as the result of molding by intergenerational and cultural memories of slavery and by hardship present in everyday life. We should note that in Burdick's ethnography, singers and audiences *of both genders* detect this intergenerational struggle and the Holy Spirit's metaphysical power in gospel voices. Whereas

Jones, in her choice of a female protagonist, emphasizes embodied memories passed on through female bodies, Burdick makes explicit the fact that bodies of both genders are susceptible to the scars left by shared experiences, and those scars are audible in both male and female singing voices.[4]

The ability to become an accomplished gospel singer is considered to be racially contingent and is often explained in physical and historical terms (Burdick 2009, 31–37, 44–45). In Burdick's ethnography, black gospel singers claim that their African ancestry endowed them with "anatomical features . . . thick vocal chords [*sic*], a wide vocal tract, capacious sinuses, and other cranial resonators—that permitted them to excel in the most physically demanding skills required by their genre, such as belting and growling" (31–32). Thus, "while acknowledging a role for training to 'polish' their voices, [informants] claimed that Blacks enjoyed a clear genetic advantage" (32). Gospel also places great importance on communicating emotion, another area in which black people are thought to excel.[5] One informant said: "We sing with this emotion because we have suffered much in the past, and still suffer, we went through slavery, and we are still discriminated against. So I think you hear all of that in the Black voice. We have a sadness that whites don't know, but they hear it" (34).

The discourse surrounding gospel invokes a shared material (physiognomic) history told in the melisma of the song. A common cultural past, rooted in ancestral slavery and current experiences of discrimination, informs the singers' ability to know and express deep suffering, all of which they sing. The idea that black singers' ability to inspire transformations by singing their suffering is a genetic ability suggests that black singers *cannot help but* sing their histories.

Contrastingly, in Brazilian gospel rap, a musical discourse-practice born of the African Jamaican and African American experience, performers attribute vocal prowess not to race but to skill. Rap is not equivalent to singing, but instead is understood as closer to speech, centering on the words, their delivery, and their message (Burdick 2009, 38–43). Black performers are not considered superior; this vocal art offers no ready means of distinguishing black performers from those of other ethnic groups.[6] Burdick writes, "The overall ideological effect of the everyday understanding that there is no distinct 'Black sound' in Brazilian rap is, quite logically, the lack of incentive to search for an organic basis of such a sound" (39). He goes on to argue that "the gold standard of rap is whether its 'voice' has integrity, is 'true,' whether it really conforms to the experience of the rapper" (40). In other words, the rapper sees himself or herself as expressing his or her "own soul," which is not reducible to his or her race or cultural history (2009, 42). Because one of his informants, Samuel, was a man who took intense pride in "himself as a Black man," Burdick expected him to connect his rapping with blackness,

> yet when it came to rap, his uniqueness trumped everything else. "No," he replied, "not my race, not my color. My ideas. In rap I express my ideas." Samuel denied that rapping "gave voice" to his "Black soul." "I believe I'm giving voice to my own soul, not my 'Black' soul," he said. "I think each person expresses their own soul. And each person has their own way of rapping. I don't think I rap as I do because I'm Black . . . I have the gift; as a white you could have the gift as well. It is not a question of color." (42)

In sum, while the Brazilian gospel singers and rappers interviewed by Burdick share a cultural and racial history, their self-narrations diverge. Although they all take pride in their identity as African Brazilians, they harbor different conceptions of the ways identity informs their musicking. For gospel singers, memory is unavoidably expressed in vocal timbre; for rappers, it is a decision expressly articulated in words and ideas. These differing perspectives suggest that gospel singers and rappers understand their bodies quite differently. In Burdick's analysis, while both rappers and gospel singers sound their bodies concretely and across generations, they tell different stories about how exactly their bodies function as "sonic archives." In both genres, vocalists seem to share the belief that experience leaves its mark on the body, altering it irrevocably; that mark—that changed, affected body—plays a formative role in their vocalizations. Where gospel singers' stories diverge from those of rappers is on this point: what *kind* of experience leaves audible imprints on the body?

For the gospel singer, Burdick suggests, it is as though his or her body encompasses historical time, involuntarily conveying the suffering of his or her ancestors and his or her race, as we described already. At the same time, according to Burdick's informants, to hear the gospel singer's voice is to hear "the voice of God . . . an overflow of the Holy Spirit," which implies that the singer's resonating body also encapsulates metaphysical bodies, entities, or voices that "overflow" into his or her own (Burdick 2009, 30–31). When the singer starts to improvise, "overflowing" the confines of the hymn to add melismas and cadenzas, it is, the informants suggest, those other voices, history and the Holy Spirit, that ring out through the singer's body. The past and the metaphysical are realms that lie beyond our control; yet in Burdick's analysis they leave their irreversible imprints on singers' bodies and enable them to make powerful, unique sounds.

In contrast, Burdick's informants reported that a rapper's vocal sounds result from his or her purposeful manipulations of his or her body in the here and now. As we discussed already, "the rappers [Burdick] got to know believed that rapping was a skill . . . in their view, most anyone who applied himself [or herself] could develop the capacity" (Burdick 2009, 40). This implies that the rapping body is not an extension of ancestral or metaphysical bodies but a deliberate effort and material movement in the present. The condition of the rapping body, and consequently the sound of the rapping voice, remains contingent on the mark of experience, but that experience is of the rapper's own making. What shapes the rapping body and resonates in the rapping voice are the rapper's own decisions to "apply" him- or herself in the manner of his or her choice to learning the art of rap.

The rappers' approach to the body-sound dynamic as a personal and practical, even mechanical matter poses an interesting contrast to the gospel singers' interpersonal, perhaps even impersonal understanding of the same dynamic as an uncontrolled phenomenon. Although the body and how it is affected by experience are central to both narratives, the gospel singers view their bodies as conduits of external forces: their bodies lack the ability (and do not need it, by their warrant) to determine their own shapes, capacities, and sounds. Rapping, on the other hand, relies on the rappers' willingness and ability to do exactly that and work at it. The rappers interviewed by Burdick maintain that their capacities and vocal sounds are fully under their control: the results of effort and deliberate physical movement.

However, Jones's ideas on interbody relations and body-sound dynamics resist falling into either of these opposing narratives: for her, the sounding body is not merely involuntarily sounded through intergenerational forces, nor does it fully control all the sounds it emits through mechanical manipulations. Reading gospel and rap practices and self-narratives *through* Jones's theory of the connection between body, sound, and history fleshes out these narratives and reveals their commonalities: of course gospel singers also make decisions—to sing gospel at all is a personal choice. Although rap is improvised—word ordering, sentence structure, and rhyming are at the rappers' own discretion—rappers also engage preexisting conditions, for instance, the established pronunciations of words, which they glean from others' enunciations of the same words in the past and in their contemporary surroundings. In that sense, rappers do resonate with bodies other than their own.

Burdick's research indicates a multilayered relationship between musical improvisation, embodied memory, and choice, yielding noncompatible understandings of these dynamics. However, when we read the two polar narratives through Jones's story, we understand that the body may be irrevocably shaped by its collective and singular experiences, but a musician can sometimes choose how to express them. Furthermore, we see that although some musicians believe that they have no alternative but to surrender to compulsions to perform their histories, others decide, through their specific discourse-practices, precisely how they will understand and to what extent they will express their embodied memories. Through *Corregidora*, Jones reveals how tension becomes apparent within the improvising body as it functions as an agent *and* a conduit, a distinct, present self and the expression of absent or faraway other.[7]

Conclusion

In our reading of *Corregidora* and brief analysis of an ethnographic study of African Brazilian musical identities, we have suggested that as much as we perform the personal and counterhistorical in music, we may also perform the interpersonal and abstract. Embodied memories contain the values and ways of life that shape our understanding: cultural memories that each performer shares with proximal, distant, familiar, and unknown others. What is improvised in music is thus interpersonal (reliant on several interacting persons) and perhaps also "impersonal" (belonging to no particular person) (Orlie 2010, 116) or "pre-individual" (established before a particular person distinguishes herself from her environment) (Clough 2008, 1).

This idea is worth considering from a political standpoint, as it evidences the potential for music to be listened *through*. My body and my bodily practices are not wholly mine; I am not simply or exclusively myself. The extent to which I can choose to be myself or another, to sing my memories or someone else's, is flexible. Layering bodies, some from the distant past, combine into one living, performing body. The image may be grotesque, but there is much we can extrapolate from it. Corporeal archaeology—awareness of one's own improvising body as a living, bleeding archive of other bodies, ideologies, and values—may help us listen through music with perceptive registers that may help us theorize generic, pedagogical, political, and even ontological relationships.

Notes

1. Brooks calls the various performances of Bess, in Gershwin's *Porgy and Bess*, a "subterranean feminist sonic archive" (2012).

2. "Open the Door, Richard" is a vaudeville number by Jack McVea (1947), first sung by Dusty Fletcher. "Broken Soul Blues" was made famous by Ma Rainey (1926).

3. For Burdick, the analytical challenge was to understand "how religious music, focused as it is lyrically on the universal, nonracial and nonethnic values of salvation and

redemption, might be a vehicle of Black identity," and how "particular musical practices might stimulate specific sentiments of collective identity" (2009, 26).

4. We should also note that Tadpole, a male character in *Corredigora*, alludes to his enslaved ancestors' harrowing past as well (Jones 1975, 13). However, because Ursa herself narrates the tale, her experiences are central.

5. Burdick notes that although accounts of the inevitable expression of suffering in "black" voices are familiar to U.S. readers, they are less so in Brazil, where their dynamic in relation to narratives of racial democracy is configured differently (Burdick 2009, 34).

6. It is crucial to point out that North American and Brazilian black vocality is configured differently with regard to speech. Speech is not racialized in Brazil, though it is in the United States (Burdick 2009, 39).

7. Perhaps this tension may be loosely compared to that between preestablished musical structures and spontaneous decisions in improvisation generally, which is driven by such tension.

13. Theorizing the Saxophonic Scream in Free Jazz Improvisation

Zachary Wallmark

> Possibly the most powerful human sound ever created.
>
> —critic Bill Mathieu, reviewing John Coltrane's *Ascension* [1965]
> (quoted in Jost 1981, 86)

> The most astounding piece of ugliness I have ever heard.
>
> —critic Philip Larkin, reviewing Coltrane's *Meditations* [1965] (1970, 172)

The sound of free jazz is famously polarizing.[1] Although arguably no less true today, this was especially the case in the mid-1960s, when John Coltrane (1926–1967) aligned himself with the nascent genre. Many of the revered saxophonist's staunchest advocates abandoned him entirely on this perceived act of defection: for these listeners, the once-great Coltrane had simply gone too far, losing himself to radicalism, self-indulgence, and (to some critics) even madness. To others, conversely, the sublime sounds of his new way of playing signaled theophanic revelation and spiritual ecstasy. Indeed, responses among listeners tended toward the extremes—free jazz saxophone playing was either viscerally rejected or viscerally embraced. Either way, reactions were highly *visceral*.

Examining the gut-level reaction evidenced in the early reception of free jazz, I argue that more than anything else, *timbre*—particularly that of the "scream" effect so ubiquitous among saxophonists—is crucial to the style's heightened powers of inducing ecstasy or revulsion in listeners. At issue in these wildly divergent perspectives is the following question: How does the same sound—what I am calling the *saxophonic scream*—signify so differently to different listeners, leading one side to empathize with this breach of music and the other to deny empathy entirely, hearing it instead as pure noise?[2]

Theorizing the saxophonic scream from the perspective of embodied cognition and vocality, and using this perceptual/cognitive approach as a hermeneutic window through which to assess the culturally and historically contingent reception of free jazz in the tumultuous mid-1960s, I suggest that musical perception does not function in the same way as the perception of other, nonmusical sounds. Indeed, the dynamic interaction between them is determined to a large extent by the listener's relative level of identification with the sounds themselves. Untangling this interaction is of crucial importance to understanding reactions to the saxophonic scream, since its sonic identity and the various meanings given to it (and to the people producing it) are bound up in how listeners make sense of its nonmusical, screaming quality. Although my analysis focuses broadly on reactions to the saxophonic scream irrespective of specific recorded examples, for the sake of illustration, I concentrate on the improvisatory style of Coltrane's so-called late period (1965–67).

By 1960, Coltrane was one of the most respected and influential tenor saxophonists in the jazz world. His innovative contributions to modal and postbop improvisation earned him high praise, but he was never content with his own achievements. By mid-decade, his tireless, purposeful search for ever-deeper modes of expression began to revolve primarily around timbre, a focus shared by the younger members of the jazz avant-garde. (Simply put, timbre—also known as "tone" or "sound color"—is the psychoacoustic category that differentiates one sound source, or player, from another. For example, timbre is what distinguishes a saxophone from a trumpet when they are playing the same pitch.) In the liner notes to *Meditations* (1965), Coltrane states: "There is never any end. There are always new sounds to imagine, new feelings to get at" (quoted in Hentoff 1996, 9–10). Indeed, the strident, altissimo sound of the saxophonic scream was part of a larger aesthetic reorientation within the free jazz community that manifested itself as a radical form of timbral experimentation. Players sought to liberate sound itself from the confines of pitch, elevating timbre to the primary expressive position in the improvisatory vocabulary, a shift into what Ekkehard Jost calls "sound improvisation" (1981, 169). As saxophone player Albert Ayler revealingly put it, he was looking to "escape from notes to sounds" (quoted in I. Anderson 2007, 113); similarly, *Ascension* (1965) alto player Marion Brown characterized this new timbral approach as "a reaching for sound and an exploration of the possibilities of sound" (quoted in Spellman 2000). Saxophonists who oriented themselves in this way came to be called "sound-players," and Coltrane fervently embraced this new approach.

Jost summarizes this aesthetic transformation: "In solos, there is a gradual emancipation of timbre from pitch that leads to a-melodic structures primarily delineated by changes in color and register. This kind of playing expresses an emotionalism heightened to the ultimate degree" (1981, 95). Jost draws an important link between timbre and emotion, an association that is invariably repeated in the literature: heightened timbral effects such as the saxophonic scream are characterized as being synonymous with heightened intensity and emotional expressivity.[3] Although this timbre plays a major role in the perceived fervor of the style, however, it is also at the root of its polarization. The direct, immediate emotionality of this raw saxophonic expression led to a bifurcation in perception and evaluation that strained against the very definition of music. By "escaping from notes to sounds," saxophonists played at the precarious border between music and its other, whether perceived as spiritual bliss or just plain noise.

The divide between music and noise permeates the literature on late Coltrane and free jazz in general. There are a number of elements to this improvisatory language that confound clear distinction along the music/noise spectrum for many listeners, including its lack of intuitive periodic structures, erratic rhythmic pulse, dense textures, and eschewal of standard melodic formulas. However, timbre is the sonic parameter that most clearly blurs the line between musical sound and noisy incoherence. Philip Larkin dismissed Coltrane's sound as "the usual tumults of noise" (1970, 232), but others saw in this same noise a form of meaningful expressive purity that transcended standard notions of music. As Coltrane biographer Eric Nisenson writes: "These screams, howls, and shrieks were pure sound, pure emotion, the last frontier of music. Coltrane had come to agree . . . that it was time to go 'beyond notes'" (1993, 191). A quality of "beyond-ness" does indeed mark the timbral approach to free jazz saxophonics; the agitated, screaming sound seems to reach past the constraints of the instrument, over the limits of the body, and beyond signification as a musical code. How listeners interpret this beyondness is a matter of considerable dissension, but one striking commonality unites both poles: reactions to the saxophonic scream are deeply centered on bodily experience.[4] It would seem that valuations of this particular timbral gesture are processed at a gut level, yet how different listeners judge the experience is largely determined by their willingness to engage and empathize with this acutely embodied sound (as blissful, physical transport), or reject it (as noisy, physical pain).

Admirers of late Coltrane tend to interpret the scream in unmistakably spiritual terms.[5] As J. C. Thomas puts it: "There had to be something else *besides* music there. . . . Call it Universal Consciousness, Supreme Being, Nature,

God" (1975, 172–73). To spiritually acquiescent listeners, Coltrane's ability to reach beyond the normal bounds of musical communication is tantamount to transcendence and ecstasy, a feeling mediated by the body.[6] For example, Nisenson compares the Coltrane concert experience to a "mind-boggling religious revelation" where "my body felt exhilaration, transport, even as much as my mind and spirit" (1993, xvii). Nat Hentoff, in his liner notes to *Meditations*, makes a similar connection when he writes that Coltrane and Pharoah Sanders play "as if their insights were of such compelling force that they have to transcend ordinary ways of musical speech and ordinary textures to be able to convey that part of the essence of being they have touched. The emotions are imperious; they cannot be braked or polished into conventional ways of 'beauty' or 'symmetry.' They must explode as felt—in the rawness of palpable, visceral, painful, challenging, scraping, scouring self-discovery" (Hentoff 1996, 5). In both accounts, sound is a vehicle for exaltation; the very fact that it pushes beyond normal definitions of music is evidence of its cosmic force. Rather than a disembodied, dematerialized sort of ecstatic rapture, most positive accounts are grounded in fleshly embodiment, foregrounding the overwhelming somatic experience of Coltrane's sonic bombardment.

The same is true, however, for negative critical assessments. Although admirers willingly followed Coltrane into this epiphanic whirlwind, transforming smoky jazz clubs into sacred spaces in the process, alienated listeners refused to do so. To them, the saxophonic scream was not spiritual revelation—the "other of music" that induces psychic ascension through profound, extreme bodily experience—but simply unredeemable noise, the "other of music" that is equivalent to an attack on the body. Like the positive accounts, critical responses to this style were physicalized from the beginning; rather than simply expressing intellectual or aesthetic qualms with the sound of free jazz, detractors rejected the style on a deep-seated level. Writer Clive James, for instance, memorably describes Coltrane's sound as "full, face-freezing, gut-churning hideosity" (2007, 191). In a 1965 review of *Meditations*, critic Joe Goldberg wrote that "[I] cannot be scoured or scraped any more," adding, "I feel only that I am being wildly assaulted, and must defend myself by not listening" (quoted in Woideck 1998, 236). The same haptic metaphors employed by Hentoff ("scour" and "scrape") are retooled here for a different purpose, suggesting that like fingernails on a chalkboard, the sound cuts deeper than any rational critique can capture. Rather than self-discovery this experience is akin to an assault, the sound of the saxophone being a source of physical pain that induces a fight-or-flight instinct to retreat. Other skeptics, while recognizing the strangely compelling intensity of the timbre, warned listeners not to be seduced by their senses, arguing that "energy and passion" do not amount to artistic achievement (Such 1993, 11). These reactions imply a certain physiological vulnerability to sound, not just an intellectual dismissal of it. Listeners are in the thrall of its power, but while some are swept up into an experience of ecstasy, others are confronted with their own threatening, bodily susceptibility to undesired aural influence.

As we have seen from reactions to Coltrane's music, nowhere is this susceptibility to affect more acute than in the realm of timbre. In Robert Walser's assessment, timbre is "the least successfully theorized and analyzed of musical parameters" (1991, 122). To be sure, our analytical toolbox is lacking when it comes to the affective dimensions of musical sound. This omission is explicable from a number of perspectives, but central to this "paradox of timbre" (as Cornelia Fales calls it) is the fact that tone color exists in two fundamentally different aspects. Timbre can be defined by its measurable acoustic parameters.[7] As Fales points out, however, the perception of timbre is highly subjective and cannot be fully captured by this "informational" model (2002, 91). Owing to its extreme variability among hearers, then, how do we make sense of timbre's affective qualities on a more general level? Nina Eidsheim (2008) proposes a bipartite scheme for addressing the phenomenon of timbre. She refers to the informational level of sound, that which can be explicated through Fourier analysis and spectrograph, as "timbre sonic."[8] Of more interest to us here is Eidsheim's second category, "timbre corporeal," which refers to our inner, embodied recognition of sound, the knowledge of timbre that is held in the body.

Every sound contains traces of its production. The material structure of the sound-producing object, as well as the physical means of initiating and maintaining the vibratory energy, are thus audible to us, and we relate the behavior of these sounding substances to our own corporeal experience, particularly our vocality.[9] Put differently, human embodiment—specifically the voice—endows us with a repository of innate motor experiences. Musical timbre is heard and appraised through the filter of this embodied knowledge. Eidsheim speaks to this point when she writes: "a deep experience of the timbre of instruments, such as intense emotion, is a manifestation of the corporeal experience stimulated by, and as an extension of, the sound of the singing voice" (2008, 251–52). Indeed, vocality is key to unlocking the way we experience the material nature of sound production, and nowhere is this truer than in the case of the radically corporeal timbre of the saxophonic scream.

Across cultures, the transmission of emotion through music is closely related to the iconic similarities of musical sound to vocal expression.[10] This is especially true of instrumental sounds that most directly operate on the level of vocal mimesis.[11] To be sure, the high register and bright, distorted timbral components of the saxophonic scream directly mimic the sound of the vocal scream and its accompanying state of bodily strain. As John Shepherd and Peter Wicke put it: "To hear a voice, a musical sound, is to 'have knowledge' of the corporeal and somatic state which produced it" (1997, 180). Wayne Bowman goes further, writing, "when we hear a musical performance, we do not just 'think,' nor do we just 'hear': we participate with our bodies; we construct and enact it" (quoted in Borgo 2005, 44). The "scream" designation, then, is not merely a felicitous metaphor for describing a fundamentally instrumental phenomenon; it is impossible to disembody the saxophonic scream by separating it from its vocal analog. Indeed, to many listeners, this sound is heard *as if* it were an actual screaming voice.

The timbre of the vocal scream is marked by signs of extreme friction and wear; there is a tearing quality, a sense that the material bounds of the body are fraying against the overwhelming force of its utterance. Screaming makes the agitated, overtaxed interior of the body audible; its sound is shot through with the physical effort required to produce it. The same is true of the saxophonic scream, which sonifies the same state of corporeal exertion and danger as its vocal correlate. Like the voice, moreover, the playing techniques required to produce this effect on the saxophone involve a relatively high degree of physical strain. Playing altissimo notes requires the player to sound the right pitch with his or her vocal tract; ascending higher into the altissimo range, therefore, requires the same vocal demands as upper-register singing (Chen, Smith, and Wolfe 2008, 776). The timbre of the saxophonic scream, rich with upper-partial energy and noise, thus communicates extreme exertion in the same manner as a vocal scream.

Hearing the sound of the saxophonic scream forces the listener to enact the process and experience of screaming and all the physical and emotional associations this act carries. We *empathize* with the palpable strain of the scream, and the nature of this empathetic connection between sounding bodies—the "timbre corporeal" of the performer and the embodied perception of the listener—is just beginning to be understood and verified from a biological perspective.[12] Recent research into the neurophysiology of audition and its relationship to the human mirror neuron system, a network of motor neurons that fire both while performing an action and while observing (or hearing) an action performed by another, offers some compelling empirical evidence for a phenomenon that has been intuitively understood by musicians and philosophers for centuries.[13] Investigating emotion and its relationship to musical experience, researchers theorize that the mirror neuron system works sympathetically to engage musician and listener alike at the site of the same motor network, which "allows for co-representation of the musical experience, emerging out of the shared and temporally synchronous recruitment of similar neural mechanisms in the sender and the perceiver of the musical message" (Molnar-Szakacs and Overy 2006, 236). Indeed, studies indicate that a range of communicative signals—musical, linguistic, and otherwise—transmit complex patterns of expressive motor acts and their associated emotions through an intercorporeal mirroring of bodily states, a phenomenon referred to as "shared affective motion experience," or SAME (Overy and Molnar-Szakacs 2009, 492). The authors conclude that "the expressive dynamics of heard sound gestures can be interpreted in terms of the expressive dynamics of personal vocal and physical gestures" (492; see also Cox 2001; Leman 2008). To listen to the saxophonic scream, then, is in some way to participate in it.

Not all sounds, however, produce neuronal discharge consistent with the SAME model. Audiomotor mirror neurons only fire in the presence of *action* sounds, those with identifiable intention; white noise, for instance, excites no response (Kohler et al. 2002, 846). Other studies show that goals take precedence over the specific motor actions involved in their execution, indicating that we mirror the meaningful outcome, not just the mechanical body motions (Gallese 2007, 660). This seems to suggest that mirroring depends on whether a sound is perceived as invested with intention, purpose, and meaning, a conclusion that has stark (and as yet unexplored) consequences for our understanding of music perception. A study using functional magnetic resonance imaging (fMRI), for instance, suggests that people respond with discharge in areas of the brain related to vocal expression only when listening to music that they find pleasant; unpleasant music is not perceived as having meaningful structure, and thus does not excite the mirror neuron system (Koelsch et al. 2006, 247). Listening to "music" involves some level of "inner identification" with the sound patterns as they pass; listening to "noise" involves no such sympathetic neurophysiological resonance. Relating musical sound back to the bodies that produce it, we see that a failure of empathy in listening is also a failure to hear the sounds of another as meaningful, an inability to perceive the goal that drives the motor activity underlying the sound production of another. In certain extreme cases, it is a collapse of empathy toward the people making these repudiated sounds. It is indeed suggestive that those who exhibit the most mirror activity also score highest on "perspective taking" tests, a common metric for measuring empathy (Iacoboni 2009, 665).

By unconsciously arousing our empathy, the saxophonic scream forces the listener to respond. This is essential to its intercorporeal potency: it impels us, involuntarily, to identify with its voice-like qualities, both consciously and through sympathetic mirroring mechanisms, and it demands that we take notice and act. To engage—to accept the scream and, in a sense, allow oneself to resonate with it and "scream" along internally—is to cede a certain level of control to the sound itself and the strained musician's body that manifests it. It is also to embrace the motivations and meanings underlying the effortful production of this sound. In a sense, empathizing with the scream— hearing it as "music," or paradoxically as something "beyond" music—leads us to identify with its implied anguish or ecstasy, inviting it into our bodies to mingle with our own embodied knowledge of screaming. We are also led to co-experience the impetus behind it, which for many adherents resembles a form of spiritual ecstasy.

To many listeners, however, the permeability of our bodies to sound is a point of great anxiety. Receptivity to this sound requires that on some level, we allow it in, that we want it to affect us; otherwise it feels like an assault. Our initial exposure to the saxophonic scream confronts us with our own vulnerability to affect, but how we answer its demands is determined to a large degree by conscious choice. Music phenomenologist Thomas Clifton argues that sound will only be perceived as music if the listener feels as if he or she "possesses" it, an act that requires us to interpret it *as* music (1983, 273–81). If one is unable to countenance an answer to this question of receptivity, if one does not want to "possess" the sounds in question (as music or its spiritually illuminating "other"), then the intercorporeal flow of communication shuts down, and the code will turn to pure, unredeemable noise. This allows the listener to stay in control, not submitting power to the performance, as fans readily do. In fact, the breakdown of empathy in response to the saxophonic scream is perhaps the only form of control that a listener can exert over this particularly vulnerable aesthetic experience. If one hears it as noise, then it is easy to expel from bodily experience. As our critic from earlier put it, "I must defend myself by not listening" (quoted in Woideck 1998, 236).

What is at stake in this interaction, and why does it matter whether we hear another person's sounds as music or as noise? To begin gesturing toward a response, we would do well to turn to the metaphors commonly used to describe this saxophonic timbre, most notably terms like *scream*, *shriek*, and *cry*. Designations like these are ubiquitous among all listeners and performers of this style, regardless of their level of empathy. Nevertheless, "screaming" is not a neutral act. It is impossible to dissociate these vocal expressions from their archaic connotations in the Western world: *screaming*, *shrieking*, and *crying* are heavily gendered terms, associated since the Greeks with uncontained female vocality and hysteria.[14] Indeed, as Anne Carson points out, women in classical literature are "a species given to disorderly and uncontrolled outflow of sound—to shrieking, wailing, . . . screams of pain or of pleasure and eruptions of raw emotion in general" (1995, 126). High-pitched voices, especially those marked by the stress of screaming, are the sounds *women* make, and although free jazz saxophonists (most of whom are male) use these words to describe their own sounds, such designations tap into an implicitly gendered discourse of power. On the scale of empathy outlined above, the distinction between music and noise is also an operative category in the determination of whether this sound represents the masculine overriding of earlier connotations, or simply an "ideological association of female sound with monstrosity, disorder and death" (121).

Such gender considerations played a major role in the way listeners interpreted Coltrane and other performers in concert, where audience members were confronted with the sheer, unbridled physicality of black male performers "screaming" through their instruments. As Michael Spence Washington explains, in the 1950s Coltrane played with great physical restraint, an essential quality to appearing "dignified" in concert (2001, 284–85). His free jazz period, however, was marked by complete kinetic abandon. Nisenson vividly speaks to this point in his description of a mid-1960s concert, where Coltrane was "playing roiling arpeggios ... often accentuated by saxophone cries and wails. Playing at this level for even a few minutes would have exhausted most musicians, in terms of both imagination and sheer physical taxation. But Coltrane kept up at this level for what seemed hours ... Coltrane was eventually almost completely bent over forward, his face flushed, and at one point saliva poured out of the side of his mouth" (1993, xvii).

As the author goes on to observe, Coltrane's uncontrolled, even slightly grotesque physicality made him appear to be "not in this world," a reaction consistent with the transcendent interpretation of the scream. It is easy to see how the same experience could lead observers to default to a different set of presumptions: by appearing to relinquish control of his body to the gendered sounds coming out of his horn, the scream has the power to feminize. Coltrane was aware of this precarious balance between transcendent power and (female) hysteria, sometimes to the point of his own embarrassment (Washington 2001, 285). Such uncontrolled sounds and bodily movements are a threat to culturally constructed notions of masculinity, a risk to which Coltrane felt vulnerable.

The gender connotations of the scream are further complicated when the issue of race is brought into the discussion. Indeed, the "screaming," "shrieking" sound quality of the saxophone, in addition to its gendered link to uncontained vocality, carries strong racial associations that show up in critical and sympathetic accounts by both black and white writers. As Jon Cruz has shown, black music was once considered noise to white listeners, and whites have long linked unruly vocality to blackness.[15] Although white unease over black sound is a topic too big adequately to tackle here, suffice it so say that perhaps it is not surprising that many white critics have interpreted free jazz in explicitly racialized terms, as the sound of black nationalism. In 1965, a year of race riots and civil rights tension, the image of a black man scream-ing was particularly potent, and even many critics who viewed the movement positively interpreted these sounds through the lens of racial anxiety. Black writers Amiri Baraka and Henry Dumas did their part to cement this associa-tion,[16] but the interpretation was repeated often in the white press, where the sound of the scream was linked, in the words of Frank Kofsky, to "the ghetto's vote of 'no confidence' in Western civilization and the American Dream" (1970, 131).[17] In particular, the saxophonic scream was conceived as an explic-itly African form of vocal mimesis. Baraka labels the vocal elements of the free jazz saxophone as "quintessentially African" (quoted in I. Anderson 2007, 110), and Kofsky writes of the "growling, raspy" sound quality and "eerie shrieks," concluding that these are the "quintessence of Negro vocal patterns" (1970, 134). In an oft-cited interview, Kofsky pressed Coltrane to own up to the racial and political valence of his music (1998, 435). To writers like Kof-sky, the sonic qualities of free jazz—particularly its timbral attributes—were simply too black sounding *not* to be related to radical racial politics. Col-trane demurred and, indeed, few musicians explicitly related their music to political movements or civil rights issues, despite repeated attempts by writ-ers to draw the connection (Gridley 2007, 139–55). Perhaps the most egre-gious example, however, comes from Larkin, who described the saxophonic scream as "death-to-all-white-men wails," adding that Coltrane's "dervish-like heights of hysteria [are] the musical equivalent to Mr. Stokely Carmichael" (quoted in Ratliff 2007, 179). Indeed, many listeners were acutely aware that this sound of violence and rage (or so they believed) was coming out of the bodies of black men.

There is much more to be said about the gender and racial connotations of the saxophonic scream and how this played into the reception of the sound, a reception indelibly marked by the cultural and historical circumstances sur-rounding its audition. I broach these issues in conclusion only to demonstrate the potentially high stakes involved in how we hear and evaluate timbre; indeed, our ability to empathize with the quality of a sound is inextricably bound to our ability to empathize with the gendered and raced body that conveys it. Timbre, by articulating the motor actions and bodily states in-volved in its creation, draws people into an intercorporeal dialog, the effect of which is simultaneously outside of our control and mediated by a variety of internal and cultural factors. Because judgments of timbre often take place on a preconscious, subliminal level, we are susceptible to this element of music in a uniquely intense and highly emotional way.[18] Timbre is not a neutral, unmarked category of sound; rather, it is deeply invested with both biologically and culturally situated meanings, and these values seep unconsciously to the surface when we form critical evaluations of music. Though it would be wrongheaded to claim that a lack of empathetic connection to a particular music is automatically equivalent to a lack of empathy with the people producing it (or the larger social category they represent), there is often a covert, unrecognized ethics of timbre at play not only in the reception of polarizing styles like free jazz but also (for example) in heavy metal, gangsta rap, country and western, and avant-garde concert music, arguably contributing to the visceral reactions they arouse in some listeners.[19]

Our embodied cognition of sound is poorly understood and woefully undertheorized by music scholars. Despite the fact that the sound of free jazz—particularly the scream—figures prominently in the reception history of the style, most of the published scholarship on late Coltrane and free jazz improvisation tilts in favor of transcriptions, structural analyses, and assessments of the soloists' motivic development and harmonic language.[20] Although such analyses can tell us a lot about the structural underpinnings of a particular improvisation, by eliding timbre, scholars have inadvertently covered up one of the most important parts of the story. This lacuna is understandable, given the methodological poverty when it comes to timbre; it is also possibly the result of an attempt to validate this often-maligned music by demonstrating its "seriousness" and complexity through the rigor of traditional musicological analysis. But part of it, I contend, has to do with the uncomfortable corporeal realities that the saxophonic scream is capable of conveying—matters that evade traditional transcription. Free jazz improvisation has the capacity to both enrapture and repel, and key to this polarization is the dynamic relationship between its most iconic timbre—the saxophonic scream—and the sensing, feeling body.

Notes

1. "Free jazz" refers to a form of collective improvisation that originated in the early to mid-1960s.

2. Saxophonic screaming has a long history as an R&B "freak effect," and in this context, it carries vastly different meanings and associations (Nisenson 1993, 188). In this chapter, I focus exclusively on the scream as employed by saxophonists like Coltrane, Albert Ayler, Pharoah Sanders, and Archie Shepp in the context of free jazz improvisation.

3. See I. Anderson (2007, especially 71 and 115); Liebman (1996, 177–80); Such (1993, 17 and 56); and Borgo (2005, 50).

4. Spellman (2000) speaks directly to these somatic effects when he indicates that by the end of *Ascension*, the listener's "nervous system has been dissected, overhauled, and reassembled."

5. See Franya Berkman (2007), McDonald (1995), Borgo (2003), and Ratliff (2007), especially chapter 9, for more on the spiritual side of Coltrane's music.

6. See Borgo (2003) for the link between ecstasy and embodiment in free jazz saxophonics.

7. For an overview of various paradigms for conceptualizing timbre, see Hajda et al. (1997).

8. Fourier analyses visually represent the waveform of a steady-state sound; spectrographs show the relative strength of harmonic and inharmonic partials (in hertz) over time.

9. More on embodied music cognition can be found in Leman (2008) and Cox (2001).

10. For a comprehensive literature review, see Juslin and Laukka (2003).

11. Juslin, in his "super-expressive voice" theory, contends that instruments have the capacity to transmit a sense of *extreme* emotion because, while resembling a voice, they "go far *beyond* what the human voice can do in terms of speed, intensity, and timbre" (Juslin and Västfjäll 2008, 566). It should be noted that players and observers explicitly conceived saxophonic screaming along vocal lines. Archie Shepp, for instance, commented that "[extended timbral effects] gets a quality of like male and female voices" (quoted in Simpkins 1975, 188).

12. Although the term *empathy* is usually applied only to human subjects, Leman suggests that in its sonic articulation of patterns of intentional movement, music can act as a "virtual social agent," and thus a "domain where aspects of empathic involvement can be demonstrated" (2008, 126, 124). Clifton concludes: "The 'other' need not be a person: it could be music" (1983, 285).

13. For a concise summary of important findings in this field, see Iacoboni (2009). Perspectives from mirror neuron research were first applied to the free jazz saxophone (though quite simplistically) in Gridley and Hoff (2006).

14. See Julie Dawn Smith, "Perverse Hysterics: The Noisy *Cri* of Les Diaboliques" (2008) for an illuminating reading of "noisy" female sound in the context of free improvisation.

15. See Cruz (1999), especially chapters 2 and 3.

16. In particular, see Baraka's short story, "The Screamers" (1967) and Dumas's "Will the Circle Be Unbroken?" (2004), which features a black saxophonist whose sound kills white listeners.

17. For more on the racial overtones of free jazz reception, see chapter 2 of Grey (1986).

18. Cornelia Fales suggests that timbre acts "with subterranean impact," and that "the very subliminality of these sensations is a clue to their power" (2002, 77).

19. Such polarizing timbres can evoke feelings of fear, disgust, contempt, and ridicule in listeners who do not identify with them.

20. For representative examples of structurally oriented free jazz scholarship, see Grey (1986), Hester (1990), Liebman (1996), and Such (1993).

14. Extemporaneous Genomics

NICOLE MITCHELL, OCTAVIA BUTLER,

AND *XENOGENESIS*

Kevin McNeilly and Julie Dawn Smith

Chicago-based flautist and improviser Nicole Mitchell composed *Xenogenesis Suite* in 2008 as an homage to the Afro-futurist science fiction of Octavia Butler, whose work Mitchell's mother had read and admired. The hour-long suite was recorded by Mitchell's Black Earth Ensemble and released in April 2009 on Firehouse 12 records, produced by cornettist and fellow improviser Taylor Ho Bynum, with whom Mitchell collaborated in Anthony Braxton's thirteen-piece performing ensemble, the 12(+1)tet.[1] Mitchell is one of a handful of women members of Chicago's AACM (Association for the Advancement of Creative Musicians), a cooperative of experimental musicians that emerged from the city's south-side African American community in the 1960s. Notably, she served as the first female president of the AACM,[2] and she continues to act as a mentor for a new generation of AACM women. Currently she is professor of integrated composition, improvisation, and technology at University of California, Irvine. Mitchell's work has garnered significant recognition in recent years; she has received many awards, most notably the prestigious 2011 Alpert Award in the Arts, an award aiming to recognize, as its website asserts, "experimenters who are making something that matters," and the inaugural Doris Duke Artist Award (2012) that provides "a deeper investment in the potential of dedicated artists, empowering them through the freedom of unrestricted support while celebrating past achievement."[3] These legacies and intersections offer significant starting points for listeners to engage with Mitchell's music because of the inherently collaborative nature of her artistic practice. *Xenogenesis*—Butler's trilogy and Mitchell's musical reimagining—investigates how tactics of hybridity, miscegenation, mixing, differentiation, and negotiation operate formally and genomically within sound, voice, and text.

Mitchell's work, alongside Butler's, approaches corporealities in performance, inviting listeners to question how bodies are both shaped by and resistant to social and sexual hegemonies. Inspired by *Dawn*, the first book in Butler's trilogy, Mitchell's exploration traces the problematic salvation of humanity by alien genetic "traders" after an imagined nuclear apocalypse, addressing the rebirth of humanity from the perspectives of an unwilling and compromised earth-mother—aptly named Lilith, an anti-Eve—and her descendants. Although in Butler's novel Lilith is saved from the destruction of Earth by the alien race the Oankali, she (along with several other humans) has been held captive in suspended animation for 250 years on an extraterrestrial spaceship. Lilith is the first human to be awakened and was carefully selected to breed with the aliens for the propagation of a new interspecies. Human breeding is renewed through the mediation of a third Oankali gender, the ooloi, who are sexually stimulating and can also penetrate the DNA and consciousness of others. Lilith is assigned to act as surrogate mother to the group of humans who will eventually be awakened from their suspended animation to repopulate a restored Earth.

Mitchell's *Suite* takes up Butler's challenges to biological purity, cultural sanctimoniousness, and socially engineered heteronormativity and attempts an improvised music that confronts normative concepts of how listeners and performers make sense of what they hear and feel. Sense—as sensation and meaning—emerges in Mitchell's sound-world as a recombinant amalgam that like the tentacles of Butler's Oankali prods us to question how and where our own bodies begin and end, how self and other interpenetrate, collaborate, dissolve, and (mis)comprehend, and how community can arise from cohesion and from misfires.

"*Xenogenesis*, written from an African American perspective, raises questions on how concepts of alien and other are used negatively to marginalize people."

Butler's narratives trouble static notions of human subjectivity and suggest hybrid alterities for future generations to inhabit the landscape of imagined alien worlds.[4] Drawing from historical accounts of slavery and colonization amid current realities of racism, sexism, and dislocation, Butler's work is squarely located alongside the work of Afro-futurist artists who imagine "*other* stories to tell about culture, technology and things to come" (Dery 1993, 738). Lilith embodies the complex lived experience of African American women who exist on the margins of hegemonic structures; her doubleness challenges the status quo—whether alien or human—as she simultaneously inhabits her power and confronts her powerlessness. Lilith acts as both witness to and unwitting participant in alien breeding, and by way of her protagonist Butler speaks to the horrors of eugenics and a host of other medical atrocities inflicted on the black community throughout U.S. history. Her agile approach to science fiction demonstrates the effectiveness of Afro-futurist interventions to radically reinvent complex African American histories with remarkable resilience. "You can be backward-looking and forward-thinking at the same time," notes writer Greg Tate in an interview exploring Afro-futurism: "Ironically, one of the things that's allowed black culture to survive is its ability to operate in an iconoclastic way in regard to the past; the trappings of tradition are never allowed to stand in the way of innovation and improvisation" (quoted in Dery 1993, 767).

Mitchell was drawn to Butler's Afro-futurist vision precisely for its backward-looking and forward-thinking approach, a call-and-response between particular historical moments and their future incarnations. "[Butler's] words, her work is very unusual," remarks Mitchell in a 2011 lecture. "As science fiction it's not just based in fantasy; it makes you reflect on your present reality because she's always creating these tensions that make you reflect on [the] social problems that we have" (2011). Mitchell's own Afro-futurist expressions are similarly reflective and visionary, referencing the musical flights of the iconic Chicago musician, composer, and interplanetary inhabitant Sun Ra. Mitchell explains Sun Ra's music as "very focused on this idea of the future and creativity and imagination and community" while drawing on the AACM concept of artistic trajectories "ancient to the future." Sun Ra's sonic visions acted as a launching pad for African Americans to imagined worlds that escaped the restraints of a racist society. His epigram "Space is the Place" became a mantra that sounded space as "both a metaphor of exclusion and of reterritorialization, of claiming the 'outside' as one's own, of tying a revised and corrected past to a reclaimed future" (Szwed 1998, 140).

Much like the compositions of her intergalactic ancestor Sun Ra, Mitchell's *Xenogenesis Suite* takes the listener to the far reaches of inner and outer musical space, exploring complex, densely textured soundscapes that depict (as she puts it) "the horrifying reality of human self-destructiveness," or as Butler's alien Oankali describe it, the incompatible human characteristics that led to the Earth's destruction—intelligence and hierarchy. Lilith is warned by the aliens that "a complex combination of genes that work together to make you intelligent as well as hierarchical will still handicap you whether you acknowledge it or not" (O. Butler 2000, 39). The aliens fear, yet are also strangely attracted to, the human contradiction, and their desire for Lilith is reciprocally genetic: "You're filled with so much life and death and potential for changes" they tell her (80). Mitchell's compositions are equally fascinated by the human contradiction "of all this potential that we have in creativity, intelligence and yet the self-destructiveness in the human spirit and how that plays out in our realities" (Mitchell 2011).

"So this is like, her on the ship. And there's no windows, there's no doors. It's like being inside of an egg. So what do you do? You're just looking for some crack, some way to get out."

The opening lines of *Dawn* present the first moments of Lilith's posthumous and posthuman life, her return to self-awareness at the hands—or the tentacles—of the Oankali:

> Alive!
> Still alive.
> Alive . . . again. (O. Butler 2000, 5)

We overhear Lilith's interior monologue, and the narrative firmly links Butler's readers to Lilith's point of view. As Lilith awakens to discover the meaning and details of humanity's survival, its collective life beyond its scripted end, Butler's readers are gradually awakened to her sense of a fatal determinism coded into the human genome—the "lethal" combination of intelligent self-awareness and hierarchical world-ordering mentioned before—and to our potential for rescue through genetic mixing: not for improvement or betterment but for differential miscegenation, through fleshly blending and trade with what is alien or strange, with what we are not. This identification with Lilith, however, is more than an epistemological device borrowed from quest narratives; as those first words of the novel make clear, we are meant to reexperience that awakening parasitically or vicariously along with Lilith. The opening exclamation is a birth cry, a reentry into life but as a self-aware adult, able to track the sensation—for her readers, through the secondhand accounting of text.

The voice of Butler's novel, despite its even textual surface, is thoroughly compromised, a hybrid stylistic and conceptual amalgam. This compromise needs to be understood, if we are to approach it through Mitchell's music, as inherently plural and porous: not so much parasitic as symbiotic, reciprocal. Lilith sounds herself out, declares her presence in the novel's opening words. But what sounds like Lilith reasserting herself as a discrete being also remains enmeshed in audience, in audition. Within a few pages, Lilith discovers that she has been medically, genetically altered by having her flesh broached—her body's "talent" for cancer converted chemically and surgically into a capacity for self-healing; moreover, this capacity is framed as a significant instance of genetic trading, a leveling exchange among bodies that, both sexually and cognitively, the Oankali enable. Whoever or whatever declares herself alive is no longer merely human: not a fixed or remediated body but a mixed and mediated self. This compromising of voice and self—much the same thing, for Butler—sounds itself differentially in her text. Although the exchanges between Lilith and her captor Jhadya tend to feel more expository than enactive—explaining who the Oankali are and what has become of humanity—Lilith craves the performance of conversation as much as its substance, even conversation with her tentacle-covered alien captors:

> The tentacles were elastic. At her shout, some of them lengthened, stretching toward her. . . . She imagined small, tentacled sea-slugs—nudibranchs—grown impossibly to human size and shape, and, obscenely, sounding more like a human being than some humans. Silent, [Jhadya] was utterly alien.
>
> She swallowed. "Listen, don't go quiet on me. Talk!" (O. Butler 2000, 14)

As the organs of trade—through contact, cellular penetration—Oankali tentacles figure, frighteningly and "obscenely," the exchange of flesh. Significantly in this passage, that exchange, a bridging of alienations, also manifests as a demand for quasi-human conversation.

"And then there's the unknown, there's that place—I want to be like a bridge where I'm taking you as a listener to somewhere else that you may have never been before."

Butler names this simultaneously metaphorical and literal discursive exchange her "radio imagination"; she privileges hearing words over using them as vehicles for descriptive visualization: "I have the kind of imagination that hears. I think of it as radio imagination. I like radio a lot better than I do television" (quoted in Francis 2010, 101–2). The self, as voice, figures forth as hearing and heard. Jean-Luc Nancy refers to this double movement as a sounding of body, a listening "self"—a medial awareness that is both interior to and outside of its membranous boundaries, its tympanums and skin: "to sound is to vibrate in itself or by itself: it is not only, for the sonorous body, to emit a sound, but it is also to stretch out, to carry itself and be resolved into vibrations that both return it to itself and place it outside itself" (Nancy 2007, 8). Moreover, for Butler the self as partial and uncontained is also definitively embodied, or as she puts it, the self can be experienced "pretty much" as body (quoted in Francis 2010, 110), although it remains at least in some small part unfinished, unclosed, approximate. That unfinishedness is what, for Butler, the body is. Lilith's attention is drawn obsessively throughout *Dawn* to the inhuman grotesqueness of Oankali anatomy, their repulsive bodies to which Lilith has already begun to adapt. The interpenetrative porousness that disgusts and allures her is what Butler often refers to as "community," the fraught but desirable, embodied spaces of shared human living. A community, after all, is what the Oankali are attempting to foster among the rescued humans they want to return to Earth.

Building on the profound ambiguity of the human contradiction, Butler creates an uncanny codependence between the humans and the aliens that attracts as well as repels. Throughout the narrative Lilith is both coerced and seduced by her abductors while she in turn seduces and resists them, struggling with the contradictory existence circumscribed for her in this alien environment. Mitchell, aware of the conflict, musically articulates Lilith's psychic, emotional, and physical predicament:

> In my music I really wanted to explore that possibility of fear. Imagine being one person on this ship where there are no other people around, your whole past has been taken from you—your home, your family, anything familiar. You're just in this alien space and you're alone. What does that feel like? How do you survive minute-to-minute, day-to-day, month-to-month in this situation? In creating the music I really tried to get into that emotional space. And so I used instruments to create the feeling of the ship and the strangeness and then I have a vocalist to deal with the emotional aspect and the voice of this one woman. But she's not going to be using any words, so not using any words and only emotional expression actually creates an alien language, so she has a double identity of being the alien and at the same time of being the one human sound in the music. (2011)

Deeply disturbed by her conflicted position, Lilith nonetheless demonstrates remarkable dexterity in her ability to adapt to the strange communal exchanges, establish her own agency, and negotiate (at least some of) the terms of her transformation, as well as mitigate the genetic alteration of her progeny. Her bargaining with and on behalf of the reawakened humans is a more complex affair and the kinship—humans to Oankali, human to human—never fully gels. Although the Oankali genuinely attempt to foster a community among the rescued humans they want to eventually return to and repopulate Earth, the humans are resistant to the requisite transformation they will have to endure.

"The AACM . . . this is a group of black artists that were thinking about music in terms of research, in terms of investigation: what are the possibilities of sound?"

Mitchell's Black Earth Ensemble is arguably a realization of the performative, creatively incoherent community Butler conjures in her writing. Taylor Ho Bynum, who produced the recording of the *Xenogenesis Suite*, suggests that Mitchell's approach to ensemble composition, which he characterizes as focusing on a "sonic otherness," is not based in conformity or in deferential mutuality, but in enabling particular instrumentalists to converse, to exchange sounds:

> The way [Nicole Mitchell] uses the vocalist in that piece, particularly, as really existing within the ensemble and outside of the ensemble. But very much not the idea of the traditional vocalist in an ensemble, where you're singing with a background. It was much more both integrated within the group and then also reactive to the group. Where the music prods the vocalist into places as opposed to acting as a padding for it. And so I think that idea of really freeing up the different cells of the ensemble to have independent agency was very appropriate for *Xenogenesis* as a narrative, because [of] that idea of alien bodies, and the idea of the interaction of alien worlds. (Taylor Ho Bynum, interview with Kevin McNeilly, Vancouver, February 5, 2010, transcribed by Jessamyn Swift)

Bynum associates this compositional practice with Anthony Braxton, particularly with what became Braxton's plural communitarian performance of his "sonic genome." Mitchell has credited her work in Braxton's 12(+1)tet—in which she performed Braxton's multivoiced, sonically layered, and improvisational scores—with opening up improvisational and compositional possibilities in her own music (Mitchell 2007, 19). If we listen to the opening section of her *Xenogenesis Suite*, we can hear how the ensemble textures and the kind of vocal interactions Bynum is describing operate as instances of porous reciprocity.

"With my own work, what I am really interested in is the balance between two things, the familiar and the unknown."

The first section of the recording, "Wonder," musically enacts this differential ensemble form as music, operating "within" and "outside" its own formal structures. The experience of wonder, Mitchell asserts in her notes, contains both beauty and power: "This power can be equally beautiful and horrific, echoing the power of humans who are so creative and yet so destructive to planet Earth and to ourselves." The fanfare with which the piece opens announces immediate concord in bright, ascending unisons (flute, trumpet, saxophone, wordless voice), but that strident upwelling of voices is quickly crosscut as it repeats and modulates by metallic patter—cymbals and cowbell, along with rolling snare drum—that introduces what George Lewis (1996) might call an "Afrological" texture to the performance (the percussion includes a jazz drum kit) as well as a deliberate unruliness that propels the music forward. Bowed cello and bass syncopate and extend the opening horn phrase, entering into dialogue with the guttural yodels, hoots, squeals, and hollers of Mankwe Ndosi's improvised vocals. The fanfare returns, gesturing toward contingent order through recurrence, to insist on a compositional cohesion—the composer's flute forms part of the wind trio—that continues to be expansively and subversively interpreted by voice and soon by freely extemporizing piano. The graphic score for *Xenogenesis Suite* offers direction and shape for the performance while inviting free interpretation and even subversion. On the first page of "Wonder," for example, snippets of musical staves are dispersed over the paper surface, gesturing at traditional Western music notation—notating chords and intervals, as well as frittered meters—but each fragment is interspersed with hand-drawn squiggles, arrows, and text (indexing dynamics and instrumentation, although lyrics soon appear as well). The score presents a mixed idiom, a hybrid of manuscript graphic and musical typography that echoes, to some degree, Sylvano Bussotti's tangled compositions (reproduced at the head of the introduction to Deleuze and Guattari 1987, 3). The score is a recombinant admixture of the transparently decipherable and the plural, the rhizomatic, the indeterminate. "Wonder" does not offer a washy orchestral soundtrack to contrived awe but rises and falls in surges of tension and what Mitchell refers to as "emotional instability"; voices play across their own feeling bounds, at once deferring to and refusing genetically coded behavior.

"Because what happens when you deconstruct melody, if you don't have something you can sing and hum to, is it still music?"

Despite Butler's highly aural sense of language and narrative, her "radio imagination," her intervening aliens—the agents of necessary transformation and the reauthors of human biology—hate and actively refuse human music:

> People had clustered at the guest house where someone was telling a story, and another group had gotten out flutes, drums, guitars, and a small harp. . . .

Oankali did not like music. They began to withdraw into the houses—to save their hearing, they said. Most constructs enjoyed music as much as Humans did. Several Oankali-born construct males had become wandering musicians, more than welcome at any trade village. (O. Butler 2000, 439)

That the Oankali have no predilection toward music is telling. Music is clearly unique to humans, a dominant gene that endures, passed down to future generations of interspecies. The jam session is a form of human community that the Oankali do not wish to hear, a demonstration of extemporaneous genomics outside of their immediate control; gene trading offers no definitive blueprint for human creativity.

It may seem strange both for Butler to describe the beings who heal humanity as antipathetic to the healing powers of sound and for Mitchell even to write a piece of music called "Oankali" (the fifth movement of her suite) honoring those antimusical beings, but there is an important point to be made around the work of hearing, and hearing well; listening, enacted in music such as Mitchell's or text such as Butler's, is neither deferential nor passive but involves tangible, material, embodied difference. Mitchell's music is not designed to be likable, nor is it aimed at repelling its audience. Rather, listening is a community-based species of pleasurable debate, a collision of beauty and horror, of the known and the alien: not easy agreement, but what Nancy calls "stretching." In such listening, the self accretes and coheres around its own unresolvable estrangements.

Oankali resistance to music also opens up to scrutiny their seemingly utopian aspect; they aren't offering humanity a panacea, but, through mixing, trade, through biological "community," the possibility of surviving beyond our genetically coded doom; the fatally conflicted, biologically determined end of humanity, our awful blend of intellection and hierarchy, can be reshaped into productive tension and creative conflict by engaging in a wider practice of miscegenation, of self-refashioning. In an afterword written for one of her short stories, Butler disavows utopian impulses: "I don't like most utopia stories because I don't believe them for a moment. It seems inevitable that my utopia would be someone else's hell" (2005, 214). Although clearly playful, Butler is also characteristically aware of audience, of other reading minds. She expects readers to disagree with her, hopefully creatively, which is why she is drawn to composing not introductions to her works but afterwords: "I like the idea of afterwords rather than individual introductions since afterwords allow me to talk freely about the stories without ruining them for readers. . . . I feel that what people bring to my work is at least as important to them as what I put into it" (viii). She doesn't want to put her readers through hell but to enable their responses—precisely what a radio imagination wants to do: to converse, exchange, react. Mitchell's suite is not musical allegory, nor is it programmatic, nor is it a soundtrack to Butler's text. The words Mitchell sets in some of the sections are her own, not Butler's. It's an homage or a tribute, certainly, but it's better understood as an improvisation on Butler, a musical afterword. By circumstance, Mitchell notes, the suite became a dedication posthumously to Butler: "In February 2006, I submitted my proposal for *Xenogenesis Suite* to Chamber Music America and was shocked to discover that Butler suddenly transcended from this earthly realm the day after I dropped the proposal in the mail. Her unexpected passing further strengthened my determination to pursue this project."

This homage does not take up Butler's writing as closed by her death. Instead, in the spirit of her afterwords, Mitchell finds moments of dialogic instability within Butler and gives those moments musical extension.

"I tried to make a soundtrack as if there was a bombing and what that would sound like."

Mitchell's text for the eighth section, "Before and After," consists of a string of single-syllable words: "light / time / dark / sand / leaf / ma / why / seed / hope / fear / child / grass / love / death." The collation describes a trajectory in time concluded by death. But the title suggests that listeners and performers come to inhabit an auditory space outside the limits of formal closure. The music begins with long, sustained tones that, with slightly roughened timbres, tend to resist resolving but are soon replaced by a vestigial, minor mode piano vamp—an unclosing repetition that feels as if it will cycle endlessly, with incremental variations, until it is interrupted by a fierce ensemble *tutti*. The words are spoken, not sung, in the last minute of the piece, accompanied (as if to regiment its recurrence) by a single-note piano *ostinato*. However, the vocalist doesn't repeat the words in their given order, and even adds a few of her own ("sky," "I"), as the text emerges from and then descends into a sparse, unorganized welter of percussion and breath. This is proto-language, an elemental vocabulary feeling its way toward articulation, collapsing into its phonemic constituents.

Julia Kristeva's description of what she calls the "semiotic," the sensual upwelling, prior to sense-making, of the human capacity to signify, of sound and rhythm, offers a theoretical hook for understanding how Mitchell's "setting" of words to music operates (1984, 24). The one word in this string that gestures definitively at Kristevan semiosis is *ma*—a colloquialism for mother and also a nonsense syllable. Tropes of "ma," of motherhood and reproduction, occupy a contested and yet potentially transformative corporeal and psychic space within Butler's text. Rosi Braidotti notes how "recent feminist readings of the maternal function have stressed the double bind of the maternal issue. Motherhood is seen as both one of the patriarchal dominations of women and one of the strongholds of female identity" (1994, 181). Butler's narrative pivots on the theme of reproduction and the role of mother in the (dis)continuation and alteration of the human species. *Xenogenesis* etymologically suggests alterity, referencing the propagation of offspring that have undergone profound mutation. Lilith, held captive on a mothership far from her earthly origins, is chosen to become the first mother of a new interspecies; she is also assigned to act as surrogate mother to a group of humans who will eventually be awakened from their suspended animation to repopulate a restored Earth. The alien ship is like a womb, a smooth enclosure with no angles or openings; it is the space where Lilith is literally "reborn." The pods encasing the sleeping humans are also womb-like, and Lilith is required to act as midwife in the rebirth of the humans who have been assigned to her care. When probed about their homeland by Lilith, the Oankali describe it as a womb to which they cannot return because it was "time to be reborn" (O. Butler 2000, 37). At the end of *Dawn*, Lilith is impregnated by the Oankali ooloi, the third gender being who facilitates interspecies sex and reproduction. Lilith is told that the ooloi Nikanj has mixed the genes of multiple Oankali/human "parents" to create the child inside of her without her consent (246–48). The outcome of this new gestation will be both hybrid and monstrous, a creature of wonder and fear. The Oankali subsequently coerce Lilith's agreement by rationalizing their betterment of human biology through mixing and splicing, but she remains resistant, both to the utopian possibilities presented by the Oankali and to her own role as species mother:

> "But it won't be human," she whispered. "It will be a thing. A monster." . . .
> "Our children will be better than either of us," it continued. "We will moderate your hierarchical problems and you will lessen our physical limitations." . . .
> "But they won't be human," Lilith said. "That's what matters. You can't understand, but that *is* what matters."
> Its tentacles knotted. "The child inside you matters." (247–48)

Lilith's pregnancy involves a profound ambivalence that remains unresolved at the end of the novel; this ambivalence—coupling love and loss, horror and beauty, abjection and transcendence—also sounds itself musically throughout

Mitchell's suite as a tension within the performing community of her ensemble between accepting the maternal shaping influence of the composer's vision and expanding, extemporaneously, on the guiding framework of the graphic score—an elaboration that the indeterminate visual form of the score actually requires from performers. Mitchell herself, as both composer and ensemble member, enacts this tension within her own playing, when, as an improviser, she simultaneously attends to and departs from her (and Butler's) provisionally written material, producing an inherently hybrid, temporary music. She becomes, arguably, a musical ooloi.

Butler's strategic use of the mother metaphor throughout the trilogy draws from the embodied exploitation and resistance black women have negotiated within the racist confines of colonization, slavery, and modern society. Grounding her work in particular historical moments, Butler's black feminist positioning weaves the stories of iconic black women into Lilith's chronicle, giving voice to a history of omission that exposes "the ascendance of medical theories about the "alien" attributes of black women" in regard to corporeality, sexuality, and reproduction (H. Washington 2008, 83).[5] By embedding particular historical moments in the fabric of her futuristic parables, Butler's radio imagination listens backward then writes forward in a call-and-response that intones the complex genetics of community. Butler hears Lilith's voice reverberate in accounts of the disturbing exploitation of black populations in the name of Western science, and she allows unspeakable atrocities, such as the Tuskegee experiments that seem to belong more to the stuff of science fiction than to modern medicine, to haunt her narratives.[6]

Studied and probed by the Oankali, Lilith conjures Saartjie (Sarah) Baartman,[7] an African woman often referred to as "the Hottentot Venus," who was anatomically scrutinized for her steatopygia (protruding buttocks) by medical professionals in England and publicly displayed at circuses and lavish parties in Paris during the early nineteenth century. When Baartman died in Paris in 1815 around the age of twenty-seven, an autopsy was performed on her body and famously published by Georges Cuvier. Most notably the postmortem mutilation of Baartman's body preserved her genitalia and became a permanent display at the Musée de l'Homme in Paris until the 1970s. The spectacle of Baartman's defaced corpse served as a cautionary tale of the pathological black female body associated with degeneracy, disease, and prostitution; such appraisals were reinforced by the nineteenth-century medical model that constituted black women's bodies as alien, justifying both abuse and voyeurism (Gilman 2010, 17).

"By having intelligent and paternalistic aliens rescue humanity from the self-destruction of nuclear war, Butler may ask of us: why do we see difference of color, culture, ideas and religion as bigger than our similarities or biology?"

Although she retains her horror and disgust at the authoritarian, callous, and abusive treatment she receives from the Oankali, Lilith also embraces the fraught but tangible transformative potential that her captors necessarily offer her. Baartman could do little to rescue herself, but Butler's Lilith—and especially Mitchell's posthumous reimagining of her—enables a creative vitality in survival beyond her humanity. Mitchell's music materially re-members, as what she calls "the smell of fear," the atrocities committed on black women's bodies, but also converts oppression into reciprocity, domination into physiological call-and-response, a trade. "Find humor in your captors," she writes in her notes to "Oankali," "identify with them, so you can save your mind." The "you" here concatenates figures of Lilith, Mitchell herself, Butler's readers, Mitchell's listeners, and the members of the Black Earth Ensemble performing the music. This transformative "humor" (a term for laughter and for the personality-determining fluids that medieval physicians believed governed human physiology) sounds in "Oankali" as a tension between a fractured polka bounce in the string bass and the stuttering vocals, as in the opening section of the suite; Ndosi's voice doesn't so much laugh as gasp, yodel, and yawp. Playing against the parodic, dour comedy of what could almost be a circus-music bass line (recalling Baartman's public display), the vocalist refuses the violence of regulation and instead sounds a provisionally bittersweet chuckle, her reappropriation of an aural practical joke.

Admittedly, the second-line musical representation of power struggles over black women's bodies remains at a remove from the historical and material fact of atrocity, but the corporeal immediacy of performed, extemporaneous sound in Mitchell's work touches on their lived experience as text cannot quite do, producing contiguities, moments of felt contact, as we listen. Lilith's "talent" for cancer also summons the ghost of Henrietta Lacks, a poor descendant of slaves who worked the tobacco farms in Virginia and sought medical treatment on the "colored" ward of Johns Hopkins Medical Center, despite her general apprehensiveness of the medical profession amid rumors of illicit experimentation conducted on African Americans. The "knot" Henrietta felt in her body was diagnosed in 1951 as a malignant cervical tumor and was harvested without her consent by researchers at Johns Hopkins. George Gey, the director of tissue culture research whose career-long quest was to find an "immortal" cell line, cultured Henrietta's cells and found that they were uniquely virulent, reproducing as no other cells had in a laboratory environment. Gey named these cells HeLa and began to ship them worldwide to researchers, eventually spawning a multimillion-dollar biogenetics industry.

The radium treatment Lacks received proved unsuccessful, and she died shortly after her diagnosis, unaware that her contribution to science would revolutionize medical research; contribute to countless vaccines for diseases such as polio, human papillomavirus, and cancer; develop cloning and gene mapping; and form the basis of the Human Genome Project. Lacks's family, similarly unsuspecting, was also used in research without consent once they were identified as Henrietta's blood relatives. The family was neither informed nor compensated for the unwitting role they or Henrietta played in scientific research, revealing post-antebellum exploitation of African Americans, carved with particular cruelty on the corporeality of black women (Skloot 2010).

Fannie Lou Hamer fell victim to the same cruelty and violence when she entered a Mississippi hospital for a procedure that would remove a benign fibroid tumor from her uterus. She was later informed by means of local gossip that the surgeon who performed the procedure had removed much more than a fibroid from her body; without her consent he had given her a hysterectomy. Hamer, a poor sharecropper, confronted the doctor, who offered no explanation for his actions, propelling her toward political engagement. Although "mother" to many in the civil rights movement, Hamer often referred to her "Mississippi appendectomy" with deep regret. Forced sterilization for African Americans was linked to the practice of eugenics in the United States, sparking a fear that reverberates in Lilith's consciousness:

> "You had a growth," he said. "A cancer. We got rid of it." . . .
> "What did I lose along with the cancer?" she asked softly.
> "Nothing."
> "Not a few feet of intestine? My ovaries? My uterus?" (O. Butler 2000, 21)

We need to remember, as listeners and readers for *Xenogenesis*, that the dreadful, tampered, creatively enabling corporeality addressed in text and music is materially sounded as maternal. For Kristeva, motherhood presents this address as necessarily conflicted, a concatenation of sense, flesh, and social materiality. The mother subtends a concurrent existence of self and other—a paradox of "being oneself and someone else at the same time" (1984, 223) and mediates mind and body. The mothering manifest by Butler and Mitchell is not merely figural but has had very real consequences for the lives and identities of black women. "Throughout the ages," Mitchell writes in her "Composer's Notes" to *Xenogenesis Suite*, "countless people have been victimized by others, torn from the familiar and subjected to foreign ways of life." This violent estrangement is not merely a matter of encounters with foreign cultures, but has also happened and continues to happen within the boundaries of the United States as racially marked violence, a dire estrangement to ourselves.

For black women, motherhood is often a strategic site of embodied political consciousness, resistance, and agency. As Patricia Hill Collins notes, mother is an expansive role, one that must also be adaptable; "Motherhood—whether bloodmother, othermother, or community othermother—can be invoked as a symbol of power by African-American women engaged in Black women's community work" (2009, 207). This stance does not rule out ambivalence toward motherhood by some African American women, but it speaks to the importance of a strategic standpoint that understands the complexity of mother in a legacy of reproductive coercion. Within a constellation that reflects a similar kind of control, Lilith must negotiate mother on her own terms as best she can:

> She was intended to live and reproduce, not to die. Experimental animal, parent or domestic animals? Or . . . nearly extinct animal, part of a captive breeding program? Human biologists had done that before the war—used a few captive members of an endangered animal species to breed more for the wild population. Was that what she was headed for? Forced artificial insemination. Surrogate motherhood? Fertility drugs and forced "donations" of eggs? Implantation of unrelated fertilized eggs. Removal of children from mothers at birth . . . Humans had done these things to captive breeders—all for a higher good of course. (O. Butler 2000, 60)

Priscilla Wald links Lilith's fate to the genetic and medical experimentation enabled by HeLa, noting that "Lilith's sense of being tampered with—of no longer owning herself (which is her first thought on awakening among the Oankali)—anticipates the outraged response (and charges of racism) of indigenous groups to population geneticists' proposals to collect the DNA of indigenous populations allegedly facing 'extinction'" (2012, 261). Wald ties this outrage to the tangible fear among African American women of the destruction of racial and cultural memory. Hybridity, in her reading, offers humanity real transformative potential, but also carries the residues of oppression and loss in miscegenation. "Mixed-race hybrids at once embody the principle of ecology—the health of the population—and represent a threat to the reproduction of a 'humanity' that defines itself by stasis—the ability to look into the future and imagine a mirror image of contemporary social and biological configurations" (261). Mitchell's musical "reading" of Butler departs from Wald's in its more sanguine sense of transformative possibilities, but it also retains something like Wald's insistence on remembering the material, historical facts not only of corporeal abuse but also of a strategically essential racial identity tied to mother and community.

"It's kind of like putting your lab coat on and trying to find a whole new world through playing one of these instruments or through electronic music."

Mitchell's revitalizing working method for *Xenogenesis Suite* might be grasped as an instance of what Isabelle Stengers has called "reciprocal capture." As a philosopher of science, Stengers interests herself in the capacity of the scientific imagination to engage exactly in what Butler calls trading; that the study of scientific fact—particularly as work on particle physics or on the human genome progresses in the scientific community—increasingly manifests itself in terms of reciprocities and instabilities, or what Stengers might want to call, under the influence of Gilles Deleuze and Félix Guattari, multiplicities. Her overarching science is ecology, conceived in a particular sense, as "the science of multiplicities, disparate causalities, and unintentional creations of meaning" (Stengers 2010, 34). Reciprocal capture is a definable biological practice of interdependency, an interdependency that is also a discursive practice. An "immanent process of reciprocal capture" (as distinct from either parasitism or mimetic defense), involves not so much autopoeisis—self-sustained making—as heteropoeisis—other-making, or the mutual making of self both within and outside of itself, relationally: "we can speak of reciprocal capture whenever a *dual* process of identity construction is produced: regardless of the manner, and usually in ways that are completely different, identities that coinvent one another each integrate a reference to the other for their own benefit" (36). This practice of coinvention suggests an improvisational ecology that informs Mitchell's performances, which are thoroughly collaborative and musically both accretive and heterogeneous. Their call-and-response structure involves not simply a trading of phrases among soloists or an interdependency of improviser and accompanist, but a fundamentally interwoven exchange—a combination of deference and resistance, of historical acknowledgment and forward-moving departure "ancient to the future"—that converts the potential victimization of being captured, suppressed, and determined by identitarian authority (whether social, cultural, or musical) into a realization of self and voice, turning strategies of control not only into tactics of resistance or backtalk but also into recombinant identities, genomic communities, new selves.

"A lot of my music actually tends to be very joyful and celebratory and to actually go in this direction to make you feel this gripping feeling was a real challenge for me."

The "dawn of a new life" promised in the final section of Mitchell's suite is not a naively conceived utopia but a restless and—as Mitchell says of Butler—unsettling desire for creative exchange, for living community. When the vocalist sings that "we collide / transformation looms / memories ripped and shredded for your greater pleasures," she is refiguring the race-marked fear of social death, embodied vestigially in Butler's text through the specters of (m)other-figures such as Baartman, Lacks, and Hamer, into an "intelligent creation" mixing "fear and wonder," drawing "different orbits" into momentary rapturous conjunction. What matters even more, as we listen to Mitchell's ensemble perform this piece, is that the vocalist's articulation is muddled and indistinct; often, it's not clear—within a panoply of glisses, slurs, and mutterings—that she is singing words at all. Voiced at the margins of audible or legible speech, the lyrics are simultaneously uttered and disavowed, converted into upwellings of semiosis, of both sense and nonsense, of sensuous happening. This last section of the suite is deliberately composed in the tradition of the jazz ballad; it speaks about love and loss, or perhaps more specifically, the anguish of love and loss. The flute is very melodic throughout, in dialogue with and in contrast to the anguished vocals depicting the conflicted position of the humans walking into the sunset "together" with the Oankali. There is both love and loss in the dawn of this new life. Within the fabric of a multiplicitous female voice (Butler's, Lilith's, Mitchell's, Ndosi's), we hear the tug and tear of mixing realize itself: an embodied reciprocity *and* resistance, sounding and sharing its survival.

Notes

1. For more information on Anthony Braxton and his oeuvre, see www.tricentric foundation.org.

2. Mitchell was AACM president from 2009 to the end of 2010, vice president from 2005 to 2007, and co-president with Douglas Ewart from 2007 to 2009.

3. For more information on the Herb Alpert Award for the Arts see www.alpertawards .org (accessed October 15, 2012). For more information on the Doris Duke Artist Award see www.ddpaa.org/program (accessed August 7, 2013).

4. All headings are taken from Nicole Mitchell's "Lecture: Afro-Futurism" (2011).

5. *Black feminist* is a contested term. See, for example, Collins (2009).

6. The Tuskegee Syphilis Study was an infamous clinical study conducted in Tuskegee, Alabama, between 1932 and 1972. Poor, rural black men were coerced to participate with

the promise of free health care but were left to suffer and die from the untreated disease. See H. Washington (2008). Don Byron's CD *Tuskegee Experiments* is a musical response to the experiments that Byron calls "metaphors for African-American life" (Electra Nonesuch, 9 79280–2).

7. Naming Saartjie (Sarah) Baartman is fraught with difficulties. Her Khoikhoi birth name is unknown. "Saartjie," a Cape Dutch diminutive of "Sarah," appears to be the earliest name by which she is known, so we have elected to use it here.

PART V

Representation and Identity

15. Faster and Louder

HETEROSEXIST IMPROVISATION IN
NORTH AMERICAN TAIKO

Deborah Wong

Jazz has served as a platform for deeply held ideas about difference and democracy in ways inspired and troubled, inspiring and reactionary. Social
transformation is always incomplete; antihegemonic practices often carry
stowaways from incompatible histories. Progressive musical practices are almost always imperfect and uneven.[1] Here I focus on how the powerful ideological links between jazz improvisation, race, and gender were transported
into *taiko*, the dynamic contemporary Japanese tradition of drumming now
firmly established in North America. I trace the effects of this history and
ask why so many Asian American women who play taiko are uneasy about
improvising, don't think they're good at it, and are afraid to try. More deeply,
I consider the fraught interface between improvisation and women. Certain
traditions of improvised jazz have offered powerful progressive ideals of social transformation but almost always without addressing the overwhelming
presence of men in their midst.

Liberatory discourses always walk a fragile line, and progressive identity
formations that push against prevailing models of race and gender are especially tough to sustain. Falling back on common-sense understandings of difference is too easy, and sometimes it seems to me that every new gesture draws
on contradictory moves that can undermine the progressive potential of the
experiment. In this chapter, I focus on improvised solos in taiko. Effective
community building through performance takes a great deal of vigilance, and
taiko is no exception. Asian Americans literally play themselves into visibility and audibility through taiko in fraught environments defined by the low-
est common denominator principles of corporate multiculturalism. These
paradoxes set up a number of traps. Taiko invites a reading of performance

practice as social formation: the pleasures and seductions of such a structural reading are nearly irresistible. Taiko is loud, choreographed, and a post-1960s presence in the face of Chinatowns burned and Japantowns "evacuated" (in the paternalistic language of the U.S. and Canadian governments during World War II). Many Asian Americans accept invisibility and inaudibility as a condition for safety and citizenship. The area of improvisation studies represented by this book and indeed by the Improvisation, Community, and Social Practice project[2] that generated this collection, is energized by a problem: How can we avoid valorizing improvisation while still insisting on its potentially progressive power? What are the relationships between musical and social practices, and between musical aesthetics and social aesthetics? Rather than exalt improvisation as a catchall praxis of liberation, we must also attend to how improvisation can be hardened and assert other kinds of clout. We can celebrate improvisation as a space of freedom but must also recognize that it sometimes offers a stage for some pretty tired ideas about ability and authority. As Vijay Iyer has said, improvisation isn't always a model for progressive social change, and it certainly won't be unless we insist on it.[3] Writ large, improvisation is alternatively *de*valued (as black, as low culture) and sometimes *over*valued (as black, hip, and interventionist). All this gets played out—often quite loudly—in taiko.

Taiko is both new and old. The Japanese practice of playing a large, barrel-shaped drum in Shinto and Buddhist ritual is very old[4] and quite alive; taiko playing is often spectacularly featured in the thousands of regional festivals (*matsuri*) in Japan. In the wake of World War II, young Japanese musicians used taiko to assert a new modernity by drawing on it as a "traditional" music while infusing it with the Japanese martial arts movement and other musics. I revisit this later by examining taiko's originary moments in the 1950s, the period when taiko was first influenced by jazz. This "new tradition" is called *kumi-daiko*, "group taiko," because taiko ensembles usually feature numerous drums of at least three different sizes usually played in fast, loud, virtuosic, athletic style that are quite unlike the dignified, minimalist solo drumming that continues to accompany Shinto and Buddhist ritual.

I studied taiko intensively as a performer from 1997 to 2009, and my ongoing ethnographic research addresses taiko in Southern California and its place in Japanese American and Asian American communities. As I have written elsewhere (D. Wong 2004, 2008), I was drawn to taiko precisely for the loud, graceful, and powerful promise it extends to Asian Americans . . . especially to Asian American women. Ideas about race, ethnicity, and gender are played out through taiko in a transpacific flow of performative exchange. In any musical tradition, the ability to improvise is always gendered and raced because it usually emanates from a powerful nexus of ideas about musical mastery, skill, and authority. Taiko solos are thus racialized and gendered in complicated ways that reveal how the tradition is located in transnational circuits of desire. Here I address how certain taiko players improvise and when; how they think about improvisation; how improvisation acts out deep values; how it performs contradictions; how it is loved by performers and audiences alike; how it is an intense locus for intercultural expansion within taiko; and how ideas about gendered mastery are sometimes carried forward in improvised solos in unthoughtful ways. Improvised taiko solos are thrilling: they allow us to see and hear how pleasure is shaped through performance. I have found that Asian American women are often unwilling to perform improvised solos, and when they try, many are uneasy and uncomfortable because fraught histories of gendered and racialized powerlessness are suddenly put up against the expectation that the soloist should want to revel in the display of her individuality and prowess. Improvised taiko solos are thus most frequently performed by men. Although I am always stirred by the sight of Asian or Asian American men performing strength and power through taiko, at the same time I long for a woman to (at least sometimes) take their place, even as I remind myself that those performatives of strength and mastery are inevitably masculinist, and even as I confront, all over again, the contradictions bundled up in my own pleasures as a taiko player, student, fan, and culture bearer.[5] Let me offer some moments of improvised confusion and triumph, all from my perspective as a taiko player and witness.

Lost in Improvisation

I am a member of the Taiko Center of Los Angeles, and we perform frequently. In March 2008, we performed a full-length concert in Banning, California; just after intermission we played "Aranami," our signature piece, composed by our teacher, Rev. Tom Kurai. *Aranami* means "turbulent waves," and the piece is meant to impress: it is heavy, dramatic, and high energy. Fifteen of us were there that day to perform it, which was ideal because "Aranami" works best with a lot of drums and drummers. "Aranami" is only twenty-eight measures long, and we play it in several different arrangements. In more informal performances (for example, at street fairs), we often just play it through four times in a row with the fourth round at a faster tempo, which takes about three and a half minutes total. At more formal performances, when our most skilled and experienced musicians are present, we often extend "Aranami" by inserting a long section of improvised solos in the middle. On the evening in question, the "corps" of the group was fifteen musicians (fourteen women

and one man) of varying skill levels filling much of the stage, all of us on individual *chudaiko*, a drum roughly the size of a wine barrel. Gary and Rev. Tom[6]
were off to the side of the group: Gary led us from a small, high-pitched drum
(*shime-daiko*) and Rev. Tom improvised throughout on a set of three fan-
drums (*uchiwa-daiko*), that is, small frame drums with different pitches. Judi
and I were both on chudaiko in the front center of the mass of chudaiko. We
played through "Aranami" twice with Gary maintaining time on shime with
a straight *teke-teke-teke-teke* pattern,[7] an ostinato used in many taiko pieces.
When we finished the second round, everyone except the soloists knelt—that
is, Rev. Tom and Gary remained standing, and so did Judi and I. Rev. Tom
had assigned the order of the solos ahead of time: me, Gary, and then himself.
Judi and I started off with a fixed phrase (DON *doko do-*DON) that we played
four times. Then I played an improvised solo while Judi kept time beside me
(*doko doko doko doko*), then Gary played a solo, and then Rev. Tom played a
solo. After he finished his solo, Rev. Tom was supposed to give us all a cue:
DON DON DON DON DON DON DON DON *doko doko doko doko* DOKO DOKO
DOKO DOKO, so the entire group could dramatically leap to its feet en masse
and play "Aranami" one last time.

The middle section of improvised solos is meant to crank up the energy
and excitement of the performance. Usually our two youngest members play
the solos, but they weren't there that night, so the three of us were substitutes.
I wasn't used to soloing. Rev. Tom was pushing me a bit, giving me a chance
to try something new. It is entirely his call who gets to play solos, and indeed
everything is his call because it is his group: he is the sensei, the teacher and
artistic director. I knew ahead of time I would be playing a sixteen-measure
solo, but I foolishly decided to actually improvise, that is, not precompose
something and memorize it, as so many taiko players do. Frankly, I *should*
have precomposed it: my short improvised solo wasn't good at all. My rhythms
were pedestrian; I offered a pretty dogmatic regurgitation of standard phrases;
I lagged behind the beat. My solo was downright lame, but I finished and
handed it off to Gary.

Gary and Rev. Tom are fantastic musicians, and they are used to playing together, so there was a nice dialogue between them, and the rest of us
supported them like crazy. Supporting a fellow musician is not an abstract
concept in taiko. An articulated, explicit theory of energy and social aesthetics means that taiko players express, channel, and intensify their *ki* (energy) in
a number of codified ways, especially by shouting. As Rev. Tom's and Gary's
solos took off, we urged them on with *kakegoe*, the shouts used in the Japanese martial arts for the same reasons, so their playing was punctuated with
spontaneous shouts of *Ho! Yo! So-re!*, all formulaic syllables, all used to raise

the energy level and encourage the soloists. Since Rev. Tom and Gary mostly used formulaic duple rhythmic patterns, we also knew where best to insert kakegoe—that is, although kakegoe are spontaneous and improvised, they are not arbitrary, and in fact we learn how to fit them in, rhythmically and structurally. Gary's solo was fast and intricate. He combined taiko rhythms and rock and roll riffs in ways that we've come to expect from him and never tire of. Next came Rev. Tom's solo on the fan drums, which was more taiko-esque, drawn more literally from traditional taiko rhythmic patterns but also nicely melodic since he had three pitched fan drums with which to play. But then Rev. Tom went into a big decrescendo and we got ready for him to bring us back in . . . except he didn't—he kept going. And going. I felt a ripple of awareness run through the rest of the group. He couldn't remember the cue to bring us all back in! We had a problem. Gary came back in and we all thought he would take matters in hand. Gary started a long solo, pure rock and roll, and Rev. Tom stopped soloing and just kept the beat. Then they started to trade phrases back and forth, call-and-response, and it was nicely done, but they kept going back and forth, pounding away, and eventually the rest of us realized we had another problem: *neither* of them could remember the cue! They didn't know how to get out of their solos! The rest of us kept waiting, and finally I did something I'm rarely in a position to do. I took it away from them: I shouted a kakegoe, played the musical cue, Judi and I repeated it in unison, and everyone jumped up and came back in. We played one final round of "Aranami" at top speed and ended with a flourish.

I have watched our video of this performance a number of times, and now I think I should have cut in earlier. I can see several points where I had already assessed the situation and could have taken action; in fact, I can see from my own body language that I almost did so but pulled back, waiting for Rev. Tom or Gary to save us. Actually, I can see that Judi was having similar reactions, and she's quite accustomed to leading. This performance, in all its drama, is emblematic of the American taiko scene. The corps/body of the massed women offers energetic support to the virtuosic soloing men. I also acknowledge my (woman's) improvisational ability to get back together, to go from mass to individual and back to mass, and the gendered/raced dynamics that made it possible. It was actually a terrific performance due precisely to our improvised responses—among Gary, Rev. Tom, and me, and among the rest of us who knew how to wait, listen, assess, and respond. All of this occurred in a diasporic environment where 75 percent of North American taiko practitioners are women but teaching taiko and improvising remain primarily male domains.[8]

A Kōan: When Is a Solo Not Heterosexist?

At the time of this writing, there are perhaps five thousand taiko groups in Japan, around two hundred in North America, and another fifty or so spread out across Western Europe (featuring mostly non-Japanese musicians) and Brazil (in diasporic Japanese communities).[9] Taiko is the music du jour in North America. While taiko was based in the Japanese American community from the late 1960s through the late 1980s, by the early 1990s it had become more broadly Asian American and by the late 1990s was attracting performers from many different ethnic backgrounds, especially white Americans.[10]

Jazz and free improvisation are the two North American modes of musicking where improvisation reigns supreme, and both are strongly, deeply, and historically male.[11] Kumi-daiko was intercultural from its beginnings, and improvisation's specific place within it is, at the heart, a gesture taken wholesale from jazz and transplanted into taiko. It is simply understood that certain things are supposed to happen in an improvised taiko solo: great technique will be displayed, and it will be exciting. The individual's prowess is on display and only "good" musicians do it in public. All those factors—technique, excitement, prowess, excellence—are defined in masculinist terms lifted directly from jazz (and a bit from rock). Kinnara Taiko in Los Angeles is the only group I know that takes the exact *opposite* approach to soloing: everyone in that group is expected to solo, improvised group jamming is constant, and the point is not to show off but to learn to play in response to one another. Kinnara's approach to improvisation is central to their Buddhist group philosophy and is explicitly articulated. Indeed, it is so unusual—so different—that it is almost always mentioned, and their soloing doesn't emulate the model I just described. Instead, Kinnara members' solos are often soft, loose, and even playful, in marked contrast to the "power taiko" soloing that is now the norm.

In comparison, Asian prowess and skill is central to the international world of classical music. Mari Yoshihara has shown how Asians are regarded as overly adept performers of Western European art music and that East Asian investment in classical music is based in certain ideologies that have traveled far. As she puts it, "Many Asian families associate classical music with Western modernity, cultural sophistication, and upper-middle-class status" (Yoshihara n.d.). One result is the "overrepresentation" of East Asians in U.S. conservatories (Yoshihara 2007, 4–5). Yoshihara notes pervasive beliefs that East Asian approaches to Western European art music tend to emphasize discipline and structure rather than innovation or change (42–45). In comparison, nonconformity is often valued if not overdetermined in U.S. ideologies of creativity, but in the taiko community, conformity is regularly encouraged in every way except in the solo. The social aesthetics of taiko maintain an environment where stepping out from the group even in mundane ways may be seen as tantamount to selfishness or an arrogant insistence on putting your needs above everyone else's. The taiko solo is thus a space in which a strikingly different set of values is highlighted, yet its inherent contradictions are far from arbitrary.

I must now disclose that I'm ashamed of my badly executed improvised solo, described already. Furthermore, I'm ashamed of my habitually bad soloing. I wish I were better at improvising solos, but I've had little chance to try and I'm extremely anxious about doing it. Whenever I get to solo, I'm not very good, thus proving that taiko doesn't automatically reset the interconstitutive relationship between race and gender. Many Asian American women go to taiko in search of a subjectivity they don't already have, as I have written elsewhere (D. Wong 2004). Many of us long for the strength, discipline, and presence that taiko clearly provides, and many of us find it. Most of us find it in the act of playing alongside others, as I address in more detail shortly. When Asian/Asian American men improvise in taiko, however, they generally draw on the model of the jazz solo—that is, the powerful model of African American male improvisation—at the cost of Asian American women, who come to believe that we can't pull it off.

The Asian/American man labors under a long history of feminization, as most famously depicted in *M. Butterfly* (Hwang 1989). Indeed, his femininity is one of the key means through which the slippery ambivalence between "Asian" and "American" is maintained. Whether undersexed, effeminate, or literally feminized, the Asian/American man is either asexual or a bottom. He is defined through a dynamic binary relationship with the hypersexualized black man: as Richard Fung notes, "the Asian man is defined by a striking absence down there" (Fung 1998, 117). David Eng argues that the Chinese immigrant bachelor communities created by U.S. immigration laws had far-reaching effects on the social construction of the Asian American man. As he puts it, "Asian American masculinity must always be read as an overdetermined symptom whose material existence draws its discursive sustenance from multiple structures and strategies relating to racialization, gender, and (homo)sexualizing" (Eng 2001, 18). In sum, the Asian American man cannot be masculine or even, really, straight. He may try to mobilize masculinist tropes such as sports and the martial arts, but these discursive efforts often activate, in turn, the need to keep Asian American women in their place. That is, such performative efforts come at a cost. King-Kok Cheung flatly states, "The refutation of effeminate stereotypes through the glorification of machismo merely perpetuates patriarchal terms and assumptions" (2004, 165). She argues that Asian American antifeminism ultimately builds up Asian American masculinity by aligning it with heterosexist white dominance. Asian American sexism thus serves a real purpose: the Asian American man can only be rehabilitated at the expense of the Asian American woman.

These problems are imported wholesale into the raced and gendered politics of North American taiko. In his work on the postwar "tradition" of Japanese men soloing on the largest drum (*odaiko*), Paul Yoon flags multiple anxieties driving the performance of masculinity. He notes that men in North American taiko look to Asia for models, stating that "positive stereotypes typically flow from Asia into the Asian American imagination and not the other way around. Whether it's the *kung fu* master, *samurai*, *yakuza*, Ultraman, or ruthless Korean *gangpae*, these Asian male bodies are agentic and powerful, all of which are traits recognizably aligned with (at the very least) Western notions of masculinity that are typically constructed as 'good'" (Yoon 2009, 100). Furthermore, he documents gay taiko players' profound anxieties over acceptance by the U.S. taiko community (123), and he dwells on a well-known performance by a young Japanese American male taiko player (Bryan Yamami) who relies on parody to reconstitute the masculine Asian American taiko player.[12] I would go further than Yoon and say that the North American taiko community is generally imagined as heteronormative and in practice is often heterosexist.

The taiko solo is thus a fraught node of racialized heterosexist display and control. It carries with it a constellation of attitudes and needs. I am attempting the kind of "ear training" advocated by Sherrie Tucker (2001/2002, 377), who has argued that jazz studies needs to attend more closely to "historically contingent ideas about masculinity and femininity, in conversation with multiple and shifting ideas about race, ethnicity, class, sexuality, national identity, empire, and capitalism" (379). Tucker asks in no uncertain terms why gender analysis is largely absent from jazz studies. As she puts it, "even in academic jazz studies, to raise the specter of feminist theory, or even of gender as a pertinent consideration, is often to invite an eerie parallel of what it must feel like for a woman horn player, of any number of historical time periods, to enter a cutting contest where the rules of what counts as virtuosity, prestige, authenticity, and value have been laid down by people who, quite possibly, do not want you there" (383).

It should come as no surprise that many woman taiko players, especially Asian American women, approach soloing with a lot of trepidation. Many don't want to do it at all. When pushed, some take a back door into it by creating and memorizing a solo and then playing it whenever they are called on to "improvise." Soloing is the antithesis of what draws many women into taiko to begin with. Asian American women tend to like that feeling of being strong *and* being part of a group, of being bigger and stronger than yourself, of drawing strength and presence from that totality. Brenda Joy Lem, a long-time member of the feminist taiko group Raging Asian Women and now the director of the all-women Inner Truth Taiko Dojo, writes:

> Taiko originally were played only by men. Many traditional cultures believe it is the men's role to play the drums. By women-centred taiko I mean Inner Truth Taiko Dojo is a space which not only allows women to drum, but works with and values qualities often considered weakness or limitations in women: openness of emotions, grounded energy, internal strength, softness or fluidity, and brings them to the centre of our practice. This is not to assume these qualities are always or only found in women. I find in general these qualities are not valued in our society and not found in most people. There are hundreds of taiko groups in North America and, although most groups tend to have a larger membership of women than men, only a few are led by a woman. Even groups which are led by women often focus on dominating values of power, aggression, speed and elitism. (Lem 2008, 6)

When you are pushed forward to solo, suddenly you are on your own, alone, called on to do something profoundly different from the skills you have spent so much time developing—skills like the ability to lock in with others, to put aside your ego, to be part of something bigger than yourself. Suddenly you're expected to do the exact opposite: you're supposed to step forward and say, in effect, "Look how great I am! Look at what I can do all by myself! Look what I've come up with that's mine, distinct from the group!" You have neither the heart nor the stomach for it. More deeply, you don't think you have the skills for it. You have no confidence, and of course improvised solos are all about confidence.

I have not mentioned the absence of Amy and Taylor, both then nineteen years old and the two strongest musicians in the Taiko Center of Los Angeles, on the night of the endless solos. They usually play the parts that Judi and I played, and they usually play brilliant solos. Both grew up through, and in, taiko. They each started playing when they were seven or eight years old, and both accept the terms of the contract: play louder, faster! Amy usually improvises her solo, and Taylor usually plays something she works out ahead of time. They are impatient with my questions; both play with a freedom and mastery that I envy. They are both beautiful, confident, skilled young women who seem to disrupt the masculinist paradigm but mostly reinforce it . . . and I am in awe of their skills.

Solos have a special place both in jazz fan culture and in jazz scholarship. Jazz journalists and jazz scholars have often assumed that solos are the locus of a performer's "genius." Post-1980s jazz studies include an impressive number of articles and dissertations devoted to close examinations of improvised solos. Most academic scholarship on soloing has emphasized notes and structures over social relationships, with the significant, groundbreaking exceptions of Ingrid Monson's (1996) and Paul Berliner's (2012) work. Transcribing recorded performances of solos is a time-honored practice in jazz scholarship. A significant body of jazz scholarship has focused on the notes, addressing how soloists make improvisatory decisions and come up with those sounds. Thomas Brothers's work, for instance, has delved deeply into syntax and soloists' abilities to move within, or to step beyond, structures created by harmony and melody. As Brothers puts it, soloists' "radical detachment from the harmonic cycle" by the early 1940s was built on soloing "techniques developed by Armstrong, Young, Hawkins, and others," and "were extended and intensified" (1994, 498).

At another level, soloing is all about the gendered social psychology of confidence and presence. Erin Wehr-Flowers writes that "as jazz study becomes more specialized and advanced, there appears to be an increased expectation for improvisation and a decrease in participation by women" (2006, 338). Wehr-Flowers surveyed 332 students,[13] all instrumentalists, in middle school, junior high school, high school, college, and community jazz programs and found that "females are significantly less confident, more anxious, and have less self-efficacy (attitude) towards learning jazz improvisation" (345). In her landmark study of "all-girl" swing bands of the 1940s, Tucker found that most white woman musicians did not take solos (though some did), and those who did learned how to improvise by sitting in with African American musicians (2000, 52–53). She notes that "white women who improvised sought membership in bands where they could focus on these skills, which were not always prized in white all-girl bands" (53). Tucker looks closely at how gender and race intersected with ideologies of skill. She follows the compliment of "she plays like a man!" through jam session showdowns between two all-girl bands of color and through newspaper reporters' surprise that "they really play" (204). "Girl" soloists' abilities in the 1940s set the foundation for the raced/gendered ideologies of improvisatory skill that persist in the early twenty-first century:

> "She plays like a man" was a compliment, one freely doled out by the press, men musicians, and audience members, and one about which women sometimes complained during our [oral history] interviews. But playing

"like men" was also seen as a positive thing in that it made it possible to describe women's playing as undifferentiated from—not just equal to—men's. [. . .] To perform jazz without audible gender difference meant women playing instruments and styles that were associated with men. It meant women refusing to restrict themselves to soft or sweet timbres. It meant women improvising. And such women, whose jazz did not produce *feminine difference*, challenged both audiences' definition of *woman* and men's exclusive possession of the most highly valued instruments and styles. (209–10)

Tucker thus identifies the pernicious and pervasive ways that gendered musicking was habitually remasculinized during the war years as a condition for success, despite women who refused binary assumptions and quotidian expectations in jazz.

Jazz carries powerful gender ideologies, and although jazz scholarship has long paid almost obsessive attention to the black/white binary (by sometimes questioning it, sometimes romanticizing and essentializing it, and often reifying it), the task of following gendered epistemologies through jazz histories has barely begun despite Tucker's groundbreaking work. If tracing gender ideologies through jazz to taiko is already a challenge, we must also theorize geospatial movements and intercultural encounters between musicians and musical styles. Too frequently, we discuss the movement and migrations of musical styles as if they were viruses or bacteria, or in some cases as if "borrowing" were a matter of idiosyncratic decisions by individual composers. In fact, it isn't necessary to gesture vaguely toward the influence of jazz on taiko: it was right there at the beginning, in an origin story that I now revisit.

A Jazz Drummer in Japan

Daihachi Oguchi (1924–2008) almost single-handedly created the contemporary taiko phenomenon. Oguchi-sensei, as he is known among taiko players worldwide, founded Osuwa Taiko, the first kumi-daiko group, in 1951 in Suwa City, Japan. His influences on kumi-daiko were profound: he put together different-sized taiko into a large ensemble, he assigned different roles to different size drums, he created new drums and additional instruments, he divided traditional taiko rhythms into simpler patterns that could be played by many people at once, and he added new rhythms. Before he turned to taiko, however, Oguchi was a jazz drummer.[14]

E. Taylor Atkins has painstakingly documented that history of jazz in Japan, showing that it was well established in Japan during the 1920s and 1930s and central to ideas about modernization and internationalism. During the war, however, Japanese jazz musicians struggled. The dance halls were closed in 1940 and jazz was declared an "enemy music" after Pearl Harbor (Atkins 2001, 130). In an interview conducted years later in 1972, jazz drummer Okuda Munehiro remembered that while playing with a wartime movie intermission band, he managed to get away with "flashy drum solos" by mixing in Japanese folk songs and military tunes (129). Atkins notes that wartime Japanese jazz was "subject to extreme measures of control" (131) that were paralleled in Germany and the Soviet Union (159), and a self-consciously Japanese jazz and "Asianified jazz" was generated in response. He writes, "The jazz community's response to state pressure entailed a musical compromise: jazz could remain in Japanese society, could even be made useful to the war effort, if it could be *made authentically Japanese*. Thereby the jazz community could carve out a constructive role for itself within the New Order, something which its early association with frivolous and decadent modernism had prevented" (160). The wartime dark age of Japanese jazz was followed by a postwar golden age supported by the U.S. occupation and a renewed emphasis on modernization. Against this backdrop, Oguchi-sensei was drafted during World War II while still a student and sent to China to fight, where he was taken prisoner. He returned home to Suwa City in 1947 and formed a local jazz band in which he performed as a drummer. Atkins notes that "in the early postwar period jazz came to represent the cultural power of the victor" (171). In the late 1940s, one of Oguchi's relatives shared an old document that contained taiko rhythms. Intrigued, Oguchi tried to figure out the rhythms and decided he wanted to perform them at Osuwa Shrine, a major Shinto shrine in his town. Although the early 1950s are known as the "jazz boom" era in Japan (184), other scholars have shown that younger Japanese struggled to address the overwhelming forces of lingering Japanese authoritarianism and U.S. control by turning to potent symbols of traditional Japanese culture.[15] Oguchi did just that. He gathered together taiko from antiques stores (some sources say) and probably from local temples and festival (matsuri) groups. He then invited local musicians to work on the rhythms with him. Oguchi found the traditional "piece" monotonous, and he added to it and evidently spread the parts of the rhythmic patterns out over different drums and performers, drawing on his jazz experience (R. Robinson 2008).

In short, this formative moment—the birth of kumi-daiko and the emergence of a new genre that has since been a lodestone for Japanese traditionality—emerged from a nexus of things, including intercultural contact, the transnational movement of jazz from North America into East Asia, and thoroughly improvisational sensibilities. Oguchi was far from a traditional Japanese musician: he was a jazz drummer who very openly brought his jazz experience and sensibilities to bear on Japanese rhythms and instruments, and the rest is quite literally history.

In a performance filmed around 1980, Oguchi-sensei performed a solo at the Osuwa Shrine with other members of his group, Osuwa Taiko.[16] Oguchi-sensei performed this piece many times over many years, calling it "Yuki Oroshi" and never performing it the same way twice;[17] the improvisation is based on a set of key rhythmic phrases that Oguchi used as a loose framework. *Yuki* means "snow," and *oroshi* is an instantly recognizable musical gesture from Buddhist and Shinto taiko—a drumroll that starts very slowly and gets faster and faster, originally from traditional Japanese music drama (e.g., Noh and Kabuki) and now used more generally in kumi-daiko to begin and end everything from individual pieces to entire practice sessions. The filmed footage of Oguchi-sensei's solo is interesting for several reasons. First, Oguchi-sensei has drawn a group of different drums together, creating a kind of trap set out of taiko, with four or five drums of different sizes arranged so he can move between them quickly and easily.[18] His solo was supported by a second drummer (on shime) and a flute player (on *fue*). Furthermore, the solo was about more than music qua music or rhythm alone. The display and integration of the body and specific gestures was centrally part of the phrases: when Oguchi strikes the chudaiko and allows the rebound from the drumhead to push his arms into the air, raising his arms and holding the pose, these are not mere performance details but evidence of his emphasis on kata, or bodily form. Oguchi's solo vividly demonstrates how, in his hands, taiko was a combination of "traditional" Japanese musics, jazz, and other Western influences. His approach to this taiko solo was foundationally informed or even defined by the masculinist trope of the jazz master musician.[19] The masterful male taiko soloist with an array of drums was in place from the very beginning.

Asian American Improvisation and Other Oxymorons

What happens when Asian Americans improvise? African American improvisation is normalized thanks to deep-seated American expectations that African Americans can, should, and must improvise. The circle of Asian American improvisers and composers loosely connected through Asian Improv aRts—particularly Francis Wong, Tatsu Aoki, Mark Izu, Glenn Horiuchi, Jon Jang, Vijay Iyer, Fred Ho, Hafez Modirzadeh, and Anthony Brown—has received quite a bit of scholarly attention.[20] They are not the only Asian American musicians who improvise, nor the only ones who do so with an articulated Asian American sensibility, but most of them explicitly connect their work to the Association for the Advancement of Creative Musicians' vision for self-determination, thus politicizing their work by asserting its location in the U.S. racial polity and emphasizing their own connection to black improvisation.[21]

So I ask again: what happens when Asian Americans improvise? Any insistence on Asian American visibility and audibility carries risks and automatically broadcasts an astonishing shift in subjectivity, a willingness to be seen and heard. An unapologetic performance of self-determination isn't easy for many Asian Americans. In nearly any environment and especially in the racial politics of the United States, the very act of Asian American improvisation constitutes a challenge. When Asian Americans improvise, they put themselves into interethnic conversation with other communities. Francis Wong, Jon Jang, Mark Izu, Tatsu Aoki, and Hafez Modirzadeh do this self-consciously, to pay respect to African Americans and beyond. They cultivate vigilant, respectful relationships with leading African American improvisers; their call for Asian American self-determination is carefully linked to black political models. When taiko players perform solos, we are in conversation, knowingly or otherwise, with deep ideas about improvisational play that come to us directly from the world of improvisational jazz, and a lot of things come along with that, especially values about skill.[22] It is understood that that skill lies in technical ability (rather than personal character or spirituality), and this is framed by an uninterrogated understanding that men are the "best" improvisers and soloists.

How and When to Play a Taiko Solo

Improvisational play is most frequently found in two taiko environments: jam sessions and improvised solo sections within composed pieces. Jam sessions have a time-honored place in the North American taiko community.[23] Unlike other traditions (e.g., old-time music or jazz), a taiko jam session features a group of musicians improvising simultaneously, often without any set repertoire or guidance. The effect of a taiko jam is pure cacophony, and the experience of playing in a jam is (at its best) euphoric. You play with all you've got, but it vanishes into a wall of furious sound. Individuals are neither emphasized nor the point: it's all about the collective roar. You are heard but not heard, your sound matters but doesn't matter. You may be doing something interesting, and you may even be interacting with nearby musicians, but the point is the sum total of the sound and the activities within it. Taiko jams are metaphor from start to finish: the relationship between the individual and the community is both broken down and reasserted in exactly the ways that taiko players are taught to let go of the ego and any sense of self-importance, and instead work for the good of the group.

However, improvised solo sections within composed pieces are far more common. As I stated earlier, solos in which individual musicians briefly perform alone are almost always a moment of virtuosic display where the soloist shows off his or her chops and spirit, and therefore (the logic goes), solos should be exciting to watch and hear. Strikingly, even though solos are supposed to appear improvised, many performers precompose them, revealing the valorized place of the improvised solo in the kumi-daiko tradition: "improvised" solos are so important that some performers aren't willing to risk doing it badly. It also suggests that the moves used in taiko improvisation are recognizable enough that they can easily be assembled into something that can pass as "real" improvisation. Furthermore, this kind of "passing" is found at both ends of the spectrum of skill, from relatively inexperienced musicians to the very best. Kōdo is a Japanese taiko group featuring (arguably) some of the best taiko players in the world, all known for their virtuosic technique. Many of their solos are not improvised, even though they are supposed to look as if they are. The fact that such first-rank performers feel compelled to pretend they're improvising is strong evidence that improvised solos carry important values. They're too important to risk messing up, and it's possible to appear spontaneous even when completely rehearsed, fixed, and precomposed. Taiko solos are central to the performance of mastery. The trope of African American jazz improvisation with all its attendant coolness, control, and brilliant responsive spontaneity is so central to the taiko solo that nothing can be left to chance.

Improvised solos in Japanese American drumming are a site of experimentation, where ideas about tradition and intercultural fusion run into one another, where gendered ideas about skill are put front and center, and where fear and machismo crystallize. To return to my bad solo and Gary's and Rev. Tom's much better ones, I stuck entirely to phrases lifted from other pieces that I know, whereas Gary in particular went straight into the vocabulary he has acquired from rock, and Rev. Tom is somewhere in between, drawing both from taiko pieces and from his base in rock and pop. I think of Amy and Taylor, now in their early twenties: they don't carry my burdens, but they have their own, and I wonder how and when they will carry the contract forward. Some taiko players are extremely good at leaving the script behind and embracing the black aesthetics of the solo. Yet mistaking mimicry for mastery is the looming danger. The ideal of improvised, complicated rhythms played fast and loudly is neither the best nor only possibility. I regard the ability of the waiting corps of woman taiko players to respond, together, and save a performance about to fall apart as another kind of improvisation, a crucial kind. Any musicking activates multiple histories of sound and directs them toward the most pressing matters. Taiko is permanently embedded in intricate Pacific Rim choreographies of power and exchange: its shape at any given moment carries forward the very tools for learning how to set the intercultural encounter into motion, and it does so viscerally, in ways that allow Japanese Americans and Asian Americans to sweat and rumble together.

Maybe I'll get better at soloing or maybe I won't; maybe I'll choose not to. In fact, I long to be masterful in those ways, even knowing that musicking is always compromised. But the deeper choice is whether improvising and soloing teaches me what I most want to learn. The things I value most about taiko—group knowledge, communal memory, and the gift of becoming bigger than yourself—are the skills taught most deeply by taiko. My discontents force me to try to think of better ways to improvise, ways that might resituate accepted gendered wisdom. In the meantime, I continue to love the sight and sound of Asian American men and women virtuosically playing themselves into view and into intelligibility.

Notes

1. As one of the Improvisation Community and Social Practice (ICASP) Gender and the Body research group members wrote, "To put it bluntly, while sounding the body may be creative and fluid, it may also be a mode of discipline, albeit embodied and performed, through which subjects are produced" (Barg et al. 2009).

2. For more information, see http://www.improvcommunity.ca. Some of my observations are formed by the liberatory politics of the Guelph Jazz Festival, which collaborates with the ICASP project to mount an annual international colloquium on improvisation. For more information, see http://www.guelphjazzfestival.com.

3. Said at a Guelph Jazz Festival Colloquium talk titled "Improvising Digital Culture," with DJ Spooky, September 3, 2008.

4. See de Ferranti (2000, 40–54) for an overview of percussion in traditional Japanese dance drama and Buddhist ritual. He states, "Drums have been central to ceremonial music in Japan since earliest times. The power associated with drumming is evident in the sole form of traditional music still heard 'live' by most Japanese: the sounds of Shinto ritual and the festival ensembles of large and small shrines" (de Ferranti 2000, 28–29).

5. Writing about taiko in Japan, Shawn Bender notes, "As much as taiko drumming is a new practice that allows for the participation of new groups of people, its development has had a distinctly masculine orientation" (2012, 144). For more information, see his book, *Taiko Boom,* especially chapter 6, titled "Woman Unbound? Body and Gender in Japanese Taiko."

6. I refer to most of my fellow taiko players by first name only. All those mentioned are Japanese American or *hapa haole*/multiethnic Japanese American. Rev. Shuichi Thomas

Kurai (b. 1947), known as "Rev. Tom," is a Zen Buddhist priest and a master taiko teacher. As I describe elsewhere (D. Wong 2004), he emigrated from Japan to the U.S. when he was five years old and is thus both Japanese and Japanese American.

7. These mnemonics are standard for taiko players. Many groups learn pieces orally, by rote. Western staff notation is only rarely used in most West Coast community groups; when pieces are written down, mnemonics are most common, though even this is not standardized (e.g., some groups put the syllables in boxes, with each box representing one four-beat measure). *Don* means a quarter note at medium volume; *DON* is a loud quarter note; *doko* is two loud eighth notes, usually right hand followed by left hand; *tsuku* is two soft eighth notes, usually right hand followed by left hand; *teke* is two eighth notes on the small high-pitched drum (shime-daiko); and so on.

8. In North America, some of the very few women who lead or have led groups include P.J. Hirabayashi (San Jose Taiko), Elaine Fong (Odaiko New England), Tiffany Tamaribuchi (Sacramento Taiko Dan), Michelle Fujii (Portland Taiko), and Brenda Joy Lem (Inner Truth Taiko Dojo in Toronto).

9. Regarding the title of this section, a *kōan* is a Zen Buddhist teaching that is usually concise and irrational, paradoxical, or contradictory. Meditating on a kōan can compel enlightened understanding.

10. Very similar demographic shifts are found in the U.S. histories of the Japanese martial arts (karate in particular) and Zen Buddhism.

11. These histories need far more attention. A fair amount of scholarship addresses how different modes of black and white masculinity have both shaped jazz and been shaped by jazz (Burke 2006; Costa Vargas 2008b; Rustin 1999). A few scholars have acknowledged the dominance of white men in the free improvisation scene. For example, Julie Dawn Smith writes, free improvisation "is exercised within a predominantly white, male improvising community existing on the margins of avant-garde and mainstream music . . . Neither free improvisation nor free jazz, however, extended their critiques to include the aesthetic, economic, or political liberation of women. For the most part, a practice of freedom that resisted gender oppression and oppression on the basis of sexual difference was excluded from the liberatory impulses of male-dominated improvising communities" (2004, 228–29). Pauline Oliveros puts it even more bluntly: "Improvisational music, as well as composition, appears to remain the province of men" (2004a, 57). Similarly, Ellen Waterman writes that free improvisation communities of practice are not only literally dominated by men but usually invested in maintaining male dominance as a social structure: "however collaborative and experimental it might be, creative improvisation is nevertheless a field dominated by men, and in this sense it resembles the most regulated of Western musical practices. Arguably, the professional field of creative improvisation has often served to replicate, not critique, patriarchy" (2008b).

12. Bryan Yamami and his ensemble TAIKOPROJECT have made a 2010 performance of "Behind the Odaiko" (BTO 2010) available online at http://www.youtube.com/watch ?v=7fahIzdxyZY (accessed May 2, 2013).

13. Wehr-Flowers notes that she received responses from eighty-three men and fifty-four women (2006, 340); she offers no information about the respondents' race or ethnicity and does not appear to have considered it in her analysis.

14. I am indebted to Shawn Bender's extraordinary historical and ethnographic work on Osuwa Daiko (2012, 49–52, 174–76).

15. See Yoshimi (2003) on Americanization, and anthropologists Marilyn Ivy (1995) and Jennifer Robertson (1997) on the postwar rise in emphasis on *furusato* (native place).

16. I am very grateful to Kiyoshi Nagata, director of Nagata Shachu in Toronto, for sharing this footage with me.

17. Again, my thanks to Kiyoshi Nagata for this information.

18. This set-up has become standard for young taiko players, mostly Japanese male drummers who aspire to a solo career. For example, Shuichi Hidano (b. 1969) plays multiple taiko as if he were a rock drummer. See http://www.hidashu.com/PROFILE-E /profile-e.html for streaming video of Hidano playing solos on multiple taiko drum sets.

19. In Oguchi's hands, the presence of that trope was low-key, but it has since been blown up into larger relief in Hidano's solos into something closer to a rock star, a larger-than-life Stewart Copeland–esque performance of ecstatic/cathartic virtuosity.

20. See Asai (1995, 1997, 2005), Dessen (2003, 2006), Fellezs (2007), Ho (2006), Lam (1999), J, Robinson (2005), and D. Wong (2004). Far less attention has been paid to the prominent Asian/Asian American women improvisers who have contributed to this environment, including Miya Masaoka, Susie Ibarra, Ikue Mori, and Keiko Uenishi.

21. The Association for the Advancement of Creative Musicians (AACM) was founded on the south side of Chicago in 1965 by a group of African American musicians centered around pianist Muhal Richard Abrams. Explicitly community-based, Afrocentric, and experimental, the AACM represents a sustained critical and aesthetic approach to improvised music focused on black self-determination that has had profound influence over many decades. It offered a critically grounded approach to improvised music-making as well as practical strategies for the black arts movement, including the community-based AACM School of Music. See George E. Lewis's monumental and comprehensive study for more (2008).

22. Costa Vargas notes that he found the African American jazz musicians he followed in Los Angeles's Leimert Park inspiring precisely for their utopian efforts to create an Afrocentric musical environment and "black male agency" (2008a, 341) even though, "in such a heteronormative male-centric context, where black men are the overwhelmingly majority of performers, when not producing satisfactory results, blacks and nonblacks, men and women may be charged with 'playing white,' 'not swinging,' 'not saying nothing,' 'just going through the [chord] changes,' or not 'putting feeling into it'" (2008a, 329).

23. I discuss taiko jams in more detail in D. Wong (2008).

16. Improvisation and the Audibility of Difference

SAFA, CANADIAN MULTICULTURALISM, AND
THE POLITICS OF RECOGNITION

Ellen Waterman

Improvisation is an unruly domain. Multilayered and multivocal, improvisation can be a site of both conflict and concord, of both colonization and revolution, of both authenticity and contingency. Musical improvisation may therefore be understood as the negotiation of subjectivities in the immediacy of the intercorporeal encounter.[1] Effective improvisation depends on dialogical techniques of listening, recognition, and responsiveness. Improvisers are listening and sounding bodies alert to absorb the nuanced expressions of other improvisers even as they assert their own voices in a polyphony that exceeds the individual body. Improvisation might also be considered in terms described by philosopher Jocelyn Maclure in relation to the hurly burly of identity politics: "not only as struggles for recognition, but also as games of disclosure and acknowledgment" (2003, 4). Conceptualizing improvisation as agonistic contest troubles improvisation studies' tendency to define it as nonhierarchical and democratic and therefore inherently ethical.

In this chapter, I analyze a performance by the intercultural trio Safa to think through a particularly fraught area of identity politics: Canadian multiculturalism. This is a discourse that hits me where I live. As a Canadian, I understand multiculturalism as both an official federal policy that enshrines difference in law and a complex and contentious political discourse. Recognizing difference may serve conflicting goals: celebration or denigration, advocacy or containment. For the state, multicultural policy is about managing difference; for minorities seeking justice, multiculturalism means asserting difference to decenter power. Safa makes difference audible. The embodied practices and improvisational techniques activated by Safa are rendered in deeply engrained and diverse musical traditions modulated by receptivity and adaptability. The ensemble comprises Iranian-Canadian *tar* player and singer Amir Koushkani, Puerto Rican–Canadian percussionist Sal Ferreras, and French-Canadian clarinetist François Houle.[2] Safa interwove influences from Iranian classical music, Latin American rhythms, and creative improvisation in a moving 2007 performance at the Open Ears Festival of Music and Sound in Kitchener-Waterloo, Canada. My analysis draws on audiovisual documentation of the performance, interviews with the musicians, and an audience focus group that I conducted immediately after the performance.[3]

I characterize Safa's musicking through the term *intercultural* to respect the roles that mutuality and reciprocity play in their intercorporeal encounter. Intercultural improvisation is marked by both the "ability to juxtapose different histories without sacrificing identity" and the "reflexive use of notions of cultural difference as a basis for collaboration" (Stanyek 2004, 89). The language used by the members of Safa to describe their improvising affirms this characterization; however, in analyzing their performance, I am also listening for productive disjunctions and contradictions. What cultural and musical attitudes do these musicians bring to their improvising? How do the members of Safa safeguard their individual identities while simultaneously and expertly working to build a musically satisfying ensemble? How do audience members (including me), each from one's own cultural vantage point, interpret Safa's performance?

I begin by discussing Canadian multiculturalism in the context of philosopher Charles Taylor's influential concept of the politics of recognition and Smaro Kamboureli's critique of Taylor's ideas. This discussion provides the basis for a close reading of "Whisper of Love," the first piece Safa performed at their 2007 concert. Their intercultural improvisation provides many productive moments that help me follow the threads of authenticity and contingency that weave through the discourse on multiculturalism in Canada. Working out from this situated performance, I consider ways improvisation might contribute to the discourse on multiculturalism by extending Maclure's insight that if our goal is to build a just society, a focus on *processes* of recognition may be more productive than a focus on the end result. His conception of the politics of recognition is dynamic, even combative; it opens up a space for dissensus that sits uneasily with the traditional Canadian tendency toward accommodation but that also emphasizes opportunities for effecting social change. Improvisation, I contend, offers useful strategies for the process of negotiating—but not necessarily resolving—difference in a multicultural society.

The Politics of Recognition

In his highly influential 1992 essay "The Politics of Recognition," philosopher Charles Taylor addresses multiculturalism in terms of the increasing demand for public recognition put forward by minority groups and individuals in contemporary societies.[4] Recognition, he argues, is crucial because "our identity is partly shaped by recognition or its absence, often by the *mis*recognition of others, and so a person or group of people can suffer real damage, real distortion, if the people or society around them mirror back to them a confining or demeaning or contemptible picture of themselves" (1994, 25). Taylor illustrates his argument with examples of misrecognition in Canadian culture, in particular discontents over the failure to recognize Quebec as a distinct society that brought the province to the brink of separation from Canada just three years after the essay was first published.[5] A contemporary example may be found in the Truth and Reconciliation Commission in Canada, which is an attempt to redress the failure to recognize the cultural integrity of aboriginal peoples, a failure that resulted in draconian assimilation policies with long-term and frequently tragic effects.[6]

At the heart of Taylor's argument, which is variously influenced by Hegel, Rousseau, and Herder, is the modern idea of the authentic self, an idea that is predicated on the move from "honor" to "dignity"—where *honor* refers to privilege (some are honored because all are not) and *dignity* refers to a liberal democratic view that confers equality on all citizens (C. Taylor 1994, 27). Liberal democratic societies create policies that emphasize the "equalization of rights and entitlements" (35), as exemplified by the U.S. Constitution and, more recently, the Canadian Charter of Rights and Freedoms (1982). As many have argued, however, this putative equality often serves to elide the very real struggles of minority groups for recognition and rights. Too often, an emphasis on equality for all means a refusal to recognize difference with the result that nominal equality paradoxically creates injustice.

Along with the importance of individualized identity that arose at the end of the eighteenth century comes the notion of being "true to myself and my own particular way of being" (C. Taylor 1994, 28). Authenticity, for Taylor (following Herder), is an essentially moral ideal because it is the basis of self-esteem, without which it is impossible to grant the same kind of respect to others. Crucially, Taylor insists that the authentic self is formed in dialogue with others: "We become full human agents, capable of understanding ourselves, and hence of defining our identity, through our acquisition of rich human languages of expression" (32). The dialogical self not only is formed by foundational early relationships (such as with our parents) but is in a process of continual development. We negotiate our identity "through dialogue, partly overt, partly internal, with others. That is why the development of an ideal of inwardly generated identity gives a new importance to recognition. My own identity crucially depends on my dialogical relations with others" (34). For Taylor, dialogism is what enables the authentic self to recognize and respect difference and thus avoid the structural injustice many identify in democratic liberalism.

It is easy to see why this is an attractive idea for improvisation studies. George Lewis has persuasively argued that improvisation is a "social location" (1996, 110) constituting dynamic and dialogic processes of communication in which individual histories are brought to bear on immediate articulations of social relationships. Taylor's rich languages of expression include artistic and emotional expressions (1994, 32), so that the give and take of nuanced ideas expressed through musical improvisation may thus be understood as a kind of dialogism-in-action. If we listen carefully, we may hear subjectivities change and grow in the moment! Certainly, I have experienced the sensation of existential (ex)change in the heat of improvisation, when the sonic gestures of another player provoke an unexpected reaction in my body. Vibrations absorbed by receptive ears are translated through nerves, fingers, mouth, and breath. New timbres and sonic effects emerge in response; my vocabulary of expression is enriched and my playing is forever changed.

It is, however, a slippery slope from this argument to the highly problematic idea that "improvisation is good." Many improvisers, including the members of Safa, speak about the importance of personal authenticity in the musical encounter. Echoing Taylor, their strong sense of self empowers the musicians to be open to the exchange of ideas generated through improvisation. The meaning of the exchange, however, may be understood in radically different ways by the individual musicians and by other listeners, as I discuss later. Even if one accepts the idea of an authentic self, its actions, however dialogical, do not guarantee recognition; indeed, they may lead to patent acts of misrecognition. To illustrate the problem of the authentic self, it is useful to examine a cogent critique of Taylor's politics of recognition along the fault lines of multiculturalism.

Canadian Multiculturalism

Multiculturalism has a conflicted history in Canada that Smaro Kamboureli neatly summarizes:

When the Canadian government introduced multiculturalism as an official policy in 1971, entrenched it in the Charter of Rights in 1982, and tabled the Canadian Multicultural Act in 1988, it made substantial proclamations of responsibility concerning ethnic diversity. The Multiculturalism Act (also known as Bill C-93) recognizes the cultural diversity that constitutes Canada, but it does so by practicing a sedative politics, a politics that attempts to recognize ethnic differences, but only in a contained fashion, in order to manage them. It pays tribute to diversity and suggests ways of celebrating it, thus responding to the clarion call of ethnic communities for recognition. Yet it does so without disturbing the conventional articulation of the Canadian dominant society. The Act sets out to perform the impossible act of balancing differences, in the process allowing the state to become self-congratulatory, if not complacent, about its handling of ethnicity. (2009, 82)

Kamboureli, along with many other cultural and political theorists, nevertheless continues to view multiculturalism as important to issues of identity in Canada. To abandon the concept would be to elide the politics of difference and deny the pluralism that is central to Canadian society. Rinaldo Walcott agrees, adding that, "Stuart Hall's claim that migration is the question of the twenty-first century is crucial to this conversation" (2011, 25). For Walcott, the point is to get beyond narratives of arrival and take the multicultural encounter as an inevitable starting point of society, and therefore "always the place from which human engagement and thus negotiation proceed" (25). Instead of merely managing (and thus containing) diversity, these theorists argue, a fair and effective policy of multiculturalism would wake up to the challenge of negotiating pluralistic and competing demands for recognition even at the risk of upsetting the status quo.

In her book *Scandalous Bodies*, Kamboureli is critical of Taylor's politics of recognition because (despite his undoubted respect for minority rights) his emphasis on the authentic self stems from a Western liberal ideal, which in turn reinforces the very universalism that Taylor sets out to critique. The contradiction that Kamboureli identifies is this: although Taylor insists that individual identity is formed dialogically he also warns that this identity must not be too porous. The state must maintain a set of national principles while meeting reasonable demands for recognition. Kamboureli interprets this caveat as an anxiety of contamination by the Other, an anxiety that is all too readily observable in a variety of current debates in Canada from aboriginal self-government to Sharia law. The authentic self, she argues, closes off the possibility of alterity. In contrast to Taylor, Kamboureli believes that difference is socially constructed and that identities are always therefore contingent. Furthermore, she insists that "comprehending, and dealing with, diversity is a continuous process of mediating and negotiating contingencies" (2009, 93).

Like the authentic and dialogical self, the notion of contingency is highly resonant with critical studies in improvisation. If subjectivities are formed during moments of improvisational dialogue, they are also susceptible to continual adaptation and re-formation. To improvise is to be in a continual state of "mediating and negotiating contingencies" (Kamboureli 2009, 93). This abstraction is easily put into concrete musical terms. In the course of some types of musical improvisation, such as free jazz and creative improvisation, players move fluidly between harmony and dissonance. Players form temporary alliances (for example, by harmonizing with another player or by playing an accompanying figure), assert difference (by playing contrapuntally or through marked dissonance), signal change (by introducing a new idea or a distinctive accent), and practice forms of compliance or resistance (by going with another player's idea or playing in opposition to it). The result is often playful and agonistic, producing lively musical discourse, but the result is most effective if all players operate in a spirit of mutual trust and with the common goal of cocreation. If we listen carefully, we can hear the mobile shifting of power relations in the moment of improvisation. A good musical result does not necessarily mean harmonious consensus; instead, it may be the powerful musical delineation of discord, or, in Kamboureli's terms, the envoicing of alterity.

Kamboureli's discontents with the politics of recognition remind us that power is unevenly distributed in negotiations of identity, and there is no guarantee that recognition, once granted, will hold firm. Indeed, it is the very notion of *granting* that she most objects to in Taylor's politics of recognition. To grant recognition is to hold power that one may confer on another and naturalize the holder's right to retain that power.[7] Mediating and negotiating contingencies suggests, instead, that alterior subjects can exercise agency in the process of demanding recognition. Instead of waiting for a hegemonic power to grant recognition, the alterior subject recognizes itself (and consequently builds self-esteem) through the very process of democratic public discourse. The success of this strategy, of course, depends heavily on the degree to which a society promotes and protects the ideal of democratic discourse. To put it in musical terms, it depends on how well we are prepared to listen.

I turn now to the example of Safa's performance to explore ways that the ideas discussed so far, the dialogical self and mediations and negotiations of contingency, are operationalized through an improvisational intercultural encounter.

Safa is a Farsi word meaning inner purity, sincerity, sincere affection. Safa's publicity bio describes the group's genesis in ways that highlight intercultural encounter and musical mastery:

> Safa was born when Amir Koushkani appeared at the door of uber-percussionist Salvador Ferreras. It was ostensibly an audition for a spot in the music program at Vancouver Community College, but after hearing just a few notes of Amir's Persian lute, Sal rushed over to a neighbouring office to get clarinetist François Houle. Sal wasn't looking for a second opinion. He wanted to jam! Major musical chemistry ensued and Safa started to build a reputation as one of Canada's premier global music ensembles. While Safa's music continues to be informed and inspired by Amir's classical Persian traditions, the group brings the prodigious talent and diverse musical experience of its other two members to its stellar mix of composed and improvised performance.[8]

It is important to know that Amir was trained in Iranian classical music through a private apprenticeship, since musical training was not widely available in Iranian universities when he was a young man during the early 1990s. He left Iran for Canada because he felt that the regime's ideological opposition to music left him unrecognized, with no proper place in his own country (interview with Ellen Waterman, Toronto, June 3, 2012). Amir came to Vancouver a couple of years after immigrating to Canada, when he decided it was time to pursue more formal training in music. He later completed his doctorate in ethnomusicology and is a published authority on Iranian music, but when he first met Sal and François, Amir was a newcomer and they were musicians with well-established careers.[9]

Vancouver Community College (VCC) is a highly regarded training ground for improvisational musicians and also positions itself as a program that embraces "world music" traditions. Sal Ferreras, who was director of Music at VCC when he first met Amir, is a sought-after percussionist in the Vancouver scene and also an ethnomusicologist who studies Puerto Rican music.[10] Sal proudly describes VCC's approach to curriculum as meeting the needs of "the people in our neighborhood" by which he means both ethnic and musical diversity in Vancouver (Ferreras 2007). François Houle is a clarinetist and composer who has an international career playing both creative improvisation and contemporary classical music (his extensive discography includes recordings with Benoit Delbecq, Joëlle Léandre, Marilyn Crispell, and Evan Parker). He is one of a handful of francophone improvisers who left the distinctive and dynamic *musique actuelle* scene in Quebec in favor of a career in English Canada.

Sal and François's first meeting with Amir, as described in their bio and substantiated by my interviews with the musicians, may readily be analyzed as an act of recognition: the two senior musicians recognized a fellow player with a high degree of musical competency and a rich cultural archive with which they could engage. Although the musicians characterize their meeting as recognizing their "soulmates," a condition that for them transcends technical and musical "language" barriers, Amir was fortunate to have chosen VCC, with its mandate to reflect musical multiculturalism. In another context, he could easily have been misrecognized or gone unrecognized altogether. Most Canadian university music departments would not accommodate an undergraduate student playing tar, the "Persian lute," because they only "recognize" standard Western orchestral and concert instruments. Extending Kamboureli's critique of liberalism, despite the fact that many postsecondary music programs embrace jazz, ethnomusicology, and popular music to some degree, Western classical music continues to dominate the academy, thus privileging a Eurocentric form of music as normative.

By the time of Safa's 2007 concert at the Open Ears Festival, they were a well-established group. The performance took place in the intimate Registry Theatre in front of a sold-out house during a noon hour concert. Safa has built its repertoire mainly around songs that Amir has brought to the group from traditional Iranian music or that he has composed himself, but they also play some Kurdish songs and have improvised freely on occasion (including a track on their first album).[11] Although Amir primarily plays the tar, his singing, which is deeply informed by Sufism, is central to Safa's sound world.

Safa's interculturalism is marked by the encounter between two radically different approaches to improvisation: creative improvisation (a freely structured form of improvisation that embraces a wide spectrum of sonic expressions and whose origins lie in various 1960s avant-gardes) and Iranian classical music (based on a repertoire known as the *radif*, an ancient oral tradition first codified in the nineteenth century).[12] The radif is organized around a set of modes or *dastgah* that incorporate over 250 melodic models called *gusheh*, which in turn provide the basis for improvisation. It is a robust system that gives rise to a variety of compositional genres that are elaborated in performance through improvisation. To be considered a master musician in the Iranian tradition, one must first know the radif intimately.[13]

Improvisation works quite differently in each of these styles. Creative improvisers draw on a broad (often highly personal but also genre-based) lexicon of musical techniques and gestures, and musicians place a high value on active listening and responsiveness. George Lewis emphasizes the importance of the improviser's ability to "code-switch" in response to the utterances of other players (quoted in Smith and Waterman 2013, 65), that is, to move flexibly among musical gestures from different genres and styles. Improvisation in Iranian classical music "often involves the abstraction and recombination of previously learnt material and compositional principles" derived from memorizing (indeed internalizing) the radif (Nooshin 2003, 269). Here, improvisation is the result of mastering a specific musical tradition. Arguably, creative improvisation and Iranian classical music represent oppositional methods for improvising. Creative improvisation emphasizes contingency while Iranian classical music emphasizes authenticity in improvisation.[14] In Safa's performance, these impulses are cocreative, in ways that defy simplistic either/or analysis.

"Whisper of Love" is a *tasnif*, a composed song in a slow meter. Tasnif are compositions that serve as models on which to improvise, and for this reason, no two renditions are the same, even when played by the same performer.[15] Nevertheless, the song is recognizable by its lyrics, its particular melodic patterns, and the mode in which it is played. The title "Whisper of Love" is Safa's name for their rendition of a tasnif that was composed by Majid Derakhshani inspired by a poem by Mohammad Reza Shafii Kadkani, *Safar Bekheir (Bon Voyage)* (2000, 101). The poem is a dialogue between a forlorn desert plant, the camel's thorn, and the restless breeze. The camel's thorn yearns to leave the horror of the desert and longs to accompany the breeze to distant lands. Like much Iranian poetry, it is allegorical. In some interpretations, the camel's thorn, *gavan*, symbolizes captivity while the breeze, *nasim*, symbolizes the yearning for freedom from oppression.[16] *Safar Bekheir* is widely recognized in Iran as a metaphor for the restrictions imposed on intellectuals, and when Shafii Kadkani left Iran to teach at Princeton University in 2008, numerous fans quoted the poem online as they wished him good luck in his new life.[17] Safa's title masks this political resonance, at least for a non-Iranian audience that may be more inclined to code the song in Western genre terms, and, given the title, to read the intimacy of Koushkani's soulful performance as a love song.

The fact that the audience was unable to comprehend the lyrics is culturally significant, given the importance placed in Iranian classical music performance on a master singer's interpretation of allegorical lyrics for an "informed, knowledgeable audience" (Simms and Koushkani 2012, 17). Writing about Mohammed Reza Shajarian, a master singer of avaz, Simms and Koushkani emphasize both the techniques used by the singer to "add new layers of emphasis to the allegory" of the poem through his avaz, and the singer's "intuition and spiritual connection with the messages and the contexts of those messages. . . . An informed, knowledgeable audience receives this message as it is conveyed and through this interaction a rare and unexplainable unity occurs between the artist and the listener" (17). If authenticity in the reception of Iranian classical song hinges on common textual understanding, something important was absent from Safa's performance that day.[18]

For me, in the absence of an explanation, the lyrics to "Whisper of Love" simply disappeared into the sensuous textures of the performance. Despite our lack of understanding, the performance of this first piece on the concert provoked a standing ovation. As Sal later recalled, "Each one of us knew it at the beginning of the show: the first piece. I don't know whether it was a reaction [to the music] or a deep intake of breath that people take in certain kinds of phrases where you know that they're not just breathing, that they just took in exactly what you were sending out in terms of an expressive message" (interview with Ellen Waterman, Vancouver, September 27, 2007). The members of my audience focus group expressed deep appreciation for the concert. Like Sal, we marveled at the aura of consensus that radiated through the space, which we read as a sign of artistic authenticity. Not one of us thought to question the lyric content of the songs, thus participating in a collective act of misrecognition that seems completely at odds with Sal's idea that the audience perfectly understood the musicians' intentions. Did everyone "get it wrong," or was it simply an example of the multiplicity of meanings that coexist in shared social spaces? Perhaps meaning in this intercultural improvisation depended less on correct cultural recognition than on our appreciation of the rich complexity of the musicians' interactions: sounds signified where text did not.

Safa approached "Whisper of Love" through improvisation, as they do with their entire repertoire. When encountering a new piece, the members of Safa approach it with little strategizing. They do discuss the mode, and Amir occasionally provides notation when introducing a new song to the group, but all members insist that their process is otherwise improvisational. Each musician draws on his own lexicon of musical gestures rooted variously in creative improvisation, Latin American music, and Iranian classical music. Their improvising is a negotiation across these musical traditions, and I argue that in the process they simultaneously maintain strong feelings of personal authenticity and produce music that is the very model of contingent subjectivity.

Before I demonstrate how this works in "Whisper of Love," it is important to note that none of the members of Safa describe the group's project as political. There is, however, an implied position on multiculturalism in their self-representation "as one of Canada's premier global music ensembles." Sal and François are "informed and inspired" by Amir's Persian traditions, to which they bring their "diverse musical experience." It is the combined expertise of the group that allows a successful negotiation of this diversity—characterized in their bio as "musical chemistry" (Safa bio).[19] As Sal told me: "I don't have to be worried about relinquishing my identity in this group because we're more concerned with a common expressive core. You can't see Sal, the guy from Puerto Rico; François, the guy from Quebec. You can't really see that. There's nothing that we do that aims to focus on our identities." Similarly, Amir insists: "When I play with Sal and François I feel great autonomy. I do whatever I want and I'm sure they do whatever they want" (Fererras interview; Koushkani interview).

There is an interesting contradiction here: representationally, ethnicity is a key signifier of Safa. It is found in their press, in the presence of culturally distinct instruments on stage, and in the Farsi song lyrics, and it is marked in their appearance (see figure 16.1). It is audible in their music. Despite this evidence, the musicians highlight ethnicity as something to be transcended, a troubling move for some theorists of multiculturalism who worry about masking the alterity of cultural minorities in Canada. From Kamboureli's point of view, Safa could be seen as colluding in the "sedative politics" of official multiculturalism by articulating difference as sameness. From Taylor's point of view, however, Safa could be seen as modeling a successful multicultural consensus based on mutual esteem. Just how do the musicians both mark and transcend cultural difference?

I illustrate this complex signification through an examination of an improvisation between François and Amir based on the principle melody of "Whisper of Love" (example 16.1). After introducing it, Amir begins to improvise variations on this melody, which is in the *dastgah-e Bayat-e Esfahan* (Esfahan F).[20] François follows him by playing quite similar patterns in a call-and-response process. In this section François remains mostly in what Mehrenegar Rostami calls "the atmosphere of Persian music";[21] however, he deviates slightly from traditional Iranian melodic patterns that exclusively use small intervals of a second or third within a limited range.

During his subsequent improvisation, François departs from the "Persian atmosphere." Having previously imitated the tetrachord that marks a typical *gushe* in Bayat-e Esfahan mode (F–G–A-flat–B-flat), François now asserts his own musical subjectivity in an increasingly active passage with wider and wider intervallic leaps. When this happens, Amir drops right to the background and

FIG 16.1: Safa publicity photo. Courtesy of François Houle.

EX 16.1: Melody of *Whisper of Love* in *dastgah-e Bayat-e Esfahan*. All transcriptions are by Mehrenegar Rostami and have been approved by Safa.

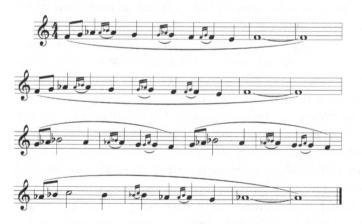

merely strums a supporting pattern. The skeletal transcription of the clarinet improvisation shown in example 16.2 shows both this increasing divergence and François's eventual return to Bayat-e Esfahan mode. The rectangular boxes indicate material with the tetrachord typical of Bayat-e Esfahan mode.

EX 16.2: Skeletal transcription of clarinet improvisation from *Whisper of Love*. Note that the transcription is skeletal and is meant to indicate only important changes of pitch and registration. It does not try to capture all nuances of ornaments and timing, and some repetition of figures has been eliminated. The key signature is used for convenience; it does not indicate a tonal basis for the improvisation. Accidentals apply only to the note immediately adjacent.

Another sign of divergence is the much wider registration as the clarinetist moves increasingly "outside" of the pitch world of the main motif in a rising sequential pattern, here drawing on codes from jazz improvisation. A further code-switch is evident at the climax of the improvisation, with a wailing motif that is generically Middle Eastern but is foreign to Iranian classical music. In short, François maps a creative improvisation strategy onto the musical materials of this Iranian tasnif. At the end of his free improvisation, he reasserts not only the pitches but also the pattern typical of the principal melody of the tasnif (just like a jazz improviser returning "inside" to the "head" or main melody of a piece).

I read this improvisation as dialogical in Taylor's sense of the word. The musicians have divergent interpretations of the event based on their strong senses of self, but each is also open to being changed by the other's "rich language of expression." When I played *Whisper of Love* to Amir, he commented on François's improvisation: "I'm mostly listening to him. At this moment I close my eyes and I try to communicate as much as possible, I'm trying to complete his work as much as possible. This is about you making a bridge for each other; you become a bridge for another person" (interview). François, however, describes his own role in Safa as one of self-imposed restraint. He contributes his jazz-based ability to "take a mode and really turn it around and create momentum" but maintains that in the context of playing with Persian classical forms "you can only go so far before you run into trouble" (interview). He works hard to ensure that his musical gestures will complement Amir's.

Indeed, François recognizes distinctive differences between his and Amir's approaches to improvisation: "Amir improvises as well: he does solos. But very often his solos are constructed on very deeply rooted sets of rules and parametric modulations . . . that are true to Persian classical music. I don't have that point of reference, except what I hear Amir do. So, I try to emulate what Amir does in his improvisation in my improvisations, and we've got to the point where we can actually have a whole conversation in the Persian classical idiom without me really knowing what I'm saying" (interview). This astonishing admission echoes the group's decision not to inform the audience about the lyric content of their songs. As we have seen, François also engages in code-switching by referencing musical ideas from a variety of genres as part of the dialogue.

Amir, in turn, is unequivocal in describing improvisation as a deep expression of individual mastery of the radif, stating that "true improvisation in Persian classical music is different. And the novelty comes from those people they never think about this organization anymore. They just want to become one with their own instrument and express their own feeling. And everything else is in their psyche, in the background and they still react to it. If you still feel your finger and breaths, if you are still looking for 'oh, what dastgah I am, where this melody comes from?' you are far from becoming a good improviser. You shouldn't even feel that you are hitting the strings" (interview). For Amir, musical mastery is culturally embedded, so deeply entrained that the musician is oblivious of technique, instrument, and body.

These different subject positions suggest that power relations are constantly in play even within this highly collegial ensemble. As a member of the dominant Canadian society (and a musician trained in an improvisational tradition that prizes versatility), François has the agency to engage with Iranian traditions in a Canadian context, but he acknowledges that he "can only go so far" in bending these traditions without "getting into trouble." In Taylor's terms, he engages the dialogical self: he grants Amir recognition and indeed considerable respect; he recognizes, and his playing is affected by, the nuances of Persian music, but he does not consider it necessary to undertake serious study of the radif to engage in the dialogue. In the end, he relies on the cultural normativity of his subject position. Although this might seem to place Amir in a position of alterity, as a traditionally trained Iranian musician, he is proud of his mastery. He plays entirely within this idiom, falling back to make "a bridge" during François's improvisation and allowing the clarinetist quite a lot of latitude. After all, he cannot be held to the same cultural standard as someone steeped in the radif. Amir asserts his own subjectivity, on his own terms, and he is confident enough to make space for François to do the same.

In fact, there is a nexus of recognition among the group's members that arguably trumps (the musicians would say "transcends") ethnicity. As their origin story demonstrates, the members of Safa meet on the common ground of musical mastery, something that was instantly recognizable to Sal when he first met Amir. Interestingly, all three musicians see themselves as the glue that binds the ensemble together. Amir provides a "bridge" for François to solo. Sal needs only "one transfer point" between Iranian rhythmic ideas and his own—"It's a little three-note cycle that comes from Amir's plucking of the drone [that characterizes tar playing]"—and sees himself as the "anchor" that allows François to play in dialogue with Amir. François sees himself as able to improvise in Amir's language and describes Safa's improvisation as "a really dynamic system. And it shifts around; every few seconds something happens, and there's a certain synergy. Mathematically, all the possible permutations are constantly present and possible" (interview). Indeed, François's description here invokes processes of mediating and negotiating contingencies. These musicians don't hesitate to invoke the language of authentic selves, but their musicking models the mutability of subjectivities in the improvisational encounter. What most strongly characterizes Safa is the musicians' ability to hold contradictory cultural and musical positions intact while consciously supporting and learning from one another in their engagements with the musical material at hand.

I turn now to a second musical detail in "Whisper of Love" to demonstrate that musical communication may occur successfully despite radically different interpretations of fundamental musical materials. The articulation of difference demonstrated here offers a valuable lesson for the politics of recognition as applied to multiculturalism. Throughout the dialogue between creative improvisation and Iranian classical music played out in "Whisper of Love," Sal Ferreras plays a repeating rhythmic pattern on an African clay pot drum, the *udu*. This intricate and hypnotic pattern provides a seemingly constant texture of support for the other musicians. As Sal describes it in an email to Mehrenegar Rostami (May 28, 2012):

> My approach is to provide a basis for Amir and François to carry a longer note value melody with a solid rhythmic background. On occasion I will depart from the rhythm to create mini-cadences to correspond with Amir's resolutions of melodic fragments. Other times I use the bass tones of the udu to drive listeners towards the beginning of a new phrase or section of the melody. It is imperative that the feel of 2/2 remain throughout (except for one section where we sometimes stop the time altogether) and the rhythm be strong yet subtle to match the beauty of the melody on the tar or the voice or clarinet.

Sal hears the pattern as a syncopated division of two beats to a measure in which we can hear eight subdivisions; the first, fourth, and seventh beats are accented and the other beats are "ghosted" (played faintly). This 2/2 feel is not just a description of the rhythm; it is "imperative," vital, in Sal's view, to the success of Amir and François's performance. Furthermore, it is a means by which he guides the listener through the piece. To my ear, this pattern is similar to the first part of an Afro-Cuban 3–2 *son-clave*, a syncopated rhythm often transcribed in two measures of duple time.[22] Although Sal did not invoke this particular ethnocultural reference in his description of the pattern, he did tell me about the other overlapping points of reference he generally finds between Latin American and Iranian rhythmic sensibilities in Safa, such as hemiola-like overlays of triplets in groups of four often found in Amir's solos that remind him of Afro-Caribbean drumming. When he first began improvising with Amir, Sal found that such reference points provided him with a "level of comfort far sooner and far more often than I expected" (interview).

Unsurprisingly, Amir also hears rhythm with culturally attuned ears. He described the rhythmic pattern in "Whisper of Love" as an additive rhythm in eight shorter beats: 3 + 3 + 2, a perception that my Iranian graduate assistant Mehrenegar Rostami confirmed is culturally normative for Iranian musicians. (She was initially almost physically uncomfortable trying to hear the pattern according to Sal's interpretation, and played it for several Iranian musician friends to confirm the correctness of her own additive perception of the pattern.) Figure 16.2 shows both ways of listening to the pattern. The top line expresses the rhythm as additive 3 + 3 + 2; the bottom line shows it

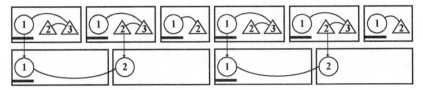

FIG 16.2: Rhythmic pattern from *Whisper of Love* expressed as both additive and syncopated rhythm.

against an underlying duple beat. When feeling the beat as duple, the small circles on the top line act as syncopated accents whenever they do not coincide with the large circle on the bottom line. The triangles are played softly, or ghosted.

As figure 16.2 illustrates, although the math is the same, the different interpretive feel between a syncopated division of two slower beats and additive groupings of eight faster beats is palpable. This difference is musically significant. Indeed, in many improvisational genres (such as jazz) getting the feel wrong constitutes bad musicianship. Amir was dismissive when I told him how Sal hears the pattern. He didn't dispute Sal's interpretation, but he made it clear that discussing (and certainly contesting) such a mundane mechanical detail with Sal would miss the point (interview). In fact, it took me awhile to get the point, but I finally realized that both musicians are right; with a little effort, as a listener I can tune my body from one feel to the other and back again without losing momentum. To do so requires opening my ears to a process of recognizing and accommodating difference, and the result is unsettling but not unmusical. The improvisational texture of Safa can accommodate two very different perceptions of this fundamental musical element. Furthermore, in my role as a listener, the simultaneous presence of these two culturally and musically significant interpretations is yet another moment of dialogism-in-action, an opportunity for me to experience a shift in subjectivity.

Or is it? As a member of the dominant Canadian society, listening from the normative point of view of the "good citizen," can I really listen to intercultural music without hearing the Canadian brand of exceptionalist official multiculturalism? Does my rush toward accommodation distract me from a more radical kind of listening? Ethnomusicologist and indigenous studies scholar Dylan Robinson challenges us to hear cultural difference and dissensus from a vantage point of radical alterity, a position that agitates my lifetime experience of sounding and listening.[23] He wonders to what extent audiences are capable of listening outside of their culturally engrained subject positions (email communication, July 29, 2013).

This uncomfortable insight invites me to consider the experiences of other listeners who attended Safa's performance that summer day in 2007. Did other listeners hear cultural as well as musical difference operating in Safa?

Transcendence, Multiculturalism, and the Audibility of Difference

Immediately following the performance, I took a group of eight audience members out to a pub to discuss our experience of the concert. Instead of asking participants what they thought about the performance, I asked them *how they experienced* the concert because I wanted to explore the agency of listeners as subjects in live musical performance. The context of the concert is important to mention briefly because it affected listeners' perceptions. The Open Ears Festival of Music and Sound is a five-day festival of experimental music that takes place biennially in the lovely small city of Kitchener-Waterloo. In 2007, founding artistic director Peter Hatch viewed the festival itself (with its various concerts, sound installations, soundwalks, workshops, and symposium) as a gigantic sound installation and his own role as that of a curator (Hatch 2013). Out-of-town audience members, many of whom stayed in the same hotel as the artists and tended to move from event to event in a loose-knit group, found that the festival engendered the transient sense of heightened togetherness that performance theorist Victor Turner calls spontaneous communitas (1969, 132).[24]

My focus group participants, who were among the one hundred or so audience members that packed the Registry Theatre for Safa's concert, felt a definite high. One listener was moved to write in her notebook during the concert: "There's nothing quite like witnessing human beings being absolutely unified to make a thrill run through me. The phenomenon defies the isolation of the human condition."[25] This reaction was received with enthusiastic nods from the other participants around the table, and it echoes Safa's self-representation of spiritual unity, a fairly common trope in creative improvisation,[26] that was expressed by all three musicians in our interviews. As François later recalled, the concert "was probably one of our most intense experiences as a trio, at least personally. We've had those responses before— quite strong responses . . . So, obviously we are able to tap into a place that transcends the rules of race and religion and musical training" (interview).

At the same time, listeners recognized and were affected by ethnocultural differences among the musicians. One listener expressed his surprise at discovering his initial perception that Safa was going to play "traditional folk music" was overturned when he saw and heard the African udu, Afro-Cuban *batá* drums, and Afro-Peruvian *cajón* box drum featured in the concert.[27] "These drums, as Sal Ferreras said, these are found nowhere in Persia and it was striking how they were able to blend . . . and [they] still stayed close to this Persian sound. I didn't know you were allowed to do that, 'cause it sounded traditional and they're not following traditional rules" (focus group). Once again, Safa's performance confronts us with two seemingly irreconcilable notions of identity: the authentic self that transcends social categories and the contingent self that must constantly negotiate cultural rules of engagement.

A dialogue between two other focus group participants illustrates the politics of recognition in action:

A: Amir was very much to me a central chord in that and there was a certain amount of really responsible kind of deferral that happened. Like not a "you're going to play the loudest all the time and we're just . . ." but there was definitely a centralization of Amir that happened that was actually very beautiful.

B: I thought so too. Yeah. "We're coming to Persia with you." It was like . . .

A: Yes!

B: It was like, "We're allowed to be . . . yeah, and here we all are" . . . so it's not like we're Canadian we're a melting pot of all, it was it's us Canadians from French Canada or from . . . Sal, I don't know where Sal's from, he's not from Canada originally I suppose, but his culture's . . .

EW: He's from Puerto Rico.

B: So they're saying "we're coming with you to Persia" which is different than saying no culture matters and it all melts into the folk fest at, you know, BC Place or something.

A: And Amir was very clearly saying "and your contributions are important and you're doing something important and we need to hear you" because he definitely pulled out when François needed to do something particularly creative, particularly different with his clarinet in order to make a sound that he would feel that contributed to that moment of the music making. Amir responded to that, and it was a really beautiful sort of dance of listening. (focus group)

These listeners have a clear idea of what should constitute appropriate multiculturalism in Canada—not a "melting pot" but a respectful recognition and accommodation of Others that fits quite nicely with Taylor's conception of the politics of difference. However, I suspect that Smaro Kamboureli would be dismayed. Meant to be celebratory and approving, the tone of this dialogue is nonetheless imbued with the liberalism that beneficently bestows recognition on the Other as a gift. Sal and François are congratulated for meeting Amir on his own cultural turf and for taking us all to Persia; Amir is lauded for not taking advantage of this generosity. Implicitly (although Sal is assumed by one participant to be an immigrant and François is identified as specifically from French Canada), Sal and François are somehow less different than Amir.[28] However, the dialogue also includes the evocative image of a "beautiful dance of listening," which reminds us again of Walcott's call to take the multicultural encounter as an inevitable starting point of society, and therefore "always the place from which human engagement and thus negotiation proceed" (2011, 25).

Sal describes Safa's work in terms that suggest that improvisation might offer useful strategies for such negotiations. Safa's improvisation, he suggests, is "a sort of triangulated translation game . . . It might not be flat or horizontal: it could be like a spiral . . . François will play something to Amir's pattern that Amir is playing to my rhythm. I hear François. I will react to him, and I will reference, say, rhythms and juxtapositions that are more common in contemporary music. Amir will hear that, and find something from his reference that will reference that, so we continue to do this strange little angular spiral. It's not smooth; it's reactive, and, as in all improvisation, it's immediate. But you only know that at the other end" (interview).

Conclusion: Improvising Processes of Recognition

Through my analysis of Safa's performance of "Whisper of Love," I have shown that improvisation can articulate quite different conceptions of subjectivity—both the authentic (dialogical) self and the socially constructed (contingent) self—fluidly and even simultaneously in a constant circulation of power, characterized by Sal as a "triangulated translation game." As a concluding gesture, I return to Maclure's suggestion that we should focus on processes of recognition rather than outcomes. He neatly summarizes the central problem, "the insistence on recognition seems to imply that a consensus on a thick identity precedes and enables the actual struggle for recognition. But what collective identity is free of internal ambivalence and dissonance? Are the politics of recognition and the critique of cultural essentialism antithetical?" (2003, 5).

To breach this impasse, Maclure (following James Tully) suggests that "identity politics must be thought of not only as struggles for recognition, but also as games of disclosure and acknowledgment" (2003, 4). These are serious and agonistic games whose underlying principle is not "dignity, self-respect, or self-esteem, but *freedom*: the democratic freedom to compete for the modification of the current structure of recognition as our identities change in the course of the very process of identity criticism and disclosure" (6). This principle is an utterly dialogical ideal that assumes that exposure to public debate necessarily informs and broadens our views. It depends on the idea that we are listening empathetically to others' demands for recognition even as we are putting our own demands forward.

Although reframing the politics of recognition as both a struggle and a game suggests that there will be winners and losers, the value of the freedom to compete lies in the fact that people's grievances are brought into the public sphere where they may educate and inform others and provide an outlet for the aggrieved people's frustrations. Maclure insists that "reflexive practices of articulating the unfairness or unacceptability of a given form of recognition, of deliberating about it, and of competing for an alternative description in a public space are, in themselves, means of enhancing self-knowledge, self-respect and self-esteem" (2003, 7).[29] Alterior subjects thus become active advocates for rights instead of passive victims of society. The subject isn't simply waiting for someone else to grant him or her recognition; instead, he or she is enunciating the terms of recognition that are acceptable to him or her. Furthermore, such reflexive debates may give voice to the differences that exist within minority groups, honoring the contingent nature of both individual and group identities. There is no definitive end to this game, which relies on the idea that in a liberal democracy, policies can always be revisited and adjusted. Maclure is counting on an always dynamic and thoughtful public debate to keep the competing needs of minorities under consideration. A focus on processes of recognition accounts for the ever-changing nature of identities, but it requires a large social appetite for risk. It seems to me that agonistic games of disclosure might too easily go unacknowledged; such contests could still fall prey to becoming spectacles that hegemonic citizens watch from the safety of the coliseum. This heavy-handed, but all too contemporary, metaphor highlights the fact that games are not neutral, that some players will have advantages over others, that some don't get to play at all, and that—in many nation-states—some are expected to accept death as the outcome.[30]

Can improvisation offer strategies for engaging in ethical and therefore effective processes of recognition? The improvisational techniques of active listening, adaptability, code-switching, and reflexivity demonstrated by Safa are powerful tools for alterior subjects and dominant citizens alike, high-performance equipment for use in the recognition games. These tools are calibrated for optimum responsiveness to changing conditions in the moment, and they stand up to a chaotic playing field in which many voices are competing for attention. Crucially, they are also tools for receptivity, for dialogism-in-action, for the kind of acknowledgment that produces change. As demonstrated by Safa's musicking, improvisation allows for both the articulation of an authentic self and the openness to self-transformation that comes from negotiating contingent subjectivities. Authenticity here may be read in Taylor's sense of knowing oneself, as the kind of self-knowledge that gives the musicians confidence to play according to their cultural traditions, or to play outside, to explore new ways of sounding the body. Improvising musicians take on the risks of performing under exposed conditions but never precisely knowing what the outcome of their interactions will be (all games are improvisational in this respect). To work, this approach requires a considerable degree of trust. Safa's very name, translating as "sincere affection," positions the group in an ethical place from which to engage in games of disclosure and acknowledgment. All members of the group express their trust that the others will respect their autonomy, and they articulate specific strategies for supporting the expressive musicking of their colleagues. Not a bad model for ethical social relations in a multicultural society.

At the same time, however, my analysis of "Whisper of Love" reveals layers of hidden meanings, areas of nondisclosure, and even blatant misrecognition as the musicians and their audience act from positions that are so deeply culturally conditioned that they are naturalized and embodied. Indeed, some aspects of improvisation, like the ability to transcend the technical aspects of one's musical training, depend on such embodiment. Nondisclosure, as Kamboureli would agree, may also occur due to our lack of conscious awareness, the taken-for-grantedness that is the luxury of inhabiting a dominant social position. If we could just listen to ourselves, we might reconsider our ideas. Remarkably, what seems like a contradiction (how can empathy coincide with intractability?) is, in the immediacy of the intercorporeal encounter, also cocreative, suggesting that dissensus might, under conditions of active listening, be an ethical domain of intersubjectivity. Listening for difference and supporting it into audibility is not the same thing as granting accommodation from a position of dominance. It means giving up some of one's power so that something new and potentially significant might emerge. An ethical and effective politics of recognition depends on our willingness to accept the conditions of both disclosure and acknowledgment played out in an unruly, improvisational domain.

Notes

1. See Stanyek (2004) and D. Wong (2004) for studies of improvisation as intercorporeal encounter.

2. My representation of the musicians in Safa via hyphenated identity markers is deliberate; it brings into relief the categorical and sometimes arbitrary ways identity is marked in a multicultural society.

3. This chapter is part of a larger comparative study of experimental music performance across Canada funded by a Standard Research Grant from the Social Sciences and Humanities Research Council of Canada. I am grateful to Daniel Fischlin, Dylan Robinson, Mehrenegar Rostami, and Gillian Siddall for their careful readings and comments.

4. The demand for recognition of course extends to many social domains, including gender, sexuality, and religion as well as ethnicity. See, for example, Susan Wolf's (1994) commentary on Taylor's essay, in which she addresses the question of gender and recognition.

5. See Bothwell (1998) for an account of the Canada/Quebec historical relationship. The politics of recognition became a contentious issue once again in 2013 with the Quebec National Assembly's introduction of Bill 60, the Quebec Charter of Values, which effectively died when the Parti Québécois was defeated in April 2014. If passed, Bill 60 would have barred public sector employees such as teachers and health workers from wearing the burqa and the niqab, a move that would effectively force some Muslim women to choose between their religious beliefs and employment opportunities. See http://www.assnat.qc .ca/en/travaux-parlementaires/projets-loi/projet-loi-60-40-1.html.

6. See the comprehensive archival website of the Truth and Reconciliation Commission at http://www.trc.ca.

7. Glenn Coulthard (2007) is similarly critical of Taylor in relation to the recognition of aboriginal identities in Canada.

8. Until summer 2015, when Safa became an inactive project, this bio was posted on François Houle's website at http://www.francoishoule.ca/?p=1162. Information about Safa may still be accessed online at http://songlines.com/release/alight/.

9. See Simms and Koushkani (2012).

10. At the time of this writing, Ferreras is vice president, Educational and Student Services at VCC.

11. Several tracks can be streamed at http://www.songlines.com/release/alight.

12. Today, there are about seven well-known radifs in general use, collected and developed by different master musicians. However, the first and the most famous radif is attributed to a nineteenth-century court musician, Mirza Abdollah. See Nooshin (2013) for more information on Iranian classical music.

13. See Nooshin (2003).

14. Nooshin's recent work with young Iranian musicians who take inspiration from the radif but work outside this tradition troubles this dichotomy. See Nooshin (2013).

15. Compared to the more open and complex genre *avaz*, the "premiere musical element" of any performance of Iranian classical music, tasnif are more strictly composed and are often "vehicles for mass appeal" (Simms and Koushkani 2012, 26). Even so, listening to different performances of the tasnif on which "Whisper of Love" is based, by its composer Majid Derakhshani, reveals a wide range of interpretation and improvisational creativity.

16. The poem was translated from Farsi by Mehrenegar Rostami, who also translated a private citizen's political interpretation of the poem found in Farsi at http://p30city.net /showthread.php?t=15235.

17. Personal communication with Mehrenegar Rostami, July 25, 2013.

18. "Whisper of Love" would presumably receive an entirely different reception at Safa's performances for the Iranian-Canadian community in North Vancouver. François Houle has fond memories of being "adopted" as an unofficial Iranian by such audiences (interview with Ellen Waterman, Vancouver, September 30, 2007).

19. See note 8.

20. Esfahan in F and Esfahan in G are both very common in playing the radif on the tar. In this rendition, F serves three functions as: the starting note (*Aghaz*), the finalis, and the witness note (*Shahed*). See Farhat (2004) for a detailed explanation.

21. I am deeply grateful to my research assistant, Mehrenegar Rostami, for her culturally attuned ears, patient transcription, and assistance with analyzing the Persian aspects of Safa's performance.

22. *Son* is an Afro-Cuban genre of song. *Clave*, meaning code or key, refers more generally to the syncopated rhythmic pattern found in either duple or complex triple meters within several Afro-Cuban genres, including rumba. The pattern has sub-Saharan African roots. See Peñalosa with Greenwood (2009).

23. Robinson leads a team of interdisciplinary scholars who are looking at the cultural components (such as concerts and plays) included in Canada's Truth and Reconciliation events. Robinson examines ideas of normative listening in the TRC context (and the assumption that positive affective responses are shared among audience members for indigenous intercultural music). See D. Robinson (2014).

24. See also Edith Turner (2012) for a discussion of how music festivals engender communitas.

25. Focus group, Open Ears Festival of Music and Sound, Kitchener-Waterloo, Ontario, Canada, April 28, 2007. Hereafter cited as "focus group."

26. See, for example, my interview with Nicole Mitchell (Waterman 2008a).

27. The *cajón* is a wooden box-shaped percussion instrument originally from Peru but also important in Afro-Cuban music; the player sits on the instrument and hits the thin front face of it with the hands. Batá drums are double-headed hourglass-shaped instruments; they come in several sizes and are closely associated with Cuban Santeria religious practices.

28. In her revealing doctoral dissertation on multiculturalism and public arts funding in Canada, Parmela Singh Attariwala (2014) describes a similar experience of being placed on a panel of "new Canadians" at a conference despite the fact that her family has lived in Canada for several generations. The (Anglo-Canadian) organizers wrongly assumed that because she appears ethnically South Asian, she must have immigrated to Canada herself.

29. See also Tully (2000) and Benhabib (1996).

30. A historical reference to the Roman coliseum has contemporary resonance for comfortable Canadian subjects, whether we are thrilling to *Hunger Games* in the cinema, watching the appalling spectacles of civil war around the world on the evening news, or passively listening to statistics about the suicide rate in aboriginal communities in the Canadian north.

17. Performing the National Body Politic in Twenty-First-Century Argentina

Illa Carrillo Rodríguez and Berenice Corti

In May 2010, Argentina's national government organized different cultural activities to commemorate the two hundredth anniversary of the first independence movement against Spanish rule (henceforth the Bicentennial). Over a period of five days, thousands of artists performed for approximately six million people, who made their way to downtown Buenos Aires to visit the Bicentennial Pathway, where an eclectic set of commemorative events was held: public debates with human rights activists, parades organized by Argentina's provincial governments and immigrant communities, and a pageant that represented nineteen key moments of Argentine history through a series of "scenes" or moving tableaux vivants performed on floats. The pageant was staged by Fuerzabruta ("Rawforce" or "Bruteforce"), a theater troupe that physically and emotionally implicates spectators in its performances through the use of musical and choreographic forms associated with aerial dance, circus arts, techno music, punk, rock, and *murga* (a carnival genre involving dance, music, and satirical texts). From 1976 to 1983, Argentina was governed by a military regime that abducted, tortured, and "disappeared" approximately thirty thousand people. These years are referred to as the period of state terrorism. In the pageant's historical scene that represented Argentina's 1983 return to democratic rule, Fuerzabruta put to work the murga's sonic and choreographic aesthetic in conveying to spectators the transformations experienced by individual bodies and the national body politic in the postdictatorship years. In this scene, hundreds of murga performers danced and chanted with audience members, compelling them to collectively reenact common citizens' reappropriation of public space in the dictatorship's aftermath.

This essay examines the forms of political subjectivation and memorialization that crystallized during the Bicentennial, in moments of rehearsed, yet improvisational interaction like the one described here. Our approach is informed by a body of literature (Bourdieu 1995; J. Butler 2004; Tilly 1993) that has recourse to the concept of improvisation as a means of "reflecting on the coordination of actions and . . . the articulation between the conventional and creative dimensions of those actions" (Bachir-Loopuyt et al. 2010, 10).[1] Even though this literature is not grounded in a sustained reflection on improvisatory traditions in the arts, it puts to use the idea of improvisation in thinking through phenomena that artists and scholars who engage with those traditions are attentive to. These include (1) the "overlapping layers of participation and interaction [and] the negotiating and trading of performance roles" (Monson 1996, 8) in cocreative practices; (2) the "continuous process of mutual adjustment [whereby] partial knowledge is shared on the fly and combined, step by step, to produce a performance" (Faulkner and Becker 2009, 183–84); (3) the ways social actors grapple with shared conventions to establish evolving frames of interaction that enable the articulation of a plurality of voices and perspectives (Bimstein 2010); and (4) the role of the lived moment and the lived body in the transformation of normative cultural scripts and the emergence of unexpected, disruptive practices within well-established frames of interaction.

The public sphere operates as one such frame. Whatever becomes apprehensible as "public" and is deemed legitimate (or anomalous) within that frame is largely determined by the shared conventions and cultural scripts that underpin commonality. Following theories rooted in Hannah Arendt's (1958) conception of citizenship, we approach the public sphere as the sphere of the common, "a shared and public world of human artifacts, institutions, and settings . . . which provides a relatively permanent and durable context for our activities[,] . . . the stable background from which public spaces of action and deliberation can arise" (D'Entreves 2014). The forms of identity and agency that take shape in these spaces bear the traces of a stable repertoire of communal imaginings and of the spatially and temporally contingent social encounters through which those imaginings are actualized. Hence, though anchored in a repertoire of conventions, the public sphere is not an unvarying script or frame of interaction. It is relational, processual, and improvisatory, "the product of the fleeting instant, . . . inhabited by action, conflict, and confrontation" (Göle 2009, 291). The public sphere is always differentially iterated by a plurality of actors in the course of interactions that entail the decoding and resignification of norms; the formulation, attribution, and negotiation of social roles; and intersubjective processes, whereby "people come to know what others have in mind and . . . adjust [their reactions] accordingly" (Bruner 1996, 161) to cocreate common spaces.

The multiple, intersecting socialities that are at work in the production of the public sphere recall the forms of intersubjectivity, agency, and cocreativity that improvisatory arts-based practices bring to the fore. Our analysis mobilizes the heuristic potential of "improvisation"—as a concept and field of critical inquiry—to explore the versions of collective identity that were performed during Argentina's Bicentennial. Through that prism, we discuss why certain iterations of nationhood were represented as disruptive enactments of the public sphere. In dialogue with Butler's theorization of political signifiers, we examine the relational construction of moments of collective agency that illuminated the set of exclusions on which normative figurations of Argentine identity and history had been traditionally predicated. To better understand the commemorative and political implications of these moments, we situate them in the context of the historiographic battles that were waged during Argentina's Bicentennial year by means of symbols of musical erudition such as the Colón Theater, Argentina's most prestigious opera house. The first part of our discussion focuses on this theater's reopening gala, which was held a day before Fuerzabruta's pageant. We posit that in this commemorative gala, the Colón and the music culture it represents were "made to sound" in a nostalgic register that conjured up conservative notions of social and aesthetic harmony. We then discuss how the musical trope of harmony, marshaled by the gala's organizers, was imbricated with media representations of contemporary Argentina's public sphere as a site of political and social strife.

In the second part of our analysis, we argue that people's celebratory, yet introspective participation in the Bicentennial festivities unsettled such representations, forcing journalists and public intellectuals to interrogate reductive characterizations of embodied, collective practices as the catalysts of potentially perilous social behavior. Here, we are particularly interested in understanding how discursive mediations of such practices may silence or make audible the memory work that undergirds collective improvisational instances.

The focus of the final part of our discussion is on two such instances, in which the crowds who participated in the Bicentennial played a key role. This part of our analysis builds on R. Keith Sawyer's research on the interactional mechanisms that are used to create collective improvisational performances. We argue that, in the two performances under consideration, improvisational interaction was mediated by a corpus of shared cultural references or "ready-mades" (Sawyer 2000, 157). Through a close reading/auscultation[2] of spectators' often silent reactions to those ready-mades, we examine the commemorative and political ethos that emerged in the course of those performances. Finally, we argue that spectators' interaction with and resignification of that corpus of ready-mades contributed to the iteration of an unconventional version of Argentine national identity during the Bicentennial.

Sounding Nostalgia

During the Bicentennial, "art" and "popular" musical forms emerged as tropes of conflicting conceptions both of Argentine history and the ideal national community of the twenty-first century. Nowhere was this dichotomy more explicit than in the gala organized by the mayor of Buenos Aires to celebrate the reopening of the Colón, after almost four years of restoration work. Inaugurated in 1908, in emulation of Europe's grand opera houses, the Colón is a symbol of the nineteenth-century elite's cosmopolitanist aspirations and of the aesthetic and social order this fin-de-siècle elite attempted to actualize through the Haussmann-inspired transformation of Buenos Aires, undertaken around the time of the 1910 Centennial celebrations.[3] The turn-of-the-century reshaping of Buenos Aires entailed, among other changes, the construction of broad thoroughfares, which facilitated the surveillance of the plebeian masses, and the creation of architectural preserves within which the elites could "maintain identification with their fantasy of a Civilization unsullied by Latin American architecture or the poor" (Needell 1995, 539). In this segregated urban space, the Colón stood as the locus of edification of the Centennial elite's model citizen: the cultivated, self-contained subject of cultural modernity and political liberalism. The erudite music culture, of which the Colón became the temple, played a central role in the enactment of this form of citizenship.

The reopening gala of 2010 commemorated this dimension of the Colón's history, in an attempt to reinforce the theater's identification with canonical forms of high culture and the Centennial elite's related prestige. The event was organized according to a spatial logic that, unwittingly, conjured up the compartmentalized public sphere of 1910. A fence built around the Colón for the gala separated the event's special guests from the crowds that had gone to the city center to attend the performance, which the city government was to broadcast on a giant screen outside the theater. As they made their way across a Hollywood-style red carpet leading to the theater's entrance, agribusiness and media corporation magnates claimed for themselves a privileged relationship with the mythical genealogy of nationhood embodied by the Colón. In the social order enacted during the gala, ballet and opera were to contribute to the production of aesthetic and historiographic harmony as part of a commemorative spectacle that endeavored to establish a consensual dialogue with the theater's past and the cultural politics of the present. Avant-garde performance practices and popular music cultures, which have entertained a tense, yet fruitful relationship with the Colón for the past century, were therefore absent from the repertoire selected for the gala: Giacomo Puccini's *La Bohème*, which represents nineteenth-century Paris as the mythical locus of Romantic poiesis and revelry, and Petipa and Ivanov's 1895 version of *Swan Lake*, a palace ball scene that is designed to display classical ballet's sartorial splendor and conventional forms of choreographic virtuosity. The selection of this repertoire and its sumptuous staging were functional to the gala's mise-en-scène, which deployed sonic topoi of legitimate culture to signify the Colón's refinement, thereby commemorating the (lost) glory of the Centennial Patria.

Throughout 2010, the Colón appeared in various media narratives as the architectural embodiment of the spirit of 1910, and Centennial Buenos Aires, as the nation's desired telos: a paradigmatic public sphere in which enlightened rationalism and liberal-republican values ensured social harmony. Prominent political and cultural figures, who subscribed to this characterization of the Centennial era, went so far as to posit the theater's reopening gala as a miniature, ephemeral version of the social and political order toward which the Bicentennial generation should strive. To this paradigm of nationhood, they opposed the Argentina of 2010, a society presumably under the sway of regressive passions and political forces that had succeeded in polarizing a formerly harmonious national community and in weakening the institutions and values that had laid the groundwork for such feats as the construction of the Colón.[4] Two concepts dominated these representations of Bicentennial Argentina: the notion that the city's public spaces were dangerous and the idea that political and cultural debates in the public sphere were the loci of extreme tension.

Improvisation as Political Dislocation

We reconsider these figurations of the contemporary Argentine body politic not in terms of progress and regression but as symptoms of a dislocating political event. For a political experience, we suggest, took place during the Bicentennial: an experience that productively disrupted the institutional and discursive practices that simultaneously actualize and naturalize what Kristin Ross, following Jacques Rancière, has called "'the police logic' of the social: the logic that assigns people to their places and their social identities, that makes them identical to their functions" (2002, 24). The police logic was power-fully at work during the Colón's reopening ceremony. However, something else happened outside the theater that involved the resignification of national symbols and values and, hence, upset the police logic that underwrote the dominant conception of the public sphere circulating in Argentina's corpo-rate media in 2010. What happened during the Bicentennial, we submit, was an "event" in the sense that Alain Badiou has given the term: "something that arrives in excess, beyond all calculation, something that displaces people and places, that proposes a new situation for thought" (quoted in K. Ross 2002, 26).

The Argentine presidency's Bicentennial Unit, which organized the com-memorative festivities, had estimated that approximately 200,000 people would attend the closing performances. A much larger crowd, however, con-gregated in downtown Buenos Aires for those performances, which included Fuerzabruta's pageant and a concert headlined by some of Argentina's most prominent popular music artists. After the Bicentennial, the national govern-ment and various commentators estimated that two to three million people attended the closing festivities (Télam 2010). In an attempt to discursively contend with this "excessive," unexpected embodiment of the Bicentennial nation, certain pundits focused on the event's statistics. "With a calculator and a map in hand," a renowned journalist wrote, "I spent some time doing a calcu-lation: it [the government's estimate of the number of participants] wasn't right. Three million could only have fitted [in the area where the closing festivities took place] if people had been on each other's shoulders" (Lanata 2010). Tak-ing distance from this "statistical" approach to the Bicentennial, Eduardo Ali-verti, another leading journalist, characterized pundits' preoccupation with "numerical accuracies" as a discursive subterfuge through which they avoided commenting on the harmonious coexistence of millions of bodies in a polis that the corporate media had heretofore construed as a space fraught with violence and social tensions. For Aliverti, the central issue of the festivities was that "the people [el pueblo] overcame the fear conveyed by the media . . . They went out on the street to see what was happening . . . and discovered themselves in all their diversity" (Aliverti 2010).

The Bicentennial multitude thus became the object of discursive media-tions that endeavored to contain—in the double sense of encompassing and controlling—unruly actualizations of "the people" that might question and usher the rearticulation of another political signifier: "the nation." Philos-opher Ricardo Forster grappled with this double-edged form of containment in his attempt to name the Bicentennial multitude, stating that "there, in the festive . . . city, there were no "people [gente]," that name forged to . . . make the other invisible. . . . There were the people [pueblo] . . . [that] shattered in a thousand pieces the discourse that taught us to establish a brutal equivalence between multitude and homogeneity . . . The pueblo is . . . a body on which the writings of history leave their indelible traces" (2010a). The distinction Forster establishes between *gente* and *pueblo* introduces a representational tension/question: why portray the Bicentennial multitude as gente and not pueblo? For Forster, choosing between these terms was not simply a stylistic matter but a way of conceptualizing political and historical subjectivities. Even though both words may be used to signify "people," *gente* does not evoke the figurations of the "popular" that the term *pueblo* immediately conveys.

As scholars of discourse analysis have shown (Díaz 2009, chaps. 3, 5; Laclau 2005, 214–22; Sigal and Verón 2004, 43–52, 231–42), *pueblo* has operated as a key semantic nucleus in the construction of social and political identities in Argentina. Throughout the second half of the twentieth century, the word *pueblo* was often conflated with signifiers that named the subjects and agents of a history of struggle and resistance; for example, the *descamisado* (shirtless) workers extolled by Eva Perón in her speeches, the unemployed picketers whose *puebladas* (popular uprisings) epitomized the struggle against 1990s authoritarian neoliberalism, and the supporters of Argentina's human rights movement, who expressed their solidarity with that movement's most emblematic figures by collectively chanting "Madres de la Plaza, el pueblo las abraza" (Mothers of the Plaza [de Mayo], the pueblo embraces you). Through this web of discursive connections, *pueblo* came to be associated with a collective subject(ivity) shaped by experiences of disenfranchisement, rebellion, and solidarity. The echoes of those experiences, which resonate in *pueblo*, are largely absent from *gente*. The word *gente*, Forster observes, was frequently used in 1990s neoliberal public discourse as "a way of agglomerating depoliticized citizens" (2010b), whom media corporations represented as peaceful, in opposition to the unemployed workers' movements that organized road blockades and "disrupted" public order.

The tension/question raised by Forster compels us to think of political signifiers, such as *gente* and *pueblo*, in relation to what Judith Butler understands as their historicity, "a signifier is political to the extent that it implicitly cites the prior instances of itself, drawing the phantasmatic promise of those prior signifiers, reworking them into the production and promise of 'the new,' a 'new' that is itself only established through recourse to those embedded conventions, past conventions, that have conventionally been invested with the political power to signify the future" (1993, 220). In other words, these signifiers are always already dialogical performative acts that are constitutive of political subjectivities precisely because they bear the traces of a chain of prior usages. Central to Butler's theorization of the sense of futurity that political signifiers may open up is what she calls the experience of misrecognition or disidentification, "the uneasy sense of standing under a sign to which one does and does not belong" (219). This experience always crystallizes in relationship to—indeed, as a reaction against—the political signifier's prior chain of usages and the set of constitutive exclusions that underwrite it. Such exclusions "return to haunt the claims of identity defined through negation" (221) and in this way enable the rearticulation of fixed identity categories. The experience of disidentification or misrecognition can thus be understood as a "haunted" (re)iteration of the signifier of identity that "commit[s] a disloyalty against identity—a catachresis—in order to secure its future" (220). It is in this "hiatus of iterability" (220)—in the "open-ended and performative function of the signifier" (191)—that Butler locates agency. In terms that resonate with Butler's, Rancière (1998, 28–30) posits the experience of disidentification with respect to a familiar order as the point of departure for the manifestation of a political subjectivity capable of troubling the order of things: the inclusions and exclusions that the police logic of the social naturalizes.

In the semantic distance separating the two political signifiers that Forster juxtaposes, there is, we believe, a hiatus in the iteration of national identity that renders audible the exclusions that signifiers of identity tend to naturalize. By choosing *pueblo* instead of *gente* to represent the Bicentennial multitude, Forster discursively replicates the "disloyal" performance of Argentine identity through which millions of anonymous bodies disrupted a representational system predicated on the police logic of the social, which "prescribes what emerges and what is heard, what can be counted and what cannot be counted" (Rancière 1998, 29). What many commentators were unable or reluctant to (re)count was not the exact number of people who participated in the Bicentennial but the way this multitude challenged assumptions about the pueblo's relationship to history, politics, and nationhood. These assumptions are connected to a racialized view of the denizens of impoverished peripheral regions as irrational, violent mobs or as the passive objects of corrupt *caudillos*. The unscripted emergence, in downtown Buenos Aires, of these obscure phantasms of middle- and upper-class anxieties in the guise of serene, celebratory families and groups of friends operated as an embodied excess that wrenched those assumptions and laid bare the racial and social prejudices that sustained them.

The Madres

The physical displacement of so many people from marginal areas to the city center entailed a disruption of implicit spatial hierarchies—a disruption that allowed for the intermingling of heterogeneous groups and atypical encounters, which temporarily diluted social compartmentalizations. Families who went to the Bicentennial Pathway in search of reified forms of cultural heritage stumbled upon the exhibition spaces of some of Argentina's most important human rights groups, whose history of struggle against state terrorism and subsequent forms of state violence contested the romanticized narrative of nationhood that reified modes of heritage production generally convey and legitimate. For visitors who knew little or nothing about this struggle, the discovery or revision of the human rights movement's political and cultural work revealed a long trajectory of resistance grounded in an experience of disidentification, not only with respect to a state that disappeared citizens in the name of the Patria, but also with respect to sectors of the national community that openly supported or passively subscribed to the ideologies of state terrorism.

Out of this experience of disidentification emerged an "unnatural" form of motherhood that disloyally iterated the paradigm of maternity on which the Patria's teleology of civilization and progress rested. The mothers of abducted political militants who denounced the disappearance of their children in the Plaza de Mayo during Argentina's last military dictatorship (the Madres) performed, indeed, a conventional version of motherhood, the Mater Dolorosa, but they did so "out of place"—in the public sphere—and through inappropriate behavior: by deprivatizing "subjective" emotions. A detailed discussion of their decades-long history is beyond the scope of this analysis; however, a brief description will elucidate the ways in which they disrupted and modified Argentina's public sphere during the country's last military dictatorship. This discussion will lay the groundwork for an analysis of Fuerzabruta's representation of the Madres in the Bicentennial pageant.

On April 30, 1977, after months of begging government officials and members of the clergy for information concerning their missing children's whereabouts, fourteen mothers decided to publicly and collectively voice their demands in the Plaza de Mayo, Buenos Aires's central square, where Argentina's House of Government is located. Under the state of emergency declared by the junta, the women's presence in the country's political and financial center was considered illegal. Thus, police attempted to break up the group by ordering them to "circulate." Through this perilous interaction with the state's police apparatus, the Madres' rounds in the plaza started to take shape. Thereafter, they walked around the Pirámide de Mayo, the plaza's obelisk, every Thursday afternoon, in groups of two, thus simultaneously complying with and disobeying the police's order to circulate. By July 1977, 150 Madres were circulating in the plaza and continued to do so throughout the dictatorship years, in spite of constant police harassment and the "disappearance," in December 1977, of twelve of the incipient movement's members (D. Taylor 1997, 187). Over the next three decades, the Madres joined or formed various human rights groups[5] and struggled to advance the rights of dispossessed sectors of the population, such as aboriginal communities and shantytown dwellers. Through their participation in these struggles, they succeeded in establishing a connection between their disappeared children's political activism, their own resistance to the military regime, and the post-dictatorship era's struggles for social justice.

Located in the interstices of normativity and transgression during the years of state terrorism, the Madres carved out a locus of moral authority in the nation's symbolic center, from which they exposed the dystopian underside of a Patria built on the violent exclusion of its undesirable Others. Wearing their disappeared children's diapers as headscarves and their photo IDs around their necks, they reappropriated public space in the form of walking, breathing palimpsests that contained the material traces of the abducted militants' intimate history and photographic elements of an "archive associated with surveillance and police strategies" (Taylor 2002, 160). These bodies in "archival drag" overperformed motherhood. As such, they embodied a grotesque excess of emotivity and memory in a willfully amnesiac Patria that endeavored to silence the disruptive set of questions they raised: What happens when bodies and their traces move or are violently moved out of their "familiar" places? What happens when subjects cease to loyally iterate prescribed identities and roles?

The Madres posited these questions through a repertoire of sonic and visual ready-mades on which they performed a series of defamiliarizing operations that drew the national community into a tense, initially silent dialogue about the legitimacy of the order of things. Their white *pañuelos*, or headscarves, evoked a Christian iconography of female abnegation and piety, which the Madres travestied by embroidering on them their "subversive" children's names and abduction dates. The silent, seemingly submissive behavior they initially adopted also played with received notions of female passivity. Their silence, however, was perceived as a dissonant utterance in a public soundscape of military marches, patriotic chants, and obedient, terror-stricken speechlessness. In 1983, the Madres visually represented the muted cry that their silence conveyed by plastering Buenos Aires's walls with silhouettes of human bodies.[6] They put to work a form of representation associated with the police's investigation procedures—the chalk outline of a dead body—to signal the absence of citizens whose abduction was disavowed by the police-state. Like the Madres' cacophonous silence, these silhouettes elicited both anxiety and repulsion:

Passersby manifested the discomfort or estrangement provoked by the feeling of being *looked at*, of being interpellated by those figures without a face. . . . The silhouettes "seemed to point, from the walls, at those guilty of their absence and seemed to silently claim for justice." . . .

[They] punctured the wall of silence erected in society during the dictatorship. (Longoni and Bruzzone 2008, 30–31)

Through this exchange of silences, the victims of state terrorism and their reluctant interlocutors improvised a public soundscape that belabored the collective numbing of the senses—the "percepticide"—that, as Diana Taylor has noted (1997, 122–24), was induced by the military regime's spectacular, disempowering show of force. This soundscape and its accompanying visual aesthetic worked as a basic representational matrix to which different layers of sonic motifs—that is, chants, songs, divers forms of silence—were added as the human rights movement changed, became fragmented, formed new political and cultural alliances, and improvised further performance strategies to contend with the politics of amnesia and privatization of the "public" that hegemonized Argentine life in the late 1980s and 1990s.

The Madres' strategies emanated, hence, from a collaborative process that resulted in dislocating performances of cultural and social identities. In this process, they mobilized representational mechanisms analogous to those that improv ensembles deploy in their performances: "In improvisational theater, . . . the actors have to rely on the group collectively, to generate the scene through dialogue. And a defining feature of improvisational theater is the involvement of the audience. . . . The actors assume that the audience shares a large body of cultural knowledge and references. In this sense, the audience guides their improvisation" (Sawyer 2000, 156). The Madres' built-in idea of their potential audiences indeed played a crucial role in the shape they gave to their public performances. When they first entered the plaza as docile women, for example, they were fully conscious that their silence and sartorial choices would elicit compassion from a citizenry who generally associated such behavior and attire with proper Catholic womanhood. Therefore, the Madres adapted elements of their representational matrix—their headscarves, silences, slogans, the tone and volume of their voices—to their audience's body of cultural references and the country's labile political situation. Notwithstanding these contingent variations, the general representational matrix remained subordinated to the same goals: to keep alive the memory of the disappeared and bring to justice those who committed crimes during the dictatorship. Their sonic and visual ready-mades operated as formulaic speech does for improv ensembles,[7] and their overarching goals had the same function as the latter's scenario does: "There are two forms of structure that guide their [improv ensembles'] emergent improvisations: scenarios that guide the overall improvisation and formulaic speech that actors use in their individual lines. These structures are always in dialectic with improvisation" (156).

Fuerzabruta: Improvising Silence

The narrative of national history staged by Fuerzabruta during the Bicentennial referenced both the "scenario" and the "formulaic speech" that structure the Madres' representational matrix.[8] In this performance, the troupe had recourse to a repertoire of ready-mades associated with the Madres' early performance history to conjure up the sensory and emotive impact that their unforeseen entry in the military regime's public sphere generated. Fuerzabruta's representation of the Madres' struggle was, of course, carefully designed. It was also an improvisational moment because the ways it resignified the past "emerged" from and through the audience's unscripted, polysemous reactions and interaction with the artists.[9] The scene we are referring to was performed by a group of female artists, who represented the Madres' rounds in the plaza on the square platform of a float on which water, simulating rain, poured (figure 17.1; "Especial Festejo del Bicentenario—parte 16 de 20," narr. Felipe Pigna and Gabriela Radice).[10] Dressed in trench coats, the artists enacted the Madres' ritual movement by walking around the borders of the platform, sporadically stopping to face the multitude that flanked each side of the float at a distance of approximately two meters. They wore the Madres' distinctive headscarves, from which a white light emanated. The float was also illuminated by blue lights located in the scaffolding's upper frame and on the borders of the platform floor, but the most striking lighting effect came from the white LEDs that were integrated into the headscarves' underlying acrylic structure. Designed by Fuerzabruta's lighting artist, Edi Pampin, the illuminated headscarves conveyed the idea, ubiquitous in songs and others forms of popular culture, that the Madres embodied "light in [the midst of] obscurity" (Gieco and Gurevich 2001) during the dictatorship years. In this performance, the obscurity surrounding the headscarves was real, since the pageant took place at night.[11] However, the scene's darkness, with its attendant associations with the dictatorship's sinister, clandestine practices, was not simply a natural lighting effect, but an aural sensation produced by the sonic mise-en-scène's main elements: the artists' silence, the sound of water falling onto the float's platform, and the score, which consisted of the intermittent rumbling of thunder layered over fragments of wailing voices and a continuous base of ambient synthesizer sounds.[12]

FIG 17.1: Fuerzabruta's representation of the Madres de Plaza de Mayo. Photo by Ángel Castro, courtesy of Fuerzabruta.

FIG 17.2: The truck that towed the float. Photo by Ángel Castro, courtesy of Fuerzabruta.

The multitude that accompanied the float as it moved from the Plaza de Mayo to Avenida Independencia participated in this soundscape with different manifestations of silence.[13] Some forms of silence seemed to express simple fascination before Fuerzabruta's synesthetic spectacle, in which the performers' bodies always appeared to be at risk, in situations that, although meticulously planned, exposed them to an unpredictable group of people and put them under considerable physical and emotional strain. The entire cast and crew experienced a moment of particularly high tension and uncertainty when the floats and trucks reached Carlos Pellegrini Street, a thoroughfare adjacent to the Obelisk. At this point, the pageant had to come to a halt because the street was overflowing with people who had been forced to move from the sidewalk to the road as more and more spectators arrived at the area surrounding the Obelisk. "It felt . . . like the place was brimming over [with people]. There was no space. . . . [It] was something . . . that we were not going to be able to control," Fabio D'Aquila recalls (interview). For approximately twenty minutes, the cast of two thousand actors did its best to continue performing the scenes, which Fuerzabruta had conceived as five-minute narratives that spectators would view only once, as the floats moved through the streets at a slow but steady pace. The technical and logistical difficulties raised by the unexpected interruption of the pageant had an impact on the aesthetic experience that Fuerzabruta had sought to create: while certain scenes were performed many times before the same spectators, the allegory of Argentina's dictatorships, a scene that required the use of pyrotechnic effects, could not be enacted because there were fire hazards in the area where that float had stopped. When it appeared that the remaining part of the pageant would have to be canceled, a collective improvised performance took over, as spectators started to work with the show's organizers, the civil defense, firefighters, and police officers to clear the way for the floats and trucks to go through. Carolina Constantinovsky, one of the street performance's executive producers, alluded to the artists' sensation of fragility in the midst of a concentration of protean characteristics: "No one is one hundred percent sure of how a human group of that size reacts. . . . [I] personally saw how the multitude drew back [to let the floats go through], without hurting or attacking each other. It was obvious that there were millions of people, but they wanted to celebrate with joy" (quoted in García 2010).

Beyond the joy that Constantinovsky emphasizes, there were silent reactions to the "Madres' scene" that doubtless expressed uneasiness before a tableau vivant in which the most visually salient element, the headscarf, did not have any of the messages or information that the Madres embroidered on their kerchiefs. For some, this image may have evoked an essentialized form of womanhood, with conservative Catholic undertones, that emptied the Madres' struggle of its disruptive political content. However, D'Aquila described the crowd's silence in positive terms: "The response was hallucinating. . . . You could hear the way in which each float elicited diverse reactions. The 'reflexive' [floats] were received by an attentive silence, which is what happened with [the floats dedicated to] the Madres de Plaza de Mayo or the Falklands War" (quoted in García 2010).

For the artists who participated in the Madres' scene, listening to that silence was an emotionally unsettling experience that according to D'Aquila modified their relationship to the past they were representing. Many of those artists were born after 1983 and therefore did not experience the years of state terrorism. Some of them had had little interest in examining that period of Argentine history prior to participating in the pageant. As the crowd grew silent in their presence, they initially felt vulnerable, for that silence communicated to them very poignant emotions in which they perceived grief: "There was . . . something . . . painful [in that silence]. . . . [The artists] felt . . . as though they were carrying [that very intense emotion], [as though] they were bearing the weight of that past" (D'Aquila interview). However, they also sensed that those poignant emotions were intertwined with feelings of admiration and respect for the Madres' courage. Hence, the silence that materialized around them also conveyed strength to them, in their role as mothers of the disappeared. That collective silence, which physically surrounded and sustained them, brought them into the fold of a set of conflicting emotions (vulnerability, strength, grief) and thereby *incorporated* them into—that is, made them embody and belong to—a history that had thus far felt foreign to many of them.

This historically charged silence was anchored in a mnemonic community that bears the traces of the "rememorating guilt" (H. González 2011) of those who lost their loved ones during the years of state terrorism. The testimony of one of those spectators suggests that this silent reaction was celebratory more than it was remorseful, because the disappeared were being co-memorated not by an ostracized group of victims but by millions of people who collectively and simultaneously recognized in the Madres' struggle an ethos of solidarity and courage on which a different national community could be modeled: "'I leave fulfilled. It was a wonderful spectacle, because of the artists and the people.' Mario Robledo, 'a seventies militant,' left joyfully with his beard and military green overcoat that survived years and forgetting" (Rodríguez 2010). That celebratory sense of fulfillment bespeaks an important change in the emotional content of survivors' rememorating guilt, a change that involved the public performance of guilt as pride, rather than shame, for having survived.

We do not mean to suggest that the Bicentennial alone ushered in such a transformation. We do think that it created the conditions for the embodied reemergence and decompartmentalization of voices and silences that had been confined to isolated spaces by the military dictatorship and its political, judicial, and economic successors. In this sense, the Bicentennial was an exercise in what Rancière defines as political subjectivation: "a form of visibility conferred upon something that is supposedly non-visible or that had been removed from visibility" (1998, 30). The different performances and people's participation conferred visibility and audibility on multiple experiences of defeat and survival. Fuerzabruta's performance in particular articulated a historical narrative that celebrated not only reified forms of heroism but also common citizens' capacity to collectively improvise and re-create, defeat after defeat, a resilient body politic.

Fito Páez's Performance and the Emergence of a Co-memorative Public Sphere

The audience's embodied involvement in Fuerzabruta's performance—sometimes respectfully silent, sometimes exuberantly noisy—transformed what could have been a univocal, essentialist mise-en-scène of patriotic pride into a surprisingly introspective political moment, in which at least two mnemonic and emotive displacements were rehearsed: on one hand, the positive resignification of survivors' rememorating guilt and, on the other, the transformation of a memorializing process into a joyful experience. These displacements were also made audible through a succession of silences, applauses, and enthusiastic interjections during rock musician Fito Páez's set. Páez closed the official festivities before a large crowd that filled Avenida 9 de Julio and the surrounding area. Toward the end of his set, he invited Cuban artist Pablo Milanés to join him on stage for the performance of "Yo vengo a ofrecer mi corazón" (I Come to Offer My Heart).[14] Páez's older fans associate this song with the years of the country's return to democratic rule. In 1985, when Páez first recorded this song, many Argentines hoped that the perpetrators of state terrorism would be brought to justice. However, these expectations dissipated in 1986, when legislation that guaranteed impunity for human rights violators was passed. The song's first lines synthesize the ambivalence—the hope and disillusionment—that characterized this period:

> Who said everything is lost?
> I come to offer my heart.
> The river took away so much blood.
> I come to offer my heart. (Páez, "Yo vengo a ofrecer mi corazón," lines 1–4)

The song's version performed by Páez during the Bicentennial included an introductory solo on piano, which was received by a focused silence, as were the song's first two lines ("Especial Festejo del Bicentenario—parte 19"). When Páez sang the third line, a roar of applause broke that silence. This reaction was disconcerting at first, since the third line evokes one of the nation's most painful aporias for many Argentines: the haunting presence of the disappeared. However, as the performance of the song unfolded and the audience intercalated expectant silences with collective singing, the applause on the third line seemed to reiterate the practice of memorialization that had also crystallized during Fuerzabruta's performance: a practice that activated a desire to recollect in the double sense of remembering and coming together (to reconstitute fractured social relations).

Visibly moved by the crowd's reactions and by their decision to take to the streets, in spite of the corporate media's rhetoric of urban insecurity and chaos, Páez turned to the audience and exclaimed: "People on the streets! Beautiful!" Different journalists asked Páez to make sense of those interjections, through which the performer being looked at by millions of people inverted the function assigned to spectators by situating the locus of poiesis in the "passive" crowds. Páez chose to represent this moment as an "emergent" moment—"unpredictable, contingent" (Sawyer 2006, 148)—in which two mnemonic registers converged: the private and the public. Upon seeing so many people, of different generations, joyfully re-collecting and listening attentively, not only to what was being sung and said onstage, but also to each other, it dawned on him that such a gathering could not have been possible when he was their age. In 1976, he remembered, he was a teenager in a militarized society that construed "youth" as a group of public enemies who had to be "disappeared."

> When I saw it [the performance] afterwards, I was also surprised. I thought: why that phrase, in that moment? And I realized it had to do with memories . . . of not being able to go out on the street until 1983. Details of that history, our history, came back to me. One doesn't know why one behaves in a certain way in a situation like that; it is so extreme that one doesn't have much control over what happens. But things like that [moment], which are profound, emerge. It was very powerful and moving to see that many people having fun. . . . [B]eing on the streets, taking over public space. That was what moved me the most: the freedom. It's a big word, but it's inevitable to look for it when one has been through so many social and political circumstances. . . . For me, it was a lesson in civility. (Páez 2010)

Through this affective historicization of the unscripted interjections that received so much media scrutiny, Paéz accounts, better than most commentators did, for the mnemonic and political density of the ethos of solidarity that emerged during the Bicentennial. Indeed, in revealing the layers of memory at work in that improvisational, emotive moment, he unearthed the politically and historically mediated affects that underwrote the audience's and the performer's subjective feelings and identified those feelings as the organizing forces that made possible the enactment of a co-memorative, celebratory countertheater of the public.

Notes

1. Here and elsewhere, original text in French and Spanish is not quoted; all translations are ours unless otherwise noted.

2. *Auscultation* refers to listening to the interior of the body, such as that heard through a stethoscope.

3. The ideological and socioeconomic underpinnings of this transformation have been analyzed by Scobie (1974), Gutman and Hardoy (1992, 113–62), Romero (1976, ch. 6), and Needell (1995). For a history of the Colón, see Caamaño (1969).

4. For examples of media discourses articulated around the Centennial-Bicentennial opposition, see Cachanosky (2010), De Arteaga (2010), and D. Katz (2010).

5. The history of some of these groups, which are still active, may be found in the online archive of Memoria Abierta (see "Who We are," Memoria Abierta, Acción Coordinada de Organizaciones argentinas de Derechos Humanos, http://www.memoriaabierta .org.ar/ [accessed May 10, 2012]), an umbrella association that coordinates the research and documentation efforts of five of Argentina's most prominent human rights organizations. Today, the Madres carry on their struggle primarily through three associations: Madres de Plaza de Mayo, Madres—Línea Fundadora, and Abuelas de Plaza de Mayo.

6. This was done in collaboration with other relatives of the disappeared, human rights activists, and artists.

7. Actors use formulaic speech, or stock phrases, to quickly communicate character traits and situations to the audience and their fellow actors. These conventional phrases "have unavoidable connotations associated with past situations of use. . . . When we use a catchphrase, or say something with a stereotypical inflection or accent, everyone can't help but think of all of the other occasions on which they've heard the same thing. . . . For example, if an actor starts talking in a southern US accent, he or she implicitly communicates to the audience that the setting for the scene is somewhere in southern USA" (Sawyer 2006, 155–56).

8. Fuerzabruta's core creative team is composed of an artistic director (Diqui James), a music director (Gaby Kerpel), a general coordinator (Fabio D'Aquila), a technical director (Alejandro García), a general producer (Agustina James), and a general manager (Fernando Moya). The troupe's practice of creating a shared public space with spectators can be traced back to the interventions staged in Buenos Aires's streets by La Organización Negra (LON), a performance collective in which Kerpel and James took part in the years after the end of military rule. LON's interventions in public space, which included the sim-

ulacrum of an execution, "recreated an atmosphere fraught with the traces of the violence experienced [in the past].... [Since the return to democratic rule] the street could be the space ... of speaking subjects.... However, ... the performers did not speak.... [T]hey developed a bond/relationship of friction with the spectator, and—rejecting the curtain, seating arrangements, and stage of theatrical convention—they explored new ways of making spectators participate. This situation showed that ... the *proxemic interaction* between bodies was a fundamental dimension of new ways of being together" (M. González 2001, 6–7). Like LON's "speechless" performances in postdictatorship Buenos Aires, Fuerzabruta's representation of the Madres in 2010 operated as a space of "co-memoration"— that is, of shared recollection (Zerubavel 1996, 294)—in which spectators were compelled to listen to how bodies sounded and communicated with each other, in the absence of verbal language, during the dictatorship.

9. We are using the term *emerge* in the sense elaborated by Sawyer in his studies on group creativity: "emergence refers to collective phenomena in which ... 'the whole is greater than the parts.' ... Emergent phenomena are unpredictable, contingent and hard to explain in terms of the group's components" (2006, 148).

10. "Especial Festejo del Bicentenario—parte 16 de 20," narr. Felipe Pigha and Gabriela Radice, TV Publica—Argentina YouTube channel, YouTube.com, http://www.youtube.com/watch?v=meoIfe71P5A (accessed May 20, 2013). The water was stored in a tank and pumped through a network of hoses and pipes in such a way that it cascaded on two opposing sides of the float. The perforated platform floor functioned as a drainage system that allowed the water to flow back into the tank for reuse. The description of the technical aspects of this performance is based on Fabio D'Aquila, Skype interview by Illa Carrillo Rodríguez, August 24, 2012.

11. The scene's natural lighting varied as the float moved from dimly lit to brightly illuminated streets.

12. The sound of water and the score, composed and prerecorded by Gaby Kerpel, were broadcast by means of a power amplification system and a set of loudspeakers, which were mounted on the truck that towed the float (figure 17.2). The power amplifier was set to a loud volume, which enabled people situated at a distance of several meters from the float to hear the water and the score. Keeping a loud volume level was also important in ensuring that the other floats' sound systems did not interfere with this scene's soundtrack.

13. These manifestations of silence were sporadically interspersed with expressions of tribute to the Madres and the disappeared in the form of solemn applause and well-known chants, such as "Mothers of the Plaza, the pueblo embraces you" and "The thirty thousand disappeared are present." For examples of this, see "Escena las Madres," recorded in Buenos Aires, May 25, 2010, 751altuna YouTube Channel, YouTube.com, http://www.youtube.com/watch?v=dPrhtZfmeV4 (accessed May 20, 2013) and "Bicentenario Fuerza Bruta—Madres," recorded in Buenos Aires, May 25, 2010, Joakkk YouTube Channel, YouTube.com, http://www.youtube.com/watch?v=AQAAGr2KQzo (accessed May 20, 2013).

14. Milanés's participation in the performance was particularly meaningful for audience members who identify his voice with the musical counterculture that, though officially banned from the military regime's public sphere, circulated among friends through cassettes and was broadcast on late-night radio shows in the last years of the dictatorship.

Deep Listening Band. "Lear." On *Deep Listening*, New Albion Records, NA022, 1989, CD.

Gieco, León, and Luis Gurevich. "Las Madres del Amor." On *Bandidos rurales*, EMI Odeón S.A.I.C., 2001, CD.

Mitchell, Nicole, and the Black Earth Ensemble. *Xenogenesis Suite: A Tribute to Octavia Butler*, Firehouse 12, FH12-04-01-006, 2009.

Oliveros, Pauline. *Crone Music*. Lovely Music Ltd., LCD 1903, 1989, CD. Commissioned by Mabou Mines and recorded 1989–90.

———. "I of IV." On *New Sounds in Electronic Music*. Odyssey Records, 32 16 0160, 1967, compact disc. Composed 1966. Out of print.

———. *Mnemonics*. Mills College Centre for Contemporary Music Archive. Recorded 1965.

———. *Reverberations: Tape and Electronic Music 1961–1970*, Important Records, IMPREC352, 2012, 12-disc box set. Recorded 1961–70.

———. *Variations for Sextet*. New York, independently produced. 1960.

Oliveros, Pauline, and American Voices. "St. George and the Dragon." On *Pauline Oliveros and American Voices*. Mode Records, Mode 401994, 1992, CD. Recorded in Pomfret, CT, 1992.

Oliveros, Pauline, with Terry Riley and Loren Rush. *Improvisations 1, 2, 3*. Mills College Centre for Contemporary Music Archive, 1957.

Páez, Fito. "Yo vengo a ofrecer mi corazón." On *Giros*, *Página/*12 and EMI Odeón, 2005, CD. Recorded 1985.

REFERENCES

Adams, Fred. 2010. "Embodied Cognition." *Phenomenology and the Cognitive Sciences* 9 (4): 619–28.

Ahmed, Sara. 2004. "In the Name of Love." In *The Cultural Politics of Emotion*, 122–43. New York: Routledge.

Ajana, Btihaj. 2005. "Disembodiment and Cyberspace: A Phenomenological Approach." *Electronic Journal of Sociology*. http://www.sociology.org/content/2004/test/ajana .html.

Aliverti, Eduardo. 2010. "El día de la escarapela." Pagina12.com.ar, *Página/12* (Buenos Aires), May 31. http://www.pagina12.com.ar/diario/elpais/1-146694-2010-05-31 .html.

Altman, Rick. 2004. *Silent Film Sound*. New York: Columbia University Press.

Anderson, Iain. 2007. *This Is Our Music: Free Jazz, the Sixties, and American Culture*. Philadelphia: University of Pennsylvania Press.

Anderson, Tim. 1997. "Reforming 'Jackass Music': The Problematic Aesthetics of Early American Film Music Accompaniment." *Cinema Journal* 37 (1): 3–22.

Anzaldúa, Gloria. 1987. *Borderlands/La Frontera: The New Mestiza*. San Francisco: Aunt Lute Press.

Arendt, Hannah. 1958. *The Human Condition*. Chicago: University of Chicago Press.

Asai, Susan M. 1995. "Transformations of Tradition: Three Generations of Japanese American Music Making." *Musical Quarterly* 79 (3): 429–53.

———. 1997. "Sansei Voices in the Community: Japanese American Musicians in California." In *Musics of Multicultural America,* edited by Kip Lornell and Anne Rasmussen, 257–85. New York: Schirmer.

———. 2005. "Cultural Politics: The African American Connection in Asian American Jazz-Based Music." *Asian Music* 36 (1): 87–108.

Ashby, William Ross. 1956. *An Introduction to Cybernetics.* London: Chapman and Hall.

Atkins, E. Taylor. 2001. *Blue Nippon: Authenticating Jazz in Japan*. Durham: Duke University Press.

Attali, Jacques. 1985. *Noise: The Political Economy of Music*. Translated by Brian Massumi. Minneapolis: University of Minnesota Press.

Attariwala, Parmela Singh. 2013. "Eh 440: Tuning into the Effects of Multiculturalism on Publicly Funded Canadian Music." PhD diss., University of Toronto.

Augoyard, Jean-François, and Henri Torgue. 2006. *Sonic Experience: A Guide to Everyday Sounds*. Translated by Andra McCartney and David Paquette. Montreal: McGill-Queen's Press.

Auslander, Philip. 2008. *Liveness: Performance in a Mediatized Culture*. New York: Routledge.

Bachir-Loopuyt, Talia, Clément Canonne, Pierre Saint-Germier, and Barbara Turquier. 2010. "Improvisation: usage et transferts d'une catégorie." Editorial. *Tracés: Revue de Sciences Humaines* 18 (2010): 5–20.

Badani, Pat, and Rebecca Caines. 2009, December 16. "Pat Badani Interviewed by Rebecca Caines." *Improvisation, Community, and Social Practice Research Collection.* http://www.improvcommunity.ca/research/pat-badani-interviewed-rebecca-caines.

Bailey, Derek. 1993. *Improvisation: Its Nature and Practice in Music.* New York: Da Capo Press.

"Ballybeen (Northern Ireland)." 2010. Caines, Rebecca, and John Campbell, eds. *Community Sound [E]Scapes, Improvisation, Community, and Social Practice.* http://soundescapes.improvcommunity.ca/index.php/ballybeen (accessed December 22, 2010).

Bap on Ballybean. 2009, September 4. Best Cellars Studio. European Union Peace II Fund. https://www.makewav.es/story/80487/title/BaponBallybean.

Barad, Karen. 2006. "Posthumanist Performativity: Toward an Understanding of How Matter Comes to Matter." In *Belief, Bodies and Being: Feminist Reflections on Embodiment,* edited by Deborah Orr, Linda López McAllister, Eileen Kahl, and Kathleen Earle, 11–36. Lanham, MD: Rowan and Littlefield.

Baraka, Amiri [LeRoi Jones]. 1967. "The Screamers." In *Tales.* New York: Grove.

Barg, Lisa, Linnett Fawcett, Ric Knowles, Andra McCartney, Tracy McMullen, Kevin McNeilly, Pauline Oliveros, Julie Smith, Gillian Siddall, Sherrie Tucker, Ellen Waterman, and Deborah Wong. 2009. "Sounding the Body: Improvisation, Representation, and Subjectivity." In *Improvisation, Community and Social Practice: Gender Body Research Group.* Unpublished.

Bartlette, Christopher, Dave Headlam, Mark Bocko, and Gordana Velikic. 2006. "Effect of Network Latency on Interactive Musical Performance." *Music Perception* 24 (1): 49–62.

Baudrillard, Jean. 1988. "The Hyper-Realism of Simulation." In *Jean Baudrillard: Selected Writings,* edited by Mark Poster, 143–47. Stanford, CA: Stanford University Press.

Bell, Vikki, and Judith Butler. 1999. "On Speech, Race and Melancholia." *Theory, Culture and Society* 16 (2): 163–74.

Bellman, Jonathan, ed. 1997. *The Exotic in Western Music.* Lebanon, NH: Northeastern University Press.

Bender, Shawn. 2012. *Taiko Boom: Japanese Drumming in Place and Motion.* Berkeley: University of California Press.

Benhabib, Seyla. 1996. "Towards a Deliberative Model of Democratic Legitimacy." In *Democracy and Difference: Contesting the Boundaries of the Political,* edited by Seyla Benhabib, 67–94. Princeton, NJ: Princeton University Press.

Benjamin, Walter. 1969. *Illuminations: Essays and Reflections.* Translated by Harry Zohn. Edited by Hannah Arendt. New York: Schocken Books.

Berger, Harris M. 2009. *Stance: Ideas about Emotion, Style, and Meaning for the Study of Expressive Culture.* Middletown, CT: Wesleyan University Press.

Berkman, Franya. 2007. "Appropriating Universality: The Coltranes and 1960s Spirituality." *American Studies* 48 (1): 41–62.

Berliner, Paul. 1994. *Thinking in Jazz: The Infinite Art of Improvisation.* Chicago: University of Chicago Press.

Bimstein, Phillip. 2010. "Composing a Community: Collaborative Performance of a New Democracy." *New Political Science* 32 (4): 593–608.

Blau, Herbert. 2011. *Reality Principles: From the Absurd to the Virtual*. Ann Arbor: University of Michigan Press.

Borgo, David. 2003. "Between Worlds: The Embodied and Ecstatic Sounds of Jazz." *Open Space* 5: 152–58.

———. 2005. *Sync or Swarm: Improvising Music in a Complex Age*. New York: Continuum Books.

———. 2010. "Semi-Permeable Musicking Membranes." *Journal of Popular Music Studies* 22 (2): 131–38.

Borgo, David, and Jeff Kaiser. 2010. "Configurin(g) KaiBorg: Ideology, Identity and Agency in Electro-Acoustic Improvised Music." Conference proceedings from "Beyond the Centres: Musical Avant-Gardes since 1950," Thessaloniki, Greece, July 1–5.

Bothwell, Robert. 1998. *Canada and Quebec: One Country, Two Histories*. Rev. ed. Vancouver: University of British Columbia Press.

Bourdieu, Pierre. 1993. *The Field of Cultural Production*. New York: Columbia University Press.

———. 1995. *Outline of a Theory of Practice*. Trans. Richard Nice. Cambridge: Cambridge University Press.

Braasch, Jonas. 2009. "The Telematic Music System: Affordances for a New Instrument to Shape the Music of Tomorrow." *Contemporary Music Review* 28 (4): 421–32.

Braidotti, Rosi. 1994. *Nomadic Subjects: Embodiment and Sexual Difference in Contemporary Feminist Theory*. New York: Columbia University Press.

Breitsameter, Sabine, and Claudia Söller-Eckert, eds. 2012. *The Global Composition: Conference on Sound Media and the Environment, July 25–28 2012*. Dieburg, Germany: Hochschule Darmstadt and World Forum for Acoustic Ecology.

Briñol, Pablo, and Kenneth DeMarree, eds. 2012. *Social Metacognition*. New York: Psychology Press.

Brooks, Daphne. 2012. "'One of These Mornings You're Gonna Rise Up Singing': The Secret Black Feminist History of *Porgy and Bess*." Paper presented at the Institute for Comparative Modernities Lecture Series, Cornell University, Ithaca, NY, April 11–12.

Brothers, Thomas. 1994. "Solo and Cycle in African-American Jazz." *Musical Quarterly* 78 (3): 479–509.

Bruner, Jerome S. 1996. *The Culture of Education*. Cambridge, MA: Harvard University Press.

Burdick, John. 2009. "The Singing Voice and Racial Politics on the Brazilian Evangelical Music Scene." *Latin American Music Review / Revista de Música Latinoamericana* 30 (1): 25–55.

Burke, Patrick. 2006. "Oasis of Swing: The Onyx Club, Jazz, and White Masculinity in the Early 1930s." *American Music* 24 (3): 320–46.

Burkholder, J. Peter. 1996. *Charles Ives and His World*. Princeton, NJ: Princeton University Press.

Butler, Judith. 1993. *Bodies That Matter: On the Discursive Limits of "Sex."* New York: Routledge.

———. 2004. *Undoing Gender*. New York and London: Routledge.

———. 2008. *Gender Trouble: Feminism and the Subversion of Identity*. New York: Routledge.

Butler, Octavia E. 2000. *Lilith's Brood: Dawn, Imago, Motherhood Rites*. 1989. New York: Grand Central Publishing.

———. 2005. *Bloodchild and Other Stories*. 2nd ed. New York: Seven Stories Press.

Caamaño, Roberto. 1969. *La historia del Teatro Colón, 1908–1968*. Buenos Aires: Editorial Cinetea.

Cachanosky, Roberto. 2010. "¿El mejor gobierno de la historia argentina?" Lanacion .com, *La Nación* (Buenos Aires), May 14 (accessed May 5, 2011).

Caines, Rebecca. 2003. "Guerillas in Our Midst, May 14: Contemporary Australian Guerilla Performance and the Poststructural Community." *Australasian Drama Studies*, no. 42: 75–90.

———. 2007. "Haunted Voices in Everyday Spaces: The Community Based Hip-Hop of Australian 'Guerrilla' Artist Morganics." In *The Community Performance Reader*, edited by Petra Kuppers and Gwen Robertson, 252–62. London: Routledge.

Caines, Rebecca, and John Campbell, eds. 2010. "Woolgoolga." *Community Sound [E]Scapes, Improvisation, Community, and Social Practice*. http://soundescapes .improvcommunity.ca/index.php/woolgoolga (accessed December 22, 2010).

Carson, Anne. 1995. "The Gender of Sound." In *Glass, Irony and God*, 119–42. New York: New Directions.

Caruth, Cathy. 2007. "Trauma and Experience." In *Theories of Memory: A Reader*, edited by Michael Rossington and Anne Whitehead, 199–205. Baltimore, MD: Johns Hopkins University Press.

Casey, Edward S. 1997. *The Fate of Place: A Philosophical History*. Berkeley: University of California Press.

Chadabe, Joel. 1996. *Electric Sound: The Past and Promise of Electronic Music*. Upper Saddle River, NJ: Prentice Hall.

Chafe, Chris, Juan-Pablo Cáceres, and Michael Gurevich. 2010. "Effect of Temporal Separation on Synchronization in Rhythmic Performance." *Perception* 39 (7): 982–92.

Chafe, Chris, and Michael Gurevich. 2004. "Network Time Delay and Ensemble Accuracy: Effects of Latency, Assymetry." Paper presented at the Audio Engineering Society Convention, San Francisco, CA, October 28–31.

Chen, Jer Ming, John Smith, and Joe Wolfe. 2008, February 8. "Experienced Saxophonists Learn to Tune Their Vocal Tracts." *Science* 319: 776.

Cheung, King-Kok. 2004. "The Woman Warrior versus the Chinaman Pacific: Must a Chinese American Critic Choose between Feminism and Heroism?" In *A Companion to Asian American Studies,* edited by Kent A. Ono, 157–74. New York: Wiley-Blackwell.

Cixous, Hélène. 2000. "The Laugh of the Medusa." In *Reading Rhetorical Theory*, edited by Barry Brummett, 879–93. New York: Harcourt.

Clabough, Casey Howard. 2006. "Toward an All-Inclusive Structure: The Early Fiction of Gayl Jones." *Callaloo* 29 (2): 634–57.

Clark, Andy. 1997. *Being There: Putting Brain, Body, and World Together Again*. Cambridge, MA: MIT Press.

———. 2003. *Natural-Born Cyborgs: Minds, Technologies, and the Future of Human Intelligence*. New York: Oxford University Press.

Clarke, Bruce, and Mark B. N. Hansen. 2009. "Introduction: Neocybernetic Emergence." In *Emergence and Embodiment: New Essays on Second-Order Systems Theory*, edited by Bruce Clarke and Mark B. N. Hansen, 1–25. Durham: Duke University Press.

Clarke, Eric. 2005. *Ways of Listening. An Ecological Approach to the Perception of Musical Meaning*. Oxford: Oxford University Press.

Clifton, Thomas. 1983. *Music as Heard: A Study in Applied Phenomenology*. New Haven, CT: Yale University Press.

Clough, Patricia T. 2008. "The Affective Turn: Political Economy, Biomedia and Bodies." *Theory Culture Society* 25 (1): 1–22.

Code, Lorraine. 1991. *What Can She Know? Feminist Theory and the Construction of Knowledge*. Ithaca, NY: Cornell University Press.

Collins, Patricia Hill. 2009. *Black Feminist Thought: Knowledge, Consciousness, and the Politics of Empowerment*. New York: Routledge.

Connor, Stephen. 2005. "Edison's Teeth: Touching Hearing." In *Hearing Cultures: Essays on Sounds, Listening and Modernity*, edited by Veit Erlmann, 153–72. Oxford: Berg.

Conquergood, Dwight. 1985. "Performing a Moral Act: Ethical Dimensions of the Ethnography of Performance." *Literature in Performance* 5 (2): 1–13.

Cope, David. 2005. *Computer Models of Musical Creativity*. Cambridge, MA: MIT Press.

Costa Vargas, João H. 2008a. "Exclusion, Openness, and Utopia in Black Male Performance at the World Stage Jazz Jam Sessions." In *Big Ears: Listening for Gender in Jazz Studies*, edited by Nichole T. Rustin and Sherrie Tucker, 320–47. Durham: Duke University Press.

———. 2008b. "Jazz and Male Blackness: The Politics of Sociability in South Central Los Angeles." *Popular Music and Society* 31 (1): 37–56.

Coulthard, Glen S. 2007. "Subjects of Empire: Indigenous Peoples and the 'Politics of Recognition' in Canada." *Contemporary Political Theory* 6: 437–60.

Cox, Arnie. 2001. "The Mimetic Hypothesis and Embodied Musical Meaning." *Musicae Scientiae* 5 (2): 195–212.

Crisell, Andrew. 2012. *Liveness & Recording in the Media*. New York: Palgrave Macmillan.

Cruz, Jon. 1999. *Culture on the Margins: The Black Spiritual and the Rise of American Cultural Interpretation*. Princeton, NJ: Princeton University Press.

Csikszentmihalyi, Mihaly. 1990. *Flow: The Psychology of Optimal Experience*. New York: Harper & Row.

Csikszentmihalyi, Mihaly, and Isabella Selega Csikszentmihalyi, eds. 1988. *Optimal Experience: Psychological Studies of Flow in Consciousness*. Cambridge: Cambridge University Press.

Cusack, Peter. 2000. "Dialogue." *Soundscape: The Journal of Acoustic Ecology* 1 (2): 8.

Cusack, Peter, interviewed by Jens Heitjohann. 2012. "Enter the Void—Peter Cusack and His Field Recording Projects." *MAP: Media Archive Performance*, no. 3. http://www.perfomap.de/map3/kapite13/cusack.

Dalton, Joseph. 2007, June 8. "Deep Listening Convergence." School of Humanities, Arts, and Social Sciences, Rensselaer Polytechnic Institute. http://www.hass.rpi.edu/pl/news-s17/deep-listening-convergence.

Damasio, Antonio. 1999. *The Feeling of What Happens: Body and Emotion in the Making of Consciousness*. New York: Houghton Mifflin Harcourt.

Davidson, Michael. 2008. *Concerto for the Left Hand: Disability and the Defamiliar Body*. Ann Arbor: University of Michigan Press.

Davis, Heather, and Paige Sarlin. 2011. "On the Risk of a New Relationality: An Interview with Lauren Berlant and Michael Hardt." *Reviews in Cultural Theory* special issue On the Commons 2 (3): 6–27.

De Arteaga, Alicia. 2010. "Del Centenario al Bicentenario." Lanacion.com, *La Nación* (Buenos Aires), January 12. http://www.lanacion.com.ar/1220876-del-centenario-al -bicentenario.

de Ferranti, Hugh. 2000. *Japanese Musical Instruments*. New York: Oxford University Press.

Deleuze, Gilles, and Félix Guattari. 1987. *A Thousand Plateaus: Capitalism and Schizophrenia*. Translated by Brian Massumi. Minneapolis: University of Minnesota Press.

D'Entreves, Maurizio Passerin. 2014. "Hannah Arendt." In *The Stanford Encyclopedia of Philosophy*, edited by Edward N. Zalta. Stanford, CA: Metaphysics Research Lab (accessed September 30, 2014).

Dery, Mark. 1993. "Black to the Future: Interviews with Samuel R. Delany, Greg Tate and Tricia Rose." *South Atlantic Quarterly* 92 (4): 735–78.

De Spain, Kent. 2012. "Improvisation and Intimate Technologies." *Choreographic Practices* 2 (1): 25–42.

Dessen, Michael. 2003. "Decolonizing Art Music: Scenes from the Late Twentieth-Century United States." PhD diss., University of California, San Diego.

———. 2006. "Asian Americans and Creative Music Legacies." *Critical Studies in Improvisation / Etudes critiques en improvisation* 1 (3). http://www.criticalimprov .com/article/view/56.

Diamond, Beverley. 2000. "The Interpretation of Gender Issues in Musical Life Stories of Prince Edward Islanders." In *Music and Gender*, edited by Beverley Diamond and Pirkko Moisala, 99–119. Champaign: University of Illinois Press.

Díaz, Claudio F. 2009. *Variaciones sobre el "ser nacional." Una aproximación sociodiscursiva al "folklore" argentino*. Córdoba: Recovecos.

Dumas, Henry. 2004. "Will the Circle Be Unbroken?" In *Dark Matter: Reading the Bones*, edited by Sheree R. Thomas, 105–10. New York: Warner Aspect.

Dyson, Frances. 2009. *Sounding New Media: Immersion and Embodiment in the Arts and Culture*. Berkeley: University of California Press.

Eidsheim, Nina Sun. 2008. "Voice as a Technology of Selfhood: Towards an Analysis of Racialized Timbre and Vocal Performance." PhD diss., University of California, San Diego.

Eng, David L. 2001. *Racial Castration: Managing Masculinity in Asian America*. Durham: Duke University Press.

Etchells, Tim. 1999. *Certain Fragments: Contemporary Performance and Forced Entertainment*. London: Routledge.

Fales, Cornelia. 2002. "The Paradox of Timbre." *Ethnomusicology* 46 (1): 56–95.

Farhat, Hormoz. 2004. *The Dastgah Concept in Persian Music*. Cambridge: Cambridge University Press.

Faulkner, Robert R., and Howard S. Becker. 2009. *"Do You Know . . . ?": The Jazz Repertoire in Action*. Chicago: Chicago University Press.

Featherstone, Mike. 2003. "Technologies of Post-Human Development and the Potential for Global Citizenship." In *Globalization: Critical Concepts in Sociology, Volume III*, edited by Roland Robertson and Kathleen White, 226–46. London: Routledge.

Feisst, Sabine M. 2009. "John Cage and Improvisation: An Unresolved Relationship." In *Musical Improvisation: Art, Education and Society*, edited by Gabriel Solis and Bruno Nettl, 38–51. Chicago: University of Illinois Press.

Fellezs, Kevin. 2007. "Silenced but Not Silent: Asian Americans and Jazz." In *Alien Encounters: Popular Culture in Asian America*, edited by Mimi Thi Nguyen and Thuy Linh Nguyen Tu, 69–108. Durham: Duke University Press.

Ferreras, Salvador. 2007. "Who Are the People in Your Neighbourhood?" Keynote address to the Northwest Chapter of the College Music Society at Boise State University, February 17. http://www.salferreras.com/writings/who-are-the -people.pdf.

Finn, Geraldine. 1995. "The Power of (De)Composition: The (De)Composition of Power." In *With a Song in Her Heart: A Celebration of Canadian Women Composers: Proceedings of the Conference at the University of Windsor, March 11–12, 1994*, edited by Janice Drakich, Edward George Kovarik, and Ramona Lumpkin, 41–60. Windsor: University of Windsor.

Fischlin, Daniel, and Ajay Heble, eds. 2004. *The Other Side of Nowhere: Jazz, Improvisation, and Communities in Dialogue*. Middletown, CT: Wesleyan University Press.

Fischlin, Daniel, Ajay Heble, and George Lipsitz. 2013. *The Fierce Urgency of Now: Improvisation, Rights, and the Ethics of Cocreation*. Durham: Duke University Press.

Fish, Stanley. 1980. *Is There a Text in This Class?: The Authority of Interpretive Communities*. Cambridge, MA: Harvard University Press.

Forster, Ricardo. 2010a. "El pueblo del Bicentenario." Pagina12.com.ar, *Página/12* (Buenos Aires), May 30. http://www.pagina12.com.ar/diario/elpais/1-146644-2010 -05-30.html.

———. 2010b. "Hubo un derrame de pueblo." Interview by Sebastián Premici, *Debate* (Buenos Aires), May 29.

Foucault, Michel. 1977. *Language, Counter-Memory, Practice: Selected Essays and Interviews*. Edited by Donald Bouchard. Ithaca, NY: Cornell University Press.

———. 1984. "The Ethics of the Concern for Self as a Practice of Freedom." In *The Foucault Reader*, edited by Paul Rabinow, 281–301. New York: Pantheon Books.

———. 1990. *The History of Sexuality, Vol. 1: An Introduction*. Translated by Robert Hurley. New York: Vintage.

———. 1995. *Discipline and Punish: The Birth of the Prison*. Translated by Alan Sheridan. New York: Vintage.

Francis, Consuela, ed. 2010. *Conversations with Octavia Butler*. Jackson: University Press of Mississippi.

Freire, Paulo. 1994. *Pedagogy of Hope: Reliving Pedagogy of the Oppressed*. Notes by Ana Maria Araújo Freire. Translated by Robert R. Barr. London: Continuum.

Freud, Sigmund. 1925. *The Collected Papers of Sigmund Freud*. Edited by Ernest Jones. New York: Hogarth Press.

———. 1989. "Beyond the Pleasure Principle." In *The Freud Reader*, edited by Peter Gay. New York: W. W. Norton.

Fung, Richard. 1998. "Looking for My Penis: The Eroticized Asian in Gay Video Porn." In *Q & A: Queer in Asian America*, edited by David L. Eng and Alice Y. Hom, 115–34. Philadelphia: Temple University Press.

Gallagher, Shaun. 2005. *How the Body Shapes the Mind*. Oxford: Oxford University Press.

Gallese, Vittorio. 2007. "Before and Below 'Theory of Mind': Embodied Simulation and the Neural Correlates of Social Cognition." *Philosophical Transactions of the Royal Society: Biological Sciences* 362 (1480): 659–69.

García, Facundo. 2010. "En zona de riesgo." Pagina12.com.ar, *Página/12* (Buenos Aires), May 27.

Giddins, Gary. 1998. *Visions of Jazz: The First Century*. New York: Oxford University Press.

Gilman, Sander. 2010. "The Hottentot and the Prostitute: Toward an Iconography of Female Sexuality." In *Black Venus 2010: They Called Her "Hottentot,"* edited by Deborah Willis, 15–31. Philadelphia: Temple University Press.

Glennie, Evelyn. 1993. "The Hearing Essay." http://www.evelyn.co.uk/Resources/Essays /Hearing%20Essay.pdf.

Goldman, Danielle. 2010. *I Want to Be Ready: Improvised Dance as a Practice of Freedom*. Ann Arbor: University of Michigan Press.

Goldstein, Malcolm. 1988. *Sounding the Full Circle: Concerning Musical Improvisation and Other Related Matters*. Sheffield, VT: printed by author.

Göle, Nilüfer. 2009. "*Turkish Delight* in Vienna: Art, Islam, and European Public Culture." *Cultural Politics* 5 (3): 277–98.

González, Horacio. 2011. *Kirchnerismo: una controversia cultural*. Buenos Aires: Colihue.

González, María Laura. 2011. "Buscando formas estéticas en pleno advenimiento democrático: Teatro en espacios públicos." *IV Seminario Internacional Políticas de la Memoria, "Ampliación del campo de los derechos humanos. Memoria y perspectivas."* Centro Cultural de la Memoria Haroldo Conti, Buenos Aires, September 29–October 1, paper, Derhuman.jus.gov.ar. Secretaría de Derechos Humanos, Ministerio de Justicia y Derechos Humanos de la Presidencia de la Nación (accessed June 15, 2012).

Gosz, James R. 1993. "Ecotone Hierarchies." *Ecological Applications* 3 (3): 369–76.

Grey, De Sayles. 1986. "John Coltrane and the 'Avant-Garde' Movement in Jazz History." PhD diss., University of Pittsburgh.

Gridley, Mark. 2007. "Misconceptions in Linking Free Jazz with the Civil Rights Movement." *College Music Symposium* 47: 139–55.

Gridley, Mark, and Robert Hoff. 2006. "Do Mirror Neurons Explain Misattribution of Emotions in Music?" *Perceptual & Motor Skills* 102 (2): 600–602.

Griffiths, Jennifer. 2009. *Traumatic Possessions: The Body and Memory in African American Women's Writing and Performance*. Charlottesville: University of Virginia Press.

Grosz, Elizabeth. 1995. *Space, Time and Perversion: Essays on the Politics of Bodies*. New York and London: Routledge.

Gutman, Margarita, and Jorge E. Hardoy. 1992. *Buenos Aires. Historia urbana del área metropolitana*. Madrid: Editorial Mapfre.

Hahn, Tomie. 2006. "'It's the RUSH'—Sites of the Sensually Extreme." *TDR: The Drama Review* 50, no. 2 (2006): 87–96.

———. 2007. *Sensational Knowledge: Embodying Culture through Japanese Dance*. Middletown, CT: Wesleyan University Press.

————. 2011. "Dancing with Sensible Objects." Paper presented at the Joint Annual Meeting of the Society for Ethnomusicology and Congress on Research in Dance: Moving Music/Sounding Dance, Philadelphia, PA, November 17–20.

Hahn, Tomie, and Curtis Bahn. 2002. "Pikapika—The Collaborative Composition of an Interactive Sonic Character." *Organised Sound: An International Journal of Music Technology* 7 (3): 229–38.

Hajda, John, Roger A. Kendall, Edward C. Carterette, and Michael L. Harshberger. 1997. "Methodological Issues in Timbre Research." In *Perception and Cognition of Music*, edited by John Sloboda and Iréne Deliége, 253–306. East Sussex: Psychology Press.

Handel, Stephen. 2006. *Perceptual Coherence: Hearing and Seeing*. Oxford: Oxford University Press.

Hankins, Peter. 2005. "Libet's Short Delay." *Conscious Entities*, June 2. http://www.consciousentities.com/libet.htm.

Hansen, Mark B. N. 2009. "System-Environment Hybrids." In *Emergence and Embodiment: New Essays on Second-Order Systems Theory*, edited by Bruce Clarke and Mark B. N. Hansen, 113–42. Durham: Duke University Press.

Haraway, Donna. 1988. "Situated Knowledges: The Science Question in Feminism and the Privilege of Partial Perspective." *Feminist Studies* 14 (3): 575–99.

————. 1991. *Simians, Cyborgs and Women: The Reinvention of Nature*. New York: Routledge.

————. 1994. "A Manifesto for Cyborgs: Science, Technology, and Socialist Feminism in the 1980s." In *The Postmodern Turn: New Perspectives on Social Theory*, edited by Steven Seidman, 82–115. Cambridge: Cambridge University Press.

Harter, Lynn M., Jennifer A. Scott, David R. Novak, Mark Leeman, and Jerimiah F. Morris. 2006. "Freedom through Flight: Performing a Counter-Narrative of Disability." *Journal of Applied Communication Research* 34 (1): 3–29.

Hatch, Peter. 2013. "Putting Concert Music Performance in Its Place: The Open Ears Festival of Music and Sound as Installation." In *The Art of Immersive Soundscapes*, edited by Pauline Minevich and Ellen Waterman, 165–78. With DVD edited by James Harley. Regina: University of Regina Press.

Hayles, N. Katherine. 1992. "The Materiality of Informatics." *Issues in Integrative Studies* 10: 121–44.

————. 1999. *How We Became Posthuman: Virtual Bodies in Cybernetics, Literature, and Informatics*. Chicago: University of Chicago Press.

Heble, Ajay. 2000. *Landing on the Wrong Note: Jazz, Dissonance, and Critical Practice*. New York: Routledge.

————. 2005. "Editorial." *Critical Studies in Improvisation / Études critiques en improvisations* 1 (2). http://www.criticalimprov.com/article/view/15/43.

Heble, Ajay, and Rob Wallace. 2013. *People Get Ready!: The Future of Jazz Is Now*. Durham: Duke University Press.

Hentoff, Nat. 1996. Liner notes to John Coltrane, *Meditations* (1965). Impulse Records. CD.

Hester, Karlton. 1990. "The Melodic and Polyrhythmic Development of John Coltrane's Spontaneous Composition in a Racist Society." PhD diss., City University of New York.

Ho, Fred. 2006. "Fred Ho's Tribute to the Black Arts Movement: Personal and Political Impact and Analysis." *Critical Studies in Improvisation / Etudes critiques en improvisation* 1 (3). http://www.criticalimprov.com/article/view/57/100.

Hodge, Stephen, Simon Persighetti, Phil Smith, and Cathy Turner. n.d. "Wrights and Sights: About." http://www.mis-guide.com/ws/about.html (accessed August 1, 2011).

Homer, Matthew. 2009. "Beyond the Studio: The Impact of Home Recording Technologies on Music Creation and Consumption." *Nebula* 6 (3): 85–99.

Honing, Henkjan. 2011a. *The Illiterate Listener: On Music Cognition, Musicality and Methodology.* Amsterdam: Amsterdam University Press.

———. 2011b. *Musical Cognition: A Science of Listening.* New Brunswick, NJ: Transaction Publishers.

Howlett, Felicity A. 1983. "An Introduction to Art Tatum's Performance Approaches Composition, Improvisation, and Melodic Variation." PhD diss., Cornell University.

Hwang, David Henry. 1989. *M. Butterfly.* New York: Plume.

Iacoboni, Marco. 2009. "Imitation, Empathy, and Mirror Neurons." *Annual Review of Psychology* 60: 653–70.

Ihde, Don. 2002. *Bodies in Technology.* Minneapolis: University of Minnesota Press.

Irigaray, Luce. 1992. *J'Aime à Toi: Esquisse d'une Félicité dans l'Histoire.* Paris: Grasset.

———. 1996. *I Love to You: Sketch of a Possible Felicity in History.* Translated by Alison Martin. New York: Routledge.

———. 2008. *Teaching.* London and New York: Continuum.

Ivy, Marilyn. 1995. *Discourses of the Vanishing: Modernity, Phantasm, Japan.* Chicago: University of Chicago Press.

Iyer, Vijay. 2002. "Embodied Mind, Situated Cognition, and Expressive Microtiming in African-American Music." *Music Perception: An Interdisciplinary Journal* 19 (3): 387–414.

Jacobs, Jane. 1961. *The Death and Life of Great American Cities.* New York: Random House.

James, Clive. 2007. *Cultural Amnesia: Necessary Memories from History and the Arts.* New York: Norton.

Järviluoma, Helmi, Meri Kytö, Barry Truax, Heikki Uimonen, and Noora Vikman, eds. 2009. *Acoustic Environments in Change and Five Village Soundscapes.* Tampere, Finland: Tampere Ammattikorkeakoulu University of Applied Sciences and University of Joensuu, Cultural Research.

Jentsch, Ernst. 1996 [1906]. "On the Psychology of the Uncanny." Translated by Roy Sellars. *Angelaki* 2 (1): 7–16.

Johnstone, Keith. 1979. *Impro: Improvisation and the Theatre.* New York: Theatre Arts Books.

Jones, Gayl. 1975. *Corregidora.* Boston: Beacon Press.

Jones, Gayl, and Michael S. Harper. 1977. "Gayl Jones: An Interview." *Massachusetts Review* 18 (4): 692–715.

Jost, Ekkehard. 1981. *Free Jazz.* New York: Da Capo Press.

Juslin, Patrik N., and Petri Laukka. 2003. "Communication of Emotions in Vocal Expression and Music Performance: Different Channels, Same Code?" *Psychological Bulletin* 129 (5): 770–814.

Juslin, Patrik N., and Daniel Västfjäll. 2008. "Emotional Responses to Music: The Need to Consider Underlying Mechanisms." *Behavioral and Brain Sciences* 31: 559–621.

Kamboureli, Smaro. 2009. *Scandalous Bodies: Diasporic Literature in English Canada.* Kitchener-Waterloo: Wilfrid Laurier Press.

Katz, Daniel. 2010. "El teatro Colón y una lección para el Bicentenario." Lanacion.com, *La Nación* (Buenos Aires), May 24.

Katz, Mark. 2004. *Capturing Sound: How Technology Has Changed Music*. Berkeley: University of California Press.

Kauffmann, Stanley, and John Cage. 1966. "The Changing Audience for the Changing Arts/Panel." In *The Arts: Planning for Change: Proceedings of the Twelfth National Conference*, 23–52. New York: Associated Councils of the Arts.

Kaye, Nick. 2000. *Site Specific Art: Performance, Place, and Documentation*. New York: Routledge.

Kim-Boyle, David. 2009. "Network Musics: Play, Engagement and the Democratization of Performance." *Contemporary Music Review* 28 (4): 363–75.

Koelsch, Stefan, Thomas Fritz, Yves V. Cramon, Karsten Müller, and Angela D. Friederici. 2006. "Investigating Emotion with Music: An fMRI Study." *Human Brain Mapping* 27 (3): 239–50.

Kofsky, Frank. 1970. *Black Nationalism and the Revolution in Music*. New York: Pathfinder Press.

———. 1998. *John Coltrane and the Jazz Revolution of the 1960s*. New York: Pathfinder.

Kohler, Evelyn, Christian Keysers, M. Alessandra Umiltà, Leonardo Fogassi, Vittorio Gallese, and Giacomo Rizzolatti. 2002. "Hearing Sounds, Understanding Actions: Action Representation in Mirror Neurons." *Science* 297 (5582): 846–48.

Kraus, Nina, and Trent Nicol. 2008. "Auditory Evoked Potentials." In *Encyclopedia of Neuroscience*, edited by Marc D. Binder, Nobutaka Hirokawa, and Uwe Windhorst, 214–18. Berlin: Springer.

Kristeva, Julia. 1984. *Revolution in Poetic Language*. Translated by Margaret Waller. New York: Columbia University Press.

Kuppers, Petra. 2006. "Community Arts and Practices: Improvising Being-Together." *Culture Machine*, no. 8. http://www.culturemachine.net/index.php/cm/article/viewArticle/45/53.

Kuppers, Petra, and Gwen Robertson, eds. 2007. *The Community Performance Reader*. London: Routledge.

Kwon, Miwon. 2002. *One Place after Another: Site-Specific Art and Locational Identity*. Cambridge, MA: MIT Press.

Lacelle, Martin, and Susan Hubner. n.d. "Da Vinci Homepage." Upper Grand District Schoolboard. http://www.ugdsb.on.ca/jfr/davinci/ (accessed August 1, 2011).

Laclau, Ernesto. 2005. *On Populist Reason*. London: Verso.

Lam, Joseph Sui Ching. 1999. "Embracing 'Asian American Music' as an Heuristic Device." *Journal of Asian American Studies* 2 (1): 29–60.

Lanata, Jorge. 2010. "Se ve que andamos necesitando actos fundacionales." Perfil.com, *Diario Perfil* (Buenos Aires), May 29.

Landgraf, Edgar. 2009. "Improvisation: Form and Event—A Spencer-Brownian Calculation." In *Emergence and Embodiment: New Essays on Second-Order Systems Theory*, edited by Bruce Clarke and Mark B. N. Hansen, 179–204. Durham: Duke University Press.

———. 2011. *Improvisation as Art: Conceptual Challenges, Historical Perspectives*. New York: Continuum.

Larkin, Philip. 1970. *All What Jazz: A Record Diary*. New York: Farrar, Straus & Giroux.

Leech, Angus. 2002. "Bending the Mirror: Notes on the Many Transformations of David Rokeby's *Very Nervous System*." *HorizonZero* 3. http://www.horizonzero.ca/textsite/invent.php?is=3&file=11&tlang=0.

Lefebvre, Henri. 1991. *The Production of Space*. Translated by Donald Nicholson-Smith. Oxford: Blackwell.

Lem, Brenda Joy. 2008. "Inner Truth Taiko Dojo." *GEMS—Gender, Education, Music & Society* 4. http://www.queensu.ca/music/links/gems/lem5.pdf.

Leman, Marc. 2008. *Embodied Music Cognition and Mediation Technology*. Cambridge, MA: MIT Press.

Leppert, Richard. 1993. *The Sight of Sound: Music, Representation and the History of the Body*. Berkeley: University of California Press.

Lerner, Neil, and Joseph N. Straus, eds. 2006. *Sounding Off: Theorizing Disability in Music*. New York: Routledge.

Lester, James. 1994. *Too Marvelous for Words: The Life and Genius of Art Tatum*. New York: Oxford University Press.

Levinas, Emmanuel. 1969. *Totality and Infinity: An Essay on Exteriority*. Pittsburgh, PA: Duquesne University Press.

Levine, Lawrence. 1990. *Highbrow/Lowbrow: The Emergence of Cultural Hierarchy in America*. Cambridge, MA: Harvard University Press.

Lewis, George E. 1996. "Improvised Music after 1950: Afrological and Eurological Perspectives." *Black Music Research Journal* 16 (1): 91–122.

———. 2000. "Too Many Notes: Computers, Complexity and Culture in *Voyager*." *Leonardo Music Journal* 10: 33–39.

———. 2007. "Mobilitas Animi: Improvising Technologies, Intending Chance." *Parallax* 13 (4): 108–22.

———. 2008. *A Power Stronger Than Itself: The AACM and American Experimental Music*. Chicago: University of Chicago Press.

Liebman, David. 1996. "John Coltrane's *Meditations* Suite: A Study in Symmetry." *Annual Review of Jazz Studies* 8: 167–80.

Limb, Charles J., and Allen R. Braun. 2008. "Neural Substrates of Spontaneous Musical Performance: An fMRI Study of Jazz Improvisation." *PLOS ONE* 3 (2), p.e1679.

Lippard, Lucy R. 1997. *The Lure of the Local: Senses of Place in a Multicentered Society*. New York: New Press.

Lock, Graham, and Anthony Braxton. 1988. *Forces in Motion: The Music and Thoughts of Anthony Braxton*. New York: Da Capo Press.

Longo, Giuseppe O. 2003. "Body and Technology: Continuity or Discontinuity?" In *Mediating the Human Body: Technology, Communication, and Fashion,* edited by Leopoldina Fortunati, James Everett Katz, and Raimonda Riccini, 23–29. Mahwah, NJ: Lawrence Erlbaum.

Longoni, Ana, and Gustavo Bruzzone. 2008. "Introduction." In *El Siluetazo*, 7–67. Buenos Aires: Adriana Hidalgo.

Lubet, Alex. 2004. "Tunes of Impairment: An Ethnomusicology of Disability." *Review of Disability Studies: An International Journal* 1 (1): 133–56.

———. 2009. "Disability, Music Education and the Epistemology of Interdisciplinarity." *International Journal of Qualitative Studies in Education* 22 (1): 119–32.

———. 2010. *Music, Disability and Society*. Philadelphia: Temple University Press.

Lubet, Alex, and Na'ama Sheffi, eds. 2008. "To Dance beneath the Diamond Sky with One Hand . . ." Special issues, *Review of Disability Studies: An International Journal* 4, nos. 1–2.

Luhmann, Niklas. 1995. *Social Systems.* Translated by John Bednarz Jr. with Dirk Baecker. Stanford, CA: Stanford University Press.

MacDonald, Ann-Marie. 1997. *Fall on Your Knees.* Toronto: Vintage Canada.

Maclure, Jocelyn. 2003. "The Politics of Recognition at an Impasse? Identity Politics and Democratic Citizenship." *Canadian Journal of Political Science / Revue canadienne de science politique* 3 (6): 3–21.

Madden, David. 2011. "Vancouver English Bay Soundwalk." Soundwalking Interactions (blog), December 20. http://soundwalkinginteractions.wordpress.com/2011/12/20 /vancouver-english-bay-soundwalk/.

Maturana, Humberto R., and Francisco J. Varela. 1998. *The Tree of Knowledge: The Biological Roots of Human Understanding.* Rev. ed. Boston: Shambhala.

Mauss, Marcel. 1979. *Sociology and Psychology: Essays by Marcel Mauss.* Translated by Ben Brewster. London: Routledge.

McCartney, Andra. 2004. "Soundscape Works, Listening and the Touch of Sound." In *Aural Cultures*, edited by Jim Drobnick, 179–85. Toronto: YYZ Books.

———. 2006. *Learning to Walk.* CBC Radio 1 Outfront documentary.

———. 2009. "Reception and Reflexivity in Electroacoustic Creation." In *Musique concrète, 60 Ans Plus Tard: Proceedings of the Electroacoustic Music Studies Network Conference, Paris, June 2008*, edited by Olivier Baudoin. http://www.ems-network .org/emso8/paper.html.

———. 2010. "Soundwalking and Improvisation." *Improvisation, Community, and Social Practice Research Collection.* August 30. http://www.improvcommunity.ca/research /soundwalking-and-improvisation.

McCartney, Andra, and Sandra Gabriele. 2001. "Soundwalking at Night." *Soundscape: The Journal of Acoustic Ecology* 2 (1): 25–27.

McCartney, Andra, and David Paquette. 2012. "Walking, Listening, Speaking: The Soundwalking Interactions Project." In *Ambiances in Action / Ambiances en Acte(s)— —International Congress on Ambiances, Montreal 2012*, edited by Jean-Paul Thibaud and Daniel Siret, 189–94. Montreal: International Ambiances Network.

McClary, Susan. 2002. *Feminine Endings.* Minneapolis: University of Minnesota Press.

McConachie, Bruce A. 1993. "Metaphors We Act By: Kinesthetics, Cognitive Psychology, and Historical Structures." *Journal of Dramatic Theory and Criticism* 7 (2): 25–45.

McDonald, Michael Bruce. 1995. "Traning the Nineties, or The Present Relevance of John Coltrane's Music of Theophany and Negation." *African American Review* 29 (2): 275–82.

McLuhan, Marshall, and Quentin Fiore. 1968. *War and Peace in the Global Village.* New York: Bantam Books.

McMullen, Tracy. 2008. "Identity for Sale: Glenn Miller, Wynton Marsalis, and Cultural Replay in Music." In *Big Ears: Listening for Gender in Jazz Studies*, edited by Nichole T. Rustin and Sherrie Tucker, 129–54. Durham: Duke University Press.

———. 2014. "The Improvisative." In *The Oxford Handbook of Critical Improvisation Studies*, edited by George Lewis and Benjamin Piekut. Oxford: Oxford University Press.

Mills, Roger. 2010. "Dislocated Sound: A Survey of Improvisation in Networked Audio Platforms." In *Proceedings of the 2010 Conference on New Interfaces for Musical Expression (NIME 2010), Sydney, Australia*, 186–91. Sydney, Australia.

Minevich, Pauline, and Ellen Waterman, eds. 2013. *The Art of Immersive Soundscapes: Contemporary Sound Art Practices*. Regina: University of Regina Press.

Mitchell, Nicole. 2007. "The Newcomer." Liner notes for Anthony Braxton, *9 Compositions (Iridium) 2006*. Firehouse 12 Records FH12-04-03-001. 18–19.

———. 2011. "Lecture: Afro-Futurism." *Sonic Healing Ministries*. April 3. http://www.ustream.tv/recorded/13758840. Transcribed by Julie Dawn Smith.

Moeller, Hans-Georg. 2012. *The Radical Luhmann*. New York: Columbia University Press.

Molnar-Szakacs, Istvan, and Katie Overy. 2006. "Music and Mirror Neurons: From Motion to 'E'motion." *Social Cognitive and Affective Neuroscience* 1 (3): 235–41.

Monson, Ingrid. 1996. *Saying Something: Jazz Improvisation and Interaction*. Chicago: University of Chicago Press.

———. 2008. "Hearing, Seeing, and Perceptual Agency." Supplement, *Critical Inquiry* 34: S36–58.

———. 2009. "Jazz as Political and Musical Practice." In *Musical Improvisation: Art, Education, and Society*, edited by Gabriel Solis and Bruno Nettl, 21–37. Urbana: University of Illinois Press.

Mori, Masahiro. 2012. "The Uncanny Valley." Translated by Karl F. MacDorman and Norri Kageki. June 12. http://spectrum.ieee.org/automaton/robotics/humanoids/the-uncanny-valley.

Nachmanovitch, Stephen. 1990. *Free Play: Improvisation in Life and Art*. New York: Penguin Putnam.

Nagel, Thomas. 1974. "What Is It Like to Be a Bat?" *Philosophical Review* 83 (4): 435–50.

Nancy, Jean-Luc. 2007. *Listening*. Translated by Charlotte Mandell. New York: Fordham University Press.

Needell, Jeffrey D. 1995. "Rio de Janeiro and Buenos Aires: Public Space and Public Consciousness in Fin-de-Siècle Latin America." *Comparative Studies in Society and History* 37 (3): 519–40.

Nettl, Bruno. 1974. "Thoughts on Improvisation: A Comparative Approach." *Musical Quarterly* 60 (1): 1–19.

Nicholls, Tracey. 2012. *An Ethics of Improvisation: Aesthetic Possibilities for a Political Future*. Plymouth, UK: Lexington Books.

Nisenson, Eric. 1993. *Ascension: John Coltrane and His Quest*. New York: St. Martin's Press.

Noland, Carrie. 2009. *Agency and Embodiment: Performing Gestures/Producing Culture*. Cambridge, MA: Harvard University Press.

Nold, Christian, ed. 2009. *Emotional Cartography: Technologies of the Self*. Creative Commons.

Nooshin, Laudan. 2003. "Improvisation as 'Other': Creativity, Knowledge and Power: The Case of Iranian Classical Music." *Journal of the Royal Musical Association* 128 (2): 242–96.

————. 2013. "Beyond the *Radif*: New Forms of Improvisational Practice in Iranian
   Music." *Music Theory Online* 19 (2). http://mtosmt.org/issues/mto.13.19.2/mto.13.19
   .2.nooshin.php.

Nora, Simon, and Alain Minc. 1980. *The Computerization of Society*. Cambridge, MA:
   MIT Press.

Novack, Cynthia J. 1990. *Sharing the Dance: Contact Improvisation and American
   Culture*. Madison: University of Wisconsin Press.

Novak, David. 2013. *Japanoise: Music at the Edge of Circulation*. Durham: Duke
   University Press.

Oliveros, Pauline. 1984. "Tape Delay Techniques for Electronic Music Composers." In
   Software for People: Collected Writings 1963–80. Baltimore, MD: Smith Publications.

————. 1995. "Acoustic and Virtual Space as a Dynamic Element of Music." *Leonardo
   Music Journal* 5: 19–22.

————. 2004a. "Harmonic Anatomy: Women in Improvisation." In *The Other Side
   of Nowhere: Jazz, Improvisation, and Communities in Dialogue*, edited by Daniel
   Fischlin and Ajay Heble, 50–70. Middletown, CT: Wesleyan University Press.

————. 2004b. "Tripping on Wires: The Wireless Body: Who Is Improvising?" *Critical
   Studies in Improvisation / Études critiques en improvisation* 1 (1). http://www
   .criticalimprov.com/article/view/9.

————. 2005. *Deep Listening: A Composer's Sound Practice*. New York: iUniverse, 2005.

————. 2006. "Improvising with Spaces." Paper presented at the Acoustical Society of
   America, Providence, RI, June 6–9.

————. 2008. "The Expanded Instrument System (EIS): An Introduction and Brief
   Hisory." *Future of Creative Technologies, Journal of the Institute of Creative
   Technologies*, no. 1: 21–24.

————. 2011. "Auralizing in the Sonosphere: A Vocabulary for Inner Sound and
   Sounding." *Journal of Visual Culture* 10 (2): 162–68.

Oliveros, Pauline, Leaf Miller, Jaclyn Heyen, Gillian Siddall, and Sergio Hazard. 2011. "A
   Musical Improvisation Interface for People with Severe Physical Disabilities." *Music
   and Medicine* 3 (3): 172–81.

Oliveros, Pauline, Sarah Weaver, Mark Dresser, Jefferson Pitcher, Jonas Braasch, and
   Chris Chafe. 2009. "Telematic Music: Six Perspectives." Online supplement to
   Leonardo Music Journal 19.

Orlie, Melissa. 2010. "Impersonal Matter." In *New Materialisms: Ontology, Agency, and
   Politics*, edited by Diana H. Coole and Samantha Frost, 116–36. Durham: Duke
   University Press.

Osthoff, Simone. 1997. "Lygia Clark and Hélio Oiticica: A Legacy of Interactivity and
   Participation for a Telematic Future." *Leonardo* 30 (4): 279–89.

Overy, Katie, and Istvan Molnar-Szakacs. 2009. "Being Together in Time: Musical
   Experience and the Mirror Neuron System." *Music Perception* 26 (5): 489–504.

Páez, Fito. 2010. Interview by Karina Micheletto. Paginai2.com.ar, *Página/*12 (Buenos
   Aires). May 30.

Pallant, Cheryl. 2006. *Contact Improvisation: An Introduction to a Vitalizing Dance
   Form*. Jefferson, NC: McFarland.

Pasler, Jann. 2007. *Writing through Music: Essays on Music, Culture, and Politics*. Oxford:
   Oxford University Press.

Pearson, Mike, and Michael Shanks. 2001. *Theatre/Archaeology*. London: Routledge.

Peñalosa, David, with David Greenwood. 2009. *The Clave Matrix; Afro-Cuban Rhythm: Its Principles and African Origins*. Redway, CA: Bembe.

Pickering, Andrew. 2010. *The Cybernetic Brain: Sketches of Another Future*. Chicago: University of Chicago Press.

Poluyko, Kristen. 2001. "Alternative Music, Jazz, and the Performance Resignification of Identity in Ann-Marie McDonald's *Fall on Your Knees* and Anthony Minghella's *The Talented Mr. Ripley*." MA thesis, Lakehead University. Thunder Bay, ON: ProQuest, UMI Dissertations Publishing.

Pressing, Jeff. 1988. "Improvisation: Methods and Models." In *Generative Processes in Music: The Psychology of Performance, Improvisation, and Composition*, edited by John A. Sloboda, 129–78. Oxford: Clarendon Press.

Puckette, Miller. 2009. "Not Being There." *Contemporary Music Review* 28 (4–5): 409–12.

Ramlow, Todd. 2006. "Bodies in the Borderlands: Gloria Anzaldúa's and David Wojnarowicz's Mobility Machines." *Melus* 31 (3): 169–87.

Rammert, Werner. 2008. "Where the Action Is: Distributed Agency between Humans, Machines, and Programs." In *Paradoxes of Interactivity: Perspectives for Media Theory, Human-Computer Interaction, and Artistic Investigations*, edited by Uwe Seifert, Jin Hyun Kim, and Anthony Moore, 63–91. New Brunswick, NJ: Transaction.

Rancière, Jacques. 1998. "The Cause of the Other." Translated by David Macey. *Parallax* 4 (2): 25–33.

Ratliff, Ben. 2007. *Coltrane: The Story of a Sound*. New York: Farrar, Straus and Giroux, 2007.

Read, Alan, ed. 2000. *Architecturally Speaking: Practices of Art, Architecture and the Everyday*. London: Routledge.

Rebelo, Pedro. 2009. "Dramaturgy in the Network." *Contemporary Music Review* 28 (4–5): 387–93.

Rebelo, Pedro, and Maarten van Walstijn. 2004. "Designing Acoustic Thresholds." Paper presented at *Les journées du design sonore/Sond Design Symposium*. Paris, Institut de Recherche et Coordination Acoustique/Musique (IRCAM), October 13–15.

Renaud, Alain B. 2010. "Dynamic Cues for Network Music Interactions." Paper presented at SMC 2010: 7th Sound Music and Computing Conference, Universitat Pompeu Fabra, Barcelona, Spain, July 21–24. http://eprints.bournemouth.ac.uk /15901/1/21.pdf.

Robertson, Jennifer. 1997. "Empire of Nostalgia: Rethinking 'Internationalization' in Japan Today." *Theory, Culture & Society* 14 (4): 97–122.

Robinson, Dylan. 2014. "Feeling Reconciliation, Remaining Settled." In *Theatres of Affect*, edited Erin Hurley. Toronto: Playwrights Canada Press.

Robinson, Hilary. 2006. *Reading Art, Reading Irigaray: The Politics of Art by Women*. London: Tauris.

Robinson, Jason. 2005. "Improvising California: Community and Creative Music in Los Angeles and San Francisco." PhD diss., University of California, San Diego.

Robinson, Randall. 2008. "Daihachi Oguchi: Taiko Drum Master Silenced." *All About Jazz*, July 15. http://www.allaboutjazz.com/php/article.php?id=29948.

Rockwell, John. 1990, March 26. "Reviews/Music; A Pianist Juxtaposes Charles Ives and Art Tatum." *New York Times*. http://www.nytimes.com/1990/03/26/arts/reviews -music-a-pianist-juxtaposes-charles-ives-and-art-tatum.html.

Rodríguez, Carlos. 2010. "Todo es historia, en versión multitudinaria." Pagina12.com.ar, *Página/12* (Buenos Aires), May 26.

Rokeby, David. 1995. "Transforming Mirrors: Subjectivity and Control in Interactive Media." In *Critical Issues in Electronic Media*, edited by Simon Penny, 133–57. Albany: State University of New York Press.

———. 1998. "The Construction of Experience: Interface as Content." In *Digital Illusion: Entertaining the Future with High Technology*, edited by Clark Dodsworth Jr., 27–47. New York: ACM Press.

Romero, José Luis. 1976. *Latinoamérica: Las ciudades y las ideas*. Buenos Aires: Siglo XXI.

Rose, Nikolas S. 1999. "Governable Spaces." In *Powers of Freedom: Reframing Political Thought*, 31–40. Cambridge: Cambridge University Press.

Ross, Don. 2007. "Introduction: Science Catches the Will." In *Distributed Cognition and the Will: Individual Volition and Social Context*, edited by Don Ross, David Spurrett, Harold Kincaid, and G. Lynn Stephens, 1–16. Cambridge, MA: MIT Press.

Ross, Kristin. 2002. *May '68 and Its Afterlives*. Chicago: University of Chicago Press.

Rustin, Nichole T. 1999. "Mingus Fingers: Charles Mingus, Black Masculinity, and Postwar Jazz Culture." PhD diss., New York University.

Rustin, Nichole T., and Sherrie Tucker. 2008. "Introduction." In *Big Ears: Listening for Gender in Jazz Studies*, edited by Nichole T. Rustin and Sherrie Tucker, 1–28. Durham: Duke University Press.

Saddleton, Hugh. 2011. "Lets Buy Up Our Beaches." *Coffs Outlook*, May 5. http:// coffsoutlook.com/lets-buy-up-the-beaches/.

Salih, Sara. 2004. *The Judith Butler Reader*. Malden, MA: Blackwell Publishing.

Sawyer, R. Keith. 2000. "Improvisation and the Creative Process: Dewey, Collingwood, and the Aesthetics of Spontaneity." *Journal of Aesthetics and Art Criticism* 58 (2): 149–61.

———. 2006. "Group Creativity: Musical Performance and Collaboration." *Psychology of Music* 34 (2): 148–65.

Schaeffer, Pierre. 1967. *La Musique Concrète*. Paris: Presses Universitaires de Frances, 1967.

———. 1990. *L'Œuvre Musicale*. France: INA-GRM.

Schafer, R. Murray, ed. 1977. *Five Village Soundscapes*. Music of the Environment Series. Vancouver: A.R.C. Publications.

———. 1994. *The Soundscape: Our Sonic Environment and the Tuning of the World*. Rochester, VT: Destiny Books.

Schechner, Richard. 2002. *Performance Theory*. Rev. and expanded ed. New York: Routledge.

Schine, Jenni. 2011. "English Bay Soundwalk Reflection." Soundwalking Interactions (blog), November 18. http://soundwalkinginteractions.wordpress.com/2011/11/23 /english-bay-soundwalk-reflection/.

Schroeder, Franziska. 2006. "Bodily Instruments and Instrumental Bodies: Critical Views on the Relation of Body and Instrument in Technologically Informed Perfor- mance Environments." *Contemporary Music Review* 25 (1–2): 1–5.

Schroeder, Franziska, and Pedro Rebelo. 2009. "The Pontydian Performance: The Performative Layer." *Organised Sound* 14 (2): 134–41.

Scobie, James. 1974. *Buenos Aires: Plaza to Suburb, 1870–1910*. New York: Oxford University Press.

Seaver, Nicholas P. 2011. "'This Is Not a Copy': Mechanical Fidelity and the Re-Enacting Piano." *differences* 22 (2–3): 54–73.

Shafii Kadkani, M. R. 2000. "In Neishabur's Garden Alley." In *The Song of Rain and Wind* [*Avaz-e Bad-o Baran*]. 2nd ed., 98–120. Tehran: Nashr-e Cheshmeh.

Shanken, Edward A. 2000. "Tele-Agency: Telematics, Telerobots, and the Art of Meaning." *Art Journal* 59 (2): 64–77.

Sharma, Anu, Nina Kraus, Therese J. McGeeb, and Trent G. Nicol. 1997. "Developmental Changes in P1 and N1 Central Auditory Responses Elicited by Consonant-Vowel Syllables." *Electroencephalography and Clinical Neurophysiology* 104 (6): 540–45.

Shepherd, John, and Peter Wicke. 1997. *Music and Cultural Theory*. Cambridge: Polity Press.

Siddall, Gillian. 2005. "'I Wanted to Live in That Music: Blues, Bessie Smith, and Improvised Identities in Ann-Marie MacDonald's *Fall on Your Knees*." *Critical Studies in Impovisation / Études critiques en improvisation* 1 (2). http://www.criticalimprov.com/article/view/16.

Siebers, Tobin. 2010. *Disability Aesthetics*. Ann Arbor: University of Michigan Press.

Sigal, Silvia, and Eliseo Verón. 2004. *Perón o muerte. Los fundamentos discursivos del fenómeno peronista*. Rev. ed. Buenos Aires: Eudeba.

Simms, Rob, and Amir Koushkani. 2012. *The Art of Avaz and Mohammad Reza Shajarian: Foundations and Contexts*. Lanham, MD: Lexington Books.

Simpkins, Cuthbert. 1975. *Coltrane: A Biography*. New York: Herndon House.

Skloot, Rebecca. 2010. *The Immortal Life of Henrietta Lacks*. New York: Crown.

Smith, Julie Dawn. 2001. "Diva Dogs: Sounding Women Improvising." PhD diss., University of British Columbia.

——. 2004. "Playing Like a Girl: The Queer Laughter of the Feminist Improvising Group." In *The Other Side of Nowhere: Jazz, Improvisation, and Communities in Dialogue*, edited by Daniel Fischlin and Ajay Heble, 224–43. Middletown, CT: Wesleyan University Press.

——. 2008. "Perverse Hysterics: The Noisy *Cri* of Les Diaboliques." In *Big Ears: Listening for Gender in Jazz Studies*, edited by Nichole T. Rustin and Sherrie Tucker, 180–209. Durham: Duke University Press.

Smith, Julie Dawn, and Ellen Waterman. 2013. "Listening Trust: The Everyday Politics of George Lewis's 'Dream Team.'" In *People Get Ready: The Future of Jazz Is Now!*, edited by Ajay Heble and Rob Wallace, 59–87. Durham: Duke University Press.

Soon, Chun Siong, Marcel Brass, Hans-Jochen Heinze, and John-Dylan Haynes. 2008. "Unconscious Determinants of Free Decisions in the Human Brain." *Nature Neuroscience* 11 (5): 543–45.

Spellman, A. B. 2000. Liner notes to John Coltrane, *Ascension* (1965). Impulse Records.

Spolin, Viola. 1969. *Improvisation for the Theater: A Handbook of Teaching and Directing Techniques*. Evanston, IL: Northwestern University Press.

Stanyek, Jason. 2004. "Transmissions of an Interculture: Pan-African Jazz and Intercultural Improvisation." In *The Other Side of Nowhere: Jazz, Improvisation and Communities in Dialogue*, edited by Ajay Heble and Daniel Fischlin, 87–130. Hanover, CT: Wesleyan University Press.

Stanyek, Jason, and Benjamin Piekut. 2010. "Deadness: Technologies of the Intermundane." *TDR: The Drama Review* 54 (1): 14–38.

Stengers, Isabelle. 2010. *Cosmopolitics I*. Translated by Robert Bononno. Minneapolis: University of Minnesota Press.

Stern, David G. 1995. *Wittgenstein on Mind and Language*. New York: Oxford University Press.

Sterne, Jonathan. 2003. *The Audible Past: Cultural Origins of Sound Reproduction*. Durham: Duke University Press.

Straus, Joseph N. 2011. *Extraordinary Measures: Disability in Music*. New York: Oxford University Press.

Stravinsky, Igor. 1936. *Chronicle of my Life*. London: Victor Gollancz.

Such, David. 1993. *Avant-garde Jazz Musicians: Performing "Out There."* Iowa City: University of Iowa Press.

Sudnow, David. 1978. *Ways of the Hand: The Organization of Improvised Conduct*. Cambridge, MA: Harvard University Press.

Swenson, John. 2008. Review of *Piano Starts Here*, by Art Tatum. *Stereophile* 31 (9).

Szwed, John F. 1998. *Space Is the Place: The Lives and Times of Sun Ra*. New York: Da Capo Press.

Tanzi, Dante. 2001. "Observations about Music and Decentralized Environments." *Leonardo Music Journal* 34 (5): 431–36.

Taylor, Charles. 1994. "The Politics of Recognition." In *Multiculturalism: Examining the Politics of Recognition*, expanded edition, edited by Amy Gutmann, 25–74. Princeton, NJ: Princeton University Press.

Taylor, Diana. 1997. *Disappearing Acts: Spectacles of Gender and Nationalism in Argentina's "Dirty War."* Durham: Duke University Press.

———. 2002. "'You Are Here': The DNA of Performance." *TDR: The Drama Review* 46 (1): 149–69.

Télam. 2010. "Más de dos millones de personas festejaron con un espectáculo imponente." *Bicentenario.argentina.ar*. 200 Años Bicentenario Argentino, May 26 (accessed May 10, 2011).

Tenney, James. 1992. *Meta+Hodos*. 2nd ed. Hanover, NH: Frog Peak Music.

Thibaud, Jean-Paul. 2003. "The Sonic Composition of the City." In *The Auditory Culture Reader*, edited by Michael Bull and Les Back, 329–41. Amsterdam: Berg.

Thomas, J. C. 1975. *Chasin' the Trane: The Music and Mystique of John Coltrane*. New York: Da Capo Press.

Thompson, Emily. 1995. "Machines, Music, and the Quest for Fidelity: Marketing the Edison Phonograph in America, 1877–1925." *Musical Quarterly* 79 (1): 131–71.

Thoreau, Henry David. 1906. *The Writings of Henry David Thoreau: Cape Cod and Miscellanies, Volume Four*. Boston, MA: Houghton Mifflin.

Tilly, Charles. 1993. "Contentious Repertoires in Great Britain, 1758–1834." *Social Science History* 17 (2): 253–80.

Todorov, Tzvetan. 1999. *The Conquest of America*. Norman: University of Oklahoma Press.

Trevena, Judy, and Jeff Miller. 2010. "Brain Preparation before a Voluntary Action: Evidence against Unconscious Movement Initiation." *Consciousness and Cognition* 19 (1): 447–56.

Truax, Barry, ed. 1978. "Difference Tones." In *Handbook for Acoustic Ecology*. 2nd ed. Originally published by the World Soundscape Project, Simon Fraser University, and ARC Publications. Online edition dated 1999. http://www.sfu.ca/sonic-studio /handbook/Difference_Tone.html.

———. 2002. "Genres and Techniques of Soundscape Composition as Developed at Simon Fraser University." *Organised Sound* 7 (1): 5–14.

———, ed. n.d. "The World Soundscape Project." *World Soundscape Project*, Simon Fraser University. http://www.sfu.ca/~truax/wsp.html (accessed August 1, 2011).

Tucker, Sherrie. 2000. *Swing Shift: "All-Girl" Bands of the 1940s*. Durham: Duke University Press.

———. 2001/2002. "Big Ears: Listening for Gender in Jazz Studies." *Current Musicology* 71–73: 375–408.

Tully, James. 2000. "Struggles over Recognition and Distribution." *Constellations* 7 (4): 469–482.

Turner, Edith. 2012. *Communitas: The Anthropology of Collective Joy*. New York: Palgrave Macmillan.

Turner, Victor. 1969. *The Ritual Process: Structure and Anti-Structure*. Chicago: Aldine.

Varda, Agnes. 2000. *The Gleaners and I (Les glaneurs et la glaneuse)*. Documentary film. France: Zeitgeist.

von Foerster, Heinz. 1984. "Disorder/Order: Discovery or Invention?" In *Disorder and Order: Proceedings of the Stanford International Symposium (September 14–16, 1981)*, edited by Paisley Livingston, 177–89. Saratoga: Anna Libri.

Walcott, Rinaldo. 2011. "Disgraceful: Intellectual Dishonesty, White Anxieties, and Multicultural Critique Thirty-Six Years Later." In *Home and Native Land: Unsettling Multiculturalism in Canada*, edited by May Chazan, Lisa Helps, Anna Stanley, and Sonali Thakkar, 15–30. Toronto: Between the Lines.

Wald, Priscilla. 2012. "Cells, Genes, and Stories: HeLa's Journey from Labs to Literature." In *Genetics and the Unsettled Past: The Collision of DNA, Race and History*, edited by Keith Wailoo, Alondra Nelson, and Catherine Lee, 247–65. New Brunswick, NJ: Rutgers University Press.

Walser, Robert. 1991. "The Body in the Music: Epistemology and Musical Semiotics." *College Music Symposium* 31: 117–26.

Washington, Harriet A. 2008. *Medical Apartheid: The Dark History of Medical Experimentation on Black Americans from Colonial Times to the Present*. New York: Random House.

Washington, Michael Spence. 2001. "Beautiful Nightmare: Coltrane, Jazz, and American Culture." PhD diss., Harvard University.

Waterman, Ellen. 2008a. "'I Dreamed of Other Worlds': An Interview with Nicole Mitchell." *Critical Studies in Improvisation / Études critiques en improvisation* 4 (1). http://www.criticalimprov.com/article/view/510.

———. 2008b. "Naked Intimacy: Eroticism, Improvisation, and Gender." *Critical Studies in Improvisation / Études critiques en improvisation* 4 (2). http://www.criticalimprov .com/article/view/845/.

Watrous, Peter. 1990, March 4. "Why a Virtuoso Jazz Pianist Still Provokes Debate." *New York Times*. http://www.nytimes.com/1990/03/04/arts/recordings-why-a-virtuoso -jazz-pianist-still-provokes-debate.html.

Webb, Nancy. 2011. "Percussion Afternoon." artengine.ca (blog), February 1. http://artengine.ca/blog/?m=201102.

Wegner, Daniel M., and Betsy Sparrow. 2007. "The Puzzle of Coaction." In *Distributed Cognition and the Will: Individual Volition and Social Context*, edited by Don Ross, David Spurrett, Harold Kincaid, and G. Lynn Stephens, 17–38. Cambridge, MA: MIT Press.

Wehr-Flowers, Erin. 2006. "Differences between Male and Female Students' Confidence, Anxiety, and Attitude toward Learning Jazz Improvisation." *Journal of Research in Music Education* 54 (4): 337–49.

Weiner, Norbert. 1948. *Cybernetics: or Control and Communication in the Animal and Machine*. Cambridge, MA: MIT Press.

Welchman, Andrew, James Stanley, Malte R. Schomers, R. Chris Miall, and Heinrich H Bülthoff. 2010. "The Quick and the Dead: When Reaction Beats Intention." *Proceedings of the Royal Society B* 277: 1667–74.

Woideck, Carl, ed. 1998. *The John Coltrane Companion: Four Decades of Commentary*. New York: Schirmer.

Wolf, Susan. 1994. Comment. In Charles Taylor, *Multiculturalism: Expanding the Politics of Recognition*, expanded ed., edited by Amy Gutmann, 75–86. Princeton, NJ: Princeton University Press.

Wong, Deborah. 2004. *Speak It Louder: Asian Americans Making Music*. New York: Routledge.

———. 2008. "Moving: From Performance to Performative Ethnography and Back Again." In *Shadows in the Field: New Perspectives for Fieldwork in Ethnomusicology*, edited by Gregory Barz and Timothy Cooley, rev. 2nd ed., 76–89. New York: Oxford University Press.

Wong, Mandy-Suzanne. 2012. "Hegel's Being-Fluid in *Corregidora*, Blues, and (Post) Black Aesthetics." *Evental Aesthetics* 1 (1): 85–120.

Yoon, Paul J. 2009. "Asian Masculinities and Parodic Possibility in Odaiko Solos and Filmic Representations." *Asian Music* 40 (1): 100–130.

Yoshihara, Mari. 2007. *Musicians from a Different Shore: Asians and Asian Americans in Classical Music*. Philadelphia: Temple University Press.

———. n.d. "Q&A with Mari Yoshihara." Temple University Press, author interviews. http://www.temple.edu/tempress/authors/1776_qa.html (accessed August 15, 2008).

Yoshimi, Shunya. 2003. "'America' as Desire and Violence: Americanization in Postwar Japan and Asia during the Cold War." Translated by David Buist. *Inter-Asia Cultural Studies* 4 (3): 433–50.

Young, Iris Marion. 1980. "Throwing Like a Girl: A Phenomenology of Feminine Body Comportment Motility and Spatiality." *Human Studies* 3 (2): 137–56.

Yurtsever, Âli, and Umut Burcu Tasa. 2009. "Redefining the Body in Cyberculture: Art's Contribution to a New Understanding of Embodiment." In *The Real and the Virtual*, edited by Daniel Riha and Anna Maj, 3–11. Freeland, UK: Inter-Disciplinary Press.

Zerubavel, Eviatar. 1996. "Social Memories: Steps to a Sociology of the Past." *Qualitative Sociology* 19 (3): 283–99.

CONTRIBUTORS

DAVID BORGO is professor of music at University of California, San Diego, and author of *Sync or Swarm: Improvising Music in a Complex Age* (2005), which received the Alan P. Merriam Prize from the Society for Ethnomusicology. As a saxophonist, David has released eight CDs and one DVD and he performs electro-acoustic improvisation with his duo KaiBorg (http://kaiborg.com) and polymetric compositions with Kronomorfic (http://kronomorfic.com).

JUDITH BUTLER is the author of several influential books of philosophy and feminist theory, including *Gender Trouble: Feminism and the Subversion of Identity* (1990), *Bodies That Matter: On the Discursive Limits of "Sex"* (1993), and *Excitable Speech: Politics of the Performance* (1997), as well as numerous articles and contributions on philosophy, feminism, and queer theory. Butler is currently the Hannah Arendt Chair at the European Graduate School and the Maxine Elliot Professor at the University of California, Berkeley.

REBECCA CAINES is an interdisciplinary artist and scholar and associate professor in Creative Technologies at the University of Regina. A former postdoctoral fellow with the Improvisation, Community, and Social Practice research project at the University of Guelph, Caines is coeditor with Ajay Heble of *The Improvisation Studies Reader: Spontaneous Acts* (2014).

ILLA CARRILLO RODRÍGUEZ was a postdoctoral fellow with the International Institute for Critical Studies in Improvisation at McGill University (2013–15). She investigates the history of popular music in Argentina and the politics of embodied, improvisatory art and activism in neoliberal-authoritarian cultural formations. Her work has appeared in several edited volumes, including *The Militant Song Movement in Latin America* (2014) and *Ese Ardiente Jardín de la República* (2010).

BERENICE CORTI (Ph.D. Area Teoría Cultural, Doctorado en Ciencias Sociales, University of Buenos Aires) examines the discursive and performance practices of jazz in Argentina, with an emphasis on the relationship between racialized identities and the project of the nation-state. Her publications include "Del discurso a la performance: La producción de significaciones de nacionalidad en el 'jazz argentino'" (2011) in *IASPM@Journal*.

ANDREW RAFFO DEWAR is associate professor of interdisciplinary arts in New College and the School of Music at the University of Alabama. A noted soprano saxophonist, improviser, and composer, Dewar has published several articles on jazz and improvisation, including "Searching for the Center of a Sound: Bill Dixon's *Webern*, the Unaccompanied Solo, and Compositional Ontology in Post-Songform Jazz" (2010).

NINA SUN EIDSHEIM is assistant professor of music at University of California, Los Angeles. Her publications include "Sensing Voice: Materiality and the Lived Body in Singing and Listening" (2011), and "Marian Anderson and 'Sonic Blackness' in American Opera" (2011). Her monograph, *Sensing Sound: Singing and Listening as Vibrational Practices*, is forthcoming from Duke University Press.

TOMIE HAHN is a performer, ethnologist, and associate professor in the Department of the Arts at Rensselaer Polytechnic Institute. Her ethnography *Sensational Knowledge: Embodying Culture through Japanese Dance* (2007) was the 2008 recipient of the Society for Ethnomusicology's Alan P. Merriam Prize. Hahn is currently the director of the Center for Deep Listening at Rensselaer.

ANDRA McCARTNEY is associate professor of communication studies at Concordia University, and is considered a leading artist/scholar in the field of soundwalking. Her publications include "Creating Moving Environmental Sound Narratives," in *The Oxford Handbook of Mobile Music Studies* (2014), and "Soundscape and the Subversion of Electroacoustic Norms" (2000).

TRACY McMULLEN is assistant professor of music at Bowdoin College. Previously she held postdoctoral fellowships in the humanities at the University of Southern California and with the Improvisation, Community, and Social Practice research project at the University of Guelph. Her work on improvisation has been published in the *Oxford Handbook of Critical Improvisation Studies* (2013), *Big Ears* (2008), and *People Get Ready! The Future of Jazz Is Now* (2013).

KEVIN McNEILLY is associate professor in the Department of English at the University of British Columbia. His first collection of poems, *Embouchure*, appeared in 2011. McNeilly is author of over a dozen refereed journal articles on topics ranging from Frank Zappa to Canadian literature.

PAULINE OLIVEROS is Distinguished Research Professor of Music at Rensselaer Polytechnic Institute, and Darius Milhaud Artist-in-Residence at Mills College. A worldrenowned composer and pioneer of electronic music, Oliveros has published extensively on improvisation and her book *Software for People* (1984) is considered a classic in contemporary music studies.

JASON ROBINSON is assistant professor of music and affiliated faculty in black studies and film and media studies at Amherst College. An artist-scholar, Robinson is an accomplished composer and saxophonist. He has published articles and reviews in *Ethnomusicology, Jazz Perspectives*, and *Critical Studies in Improvisation*. His current book project, "(Re)-Sounding the African Diaspora," examines the role of improvisation and concepts of diaspora in collaborations involving African American and continental African musicians.

GILLIAN SIDDALL is dean of the Faculty of Social Sciences and Humanities at Lakehead University in Thunder Bay, Canada. Her publications include " 'I want to live in that music': Blues, Bessie Smith and Improvised Identities in Ann-Marie MacDonald's *Fall on Your Knees*" (2005); "Nice Work If You Can Get It: Women in Jazz," coauthored with Ajay Heble, in *Landing on the Wrong Note: Jazz, Dissonance and Critical Practice* (2000); and "A Musical Interface for People with Severe Physical Disabilities," coauthored with Pauline Oliveros, Leaf Miller, Jaclyn Heyen, and Sergio Hazard (2011).

JULIE DAWN SMITH is an associate researcher in the Centre for Women's and Gender Studies, University of British Columbia, and executive director of the Guelph Jazz Festival. She has published articles on improvisation and gender in several collections, including *Big Ears: Listening for Gender in Jazz Studies* (2008), *The Other Side of Nowhere: Jazz, Improvisation and Communities in Dialogue* (2004), and *People Get Ready! The Future of Jazz Is Now* (2013).

JESSE STEWART is associate professor of music at Carleton University. A JUNO Award–winning percussionist and composer, Stewart's research focuses primarily on experimental music, jazz, hip-hop, sound art, music pedagogy, and musical improvisation. He has published essays in numerous journals, including *American Music, Black Music Research Journal, Contemporary Music Review, Interdisciplinary Humanities, Intermedialities*, and in several edited collections.

SHERRIE TUCKER is associate professor in American studies at the University of Kansas. She is the author of *Swing Shift: "All-Girl" Bands of the 1940s* (2000), coeditor with Nichole T. Rustin of *Big Ears: Listening for Gender in Jazz Studies* (2008), and author of *Dance Floor Democracy: The Social Geography of Memory at the Hollywood Canteen* (2014).

ZACHARY WALLMARK is assistant professor of music history at Southern Methodist University in Dallas, Texas. He is coeditor (with Robert Fink and Melinda Latour) of *The Relentless Pursuit of Tone: Timbre in Popular Music* (2015) and has published articles in the *Dutch Journal of Music Theory, Ethnomusicology Review*, and *Music Research Forum*. He is currently at work on a monograph on timbre and embodied cognition.

ELLEN WATERMAN is professor of music at Memorial University of Newfoundland, and Memorial site coordinator for the International Institute for Critical Studies in Improvisation. Her improvisations for flutes/voice and electronics with James Harley can be heard on *Like a Ragged Flock* (ADAPPS 15001). Her publications include two edited collections, *Sonic Geographies Imagined and Remembered* (2002) and *The Art of Immersive Soundscapes* (with Pauline Minevich, 2013). She was a founding editor of the journal *Critical Studies in Improvisation/Etudes critiques en improvisation*.

DEBORAH WONG, professor of music at University of California, Riverside, is an ethnomusicologist specializing in the musics of Thailand and Asian America. Her books include *Sounding the Center: History and Aesthetics in Thai Buddhist Ritual* (2001) and *Speak It Louder: Asian Americans Making Music* (2004).

MANDY-SUZANNE WONG is editor-in-chief of the journal *Evental Aesthetics*. Her publications include several contributions on sound art and contemporary music to *The New Grove Dictionary of Music and Musicians* and Oxford Bibliographies Online, as well as articles in *Volume! The French Journal of Popular Music Studies* and *Organised Sound*.

AACM (Association for the Advancement of Creative Musicians), 245, 247, 251, 261n2, 278, 282n21

Abilities First, 184–85, 192–94, 196

academy: treatment of improvisation, 290

accessibility, 66, 194. *See also* disability

acoustic ecology, 39, 45, 50, 58, 70nn5–6, 89n7

Adaptive Use Musical Instrument (AUMI), 185, 192–95

African American: connection to improvisation, 14–16, 92, 95, 101, 105, 136–37, 202, 223, 225–26, 242, 271, 274, 277–79

Afrodiaspora, 3, 218, 225–27

Afro-futurism, 245–47, 261n4

Afrological, 92–93, 98, 101, 252

agency, 22–23, 27–29, 31, 59, 113–14, 121, 125–28, 148, 150, 207, 212, 259, 288, 296, 308–9, 314; of audience, 208, 300; in *Fall on Your Knees*, 207, 212; improvisation and, 2, 4–5, 8–9, 12, 17–18, 92–93, 101, 105, 116–18, 127; in soundwalking, 46, 50, 53; in *Xenogenesis*, 250–51. *See also* interagency

Alice Tully Hall, 136

Aoki, Tatsu, 277–78

Apollo Theatre, 137, 144n10

appropriation: musical, 136–37

art: adaptive, 13, 190–92; community-based, 10, 55–57, 60; computer-based, 169; conceptual, 174; digital, 190–92; interactive, 169; participatory, 175; sound, 169, 175. *See also* Community Sound (e)Scapes; *Very Nervous System*

Artrage, 190

Ascension (Coltrane), 233, 234, 244n4

audience, 17, 40, 83, 85, 89, 96–99, 103, 110n14, 111n22, 116, 122, 135–36, 299–300; agency of, 208, 300; as co-creative, 116, 205–6, 209–10; embodied involvement of, 13, 304, 322; informed, 291–92; as participant, 41–42; vs. performer, 193; role of, 128, 135, 139, 177, 183, 195, 201, 205–6, 220, 253, 284, 291–92, 317–18, 323–24

autopoiesis, 125, 260

Ayler, Albert, 234, 243n2

Baartman, Saartjie (Sarah), 256–57, 261, 262n7

Bach, Johann Sebastian, 137–38, 186, 144n15

Ballybeen, 57, 61–64, 66, 68, 70n13

Ballybeen Youth Centre, 62

banding, 12–13, 147, 149–51, 164–66, 180n1, 181; and community, 148, 152–53, 155–56, 159–60, 166; as embodied, 148, 154–55, 158, 161, 163; as sensual, 150, 152, 162, 167; as technology, 153

Baraka, Amiri, 242, 244n16

bebop, 225

Beethoven, Ludwig van, 203, 204

Bernstein, Leonard, 77

Best Cellars, 62–63, 68, 70n13

Bicentennial (Argentinian), 16, 307–25; gala, 309–12; Pathway, 307, 315; as political subjectivation, 308, 322

bin Laden, Osama, 24, 31–32

black box (theory), 120–22, 128

Black Earth Ensemble, 245, 251, 257

blues, 1, 3–4; in *Corregidora*, 14–15, 215n2, 218–19, 222–23, 226; in *Fall on Your Knees*, 201, 226

bodies: as archive, 14–15, 226; and community, 68–69; and disability, 172, 183, 196; fetishization of, 11; and improvisation, 3–4, 84, 169–70, 213; mediation of, 1, 8; and nation, 307, 314; networked, 11, 103; nonverbal, 83–84; as preconscious, 87; and sexuality/sensuality, 17–18, 214, 249;

bodies (continued)
   and significations, 201; as site of resis-
   tance, 5–6, 317–18; as social, 149, 156, 158,
   160, 162, 246; as sonic archive, 3–4, 224;
   as sounding, 2, 7, 9, 17, 163, 180–81, 238,
   283; and space, 55, 58; and subjectivity,
   12–13, 209; technological, 106–8
Braxton, Anthony, 70n4, 245, 251, 261n1
Brooklands Youth Centre, 63, 70n13
Brown, Anthony, 277
Brown, Earle, 77
Brown, Marion, 234
Butler, Octavia, 14–15, 245–61
Bynum, Taylor Ho, 245, 251

Cage, John, 77, 89nn3–4, 92
Campbell, John, 10, 56, 57, 59, 65, 67–68, 70n4
Canadian Charter of Rights and Freedoms,
   285–86
Cardiff, Janet, 39
Carmichael, Stokely, 242
Cell Theatre, 185, 191, 193
chance (operations), 77, 92
class, 16, 111n26, 137; and community art, 10,
   62; in Fall on Your Knees, 202–3, 208, 215
colonization, 246, 256, 283
Colón Theater, 309–12, 324n3
Coltrane, John: response to, 8, 15–16, 141,
   233–37, 241–43, 243n2, 244n5
communication, 7, 12, 51, 75, 107, 115, 123–26,
   128–29, 159, 175, 187, 214, 224, 286
community: 12, 17–18, 148, 152, 181, 195, 246,
   256; biological, 253; as embodied space,
   250; music-making, 15; national, 310–11,
   316, 321
community art, 10, 55–57, 60, 62–64; ethics
   of, 57, 59–61, 68–69. See also Community
   Sound (e)Scapes
Community Sound (e)Scapes, 55–69, 69n1,
   69n3
composition: vs. improvisation, 8, 75–78, 82,
   88–89, 92–93, 100–101, 108–9, 138, 142,
   218, 251–52, 279, 290–91
consciousness, 28–29, 85–87, 116–17, 119, 123,
   133, 148, 158–59, 177, 182–83, 189–90,
   196–98, 259
Cope, David, 140, 142, 144n15
corporeal archaeology, 14, 217–18, 223–24,
   226, 230

corporeality, 3, 8, 9, 132, 134, 185, 256, 258
Corregidora (Jones), 14, 217–30; as a blues
   novel, 219
Corringham, Viv, 39, 54n5
countermemory, 223
Crispell, Marilyn, 289
Critical Studies in Improvisation / Études
   critiques en improvisation, 18n1
Cusack, Peter, 58
cybernetics, 114–15, 129–30nn4–5; and the
   environment, 115, 119–21, 130n5, 130n11,
   130n14; second-order, 122–23
cyborg, 107, 114, 118

Dark Matter (Rokeby), 174–75
da Vinci, Leonardo, 57, 60–61, 67, 71n14
deadness, 19n5, 111n20, 141
deep listening, 75, 81–82, 84, 89, 104, 111n27,
   167n2
Deep Listening, 81–82
Deep Listening Band, 81
Deep Listening Convergence, 104
Deep Listening Institute, 185, 192
Delbecq, Benoit, 289
Dempster, Stuart, 81
Dessen, Michael, 95–96, 98, 106, 110n9, 111n25
Deviations and Straight Line (Tomaz), 6, 185,
   188–90
disability, 6, 12–13, 37–38, 64–69; and banding, 158–59; experience of, 186; inclusion
   of, 185; and performance, 182–98;
   stretched notions of, 183–84; telematics
   and, 94; and Very Nervous System, 172–73
diversity: in Fall on Your Knees, 202, 208; of
   Safa, 17, 287–89, 293
Dresser, Mark, 91, 96–98, 100, 103–6, 110n6,
   110n9, 110n18, 111n25, 111–12n28

ecotonality, 43, 51. See also acoustic ecology
Erickson, Robert, 76
e-Scaper, 56, 67, 68, 69n3
Eurological, 92, 101
Expanded Instrument System (EIS), 11, 75,
   79, 81, 88–89

Fall on Your Knees (MacDonald), 15, 201–15;
   and improvisation, 204; improvisation
   as resistance in, 205–8, 210, 212; jazz and
   blues in, 201

femininity, 241, 271–72
Ferreras, Sal, 284, 289–99, 301–2
Fitzgerald, Ella, 133, 225
flow, 3, 13, 84–85, 116, 151, 164–65, 170–72, 174–75, 177–80; disruption of, 98, 179–80
Foss, Lukas, 77
Fuerzabruta, 16, 307, 309, 324–25n8; pageant by, 312, 315, 318–20, 322–23

Gelb, Philip, 83
gender: identity, 5, 14–15, 22–27, 240–42; norms, 27–28; repetition of, 27–28; and soundwalking, 46, 48, 54n3; Taiko and, 16–17, 265–67, 270–73; theory, 5, 22; and trauma, 3–4, 14–16; violence, 26, 211–12. See also *Corregidora*; *Fall on Your Knees*; *Xenogenesis*
Gershwin, George, 134
gesture, 5–7, 89, 163, 170; in taiko, 265, 277; taiko and jazz, 270, 275
gospel, 208, 218, 226–29
Gould, Glenn, 137–38
Guelph Jazz Festival, 280nn2–3

Hamer, Fannie Lou, 258, 261
Harris, Ciara, 133
Hatch, Peter, 300
Hemingway, Gerry, 93, 95–96, 99, 100, 108
Ho, Fred, 277
Horiuchi, Glenn, 277
Houle, Francois, 284, 289–302, 305n8, 306n18
humanist, 23, 115, 128–29. See also posthumanism
hyper-embodiment, 8, 98, 108

iChat, 97, 104, 110n9
identity: politics of, 136, 202, 208, 283, 288, 301–3
improvisation: across abilities, 196; and adaptation, 10; and agency, 2, 4–5, 8–9, 12, 17–18, 92–93, 101, 105, 116–18, 127, 229–30; barriers to, 65, 279; collective, 309; and communication, 114; and community, 12; vs. composition, 76–78, 82, 87–89, 93, 138; definition of, 21, 41; embodiment of, 1, 91, 107, 170–72, 226, 229; erotics of, 17–18, 201–15; ethics of, 129; in *Fall on Your Knees*, 204; free, 58, 64, 76, 82, 84, 93, 98–99, 101, 109, 110n16,

115, 122, 202, 281n11, 243; and freedom, 4, 21, 23–26; and gender, 24, 266, 270; groove-based, 93, 95, 99–102, 109, 110n16, 116; and hope, 3; and human rights, 3; and identity, 12, 24; intercultural, 284, 291–92; mediation of, 64; as methodology, 57, 69, 76, 83; multisensory, 162; and new technology, 78–79; with objects, 156, 165; organizational, 60–61; as political dislocation, 311–14; and power, 1; and predictability, 28–30; and race, 266; as signifier, 206–7; as social, 29–30; and social change, 1, 124, 148, 202, 204, 211, 215, 265–66, 286; and subjectivity, 1, 3–9, 23, 283, 288, 292–93, 297, 299, 302, 304, 309; and theater, 317–18
Improvisation Chamber Ensemble, 77
Improvisation, Community, and Social Practice (ICASP), 19n6, 69n1, 70–71n14, 147, 266, 280nn1–2
improvisative, 4, 9, 27; vs. improvisation, 30; vs. performative, 33n7
indeterminancy, 77, 92–93
Inner Truth Taiko Dojo, 273, 281n8
Inspiraling: Telematic Jazz Explorations, 91–93, 96–98, 101, 108, 109n3
interagency, 8–9, 114, 116–17, 119, 128
Internet: and accessibility, 63, 68, 105, 107; use in performance, 11, 91, 94, 102. See also telematics
Internet2, 94, 96, 104–5, 110n5
intersubjectivity, 10, 15, 40–42, 51, 113, 129, 209, 223, 304, 308–9
Iranian classical music, 17, 284, 289–99, 305n12, 305nn14–15, 306n18
Ives, Charles, 204
Iyer, Vijay, 93, 101, 266, 277
Izu, Mark, 277–78

JackTrip, 94, 96–97, 104, 106
JamBoxx, 184
Jang, Jon, 277–78
jazz, 1, 3, 14, 30, 82, 116, 137, 202, 225, 265–66; free, 15–16, 233–36, 241–43, 243nn1–2, 244n6, 281n11, 288; and gender, 270–75; Japanese treatment of, 275–76; as male, 270–71; solos, 274–75
Johnson, James P., 138–39
Jones, Gayl, 14, 218–19, 223

KaiBorg, 114, 118, 127
Kaiser, Jeff, 114, 118
Kennedy, Kathy, 39
Kinnara Taiko, 270
knowledge: as embodied, 163–66, 183, 196, 237, 240
Knowles, Beyoncé, 133
Kofsky, Frank, 225, 242
Koushkani, Amir, 284, 289–99
Kubisch, Christina, 39

Lacks, Henrietta, 257–58, 261
latency, 11, 91–96, 98, 109; cause of, 94; elimination of, 94–95, 103–4, 106, 108; as inherent, 95; negotiation of, 99–102. *See also* time delays
law: embodiment of, 22–24; improvisation as, 25
Léandre, Joëlle, 289
LifeSize, 96–97
Lincoln Center, 137
listening, 249, 253, 299; as active, 42–44, 54n3, 56; and consensus, 87–88; as empathetic, 239; ethics of, 37–38; intimately, 40, 48, 51; as meditation, 82; partial, 46, 51–52; science of, 84–86, 90n13. *See also* deep listening
liveness, 11–12, 19n5, 111n20, 166; of re-performance, 131–32, 135; of telematics performance, 103
Long, Christopher, 39
Luz Jazz Festival, 83–84

MacDonald, Ann-Marie, 15, 201–15, 215n1
Madres, 16, 313–22, 324n5, 324–5n8, 325n13; improvisation by, 317–18; performing, 318–21, 325nn10–12
Mangione, Chuck, 133
masculinity, 8, 15–16, 241, 275; Asian American, 271–72; in jazz, 270–72, 277, 281n11; in Taiko, 267, 271–72, 280n5
materiality, 2, 3, 6, 102, 107, 127, 174, 188, 258
Mayer, Steven, 132, 134–39; as embodied, 138–39
Meditations (Coltrane), 234, 236
Melford, Myra, 111n25
memory, 2, 14–16, 186, 259, 309; cultural, 230, 323–24; embodied, 57–58, 218–19, 221–23, 229–30, 316–17, 324; in *Fall*

on Your Knees, 213; generational, 222, 225; performed, 217, 222; transmission through music, 222, 228
Miku, Hatsune, 142
Milanés, Pablo, 322, 325n14
Miller, George Bures, 39
minstrelsy, 208
misrecognition, 22, 285–86, 292, 304, 314
Mitchell, Nicole, 14, 17, 245–61, 306n26
Modirzadeh, Hafez, 96, 277–78
MONO Prelude (Rolnick), 184–86
motherhood, 15–16, 258–59, 315–16; in *Corregidora*, 220–21; in *Fall on Your Knees*, 210, 213–14; in *Xenogenesis*, 255–56, 259
Mott, David, 176–77
multiculturalism, 32, 51, 265, 293; Canadian, 16–17, 283–87, 290, 297, 299–302, 304, 306n28
Munehiro, Okuda, 276
music: electronic, 78–79, 81–82, 85–86, 88, 184, 191, 195, 260; as mediator, 202–3; networked, 91–95
Musical Instrument Digital Interface (MIDI), 131, 143n4, 173, 189

nationhood, 31–32, 309–11, 314–15
Ndosi, Mankwe, 252, 257, 261
neocybernetics, 12, 112n30, 114–15, 119, 124, 126, 128
networked music, 91–95; as accessible, 104–5; disembodiment of, 102; embodiment of, 103; as participatory, 99, 104–5, 107

objects: sensible, 165–66
Oguchi, Daihachi, 275–77, 282n19
OilEye (Hemingway), 93, 95, 99–101, 108
Oliveros, Pauline, 11, 54n3, 70n4, 95, 102–4, 110n6, 110n9, 110n18, 182–84, 193, 197, 281n11
Open Ears Festival of Music and Sound, 284, 290, 300
orientation through disorientation, 147–50, 152, 164, 166–67
original: vs. copy, 132–34, 137–39; fetishization of, 133, 137
Osuwa Taiko, 275, 277
Oswald, John, 176–77

Páez, Fito, 322–24

Parker, Charlie, 92, 225

Parker, Evan, 289

performance, 11, 25, 80, 89, 120–22, 150; embodiment of, 134; holographic, 141–43, 144n19; networked, 91–95, 98, 100–109; vs. re-performance, 133; of self, 132. *See also* re-performance

performativity, 3–6, 9, 23, 29, 33n7, 120–22, 126, 129, 251, 266–67, 313–14; of bodies, 138, 176, 178, 213; of identity, 25–27

Peterson, Oscar, 141

Phillips, Barre, 75, 83–84

Play the Drum Band, 185, 192–93

Plaza de Mayo, 313, 315, 319–21, 324n5

Polli, Andrea, 39

posthuman, 3, 107, 114, 124, 127, 141–42, 248

Prévost, Eddie, 95

Prometheus I (Egloff), 184–85, 191

race: *Fall on Your Knees*, 15, 201–2, 208, 213–14, 215n2; and gospel, 218, 227–28; and re-performance of Tatum, 136–37, 144n10; saxophonic scream and, 241–42; and Taiko, 16, 265–67, 269, 271–72; in *Xenogenesis*, 14–15

Raging Asian Women, 273

rap, 218, 226–29, 243

Reason, Dana, 83

recording, 8, 11, 39, 41; disembodiment of, 134–35, 143n7; vs. live, 19n5, 131–33, 191; as re-performance, 134

recognition: politics of, 283–86, 288, 290, 297, 300–304, 305n5. *See also* misrecognition

RePerform, 141

re-performance, 131–35, 141, 143n2, 144n10, 144n18; disembodied, 132; embodied, 132; as improvisation, 138–39; vs. performance, 133; treatment of error in, 137–38

repetition, 33n8; improvisation and, 3, 5; of listening, 47–49; martial, 31–32; and performativity, 9, 23–24, 27–28

resonance, 2, 9–10, 81, 178, 239

Riley, Terry, 76

Rokeby, David, 13, 116, 169–80

Rush, Loren, 76

Safa, 16–17; diverse musical traditions of, 283; as intercultural, 284, 289–99, 301–2, 306n18; as political, 292–93

Sanders, Pharoah, 236, 243n2

San Fransisco Tape Music Center, 79

saxophonic scream, 8, 15–16, 243n2; as embodied, 235, 238; as gendered, 241–42; as liberated sound, 234; as racialized, 241–42; response to, 233–35; as spiritual, 235; vs. vocal scream, 238, 240, 244n11

Schafer, R. Murray, 39, 58, 70n5

sexuality, 26–27; in *Fall on Your Knees*, 15, 210, 215n2

Shakur, Tupac: re-performance of, 142, 144n19

Shepp, Archie, 243n2, 244n11

Shrine Auditorium, 131

silence: and flow, 85; in performance, 318, 320–21; and resistance, 16, 316–17, 320–21, 325n13; and soundwalk, 41–42, 50

Skype, 68, 97, 102, 104, 110n9, 182, 191

slavery, 14, 219, 223, 226–27, 246, 256

softVNS, 175

sound: embodiment of, 2, 6; as immaterial, 7; as metaphor, 2; physicality of, 2, 187; relationship to stance, 7–9; as signifier, 2. *See also* recording

soundscape, 10, 39, 43–44, 46, 57–59, 61–64, 66, 68; as composition, 58

soundwalking, 10, 37–38, 59; as composition, 42, 50; at English Bay, 43–50; and gender, 46, 48, 54n3; history of, 39; as improvisation, 41; as performance, 40–41; structure of, 46, 50, 53

Soundwalking Interactions, 38, 43, 54n4, 54n7

spatiality, 55, 57, 64

stance: relationship to sound, 7–9

Stewart, Jesse: improvisation with *VNS*, 13, 178–80

Stravinsky, Igor, 135

Stretched Boundaries, 182–98

stretching, 12, 181–83, 192–97, 253. *See also* banding

subjectivity, 22, 246; improvisation and, 1–9, 23–24, 271, 302; and sensibility, 12

Sun Ra, 247

Supercussion, 173

surveillance: *VNS* and, 13, 169, 174–76

synchronicity, 91–92, 95–96, 98–100. *See also* latency; time delays taiko, 1, 16–17, 265–66; and gender, 16–17, 265–67, 270–73; improvisation within, 270; influence of jazz on, 266, 275–78; as male dominated, 273; and race, 16, 266–67, 269, 272; solos, 16–17, 265–73, 278–79

Taiko Center of Los Angeles, 267, 273

Tatum, Art, 143–44nn9–10; re-performance of, 11, 131–39, 142; as re-performing himself, 138–39

Telein (Weaver), 93, 96, 98–99, 108

telematics, 1, 11, 68, 91–98, 101–3, 105–9, 109n1, 110n9, 110n18, 111n22, 111–12n28

timbre, 13–15, 183, 228, 233–38, 240, 242–43; biological connection to, 233, 243; in *Corregidora*, 219–20, 222–23; as embodied, 237; of saxophone, 8, 238, 240

time delay, 11; in music production, 75, 78–79, 81–82, 85–88. *See also* latency

Tintinnabulate, 184–85, 189, 191

trauma, 3, 14–16; in *Corregidora*, 218–21, 223; in *Fall on Your Knees*, 202, 215; generational, 14, 202, 221–22, 225; memory of, 220–21

Truax, Barry, 58, 70n5

Truth and Reconciliation Commission, 285, 305n6, 306n23

Turing Test, 140

Turrentine, Tommy, 137

uncanny valley, 135, 140, 142, 143n8

unknowingness, 22–24

University of Toronto Electronic Music Studio (UTEMS), 79

UZEB, 173

Vancouver Community College, 289

Vancouver New Music, 45, 54n7

Vancouver Soundwalk Collective, 45

Very Nervous System (VNS), 13, 116, 169–80; development of, 173; and disabilities, 172–73; improvisation with, 170–72, 175–80

Victor Records, 133

Voyager, 140, 179

Walker, John Q., 131, 140–41

Waller, Fats, 138–39

Waterman, Michael, 39

Waters, Richard, 178

Weaver, Sarah, 91, 93, 96–100, 103, 108, 110n9

Westerkamp, Hildegard, 39, 70n5

"Whisper of Love," 284, 289–99, 302, 304, 305n15, 306n18; as dialogic, 294–97

Woolgoolga, 57, 64–66, 68, 70–71n14

Wong, Francis, 277–78

World Forum for Acoustic Ecology, 39, 45, 70n5

World Soundscape Project, 39, 58, 70n5

Xenogenesis (Butler), 14–15, 245–60; music in, 252–53

Xenogenesis Suite (Mitchell), 245–61; notation for, 252

Yamaha Disklavier Pro, 131, 139, 143n2

Zenph Sound Innovations, 11–12, 131–35, 137–40, 143nn1–2, 144n10, 144n13, 144n17; future of, 141–43